# BEYOND THE GATE

## THE UNOFFICIAL AND
## UNAUTHORISED GUIDE TO
# STARGATE SG-1

# BEYOND THE GATE

## THE UNOFFICIAL AND UNAUTHORISED GUIDE TO
## STARGATE SG-1

## BY KEITH TOPPING

First published in England in 2002 by

Telos Publishing Ltd
61 Elgar Avenue, Tolworth, Surrey, KT5 9JP, England
www.telos.co.uk

ISBN: 1-903889-50-2
Text © 2002 Keith Topping
Cover © 2002 Dariusz Jasiczak
The moral rights of the author have been asserted.

Internal design, typesetting and layout
by Arnold T Blumberg
www.atbpublishing.com

Printed in England by
Antony Rowe Ltd
Bumper's Farm Industrial Estate
Chippenham
Wiltshire
SN14 6LH

2 3 4 5 6 7 8 9 10 11 12 13 14 15

British Library Cataloguing in Publication Data.
A catalogue record for this book is available from the British Library.

**BEYOND THE GATE** is dedicated to:


Graeme Topping,

Jim Swallow,

and

David and Lesley McIntee.

The author wishes to thank the following for their outstanding support and encouragement: Ian Abrahams, Anna Bliss, the impressive Neil Connor (who responded to yet another computer-related disaster), Andy Cowper, Martin Day, Diana Dougherty, Clay Eichelberger, Rob Francis, Robert Halden-Pratt at C4i, the Godlike Genius of Jeff Hart, Craig Hinton, Tony and Jane Kenealy, Shaun Lyon, Paul Simpson (who, like Jim Swallow, provided unedited transcripts of his interviews with several of the cast and crew), Lily Topping and Deb Walsh. Also, my sincere gratitude to my publishers David Howe and Stephen James Walker who had such faith in this book where others faltered. To the excellent Arnold Blumberg and the great Dariusz Jasiczak and, as always, to Kathy Sullivan and Susannah Tiller for their research and contributions to this project, and so many others.

Also worth a mention: Andrew J, Boards of Canada, Barry Butlin, *Hai Karate*, Alan Hawkshaw, Ted Hemsley, Jeff (the Patron Saint of Biscuits), Dickie Krzywicki, Mac's 30-yarder at Burnden Park, Mandingo, Holden McGröyan, *Mönké*, Steve *The Trousers* Purcell, the Roses, school bullies with an agenda, the TPF, Umbongo™ (they drink it in the Congo) and the 'Wind. Respect, is *due*.

Plus a special mention for all my chums on the *Outpost Gallifrey* forum and the *Buffywatchers* and *Gallyfriends* mailing lists. Keep the faith.

*Beyond the Gate* was written on location in Newcastle-upon-Tyne, London and Los Angeles. Oh yes it was...

# THIS IS THE WAY... STEP INSIDE

Occasionally a really good TV show appears which, for some reason, although picking up an enthusiastic audience, never seems to get the respect it deserves. *Stargate SG-1* is a classic example. Once upon a time (and not very long ago either) *SG-1* was seen by many reviewers as a quintessentially horrid piece of trainspotter-SF. A kind-of down-market *Star Trek* for people who couldn't afford a *real* imagination. Like *Buffy the Vampire Slayer* it was a TV spin-off from a genre movie. Unlike *Buffy*, however, the first season of *SG-1* wasn't really very good. It had some fine actors in it, certainly, but the format was dull and pretty obvious; two-parts *The Time Tunnel* to one-part *Aliens*. Only, you know, without all the swearing. 'This will last one season and end to no great fanfare,' many critics, me included, believed. How wrong we were; and I, for one, am delighted to have been proven so. Because *Stargate SG-1* has matured, like a fine wine, into a rattling good series. And one that includes, within its arsenal of many strengths, a sly and laconic wit - influenced by the formidable personality of the show's leading man and executive producer, Richard Dean Anderson.

Okay, stop me if you think that you've heard this one before: Colonel Jack O'Neill is a representative of the "If-it-moves-shoot-it, if-it-doesn't-move-shoot-it-in-case-it-does-move," school of military intelligence. He'll take on anyone and spit barbed sarcasm at them: parasitic aliens, military superiors, career politicians, little grey men pretending to be Norse warriors... And, especially, Captain Samantha Carter. Because she's a scientist and (more importantly) *a woman* in a real-man's universe of bloodthirsty-alien-killing. Along with nerdish-but-loveable, "Hey-let's-talk" archaeologist Daniel Jackson, brave, if sour-faced, alien rebel Teal'c and their seen-it-all boss General George Hammond, SG-1 form Earth's first line of defence against the hideous Goa'uld and other intergalactic nasties. It's a pretty awful premise, let's be honest.

The *Stargate* movie, on which the series was based, was a vast commercial success, but previous examples of this *oeuvre* on TV (Fox's *Space: Above And Beyond*, chiefly) hadn't inspired much confidence that Military-SF could work within these budgetary limitations. Put simply, it's unwise to do alien invasions on the cheap unless you're *Doctor Who* and can do it with imagination and wit. But, just occasionally, even in those early days, there were odd moments in *SG-1* - a funny line of dialogue here, a well-directed sequence there - which convinced viewers that the people making this series *had* talent. Then, suddenly, without much warning, in its second season, *SG-1* did something really surprising. It got *good*.

*Beyond the Gate* will cover some serious issues - *SG-1* has taken the trouble to tackle racism, xenophobia, religious intolerance and debates surrounding individual choice - and it's right that any book on the show should reflect these. But I also want to have a bit of fun - a too-often-ignored element of *Stargate*'s popularity being its wicked sense of humour.

# HEADINGS

**THE WIT AND WISDOM OF JACK O'NEILL** The good jokes. And some of the really bad ones.

**SAM'S TRAUMATIC LOVE-LIFE** Poor lamb, she's got rotten taste when it comes to boyfriends. Amanda Tapping, who plays Sam, notes: 'It's a great source of frustration and embarrassment, being the black widow of the show.'

**ORIGINS OF THE SPECIES** Details on alien races encountered and the clever use of ancient mythologies in the series.

**SEX AND DRUGS AND ROCK 'N' ROLL** Oddly, given the military background, there's a surprising amount of all three. Well, not as much sex as the other two. 'O'Neill got nookie once,' Michael Shanks, who plays Daniel Jackson, noted sadly. 'After that nobody ever got into bed with *anybody*. The women all wear green army pants and military boots. We gotta ask ourselves which demographic we're aiming at.'

**POSSIBLE INFLUENCES** Pop-culture allusions and references, acknowledged roots and aspects which may owe a debt to other texts. There's no suggestion of any intentional plagiarism, but rather a highlighting of links that may not be otherwise obvious to readers. In any case, the *SG-1* writers are justifiably proud of their successful sampling of elements from their favourite movies and TV shows into the series' format.

**'YOU MIGHT REMEMBER ME FROM...'** The category which answers those annoying "where have I seen his/her face before?" questions.

**LOGIC, LET ME INTRODUCE YOU TO THIS WINDOW** Plot-holes, goofs and the bits of each episode that make *no sense*.

**GOA'ULD LEXICON** A word about spellings: I am aware this is something of a hot-topic in *Stargate* fandom. If a name appears written down on screen then that's the one I'll use. (For instance, 'Naqahdah' appears on a white-board in 'Singularity'.) Elsewhere, I've tended to go for those spellings included in the subtitles on official MGM DVDs, although I know that contradictions and mistakes occur even in these.[1] It's a complicated subject made worse by the fact that if a word is Egyptian-based (and many are) there *will* automatically be variations as the Ancient Egyptians didn't bother writing vowels (except in hieratic). This means technically 'Naqada', 'Naqahdah' and dozens of other spellings are all equally as valid as each other.

**QUOTE/UNQUOTE** Samples of the dialogue worth rewinding the video for.

**DID YOU KNOW?** Some *real* trivia for use at dinner-parties and conventions.

Other categories crop up from time to time. Most should be self-explanatory. **Critique** details what the press made of it all whilst **Cast and Crew Comments** are

---

1 Spelling variations between US and UK DVDs exist. It's 'Chaapa'ai' in the UK but 'Chappa'ai' in the US, for example.

A
*9*

added where appropriate. Each episode concludes with a review and notes on continuity.[2] So, you've been briefed and your security clearance is apparently adequate. What follows is *TOP SECRET*. You may not be aware of this, but there's something funny going on at NORAD.

**Keith Topping**
His Gaff
Merrie Old Albion
August 2002

---

2 *Stargate SG-1* is made by Double Secret Productions and Gekko Films and distributed by MGM Television. The first five seasons were broadcast in the US on the subscription cable channel Showtime, by Sky One in the UK, Channel 7 in Australia, TV2 in New Zealand, Global and other local stations on the WIC Network in Canada, RTL2 in Germany, M6 in France, TV3 in Norway, Veronica in the Netherlands, ORF in Austria and in many other countries. Several months after a season concludes, it appears in syndication in the US and on the terrestrial Channel 4 in the UK. In terms of episodes, Sky are usually about a month or two behind the US from June to December and, thereafter, a fortnight or so ahead from January to March (one exception: the final ten episodes of season five were all broadcast in the UK some months before America). From season six, the series has moved to the Sci-Fi Channel in the US (see 'Redemption').

# STARGATE (1994) THE MOVIE

'It will take you a million light years from home.

But will it bring you back?

Sealed and buried for all time is the key

to mankind's future.'

# JTARGATE (1994)

Carolco Pictures/Centropolis Film Productions/Journal Film/Le Studio Canal+/Metro-Goldwyn-Mayer

Producer: Dean Devlin, Oliver Eberle, Joel B Michaels

Co-Producer: Ute Emmerich

Executive Producer: Mario Kassar

Line Producer: Ramsey Thomas

Associate Producer: Peter Winther

Original Music: David Arnold

# STARGATE

US Release Date: 28 October 1994
UK Release Date: 6 January 1995
Writers: Dean Devlin, Roland Emmerich
Director: Roland Emmerich
Cast: Kurt Russell (Colonel Jonathan 'Jack' O'Neil), James Spader (Dr Daniel Jackson), Jaye Davidson (Ra), Viveca Lindfors (Catherine Langford), Alexis Cruz (Skaara), Mili Avital (Sha'uri), Leon Rippy (General W.O. West), John Diehl (Lieutenant Kawalsky), Carlos Lauchu (Anubis), Djimon Hounsou (Horus), Erick Avari (Kasuf), French Stewart (Lieutenant Ferretti), Gianin Loffler (Nabeh), Christopher John Fields (Lieutenant Freeman), Derek Webster (Lieutenant Brown), Jack Moore (Lieutenant Reilly), Steve Giannelli (Lieutenant Porro), David Pressman (Assistant Lieutenant), Scott Alan Smith (Officer), Cecil Hoffman (Sarah O'Neil), Rae Allen (Barbara Shore), Richard Kind (Gary Meyers), John Storey (Mitch), Lee Taylor-Allan (Jenny), George Gray (Technician), Kelly Vint (Young Catherine), Erik Holland (Professor Langford), Nick Wilder (Foreman Taylor), Sayed Badreya (Arabic Interpreter), Michael Concepcion (Horus #1), Jerry Gilmore (Horus #2), Michel Jean-Philippe (Horus #3), Dialy N'Daiye (Horus #4), Gladys Holland (Professor), Roger Til (Professor), Kenneth Danziger (Professor), Christopher West (Professor), Robert Ackerman (Companion), Kieron Lee (Masked Ra), Dax Biagas[3] (Young Ra), Frank Welker (Voice of the Mastadge), John Casino (Mr Russell's Double), Greg Smrz (Mr Spader's Double), Dennis Fitzgerald (Mr Spader's Double), John Rhys-Davies[4] (Shouting Arab Digger)

An archaeological artefact found in Egypt is put into storage until a team of scientists working for the US military discover its purpose; a 'Stargate' to another world. Colonel Jack O'Neil is sent with a team - including linguist Daniel Jackson - to explore the unknown. However, when they reach the desert planet of Abydos, there's no way to reopen the Stargate without the return address. They befriend the peaceful locals but discover that an alien, Ra, whom the ancient Egyptians worshipped as a God, is using the Abydonians as slaves.

**INTERNATIONAL RELEASE DATES** Spain, 24 November 1994. France, 1 February 1995. Argentina, 2 February 1995. Germany, 9 March 1995. Denmark, 24 March 1995. Sweden, 12 May 1995.

**EXTENT/CERTIFICATION** 119 minutes. PG-13. A *Director's Cut* containing approximately nine minutes of additional footage was released on DVD in 2001.

**ORIGINS OF THE SPECIES** Around 10,000 years ago Ra[5], described as a traveller from a distant star and a dying species, came to Earth and parasitically possessed a human boy. The Stargate was used to take humans to Abydos (a planet with three

3 Uncredited on cinema prints.
4 Uncredited.
5 The Egyptian sun-god (also known as Re). Re's Hymn begins *The Book of the Dead*. As the sun-god aged, humans began to plot against him. He summoned the Divine Eye, in the form of Hathor (see 'Hathor') to

moons, in the Kaliam galaxy 'on the other side of the known universe') and mine the quartz-like material from which the Gate is made (see 'Children of the Gods').

**THE CONSPIRACY STARTS AT CLOSING TIME** Catherine Langford's father discovered the Stargate buried on the Giza Plateau in 1928. The artefact then passed to the US Military (see 'The Torment of Tantalus', '1969') and was held at the Creek Mountain facility in Colorado.

**MILITARY INTELLIGENCE?** Join the Air Force. Journey to new, exotic worlds. With orders to blow them up. Meet a friendly indigenous population. And shoot at them.

**IN THE INTERESTS OF NATIONAL SECURITY** Daniel's symposium at the Park Plaza Hotel in LA is entitled *The Old Kingdom and the IVth Dynasty* (see 'There But For the Grace of God', 'The Curse'). He believes the pyramids are much older than the 5,000 years most scholars suggest.

**POSSIBLE INFLUENCES** Conceptually *The Time Tunnel, Star Trek*'s 'City on the Edge of Forever', Frederick Pohl's *Gateway* and *Time Travelers*. A mix of SF and Egyptology is central to *The Jewel of the Seven Stars, The Mummy* and *Doctor Who*'s 'Pyramids of Mars'. Amongst the homages and visual references are *Star Wars, The Empire Strikes Back, Raiders of the Lost Ark, Indiana Jones and the Temple of Doom, The Man Who Would Be King, Spartacus, Cleopatra* and *Highlander* ('there can be only one Ra'). The Gate-travel effect may have been influenced by the title-sequence of the Tom Baker-era *Doctor Who* or by *2001: A Space Odyssey*. Two of the books Daniel has with him are Christopher Frayling's *The Face of Tutenkhamun* and Michael A Hoffman's *Egypt Before the Pharaohs*.

**'YOU MIGHT REMEMBER ME FROM...'** A child-star with Disney, Kurt Russell first came to prominence on TV as Two Persons in *The Quest* and, in the cinema, starring in John Carpenter's *Escape From New York* and *The Thing*. His movies include *Tango and Cash, Backdraft, Soldier* and *3000 Miles to Graceland*. James Spader's CV includes *Wall Street, The Rachel Papers, Pretty in Pink, Less Than Zero, sex, lies & videotape, Crash, 2 Days in the Valley* and *Critical Care*. Jaye Davidson played Dil in *The Crying Game*. The late Viveca Lindfors was in *The Sure Thing, Creepshow, Girlfriends, King of Kings* and *I, Accuse!* Alexis Cruz played Rafael in *Touched by an Angel* and appeared in *That Summer in LA* and *Why Do Fools Fall in Love?*. Mili Avital played Samantha in *Kissing a Fool*. Leon Rippy was in *Midnight in the Graden of Good and Evil, Universal Soldier, Kuffs* and *Track 29*. John Diehl played Gordon Liddy in *Nixon* and Larry Zito in *Miami Vice* and

destroy rebellious mankind. He transformed the goddess into Sekhmet, the lioness, who slaughtered many men and waded in their blood until Re had a change of heart. He tricked Sekhmet into drinking a lake of blood-coloured wine and, intoxicated, she stopped the carnage, and thus humanity was saved.

6 The Old Kingdom actually began in the latter Third Dynasty whose Pharaoh, Djoser, had the first pyramid built by Imhotep, at Saqqara (see 'The Warrior'). The Fourth Dynasty lasted from 2613BC to 2498BC, and comprised the reigns of Sneferu, Khufu (Cheops, who built the Great Pyramid), Djedefre, Khafre (Chephren), Menkaure and Shepseskaf. For most of Ancient Egypt's history, the pyramids were as much a source of amazement to the Egyptians as they are to us today.

appeared in *Pearl Harbor*, *Anywhere But Here* and *Whore*. Carlos Lauchu was Slice in *Spy Hard*. Djimon Hounson played Cinqué in *Amistad* and Mobalage in *ER*. Erick Avari was Tival in *Planet of the Apes* and Dr Bey in *The Mummy* and appeared in *The West Wing*, *Felicity*, *The X-Files* and *Star Trek: The Next Generation*. French Stewart is famous as Harry Solomon in *3rd Rock from the Sun*. He was also in *Clockstoppers* and *Love Stinks*. Gianin Loffler was in *Faces on Mars* and *Babylon 5*. Christopher Fields' movies include *Fight Club*, *Apollo 13*, *Jurassic Park*, *Alien?* and *Jacob's Ladder*. Derek Webster was Dr Zoetrope in *Josh Kirby: Time Warrior*. Jack Moore was in *Love is a Gun*. Steve Gianneli played Steve in *Cheers*. David Pressman appeared in *Volcano*. Scott Alan Smith was in *Magnolia* and *The X-Files*. Cecil Hoffman played Zoey Clemmons in *LA Law*. Rae Allen was Ma Keller in *A League of their Own*. Richard Kind played Paul Lassiter in *Spin City*. John Storey was Craig Van Patten in *The Visitor*. Lee Taylor-Allen can be seen in *Very Close Quarters*. George Gray is best known as a host of the US version of *The Weakest Link* and *Junkyard Wars*. Kelly Vint appeared in *Space Jam*. Erik Holland's movies include *Titanic*, *Ghostbusters II* and *Maniac Cop* whilst his TV roles include *The Man from U.N.C.L.E*, *The Fugitive*, *Star Trek*, *Mission: Impossible*, *Alias Smith and Jones*, *The Bionic Woman* and *Mannix*. Nick Wilder was in *Orbit* and was world wind-surfing champion in 1977. Sayed Badreya appeared in *Shallow Hal*. Michael Jean-Philippe was in *Killing Zoe*. Gladys Holland played Madame Dubois in *Beverly Hills 90210*. Roger Til appeared in *Brewster's Millions*, *The Rockford Files*, *WKRP in Cincinnati* and *Laverne and Shirley*. Kenneth Danziger was a voice-artist on *Shrek*. Oscar-winning effects supervisor Kit West played Billie Jo in *Speedway*. Robert Ackerman was in *Shoot the Moon*. Frank Welker is a legendary voice-artist who's worked on over 300 films and series, including *The Jetsons*. His best known voice is Freddie on *Scooby Doo, Where Are You?*. John Rhys-Davies was Sallah in *Raiders of the Lost Ark*, Professor Arturo in *Sliders* and Gimli in *The Lords of the Rings*. He's also appeared in *I, Claudius* and *The Sweeney*.

### BEHIND THE CAMERA

Roland Emmerich and Dean Devlin previously worked together on *Universal Soldier*. Their subsequent projects include *Independence Day*, *Godzilla* and *The Patriot*. Devlin started as an actor in *Predators From Beyond Neptune* and *3:15*. Oliver Eberle produced *Eye of the Storm*. Joel B Michaels worked on *Black Moon Rising* and *Cutthroat Island*. Mario Kassar was executive producer on *Terminator 2: Judgment Day*, *The Doors* and *First Blood* (and its sequels). David Arnold scored *Shaft*, *Randall and Hopkirk (Deceased)*, *The World is Not Enough* and *Tomorrow Never Dies*. Stunt co-ordinator Andy Armstrong also worked on *Joshua Tree*, *Charlie's Angels* and *Galaxy Quest*. Kurt Russell's stunt-double John Casino's movies include *The Mask of Zorro*, *The Usual Suspects* and *Darkman*.

### LOGIC, LET ME INTRODUCE YOU TO THIS WINDOW

The camera crew are visible, reflected in Daniel's sunglasses. A crewperson's shadow is seen as Daniel puts Sha'uri in the sarcophagus. Shadow sizes and directions in the desert change with alarming regularity. Ra claims to be able to destroy Earth by increasing the power of O'Neil's weapon 100-fold. A 100 kiloton bomb, however, would cause only localised destruction on Earth. The symbol referred to as the Eye of Ra is actually the Eye of Horus. Kurt Russell's shirt is already cut before O'Neil is scratched by Anubis. When Daniel first enters the city, his pendant is tucked under his shirt; in the next shot it's hanging loose; then it's tucked in again. As O'Neil tries to defuse the bomb, Daniel's mouth doesn't move when he asks 'How much time do we have?'. Jack's reply, '45 seconds,' also appears overdubbed. When Kasuf is flattened by an explosion, the attacking ships are clearly models - their guide-wires are visible. The speed at which the bomb-timer ticks changes several times. Ra's spaceship moves too slowly to cover the distance shown before the bomb activates. O'Neil is notified he's been reactivated, indicating he's a reservist. However, reservists aren't authorised to handle Top Secret assignments, except in the event of war. When Jackson and O'Neil are brought before Ra, the guard who tries to hit O'Neil misses him and Kurt Russell falls after the staff is past his knee. Jackson 'speaks' Ancient Egyptian, but he shouldn't know what the language sounded like. Egyptologists assigned their own pronunciations to the language's symbols after the Rosetta Stone[7] was discovered. Daniel shouldn't, therefore, have understood what the Abydonians were saying unless they wrote it. Some Amarna letters had been written in other languages, so scholars *do* have an idea of how some words may have been pronounced, but the writers of the movie appear to have gone with the standard US-English transliteration conventions. If Ra outlawed written language many centuries ago on Abydos, then how does Sha'uri know what the symbols in the cave mean so she can teach Daniel? When the transport rings decapitate Anubis, Ra screams and Jaye Davidson's teeth-fillings are visible. The spellings of O'Neil and Sha'uri are different in the subsequent series. The TV spelling of Sha're is a much more appropriate Egyptian word, meaning 'daughter of Re'.

### QUOTE/UNQUOTE

Feretti, on Gate-travel: 'What a rush!' O'Neil, decapitating Anubis: 'Give my regards to King Tut, *asshole*!'

### NOTES

'We've opened a doorway to a world we know nothing about.' An excellent, beguiling opening 30 minutes eventually lead to a rather dull and formulaic 90s action-movie, albeit with some clever ideas. Spader is really watchable, though Kurt Russell struggles for a long time to make O'Neil interesting and (ultimately) likeable. It's a credit to the actor that he achieves this late in the movie.

Jack smokes cigarettes (he tells Skaara it's a bad habit). His son, Tyler, recently died in a gun tragedy (see 'Cold Lazarus', 'The Devil You Know'). Daniel's a linguist, had foster parents (see 'The Gamekeeper', 'Crystal Skull') has recently been evicted from his apartment and has dust allergies (see 'Children of the Gods'). He translates in 14 days what Catherine and her team couldn't in two years. The sarcophagus is used to resurrect both Daniel and Sha'uri after they're shot with staff weapons. Kasuf is Sha'uri's and Skaara's father. Each Stargate address is seven symbols long, the seventh always being the point of origin.

With a budget of $55m, *Stargate* eventually grossed a highly impressive $196.6m worldwide, including an opening weekend figure of $16.6m in the US.

### TRIVIA

*Stargate* was conceived by Roland Emmerich in film school in 1979. The Hazbot robot was loaned by NASA and the California Institute of Technology Jet Propulsion Laboratory in Pasadena. The language spoken by

7 A basalt tablet found in 1799 by French archaeologist Pierre François Xavier Bouchard, dating to the reign of Ptolemy V (c. 196BC). Carved with parallel inscriptions in hieroglyphics, Egyptian demotic and Greek, this provided the key to the deciphering of many ancient texts.

the archaeologists in Egypt is Swedish: 'Herregud, vad är det?' ('My God, what *is* it?'); 'Skulle önska jag visste det' ('I wish I knew'). The fingertips on the alien ribbon devices are based on golden fingertips put onto some royal Egyptian mummies. Ra's children wear the 'side-lock of youth' (a hairstyle worn until the coming of age/circumcision ceremony). The head-dress Ra wears towards the end, with a disc between two long horns, is from traditional depictions of the goddess Hathor (see 'Hathor').

Filming locations included the Buttercup Dunes in Imperial County, California and Yuma, Arizona (the same location used for the Dune Sea in *Return of the Jedi*). The scenes of Stargate Command were filmed in a large dome sited in Long Beach Harbor, next to the anchored ocean liner *Queen Mary*. Formerly the hanger of Howard Hughes' World War II troop-carrier, the *Spruce Goose*, the dome was also used for the Gotham City interiors in *Batman Forever*. Some additional scenes for *Stargate* were filmed at Santa Clarita Studios after shooting was suspended for three weeks by the January 1994 Northridge earthquake.

**CRITIQUE** The *Washington Post*'s Hal Hinson described the movie as a 'mostly entertaining sci-fi adventure,' noting: '*Stargate* holds our attention through a combination of suspense and funky wit. The latter is supplied primarily by Spader... [who] dominates the first half. He seems to get lost in the second - even when the character is on screen. By the end, the film's early promise has degenerated into routine pyrotechnics.' Most other critics weren't as kind as that, Roger Ebert memorably noting: 'The movie is so lacking in any sense of wonder that it hurtles us from one end of the universe to the other, only to end in a gunfight... *Stargate* is like a film school exercise. Assignment: Conceive of the weirdest plot you can think of, reduce it as quickly as possible to action movie clichés... and make sure something gets blowed-up real-good.' *San Francisco Chronicle*'s Mike LaSalle described the movie as: 'Imitation Spielberg. An outer-space attempt at wonder and enchantment that crashes inside 20 minutes.' *Leonard Maltin's Movie and Video Guide*, however, called *Stargate* an 'interesting odyssey, impressively mounted and jammed with visual effects.'

**CAST AND CREW COMMENTS** The main thing Kurt Russell remembers about filming? 'I was washing sand out of every part of my body for weeks afterwards!'

**DID YOU KNOW?** Many of the crowd-scenes feature mannequins, as they were considerably cheaper than extras.

# STARGATE SG-1
# SEASON 1 (1997-1998)

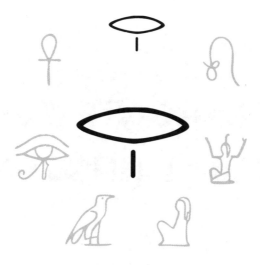

'When the gate is opened, the adventure of a
lifetime is just beginning...'

# STARGATE SG-1™ SEASON 1 (1997-1998)

Double Secret Productions/Gekko Film Corp/
Metro-Goldwyn-Meyer

Developed for Television by Brad Wright, Jonathan Glassner

Executive Producer: Brad Wright, Jonathan Glassner

Co-Executive Producer: Michael Greenburg, Jeff King (3-8)

Producer: Ron French (1-10), N John Smith (11-22)

Associate Producer: W Michael Beard (1-2)

Post Production Consultant: R Michael Eliot

Executive Story Consultant: Katharyn Powers (3-22)

Executive Story Editor: Robert C Cooper (3-22)

Regular Cast: Richard Dean Anderson (Jack O'Neill), Michael Shanks (Daniel Jackson), Amanda Tapping (Samantha Carter), Christopher Judge (Teal'c), Don S Davis (General George Hammond)

SEASON 1

# DON'T STAND ME DOWN

*Stargate* was a huge international success. However, as *SG-1* producer Jonathan Glassner recalled, writers Emmerich and Devlin were 'very bitter' about what subsequently happened to the *Stargate* franchise: 'They planned a series of movies but the studio, which controlled the rights, never had any intention [of that].' MGM decided the format would best lend itself to an episodic television series and offered the project to Emmerich and Devlin. The duo turned it down. Subsequently they heavily criticised not only the studio's decision but also *SG-1* itself. 'They've been bad-mouthing [us], which I think is very unfair,' noted Glassner. 'We've done the movie justice and stuck to the mythology created by them.'[8] 'They hate our series,' producer Brad Wright added some years later. 'They'd like to pretend it never happened. I reminded MGM that there are several million fans worldwide that may beg to differ.' It is an irony, therefore, that *SG-1* has subsequently developed far more depth and intelligence than the somewhat one-dimensional movie on which it is based. As reviewer Andy Lane observed, the series has 'better plots, better characters, better writing. The film had to be simple to get such a huge audience. Only then could the series make its bid for freedom.'

Glassner and Wright had previously worked together as producers on *The Outer Limits*.[9] (Glassner also wrote for *Star Trek: Voyager*, Wright for *Highlander*). Both were interested in developing *Stargate* for TV. 'We individually, without knowing the other was doing it, went to the president of MGM and said "You've got this movie in your library. It would make a great series,"' noted Glassner. 'He suggested we do it together.' One thing the writers wished to expand was the mythology database. If visitors from another planet shaped Egyptian culture, the argument went, why not other cultures from history? 'All good science fiction is metaphorical,' says Glassner. 'It's a way to study ourselves.'[10]

Early in *SG-1*'s development John Symes, the MGM President, suggested to Glassner and Wright that Richard Dean Anderson would be a perfect choice for Jack O'Neill. 'I had to make sure they were willing to endure my sense of humour and infiltrate it into the character subtly. Or with a sledgehammer,' noted Anderson. The search for the other actors took longer, with extensive auditions/rehearsals held in New York, Toronto and Vancouver. Pruning thousands of potential cast members down to 25, the producers flew the hopefuls to Los Angeles for screen tests. Christopher Judge was the immediate choice for Teal'c (as soon as they heard his voice, Brad Wright says, it was a case of 'Okay, he's Teal'c. Next!'), although Peter Williams, who also read for the part, impressed the production team enough to find himself offered the recurring role of Apophis.

With casting in place, filming of the pilot episode began in February 1997 in the mountains outside Vancouver.[11] The first day was a disaster, torrential rain and technical problems causing

8 It's certainly fair to say that in the 2001 DVD commentary, Devlin's comments concerning the series are somewhat dismissive.

9 Early SG-1 episodes do have a tendency to look like *Outer Limits* stories retooled for a regular cast. Given the shared filming locations and the writer/producer relationship between the two shows, perhaps that's inevitable.

10 'The film only scratched the surface,' noted Brad Wright. 'The Stargate has 39 symbols on it. Why would a race create a device capable of millions of permutations but only able to send you to one planet?'

11 Because the cost of everything is much cheaper than in Los Angeles, filming US movies and TV series in Canada has become big business over the last decade. The popularity of *The X-Files* - the first five seasons of which were also shot in Vancouver - helped to alert many in Hollywood to the potential that Canada has to offer.

most of the footage to be scrapped. Interiors were shot on the largest soundstage in North America, specifically built to house Stargate Command at Bridge Studios in Vancouver.

**DID YOU KNOW?** MGM sold a package of 44 episodes of *SG-1* to the cable network Showtime. Midway through season one, a further 44 episodes were ordered, extending the cast's initial two-year contracts to four.

# ALL THE PRESIDENT'S MEN (AND WOMEN)

Richard Dean Anderson: Born in January 1950 in Roseville, Minneapolis, Rick is the son of a jazz musician father and an artist mother and first came to international attention in 1984 playing the eponymous role in the detective show *MacGyver*. By the end of its seven year run, Rick had gained almost total artistic control over the series. A very funny man, with a deep love of *The Simpsons* and British comedy, Rick first appeared on TV in series including *The Love Boat*, *Facts of Life* and *General Hospital*. In the latter he played Jeff Webber for five years in the late 70s. When *MacGyver* ended, Rick formed his own production company - Gekko Films - with Michael Greenburg. They subsequently made two *MacGyver* TV movies and the short-lived *Legend* for UPN. Anderson's films include *Odd Jobs*, *Beyond Betrayal* and *Private Collection*.

Active in a pressure group called *Handgun Control, Inc* - in *MacGyver*, his character always refused to carry guns - Rick aspired to play professional ice hockey as a teenager but broke both arms in separate incidents when he was 16. The second was so bad he was hospitalised for three months. A year later, he rode his Harley Davidson 5,000 miles from Minnesota to Alaska. After leaving St Cloud State College, Rick performed as a mime act and a cabaret jester before turning to acting. He also fronted a country-rock duo called Rickie Dean and Dante during his college years. A keen sportsman, Rick has competed in various driving championships, twice completing the Toyota Celebrity Long Beach Grand Prix. He claims to have done everything he wants to in life 'at least twice'. He and his partner, Apryl Prose, have a young daughter named Wylie.

Amanda Tapping: 'She's got the greatest eyes,' noted director Peter DeLuise. 'You could drown in them.' Born in August 1965, in Rochford, Essex of Canadian parents, Amanda was raised in Toronto. Two of her brothers are in biochemistry and computer science respectively and her parents hoped that she would pursue a similar academic career. But acting got to her first. Graduating from the University of Windsor's School of Dramatic Art, Amanda co-founded the stage comedy group Random Acts, before making her mark in TV on series such as *Forever Knight*, *Due South*, *The X-Files* and *Millennium*. Her movies include *The Void*, *Blacktop*, *Booty Call*, *What Kind of Mother Are You?* and *Rent-a-Kid*.

Michael Shanks: Born in December 1970, in Kamloops, British Columbia, Michael Shanks studied Commerce at the state's university before pursuing an acting career and graduating with a Bachelor of Fine Arts degree. He performed for two seasons at the Stratford Shakespeare Festival and made his film debut in *Call of the Wild*. His other credits include *Highlander*, *A Family Divided* and *Andromeda*. Michael was formerly in a relationship with his screen wife, Vaitiare Bandera, and the couple have a daughter called Tatiana.

Christopher Judge: Although he seemed destined for a professional football career after receiving a scholarship from the University of Oregon, Chris Judge always knew he was going to be an actor. Whilst in Oregon, he became host of the West Coast FOX KLSR *Morning Show*. This led to guest appearances on *The Fresh Prince of Bel Air* and *The Jamie Foxx Show*. Judge studied Drama at the Howard Fine Studio in Los Angeles, played Richie Styles on *Sirens* and appeared in *Bird on a Wire*, *Cadence* and *House Party II*. A fine singer, Chris's first CD was released in 1999 and his distinctive voice was used for Magneto on the animated *X-MEN*. He has three children, Christopher, Cameron and Catrina.

Don S Davis: Something of a renaissance man; a highly-respected character-actor, a talented painter, a theatre professor and formerly a captain in the US Army stationed in Korea in the 70s. No surprise, therefore, that Don Davis has made something of a career portraying military figures: an Army major in *Twin Peaks*, a Navy captain in *The X-Files* and an Air Force general in *SG-1*. Don has appeared in numerous films including *The Fan*, *Hook*, *Needful Things* and *Look Who's Talking*. On TV, in addition to being Dana Scully's father in *The X-Files*, he was in *Broken Badges*, *L.A. Law* and *Knots Landing* and previously worked with Richard Dean Anderson acting as Dana Elcar's body-double on *MacGyver*. Don currently resides outside Vancouver and spends his spare time trying to improve his golf game.

Teryl Rothery: From Vancouver, Teryl began her career as a dancer aged 13 in the stage-musical *Bye Bye Birdie*. Teryl's movies include *Masterminds* and *Urban Safari*. She appeared in the TV movies *Who Killed My Daughter?*, *Tailhook*, *For the Love of Nancy* and *The Man Who Wouldn't Die*, and guest-starred on *The X-Files*, *The Commish* and *Cobra*. Teryl's voice talents have been used on many cartoon series including *ExoSquad*. When not working, Teryl enjoys walking, riding and roller-blading.

# 1-2   CHILDREN OF THE GODS[12]

US Transmission Date: 27 Jul 1997 (Showtime)
UK Transmission Date: 8 Apr 1998 (Sky One)
Writers: Jonathan Glassner, Brad Wright
Director: Mario Azzopardi
Cast: Jay Acovone (Charles Kawalsky), Vaitiare Bandera (Sha're), Robert Wisden (Samuels), Peter Williams (Apophis), Gary Jones (Technician) Brent Stait (Louis Ferretti), Alexis Cruz (Skaara), Eric Schneider (Doctor), Colin Lawrence (Warren), Rachael Hayward (Guard #3), Rick Ravanello (Guard #2), JB Bivens (Guard #1), Stephen Sumner (Goa'uld #1), Adam Harrington (Goa'uld #2), John Bear Curtis

12 First shown as a 14-rated 95 minute movie (and released on video and DVD in that format). Most subsequent broadcasts of 'Children of the Gods', both in the US and overseas, have been as two separate 45 minute episodes. That's how it received its UK terrestrial debut, for instance. To maintain the numbering system that has 'Wormhole X-Treme' as the 100th episode of *SG-1*, therefore, for the purposes of this book 'Children of the Gods' will be counted as two episodes. The main differences between the edits are the cutting from the two-episode version of a (brilliant) scene between Jack and Daniel at Jack's home and a snatch of full-frontal nudity as Sha're becomes a Goa'uld. For UK terrestrial broadcast, Channel 4 removed all shots of Goa'uld symbionts and blood - in the process mystifying viewers as to how Kawalsky becomes a host and making it seem that Teal'c is exposing himself to Jack and Daniel at one point.

(Primitive), John Tierney (Monk), Garvin Cross (Casey) Anthony Ashbee (Soldier), Andrew McIlwaine (Medic), Santo Lombardo (Bolaa), Sean Amsing (Tobay) Monique Rusu (Dark Skinned Woman), Janette de Vries (Female Serpent Guard)

A retired Jack O'Neill is recalled to duty by General Hammond when aliens emerge from the Stargate. Reunited with Kawalsky and Ferretti and joined by Captain Samantha Carter, he returns to Abydos where the aliens, led by Apophis, kidnap Sha're and Skaara. Jack, Daniel and a group including Sam, track the aliens to Chulak. They discover Sha're's possessed by the snakelike Goa'uld, who oppress many worlds with the aid of their guard, the Jaffa. Captured, the Stargate team are to be executed, but escape with the aid of a Jaffa, Teal'c, who realises he has worshipped false gods.

**WHO ARE THESE GUYS ANYWAY?** Returning from the first mission (see *Stargate*), Jack reported the Abydos Gate destroyed and that Daniel was dead (though he, seemingly, told Catherine the truth; see 'The Torment of Tantalus'). Jack also discovered that his wife had left him. She had forgiven him for the death of their son, but could not forget it. Jack says he will never forgive himself (see 'Cold Lazarus'; significantly, he tells Kawalsky that Skaara reminds him of his son). Most of Jack's work over the past decade has been classified (and, probably, longer; see 'The Gamekeeper', 'A Matter of Time'). Daniel married Sha're and has spent over a year with the people of Abydos, who regard him as their saviour. He promises his friends on Abydos to return in one year with Sha're. If he does not, they are told to bury their Stargate forever (see 'Secrets'). He still has allergies. Samantha Carter is an accomplished pilot (or possibly a navigator, it's never made entirely clear[13]) having logged over 100 hours in enemy airspace during the Gulf War, and a theoretical astrophysicist transferred to the Stargate programme from The Pentagon. She studied the Gate for two years before Daniel made it work and believes she should have been on the original mission (see 'Secrets'). Two-star-general George Hammond replaced General West as head of the Stargate programme. He's stern-but-fair, and committed to the safety of those under his command. On his last tour of duty, he is thinking of writing a book. Apophis is described in Egyptian mythology as the serpent god. (His Jaffa soldiers wear a snake-symbol on their foreheads.[14])

**THE WIT AND WISDOM OF JACK O'NEILL** He uses two clichés *ad nauseum* throughout the series: 'with all due respect' (usually when disagreeing with Hammond's orders) and 'for crying out loud' (when exasperated with someone).

**THIS IS WHAT SHE'S LIKE?** Sam assures her male colleagues that she played with dolls as a child and, though her reproductive organs may be on the inside, she's

- - - - - - - - - - - - - - - - - - - - - - - - - - - - - - - - - - - - - - - - - - - - - -

13 One fan myth shattered: F-16s don't have navigators, they have WSOs (weapons systems officers). However, note that Sam merely says that she flew this aircraft in simulation. Nevertheless, if Sam did fly in the Gulf War, it was more than likely as a pilot.

14 Apophis is the Greek name for Apep, the Egyptian snake-god of the underworld, who threatened the barque that carried Re. A collection called *The Book Of Apophis* contains rituals intended to thwart him. It was composed in the New Kingdom near Heliopolis, though the best surviving text is the 4th century BC Bremner-Rhynd papyrus. Some cryptozoolgists believe Apophis's legend arose from giant snakes in the African jungles.

just as tough as they are.

**ORIGINS OF THE SPECIES** The Jaffa serve as incubators for Goa'uld larva from childhood. Upon reaching maturity, the parasite is removed and transferred to a host-body. Ra was *not* the entity upon which the ancient Egyptians based their religious mythology. He merely assumed this identity when on Earth. The Goa'uld choose who will become their children. They presumably have mature symbionts ready for joining (see 'Bloodlines', 'Hathor'). Teal'c is dismissive of Daniel's belief that something of the host must survive (see 'The Enemy Within').

There are 36 hours in a day on Abydos.[15] Chulak has two suns. In addition to being the planet, it also appears to be the name of the major settlement.

**SEX AND DRUGS AND ROCK 'N' ROLL** Daniel taught the Abydonians how to make alcohol. Back on Earth, Jack and Daniel share a beer. Jack, alluding to Carter, says he *likes* women (he just has problems with scientists).

**THE CONSPIRACY STARTS AT CLOSING TIME** The President authorises the formation of nine covert teams, designated SG-1 to SG-9. Their mission is to perform reconnaissance, determine threats and make peaceful contact with the people of other worlds (see 'The Broca Divide', 'Bane'). Kawalsky is given command of SG-2. A titanium iris is installed over the Stargate which allows a wormhole to be established, but keeps objects and people from being able to access the Gate. To instruct the SGC to open the iris, each SG team is given a GDO ('Garage Door Opener') with a unique code.

**SPACE TRAVEL'S IN MY BLOOD** To create a stable wormhole, the Stargate releases a tremendous energy. On other worlds it's controlled by a so-called dial home device (DHD), on which the user simply punches the symbols in an address. This device was missing from the Giza site (see 'Watergate'). According to Carter, it took 15 years and three supercomputers to make the Gate work (see 'The Torment of Tantalus', '1969'). Most of the Abydonians seemed to have learned English from Daniel. A month after the first Stargate mission, Daniel discovered a maproom on Abydos, perhaps left by the builders of the Stargates. The walls are covered with lists of addresses for Gates across the galaxy. Daniel's even mapped some of the constellations represented in the Abydonian sky. He hasn't yet been able to dial other planets however, because the addresses of many have changed slightly over thousands of years, due to planetary drift. The Gate probably worked between Earth and Abydos because they are relatively close. Sam theorises the SGC's computers can adjust for the changes, and thus correct out-of-date addresses. The Stargate itself is made from a quartz-like substance (also mentioned in the movie) subsequently named Naqahdah (see 'Singularity').

**JACK NAMES THE PLANETS** Jack appears to be observing the Trifid Nebula (in the constellation of Sagittarius) through his telescope.

· · · · · · · · · · · · · · · · · · · · · · · · · · · · · · · · · · · · · · · · · · · · · · · · · · ·

15 Abydos was both a town in Ancient Egypt much associated with the god Osiris, and a Greek colony on the Asiatic side of the Dardanelles, scene of the legend of Hero and Leander.

**IN THE INTERESTS OF NATIONAL SECURITY** The Stargate resides within the NORAD Cheyenne Mountain Complex in Colorado,[16] having moved from the nearby Creek Mountain site seen in the movie (see also '1969').

**POSSIBLE INFLUENCES** The series begins with a glorious in-joke, Sam noting it took two years to '*MacGyver* a dialling system'. Also, Henry Stanley's famed meeting with David Livingstone in 1868 ('Dr Jackson, I presume?'), *Apocalypse Now* (the death card), *Die Hard* (Jack having to kill anybody who may read any book he should ever write), G.I. Joe and Major Matt Mason (an astronaut doll from the 1970s), *Frenzy* ('lovely!') and *Star Trek* (Ferretti does a Vulcan hand-greeting).

**'YOU MIGHT REMEMBER ME FROM...'** Peter Williams was in *Soul Survivor*, *Run* and *A Good Burn*. Jay Acovone appeared in *Crocodile Dundee in Los Angeles*, *Snitch*, *Stepfather III* and *Cold Steel*. Sean Amsing was Maurice in *Bones*. Vaitiare Bandera was in *US Marshals*. Brent Stait played Rev Bem in *Andromeda*. John Tierney has appeared in *The X-Files*, *First Wave* and *Highlander*. John Bear Curtis was Bull in *Y2K*. English-born Robert Wisden appeared in *Final Destination*, *Circle of Deceit* and *Madison*, readers may know him best as Bobby Modell in *The X-Files*. Rachel Hayward played Kate in *Watchtower*. Monique Rusu was Rosita in *Mr Magoo*. Rick Ravanello played Joe Clary in *Hart's War*. Colin Lawrence was in *Dreamcatcher*. JB Bivens appeared in *See Spot Run*, *The X-Files* and *Wounded*. Adam Harrington played Doug in *Oh Baby* and was in *Valentine*, *A Girl Thing*, *Y2K*, and *Without Malice*. Eric Schneider was Dr Cooper in *Backfire*.

**BEHIND THE CAMERA** Director Mario Azzopardi also worked on *Sliders*, *Wiseguy*, *F/X: The Series* and *The Outer Limits*. Producer Ron French worked on *Badge of Betrayal*, *The X-Files* and *Strange World*.

**LOGIC, LET ME INTRODUCE YOU TO THIS WINDOW** Where on Abydos did Daniel acquire a felt tip pen? One of the extras who goes to Abydos is, visibly, a soldier killed in the teaser. Jack theorises that because they defeated Ra, the aliens now consider Earth a threat. However, neither he nor Daniel knew there were others like Ra (they were told he was from a dying race). Doesn't Apophis check his destination is reachable before stepping through a Gate? He appears on Abydos without apparently doing so. There are seven symbols in every cartouche in the Abydos maproom. If the seventh symbol is always the point of origin, then all of the seventh symbols should be the same. They're not. Major Samuels uses a radio to tell the control room to close the iris; we never see this done again. According to Daniel, all the symbols in the maproom are on the Abydos Gate, but most appear to be hieroglyphs, not glyphs as on the Earth Gate. How do the SGC work out which planets the refugees came from to return them home? Why is Sam the only one to check her GDO? Shouldn't each SGC member have one? Evidence elsewhere ('Cold Lazarus', 'There But For the Grace of God') suggests they do. Amaunet is referred to as Apophis's Queen.[17] Subsequently, the Tok'ra state that Goa'uld are sexless. Another pair of Goa'uld take Skaara as host for their offspring but Apophis and Amaunet

---

16 Beneath the pine-studded granite mass of Cheyenne Mountain lies NORAD, the North American Aerospace Defense Command. The Defense Department built the facility in the 1960s as an 'early warning' post to spot incoming nuclear missiles.

can, seemingly, reproduce themselves (see 'Secrets'). How can a wormhole be tracked through three-dimensional space on a two-dimensional plexiglas map? As Daniel tries to find out what happened to Sha're, his robe slips off his shoulder and he fiddles with it stumbling over his next line. Ferretti is dragged out of the Gate headfirst, but when he's lifted onto the stretcher, his feet are down-ramp. Daniel says the Abydonians are about to have their evening meal, but it's still daylight later when they go to the maproom. How long does it take Hammond to realise that SG-1 are the people he met in 1969 (see '1969')? Hammond says six aliens came through the Gate - in fact there was Teal'c, six Jaffa and Apophis, a total of eight. Although only two Jaffa are killed, the SGC seems to have acquired four Jaffa corpses. When a round metallic object lands at the feet of the sergeant, she picks it up. Lucky it wasn't a grenade, really. The same prop, a remote scanning probe here, *is* a grenade in 'Within The Serpent's Grasp' and 'Redemption Part 2' (and a timed booby-trap bomb in 'Seth').

How much time elapses between Jack's recall and the briefing in which Sam first appears? Jack has acquired a uniform with all his decorations on it by then. The post-Abydos briefing takes place the morning after the return from Abydos - but how much time elapses between this and the subsequent trip to Chulak? SGC patches have been designed and manufactured, so it would seem a few days at the very least. Hammond notes at the post-Abydos briefing that Jack keeps telling him it's time for Kawalsky to have a command. But Jack and the General didn't know each other before Jack's return to the SGC, so when did they have this conversation? Kawalsky wears Captain's bars throughout and is addressed as such by one of his men on Chulak. The officers in Dress Blues wear enlisted men's uniforms. Officers' jackets have a darker blue wristband. Why is there so much fuss about getting a symbiont later in the season - didn't they take those from the Jaffa killed in the teaser? The 'molecular deconstruction in progress' graphic when SG-1 go to Chulak shows only three travellers plus FRED, the vehicle carrying their baggage. When SG-1 dial home at the end, light from the wormhole is cast on Hammond and Samuels *before* the iris opens.

**STAR MATERIAL** The glyphs on the Stargate are said to represent constellations. These are arbitrary groupings of stars arranged into a pattern which makes sense only from one fixed point - in the case of 38 of the 39 glyphs on the Earth Gate, Earth itself. But most other Gates seem to include more or less the same glyphs (with occasional differences). This suggests whoever built the Gates started with Earth as the main reference point (see 'Message in a Bottle', 'The Fifth Race').

**GOA'ULD LEXICON** The Goa'uld language is diverse and there are many dialects. The order 'Kree!' is the Goa'uld equivalent of 'Achtung', though this meaning seems to change from episode to episode.[18] 'Chaapa'ai' is used on Abydos and Chulak to name the Stargate. 'Cha'hari' is Abydonian for 'don't shoot'.

**QUOTE/UNQUOTE** Sam: 'You really will like me when you get to know me.' Jack: 'Oh, I adore you already.'

• • • • • • • • • • • • • • • • • • • • • • • • • • • • • • • • • • • • • • • • • • • • • • • • •

17 One of the Ogdoad - eight chaos divinities - Amaunet was the wife of Amon, who later became Amon-Ra.

18 In 'Point of View' Jack ask the question that everyone's been dying to know: 'What the hell does "Kree!" mean?' Daniel replies it actually has several meanings including 'attention', 'listen-up', 'concentrate' and, perhaps, even 'yoo-hoo'.

Samuels: 'I kinda wish I was coming with you.' Kawalsky: 'I'm kinda glad you're staying behind.'

**NOTES** 'The aliens could've come from anywhere.' A well-structured plot, taking elements from the movie but allowing room for the one thing it didn't have an abundance of, humour. However, that 'capable-woman-scientist-patronised-by-boorish-male-colleagues' cliché is, indeed, present and correct. And done to death. Poor Amanda Tapping gets a horrible set of lines. But otherwise, good adventurous fun, and an effects *tour de force*, well-directed and papering over the occasional logic cracks with a nice use of irony. All this, *and* a flash of full-frontal-nudity.

Jack is from Chicago (see 'The Fifth Man'). He may not be much of a computer-type (as he will subsequently tell anyone within earshot) but he *does* own one. When he's looking through his telescope you can see a laptop on the table next to him. In the year since the events of *Stargate*, Kawalsky and Ferretti have both shot through the ranks from Lieutenant to Major.

**CRITIQUE** 'O'Neill is just like MacGyver: the toughest and most skilful fighter in the business, but still with a blokey, all-American sense of humour, so we can like as well as respect him,' noted online reviewer Darrin Farrant. '*Stargate SG-1* is a bit confused, even for a science-fiction show, but the special effects are good and lovers of *MacGyver* - and sci-fi groupies - will find it a welcome addition to their viewing.'

**CAST AND CREW COMMENTS** 'I knew I couldn't remain as stoic and serious as Kurt Russell's O'Neill [sic],' Anderson told Melissa Perenson. 'So I created a bit of an irreverent military figure which, apparently, goes over very big with the Air Force.' Although not a fan of science-fiction - describing himself as more *Indiana Jones* than *Star Wars* - he concedes 'stories that have humour, humanity and action are the kind I like.'

'We had a great deal of creative freedom with that first episode,' noted Alexis Cruz. 'The director, Mario Azzopardi, was willing to let us play with our characters and try different things.'

The first day's shooting was memorable for stuntman Dan Shea: 'There's a scene where Skaara blasts O'Neill with a Goa'uld weapon that sends him flying backwards. That was me doing what's known as a ratchet. You put on this jerk-harness that's attached to a cable. When the mechanism is fired it yanks you off your feet.'

**DID YOU KNOW?** *Stargate* has a universal theme, according to MGM's TV Entertainment President Hank Cohen. 'For two years running it's been the only US import to play during prime-time in Europe.' (Actually *Deep Space Nine*, *Voyager* and *Buffy* have also achieved this.) *SG-1* airs in 64 countries and is particularly popular in Germany and Scandinavia.

# 3   THE ENEMY WITHIN

US Transmission Date: 1 Aug 1997
UK Transmission Date: 15 Apr 1998

Writer: Brad Wright
Director: Dennis Berry
Cast: Jay Acovone (Charles Kawalsky), Gary Jones (Technician), Kevin McNulty (Doctor Warner), Alan Rachins (Colonel Kennedy), Warren Takeuchi (Young Doctor)

O'Neill wants Teal'c on his team, but Hammond won't approve the appointment. O'Neill sees military intelligence treat his friend like a guinea pig. Kawalsky has been suffering headaches caused by an alien larvae attached to his brain. With guidance from Teal'c, the doctors operate to remove it, but is Kawalsky still under alien control?

**THE WIT AND WISDOM OF JACK O'NEILL** To the badly injured Kawalsky: 'If you don't make it, can I have your stereo?' And: 'Any more thinking needed?'

**ORIGINS OF THE SPECIES** The Goa'uld, Teal'c notes, rule by force and control many hundreds of worlds. Once they have exhausted a planet's resources, they abandon it. The Jaffa have a myth about a lost world where the Goa'uld harvested a race known as 'the Tau'ri' for their slaves. This seems to mean that the galaxy is largely populated by the descendants of the ancient peoples of Earth.

A Goa'uld symbiont controls its host by wrapping itself around the spinal column and controlling the nervous system. Symbionts are born with the genetic memory of all Goa'uld. A Jaffa does not communicate with the symbiont within. Later in the series we learn it's more accurate to say that the symbiont refuses to have anything to do with the Jaffa who carries it.

**THE CONSPIRACY STARTS AT CLOSING TIME** The iris is, according to Sam, less than three micrometers from the Event Horizon so as not to allow matter to rematerialise. The Pentagon is keen to acquire a live Goa'uld symbiont by whatever means necessary, subsequently paving the way for the activities of Harry Maybourne's unit (see 'Bane', 'Shades of Grey').

**MILITARY INTELLIGENCE?** Jack, on Teal'c: 'I don't think he saved the lives of my team or came over to our side so he could become a damn guinea pig for military intelligence.'

**IN THE INTERESTS OF NATIONAL SECURITY** Hammond demonstrates his chumminess with the President for Kennedy's benefit.

**POSSIBLE INFLUENCES** Conceptually, *The Man Who Fell To Earth*, the Jon Pertwee era *Doctor Who*, Marvel's *Silver Surfer*, Robert Heinlein's *Stranger in a Strange Land* and *The Tingler*. The title is an episode of *Star Trek* (and many other series, for that matter). Also, *The Wizard of Oz* ('That's right Dorothy, it was all a dream').

**'YOU MIGHT REMEMBER ME FROM...'** Gary Jones appeared in *Postcards from the Edge*, *Trixie*, *The Sixth Man* and *Sliders*. Kevin McNulty's CV includes *A Girl Thing*, *Max Q*, *Millennium* and *Generation X*. Warren Takeuchi was in *Urban Safari*. Alan Rachins played Tom Moss in *Showgirls* and Doug Brackman in *LA Law* and was a writer on *Hill Street Blues*.

**BEHIND THE CAMERA** Before becoming a director, Dennis Barry was the writer of *Chloé* and *Last Song*. Production Designer Richard Hudolin worked as Art Director on *Excess Baggage*, *Little Women*, *Timecop*, *Stakeout*, *Superman III*, *Doctor Who* and *Sherlock Holmes Returns*.

**LOGIC, LET ME INTRODUCE YOU TO THIS WINDOW** Daniel and Sam both mention the 'embarkation room' rather than the gateroom (see '2010'). The first time the auto-destruct is aborted, the sergeant does so alone; after Kawalsky sets it, it requires two ranking officers to override. During Kawalsky's surgery, the guards stationed above the operating room are wearing surgical masks but not gloves. It's fairly certain that their guns aren't sterile either. Why do they have MP5s anyway? Against a bound victim, a pistol round would surely do, with far less risk of catching the medical staff in crossfire as well? The computer monitor in the control room reads 'device idle' and the sound of the wormhole disappearing is heard, but the chevrons on the Gate are still lit. Teal'c is supposedly under guard, but when he follows Kawalsky, he passes two soldiers who let him go unchallenged. The two planets SG-1 and SG-2 are supposed to go to are P3575 and P3A577, but Jack says P3A575 on one occasion. During the DHD briefing, there's already a drawing of a cube on the white board (to explain the six-points-in-space concept), but Sam starts to redraw it just before Daniel notices Kawalsky in the gateroom. When Kawalsky is trying to Gate out, Sam says that he set the co-ordinates for Chulak. But the glyphs we see on the computer start with Taurus (first symbol for Abydos), not Scorpio (first symbol for Chulak). Why aren't the 'radiation team' called every time a team returns from offworld subsequently? What, exactly, drops out of Kawalsky's head when he dies? The husk of the Goa'uld had already been removed. Symbionts evidently shed their skins, like snakes; that was probably what had been removed earlier. Hammond describes Teal'c as being an alien. He isn't, he's human. Only the embryo within him is of an alien species. How does Jack know how to spell Teal'c?

**GOA'ULD LEXICON** 'Shol'va' means 'traitor' and is often used, by both Jaffa and Goa'uld, in relation to Teal'c. 'Tau'ri' translates from Egyptian as 'people of the land of Ra'.

**QUOTE/UNQUOTE** Hammond, to a departing Kennedy: 'Don't let the door hit your ass on the way out.'

**NOTES** 'That's kind-of a human thing. We tend to be afraid of things we don't know.' A confused mix of medical drama and espionage horror, this episode doesn't really get going until it's almost over. Well-acted, but low on the two great strengths *SG-1* would soon discover it had - suspense and humour.

Jack promises to show Teal'c his world someday (see 'Cold Lazarus'). The code to abort an auto-destruct command is 81452667 (also seen in 'A Matter of Time').

**SONG FOR MY SUGAR-SPUN SISTER** 'I had to fight for, not the woman in the character but the *human* in the character,' noted Amanda Tapping. 'They were writing [Carter] in a very one-dimensional way. I said, "women don't speak like this." Sam was very linear, sitting on her soapbox with this raging feminist diatribe about equality which I personally, as a feminist, find really boring.' Amanda's perseverance worked: 'To their credit, they said "we didn't expect you to do this with Carter. You've expanded her beyond what we thought she was going to be."'

**DID YOU KNOW?** The scene in which Sam is knocked unconscious by Kawalsky in the elevator resulted in a real-life concussion for Amanda Tapping.

# 4    EMANCIPATION

US Transmission Date: 8 Aug 1997
UK Transmission Date: 22 Apr 1998
Writer: Katharyn Powers
Director: Jeff Woolnough
Cast: Cary-Hiroyuki Tagawa (Turghan), Jorge Vargas (Abu), Soon-Tek Oh (Moughal), Crystal Lo (Nya), Marilyn Chin (Clanswoman)

On P3X593, SG-1 meets the Shavadai, a race of Mongol-like warriors who operate by a strict code, which includes lowly status for women. Sam has lots to say about this but is kidnapped by Abu, who hopes to trade her for the hand of Nya, the daughter of his father's enemy, Turghan. Carter arranges Nya's escape from Turghan's tyranny and is, herself, rescued. Turghan, however, threatens to execute his daughter unless Carter can defeat him in combat.

**THE WIT AND WISDOM OF JACK O'NEILL** Daniel: 'How is it you always come up with the worst case scenario?' Jack: 'Practice?'

**SAM'S TIRADE OF MILITANT FEMINIST DOGMA** The moral of this story seems to be, all men are horny, aggressive, misogynist bigots. Okay, so there *may* be an element of truth in that... Amanda Tapping, nevertheless, gets to show off a bit of cleavage.

**ORIGINS OF THE SPECIES** Simarkans may be descendants of the Chagatai, a nomad tribe. Moughal is Chieftain of the Shavadai ('People of the Steppe'), Turghan is Chieftain of the Toughai ('People of the Forest').

**SEX AND DRUGS AND ROCK 'N' ROLL** The Simarkans have, as a natural resource, a miraculous natural anaesthetic. In an unseen trip to P3X595, Carter drank a substance that, says Jack, made her do something she finds embarrassing. It seems to involve nudity.

**POSSIBLE INFLUENCES** *Romeo and Juliet* is an obvious one. The link to *Butch Cassidy and the Sundance Kid* (the knife fight) is more subtle. Mongol warlord Genghis Khan (1162-1227) is mentioned. Jack alludes to *The Oprah Winfrey Show*. Carter mentions the Special Forces Latin motto 'Free from Oppression'.

**'YOU MIGHT REMEMBER ME FROM...'** Soon-Tek Oh played Hip in *The Man With the Golden Gun*, Sensei on *Beverly Hills 90210* and Lt Torres on *Charlie's Angels*. He also did voice work on *Mulan* and worked on *The Invaders*, *Hawaii Five-O* and *M\*A\*S\*H*. Cary-Hiroyuki Tagawa was Commander Genda in *Pearl Harbor*, Kwang in *Licence to Kill* and Zylyn in *Space Rangers*.

### BEHIND THE CAMERA

Jeff Woolnough directed on *Dark Angel*, *Strange Frequency* and *Kung Fu: The Legend Continues*. In a long TV-writing career, Katharyn Powers' work can be seen on *The Fantastic Journey*, *Petrocelli*, *Charlie's Angels*, *The Dukes of Hazzard*, *Airwolf*, *Star Trek: Deep Space Nine* and *Voyager*.

### LOGIC, LET ME INTRODUCE YOU TO THIS WINDOW

Why didn't anyone check the rules of the contest before Sam volunteered? Turghan ought to be cut, considering how hard Sam presses the knife into his face. Where did the dress Sam is given come from? It seems much finer than any of those the planet's women are wearing. When did the members of SG-1 learn to ride a horse? Jack, maybe, but *Daniel*? A nomadic people of Mongol descent yet the Simarkans speak perfect English? The tents are completely wrong, historically. It looks as if somebody borrowed a bunch from a local Renaissance Faire and hung up a few Chinese rugs in the hope that nobody would notice. They should be made of hides and skins and they are positioned far too close together within the camp. There are a lot of very un-Asiatic faces among the extras in crowd - including Turghan's daughter. Daniel places Genghis Khan 900 years ago. Actually he died in 1227. When Carter cross-blocks Turghan, then gets him in an armlock, her knife miraculously disappears between shots, then reappears once Turghan is on the ground.

### QUOTE/UNQUOTE

Jack: 'When your back's up against the wall, and there's no tomorrow, just take it one day at a time, and remember, the bigger they are, etcetera...'

### NOTES

'I'm a human being, not property.' Oh dear, a rather obvious love story with a battle-of-the-sexes subplot tacked on and very few redeeming features besides. There's a kind of vain nihilism in the script, full of thud and blunder, signifying not a hell of a lot. Author's advice: Pretend this one never happened. Only decent bits: Jack's cheesy grin when he sees Sam in a dress and, later, Daniel's embarrassment when entering her tent.

Sam hasn't been afraid of the dark since she was two. She's a lousy cook but has level three advanced in hand-to-hand combat.

### QUARK, STRANGENESS AND CHARM

'We needed a woman who could be very strong, who you could buy as a soldier who had actually been in wars,' noted Jonathan Glassner regarding Amanda Tapping. 'And who is a brilliant scientist, and a beautiful woman. Finding an actress who could do all three of those convincingly is very difficult.'

### DID YOU KNOW?

*SG-1* films almost all of its locations in and around British Columbia. Some limited second unit footage from Cheyenne Mountain (all directed by Martin Wood in a two day-shoot in early 1997) and Washington DC, plus occasional stock footage, completes the illusion of a genuine travelogue show.

# 5    THE BROCA DIVIDE

US Transmission Date: 15 Aug 1997
UK Transmission Date: 29 Apr 1998
Writer: Jonathan Glassner
Director: William Gereghty
Cast: Teryl Rothery (Dr Janet Fraiser), Gary Jones (Technician), Gerard Plunkett (Tuplo), Steve Makaj (Colonel Makepeace), Nicole Oliver (Leedora), Danny Wattley (Johnson), Roxana Phillip (Melosha)

SG-1 arrive on P3X797 and discover a world divided between dark and light. The Untouched are Minoan-like and civilised. The Touched are primitive with the instincts of animals. When the team returns, all except Teal'c and Daniel begin to exhibit the brutality of the Touched, and their symptoms are passed on to others including Hammond. Daniel, Teal'c and Doctor Fraiser attempt to discover the reason for the transformation.

**ORIGINS OF THE SPECIES** The Touched suffer from a parasitic virus that increases testosterone levels and induces violent behaviour. Janet deduces that the cause is a histamine imbalance (and the Untouched have an acquired immunity through their diet). She and Daniel both suffer from rhinitis - inflammation of the mucous membrane - caused by allergies, and take antihistamine. The cure is large doses of Chlorpheniramine Maleate.

**SEX AND DRUGS AND ROCK 'N' ROLL** Infected by the disease, Sam stalks Jack in the locker room, pins him to a bench and seems intent on having an afternoon of hormone-crazed abandon. Much to Jack's distress, seemingly.

**MILITARY INTELLIGENCE?** The President agrees that all future SG missions will study scientific and cultural issues as well as purely military ones.

**IN THE INTERESTS OF NATIONAL SECURITY** First appearances of the lovely Dr Janet Fraiser (the SGC's resident expert on alien diseases), the MALP (Mobile Analytic Laboratory Probe) and Colonel Makepeace's happy band of bloodthirsty marines, SG-3.

Stargate Command used to be a missile silo (see '1969'). A Code Five Lockdown mandates that the mountain be sealed and anyone attempting to leave will be shot (see 'Message in a Bottle').

**POSSIBLE INFLUENCES** *I Love Lucy* ('Lucy, I'm home'). Sam and Daniel refer to Pierre Paul Broca (1824-80), French anthropologist and the founder of modern craniology. There's an oblique reference to Carl Sagan's 1979 book *Broca's Brain*.

**'YOU MIGHT REMEMBER ME FROM...'** Steve Makaj appeared in *Dark Angel*, *It*, *The Lone Gunmen* and *The X-Files*. Nicole Oliver did voice work on *The Cramp Twins*. Danny Wattley appeared in *Firestorm*. Gerard Plunkett was in *Rat Race*.

**BEHIND THE CAMERA** William Gereghty was a camera assistant on *The Godfather Part II* before graduating to directing on *Magnum PI*, *Legend*, *Viper* and *The Sentinel*. Director of photography Jim Menard worked on *Millennium* and *Frostfire*.

**LOGIC, LET ME INTRODUCE YOU TO THIS WINDOW** Michael Shanks looks utterly ridiculous as a caveman (in some shots, he's a dead-ringer for *The Simpsons'* Baby-with-One-Eyebrow). If this is a non-rotating planet, leading to a permanent dark and light side, how do the plants and trees in the dark photosynthesise? Why does Fraiser let some infected airmen beat themselves senseless against the walls? She sedates Jack very quickly so that *he* wouldn't hurt himself. Considering how contagious the virus is, why don't the medical staff take special precautions when handling the patients? The dialling sequence on the computer when SG-1 return for Daniel is for Abydos. Why is Melosha unconscious when Daniel finds her? How did he get the blanket out of his pack so quickly? The MALP doesn't send back confirmation of an intact DHD, but SG-1 go through the Gate anyway. The glass in the briefing room window breaks easily, yet in 'Spirits' an arrow goes through it without shattering it completely. Perhaps it was strengthened after this. After the two men fall from the briefing room, Sam calls for medics to 'Section C' without specifying a location. When Jack sends SG-3 to take the left flank and SG-1 to the right, SG-1 appear to goes left. Where did General Hammond go? He's put in with Jack, but when Teal'c and then Fraiser are in the cell later, the General is nowhere to be seen. It doesn't look as if Janet pushes the needle all the way in when she gives Jack anti-histamine. Why aren't the Untouched upset with Teal'c when SG-1 brings Daniel back? After all, Teal'c beat the guards unconscious and took their blood. It's hard to see how a histamine imbalance could cause reversion to primitivism. Histamines are released by basophil leucocytes causing veins to dilate. This can result in depletion of vascular fluids, known as 'histamine shock'. Allergic reactions, in which histamine is released, are similar and the two conditions are both treated with antihistamines. This might be partly responsible for difficult breathing during an asthma attack, for instance, and histamine causes contraction of involuntary muscle (especially of the gastric variety). But it doesn't, generally, turn people into cavemen.

**GOA'ULD LEXICON** 'Hylk'sha', common to several worlds, means 'Gods of the Underworld'.

**QUOTE/UNQUOTE** Daniel, when Jack tells him that Carter tried to seduce him: 'Oh, you poor man!'

**NOTES** 'Are you saying we could have brought a new plague to this planet?' The leprosy metaphor is an interesting one, mixed with laudable (if somewhat pretentious) Egalitarian rhetoric. But 'The Broca Divide' is, ultimately, something of an illogical mess. A fumble in the dark from a series that had definitely hit the ground shuffling and seemed unsure of what it actually wanted to *say*. Good performances from Anderson and Rothery however.

Note that, for this episode only, Fraiser calls Teal'c 'Mister Teal'c'. Once again, this episode was hacked to pieces by Channel 4's scissors in the UK, most notably losing the bit in which Daniel retains enough sense to take the injection, implying instead that Jack simply shoots him.

**DID YOU KNOW?** The budget for an average *Stargate SG-1* episode, after the first season, is approximately $1.4m.

# 6 THE FIRST COMMANDMENT

US Transmission Date: 22 Aug 1997
UK Transmission Date: 6 May 1998
Writer: Robert C Cooper
Director: Dennis Berry
Cast: William Russ (Jonas Hansen), Roger R Ross (Connor), Zahf Hajee (Jamala), Adrian Hughes (Baker), D Neil Mark (Frakes), Darcy Laurie (Cave-Dweller)

> SG-1 are sent to find the missing SG-9. They learn that a primitive population of P3X513 greet-ed SG-9 as gods. Captain Jonas Hanson, a former fiancé of Sam, has taken advantage of this and is forcing the inhabitants to rebuild a giant Gou'ald temple. Carter believes she can appeal to Hanson. Daniel and Teal'c, with the help of local Jamala, show the people that Hanson's power comes from technology not divinity.

**SAM'S TRAUMATIC LOVE-LIFE** Her previous character doesn't suggest a 'healer of the emotionally wounded', but maybe she's been overcompensating for her female reproductive organs (see 'Children of the Gods'). Sam and Hanson were engaged but she broke it off. He was charming but a bit dangerous. Sam isn't entirely surprised by his Messiah-complex, saying he likes control and talking about his Black Ops back-ground. She says she always had a soft spot for the lunatic fringe.

**ORIGINS OF THE SPECIES** Many Stargate worlds were terraformed by the Goa'uld over the centuries - hence the number of planets which have vegetation to support life. On planets with high UV radiation the Goa'uld had a pair of devices that created a sonic barrier turning the sky orange to protect the people from the sun.

**POSSIBLE INFLUENCES** *Lord of the Flies* and, especially, *Apocalypse Now*. Also, *Indiana Jones and the Last Crusade* ('You're sure?' 'Pretty Sure'), *The Wizard of Oz* ('We're off to see the wizard') and, obliquely, the *Stargate* movie ('Tastes like chicken'). The latter line also appears in the *MacGyver* episode 'The Gauntlet'. The title is, as Sam notes, an allusion to Exodus 20:2-3 ('I am the Lord thy God. Thou shalt wor-ship no other gods before me'). In an episode loaded with Biblical imagery, there are references to Moses leading his people to the promised land (Exodus 14) and Abraham preparing to sacrifice his son, Isaac (Genesis 21).

**'YOU MIGHT REMEMBER ME FROM...'** William Russ was in *American History X* and *Ally McBeal*. Roger Cross was Joshua in *First Wave* and Cooper in *The Commish*. Darcy Laurie appeared in *Atomic Train*.

**BEHIND THE CAMERA** Robert Cooper worked as a Story Editor on *PSI Factor*. Costume Designer Christina McQuarrie's movies include *My Son Johnny* and *A Child's Wish*.

**LOGIC, LET ME INTRODUCE YOU TO THIS WINDOW** Doesn't Daniel have his own GDO? If he does, he could have sent the iris code when Jonas was planning to push Jack and Connor into the wormhole. The shot of Teal'c firing into the trees appears to be one used in 'The Broca Divide'. Jack is on watch, Teal'c is meditating, Daniel and Connor are sleeping outside. So, why are there tents erected? Where did Jack get the blowgun? And why didn't he take an extra robe to cover Connor with? Why did Daniel eject the clip from the handgun? He might have needed it. Watch Daniel's glasses and clip-on sunglasses, especially when he's on the cliff watching the miners. They're off, they're on, they're off again.

**QUOTE/UNQUOTE** Jonas: 'All along I've been looking for God. And, here I am.'

Jack: 'We'd love to stick around but some brain-dead sycophant left my buddy out here to die.'

**NOTES** 'They believe in me.' Every hoary old cliché in Christendom crops up in this episode, particularly a needlessly overcomplicated backstory for Sam. The scene in which she's unable to shoot Jonas is one of the worst in the entire series, completely undercutting the 'woman struggling in a man's world' story. It's surprising she doesn't drop the gun and start crying. From my favourite writer on the show this is, sad to say, unremittingly poor.

**DID YOU KNOW?** 'The story idea that got me the job on *Stargate* is, for a few reasons, my least favourite,' said Robert Cooper. 'I wasn't crazy about the casting.' Cooper also regrets including the subplot about a past romance between Sam and Jonas. 'Thinking about it now, it didn't seem right for her character or the series.'

# 7 COLD LAZARUS

US Transmission Date: 29 Aug 1997
UK Transmission Date: 13 May 1998
Writer: Jeffery F King
Director: Kenneth J Girotti
Cast: Teryl Rothery (Dr Janet Fraiser), Harley Jane Kozak (Sara O'Neill), Gary Jones (Technician), Wally Dalton (Sara's Father), Kyle Graham (Charlie O'Neill), Marc Baur (Senior Cop), Jane Spence (Nurse), Carmen Moore (Lab Assistant), Charles Payne (Guard NCO)

On P3X562, SG-1 discover a valley of blue crystals. O'Neill touches one and is knocked unconscious. A duplicate is created and returns through the Stargate. Once on Earth, the duplicate seeks out O'Neill's estranged wife, Sara, and tries to find the couple's dead son. Meanwhile, Jack returns to Earth and is told he's been replicated. Sam and Daniel discover the crystals contain sophisticated energy beings who describe a tragic encounter with the Goa'uld. O'Neill finds the duplicate who helps to heal his emotional scars over his son's death.

**ORIGINS OF THE SPECIES** The crystals can mimic the speech and memories of those who touch them. They cannot survive in the Earth's intense electromagnetic field.

**POSSIBLE INFLUENCES** The title's from a classic TV play by Dennis Potter. Teal'c mentions the Chicago sports teams the Blackhawks, the Bulls, the White Socks and the Cubs.

**'YOU MIGHT REMEMBER ME FROM...'** Harley Jane Kozak was Kathy in *The Favor* and Suzanne in *Necessary Roughness*. Wally Dalton played Red in *Eden*. Kyle Graham appeared in *Scary Movie*. Carmen Moore was Deputy Molly in *Wolf Lake*. Marc Baur appeared in *Ms. Bear*, *Return to the Cabin by the Lake* and *The X-Files*.

**BEHIND THE CAMERA** Ken Girotti directed *Hangman* and episodes of *Relic Hunter*, *Xena: Warrior Princess* and *La Femme Nikita*. Jeff King wrote for *Star Trek: Deep Space Nine* and *Due South*.

**LOGIC, LET ME INTRODUCE YOU TO THIS WINDOW** Jack's son used to be Tyler (*Stargate*), now, he's Charlie. The local police are able to check Sara's address remarkably quickly. If physical death doesn't have the same meaning for the crystals as it does for humans, then how did the Goa'uld shooting them lead to their destruction? Sam misses her brother and his kids since they moved to San Diego. When we eventually meet her brother ('Seth'), she says she's never met his kids. When the duplicate runs his hand across the name on his locker, there's another locker to the left, with Ferretti's name on it. In the rest of the scene, Jack's locker is last in the row. The crystal energy reproduces Jack, including his clothes. When he changes into his civvies in the locker room, what happens to the created clothing? Does the SGC get cable? There aren't many channels available to Teal'c as he flips through them. Hammond tells SG-1 that they can do nothing to reveal the existence of the SGC whilst chasing the duplicate, yet Jack clearly invokes some form of military authority to get local law enforcement to allow SG-1 access to the hospital. Also, how will Jack subsequently explain all of this to Sara *without* revealing the existence of ... something?

**QUOTE/UNQUOTE** Teal'c: 'Your world is a strange place.' Daniel: 'So's yours.'

**NOTES** 'Your pain was from an empty place in your heart.' This one's really good, albeit an avalanche of self-indulgence. An important episode in the series' development, however, with Anderson giving a quietly impressive and vulnerable performance as O'Neill's backstory is fleshed out in an effective way. Still not perfect, but it's aged much better than many of the surrounding stories. Best bit: Jack in the holding cell.

Jack keeps a cigar box containing family photos in his locker at the SGC. Sara's address is 942 Crabrooke Lane, Winter Park, Colorado 80310. Her father suggests Jack is of Irish descent. Teal'c asks Jack to fulfil his promise from 'The Enemy Within' and show

Teal'c his world. The duplicate refuses, so Teal'c makes do with television instead, appearing to develop a dislike for punk rock.

**CAST AND CREW COMMENTS** 'Kurt Russell did a phenomenal job with the character,' noted Richard Dean Anderson, 'but I knew just by looking at his hair that I couldn't do that. O'Neil's demons from the movie were brought onto the show. "Cold Lazarus" confronted the problems that had to do with his emotional scars concerning his son.'

**DID YOU KNOW?** 'Like most new series we got off to a bit of a bumpy start,' producer John Smith freely acknowledges. 'We had some budgetary restrictions our first year. Mainly because none of us really knew how much things were going to cost.'

# 8 THE NOX

US Transmission Date: 12 Sep 1997
UK Transmission Date: 20 May 1998
Writer: Hart Hanson
Director: Charles Correll
Cast: Peter Williams (Apophis), Armin Shimerman (Antaeus), Gary Jones (Technician), Ray Xifo (Ohper), Michasa Armstrong (Shak'l), Frida Betrani (Lya), Addison Ridge (Nefrayu), Terry David Mulligan (David Swift), Zoran Vukelic (Jaffa)

> Under pressure to discover advanced technology, Teal'c reveals details of a fabled creature called the Fenri which possess the power of invisibility. Upon arriving, SG-1 encounter Apophis and his guard. An ambush goes wrong and Jack, Sam and Daniel are killed. They are revived, along with a Jaffa, by the Nox, a childlike but very sophisticated people. But, can they withstand the Goa'uld?

**THE WIT AND WISDOM OF JACK O'NEILL** To Sam, when she gets all motherly with the Nox child, Nefreyu: 'No, you can't keep him.'

**ORIGINS OF THE SPECIES** The Nox are fairy-like, and seemingly in touch with nature, but also very advanced, with amazing healing powers and the capability to make things invisible, like the Stargate and their cloud-city.
SG-5 are about to visit P3C117.

**IN THE INTERESTS OF NATIONAL SECURITY** The Government representative, Swift, says the administration is less than pleased with the results from the programme so far.

**POSSIBLE INFLUENCES** Venetian explorer Marco Polo (1254-1324) and NASA's Apollo moon programme are mentioned.

**'YOU MIGHT REMEMBER ME FROM...'** Armin Shimerman played Pascal on *Beauty and the Beast* then became a TV comedy legend as Quark in *Star Trek: Deep Space 9* and

Principal Snyder in *Buffy the Vampire Slayer*. He also appeared in *Ally McBeal*, *Blind Date*, *The Hitcher* and *Stardust Memories*. Frida Betrani played Julia in *Prozac Nation*. Ray Xifo was in *Fallen*. Addison Ridge appeared in *Double Jeopardy*. A former radio DJ, Terry David Mulligan was also a producer on the Canadian cable channel MuchMusic. He appeared in *Barenaked in America*, *Big and Hairy*, *Hard Core Logo* and in Vancouver-based punk band Gob's video 'What to Do'.

**BEHIND THE CAMERA** Charles Correll was the cinematographer on *Star Trek III: The Search for Spock* and worked on *Joy of Sex*, *Melrose Place* and *Falcon Crest*. Hart Hanson's CV includes *Judging Amy* and *Guitarman*.

**LOGIC, LET ME INTRODUCE YOU TO THIS WINDOW** How does Ohper know how a Nox year compares to an Earth year? Teal'c says the Goa'uld use a homing device to find the Stargate. So why, therefore, does a Jaffa tell Apophis that he cannot find the Gate? The Nox seemingly took not only the weapons, but also the holsters, straps, and ammunition of SG-1. Why are Antaeus and his family in the forest anyway?

**GOA'ULD LEXICON** 'Dal Shakka Mel', Teal'c tells Apophis, meaning 'I die free'.

**QUOTE/UNQUOTE** Daniel: 'I thought heaven would be a little more upscale.'
Antaeus: 'Maybe one day you will learn that your way is not the only way.'

**NOTES** 'The very young do not always do as they are told.' A beautiful and mature pacifist parable, part fairy-tale, part morality-play, featuring a mix of Maoist doctrine and existential poetry. A cracking episode that convinced this author to keep watching at a time when I was about to give up on the series. Not everything works, however. Armin Shimerman does his best to keep his face straight whilst acting with a bush on his head.

SG-1 have visited 19 separate worlds (indicating a number of untelevised adventures). Ohper says he is 432 years old after Daniel describes how humans calculate time.

**CAST AND CREW COMMENTS** 'Science-fiction fans are the most intelligent, perceptive and loyal fans you can have,' noted Michael Shanks. 'The intricacy and the detail we need to have in our scripts to keep the fans interested is so amazing. They're discerning viewers. They spend so much of their lives waiting with bated breath for each episode to air and then they want to talk about it afterwards. You can't let them down.' Interestingly, Michael himself was an SF fan as a child. 'I loved *Space 1999*, *Battlestar Galactica* and *Star Wars*,' he offers. 'They were so different from things like *Starsky and Hutch*. But I got over it as I got older.'

**DID YOU KNOW?** The original Showtime broadcast of 'The Nox' was immediately preceded by a 20 minute documentary called *The Stargate Saga*, featuring interviews with the cast and crew. This was subsequently included on the US season one DVD box-set.

# 9 BRIEF CANDLE

US Transmission Date: 19 Sep 1997
UK Transmission Date: 27 May 1998
Story: Steven Barnes
Teleplay: Katharyn Powers
Director: Mario Azzopardi
Cast: Teryl Rothery (Dr Janet Fraiser), Gary Jones (Technician), Bobbie Phillips (Kynthia), Harrison Coe (Alekos), Gabrielle Miller (Thetys)

> On Argos, Daniel helps a woman give birth. SG-1 meet The Chosen; a beautiful race who celebrate during the day and sleep the moment the sun sets. The Chosen's lifespan is just 100 days - an effect that Jack unwittingly inherits when seduced by Kynthia. The rest of SG-1 return to Earth to work on a cure. Sam finds nanocytes in the Argosians blood. But will this information be in time to save Jack's life?

**THE WIT AND WISDOM OF JACK O'NEILL** When Daniel suggests Argos is a paradise: 'Have an apple, what could happen?'

**ORIGINS OF THE SPECIES** Teal'c makes the first suggestion that there are 'good' Goa'uld.

In Greek mythology Pelops ('the giver of days') was the son of Tantalus. He seemingly brought Greeks or Cretans to Argos (in his winged chariot which hurled lightning bolts) to serve as lab rats. He shortened their life span to 100 days, to observe changes in the human condition using microbiotic nanocytes with artificial intelligence. The Goa'uld language on the base of Pelops statue is Linear A, pictographs first used by Minoans and Myceneans.

**SEX AND DRUGS AND ROCK 'N' ROLL** An inebriated Jack (drugged with a ceremonial cake) spends a day of rampant passion with Kynthia. And, seemingly, enjoys it. 'Will you live the rest of your days without making love?' Kynthia asks the aged Jack. 'God, I hope not,' he replies.

**THE CONSPIRACY STARTS AT CLOSING TIME** When Sam was at The Pentagon, she worked for a year with a group studying nanocyte technology for medical research applications.

**POSSIBLE INFLUENCES** *Logan's Run* and *Star Trek*'s 'The Deadly Years'. Oblique references to *Gone With the Wind*, Genesis 3:2 (see **The Wit and Wisdom of Jack O'Neill**) and *Gunfight at the OK Corral* ('gettin' the hell out of Dodge'). The title is a quotation from *MacBeth*. The Argosians' hedonism may have its origins in the Dionysiac Greco-Roman sex-cults of the first and second century AD.[19]

19 These usually depict initiation ceremonies with devotees of the Bacchae, and other Euripidian forms of sado-erotic pleasure, abandoning themselves to the performance of wild and erotic dancing presided over by Diké, the Greek goddess of justice and punishment.

**'YOU MIGHT REMEMBER ME FROM...'** Bobbie Phillips played Kam in *Chameleon* (and its sequels), Barbara De Santos in *The Cape*, Bambi in *The X-Files* and Julie Costello in *Murder One*. Gabrielle Miller was Joyce in *Marine Life*.

**BEHIND THE CAMERA** Steven Barnes is an SF novelist and sometime collaborator with Larry Niven. He has subsequently written for *Andromeda*.

**LOGIC, LET ME INTRODUCE YOU TO THIS WINDOW** Virtually every planet designation in the series is a six-figure one; Argos (P3X8596) is seven. (There are further exceptions to this - Cartago, Tollan, and the planet in 'The Tok'ra', for instance.) Who is Sgt Mack and why is there a cardboard sign with his name on it in the window of a military truck near the Cheyenne Mountain entrance? When Sam returns for the first time, there's a shot of her glancing back at the Gate as the wormhole disengages, then as she walks down the steps, she does so again. If Daniel and Teal'c go back to the SGC to work on translating the tablet, why do they spend all their time watching Janet and Sam working in the lab? There are papers scattered around where they sit, so they may be translating it there, but what's going on in the lab must surely be a distraction to them? Why do Daniel, Sam and Teal'c return to Argos in protective gear and then take it off straight away? Why doesn't Kynthia notice that night is falling, or comment on the darkness and the stars? Why does Jack ask Sam if they can use Pelops' transmitter, if she has already set-up the alternative equipment they brought with them? Why does Janet wear her captain's insignia on her lab coat when Sam never does? Jack's hair keeps growing as he ages but his beard doesn't. Where does the food that The Chosen eat come from? Who maintains their homes if they are all so busy celebrating?

**QUOTE/UNQUOTE** Daniel: 'It's like we stepped into the citadel at Mycenae.' Jack: 'I thought you said it was Greek.' Daniel: 'Mycenae was an ancient city in the Southern Pelopponesian region.' Jack: 'Where's that?' Daniel: 'Greece.' Jack: 'Why do I do that?'

Kynthia: 'The time of one heartbeat can become an eternity.'

**NOTES** 'To every man the creator gives one hundred blissful days.' O'Neill discovers the traditionally hedonistic 'get-your-knickers-down' approach to first contact in science-fiction can sometimes have nasty consequences. Jim Kirk didn't often have these sort of problems. There's a nice rebellion subplot but ultimately the episode is rather lightweight eye-candy despite some very likeable performances.

Jack is forty. When he believes he's dying, he starts to compose a letter to Sara whom, he tells Kynthia, he still loves (see 'Cold Lazarus'). This is the second baby Daniel has helped deliver. He learned midwifery on a dig in Yucatán (see 'Secrets'). A grateful Alekos and Thetys name their new-born son Daniel. A flustered Sam says she knows nothing about delivering babies.

**DID YOU KNOW?** The original Stargate from the movie was stored in the Californian desert and, by the time the TV series was in pre-production, was unusable. However, at least Richard Hudolin and his team were able to take a mould and, from that, build their own Gate for the series. The on-location Stargate prop does include some parts salvaged from the movie version.

## 10   THOR'S HAMMER

US Transmission Date: 26 Sep 1997
UK Transmission Date: 3 Jun 1998
Writer: Katharyn Powers
Director: Brad Turner
Cast: Galyn Görg (Kendra), Tasmin Kelsey (Gairwyn), Mark Gibson (Thor), Gary Jones (Technician), Vincent Hammond (Unas), James Earl Jones (Voice of Unas)

> In search of allies, SG-1 travel to Cimmeria - home to the legendary Norse gods, the Asgard. It was long ago declared off-limits to the Goa'uld. When they emerge from the Stargate, Teal'c is trapped in a beam of light and, with Jack, is transported to a cavernous labyrinth. This is home to Unas, the original Goa'uld host. Daniel and Sam try to rescue them, aided by Kendra, a former Goa'uld host who survived her own journey through the labyrinth.

**ORIGINS OF THE SPECIES** Daniel notes there are two distinct types of Star Gods from various mythologies; tyrants who enslave humans and use their technologies to punish, and culture bearers who, although powerful, are benevolent toward humanity. He concludes the Goa'uld probably didn't build the Stargate. The Thor's Hammer sign is the symbol of a world all Jaffa are taught to avoid. The hologram of Thor describes himself as supreme commander of the Asgard fleet (see 'The Fifth Race') and says Cimmeria is a safe world for developing sentient species. In Norse mythology, Asgard was the abode of the gods, the Aesir and the Vanir (see 'Red Sky'). Access to it was possible only by crossing the bridge Bifrost (the rainbow). Thor was the god of thunder who wielded a hammer, *Mjollnir*, which represented a thunderbolt. The gods made man from an ash tree and woman from an elm and set them to live in Midgard,[20] which Gairwyn knows is the planet from which her people originate. Thrudvang, which Gairwyn describes as Thor's 'home in the stars', was a realm in Asgard where Thor built his palace, Bilisknir, with 540 rooms. (It will be interesting to know how many rooms an Asgard ship has.) The Cimmerian name for the Goa'uld is Etins:[21] These were beings halfway between man, elf and god. Kendra is from Jebanna, where she was taken by the Goa'uld Marduk (see 'Fire and Water', 'The Tomb'). She was freed by the hammer ten years ago and her symbiont removed. This episode sees the first reference to the Goa'uld 'System Lords'.

Unas[22] is described as the first host, created from the same primordial waters as the Goa'uld themselves. It has been missing for a thousand years and became a myth to the Jaffa, much as vampires are on Earth. It has great regenerative powers.

**POSSIBLE INFLUENCES** Elements of *The Lord of the Rings* (the cave

20 Spelled 'Midgardr' on the DVD subtitles.
21 Sometimes spelled 'Ettins'.
22 Unas was the name of the last ruler of The Fifth Dynasty in Egypt (2375-2345BC). Little is known about his reign, and his pyramid at Saqqara is the smallest of the Old Kingdom monuments. However it was the first to have Pyramid Texts inscribed onto the interior walls. So, you see, size isn't really important after all.

sequences). Allusions to Wagner's 'Ride of the Valkyrie', 'The Casting of the Runes' by MR James, *Star Wars* ('you're a little short for gods') and the People's Scientist Carl Sagan (1934-97).

**'YOU MIGHT REMEMBER ME FROM...'** Galyn Görg was in *Point Peak* and *Twin Peaks*. Tasmin Kelsey appeared in *Bad Money*. Mark Gibbon played Red Six in *Dark Angel*. Vincent Hammond was in *Species* and *Predator*. James Earl Jones made his movie debut in *Dr. Strangelove*. He is best known as the voice of Darth Vader in *Star Wars* and its sequels. He also voiced Mufasa in *The Lion King*, played Alex Haley in *Roots: The Next Generation* and appeared in *Patriot Games* and *Field of Dreams*.

**BEHIND THE CAMERA** Brad Turner worked on *Andromeda*, *Poltergeist: The Legacy, Strange Luck* and *Forever Knight*. Assistant Director Bill Mizel's work includes *Blacklight, Draw!* and *Dead Ahead*.

**LOGIC, LET ME INTRODUCE YOU TO THIS WINDOW** Didn't Teal'c hear the splash when Jack did? If Jack can knock Teal'c through the beam and back into the Hall, why not try to push him out the other way? Unas is described as the First One, and Teal'c suggests it was the first host. Subsequently ('Serpent's Song,' 'Demons', 'The First Ones', 'Beast of Burden'), 'Unas' refers to a particular species of Goa'uld host, of which some still exist. Why does the holographic Thor inside the labyrinth resemble a Norse warrior instead of a little grey man? The Goa'uld know of the Asgard's true form (unless, since the first Unas is there, the trap was set up before the Goa'uld found out what the Asgard looked like?).

**QUOTE/UNQUOTE** Kendra: 'In the temple we were taught that fear is the greatest enemy.'

**NOTES** 'I know the secrets of the labyrinth'. A clever episode which makes up for the minimalism of its setting by focusing on the characters and on Norse mythology. Not entirely satisfying (the ending is extremely weak and something of an *Occam's razor*) but a clear sign that the writers were starting to get to grips with where they wanted to take the series.

**CAST AND CREW COMMENTS** What's it like to work with Richard Dean Anderson? 'It's a hoot,' said Michael Shanks. 'He's like an eight-year-old child and a grumpy old man rolled into one body. He has more boyish excitement than anyone I've ever met. He can be a downright Oscar the Grouch sometimes, but I think all of us get along famously with him.'

**DID YOU KNOW?** 'Midway through the first season, we discovered that we have the same sense of humour,' Michael Shanks noted concerning himself and Richard Dean Anderson. 'We decided to play with this in the show. The writers picked up on what we were doing. For me, that's one of the highlights of doing this show.'

# 11 THE TORMENT OF TANTALUS

US Transmission Date: 3 Oct 1997
UK Transmission Date: 10 Jun 1998
Writer: Robert C Cooper
Director: Jonathan Glassner
Cast: Elizabeth Hoffman (Catherine Langford), Keene Curtis (Ernest Littlefield), Gary Jones (Technician), Duncan Fraser (Professor Langford), Nancy McClure (Young Catherine), Paul McGillion (Young Ernest), Sheelah Megill (Martha-Maid)

Whilst studying footage of Stargate experiments from 1945, Daniel discovers that Professor Langford succeeded in getting the device to work and that a young professor, Ernest Littlefield, travelled into the wormhole, but never returned. Catherine Langford was engaged to Ernest and insists on joining SG-1 in their search for him. They find the professor, now old, in a citadel that appears to have been the meeting place of four ancient civilisations. However, the Stargate's DHD is severely damaged, trapping them.

**ORIGINS OF THE SPECIES** P3X972 is close to Abydos (and, hence can be reached despite planetary shift), but, seemingly, was not part of the cartouche of addresses that Daniel found (see 'Children of the Gods'). This proves the Goa'uld didn't build the Stargates. Ernest describes the meeting chamber as Heliopolis.[23] Here, four alien races exchanged ideas, communicating at a most basic level - by way of a periodic table, listing the building blocks of the universe, the elements. Ernest has counted 146. As Nordic runes are amongst the symbols found, Daniel speculates that Thor's people were one of the races involved (see 'The Fifth Race').

**THE CONSPIRACY STARTS AT CLOSING TIME** During World War II, the US Military experimented on the Stargate believing it to be a weapon.

**MILITARY INTELLIGENCE?** Daniel doubts The Pentagon have lost any files related to the Stargate. 'The Pentagon's lost entire *countries*,' notes Jack cynically.

**POSSIBLE INFLUENCES** Dr Manhattan's fate in *Watchmen*. Also, *The Simpsons* ('It was like that when I got here'), Douglas Adams ('This is Meaning of Life stuff'), *Scanners* ('before your head explodes'), US president Franklin Roosevelt (1882-1945) and Benjamin Franklin (1706-90) and his electricity experiments. The title refers to Greek king Tantalus, sent to *Hades* and placed, for eternity, in a lake of water which receded whenever he tried to drink.

**'YOU MIGHT REMEMBER ME FROM...'** Keene Curtis was Hill in *Cheers* and Max Pomeroy in *The Magician*. He also voiced Grand Moff Tarkin in the National Public Radio adaptation of *Star Wars: A New Hope*. Elizabeth Hoffman appeared in *Dante's Peak*, *thirtysomething* and *Little House on the Prairie*. Nancy McClure was Terry in

---

23 Greek for 'city of the sun', Heliopolis was the centre for sun-worship in ancient Egypt and is twice mentioned in the book of Genesis. Today it's a fashionable suburb of Cairo.

*Happy Gilmore*. Duncan Fraser played Sgt Regan in *Da Vinci's Inquest*. Paul McGillion appeared in *Skullduggery*. Shellah Megill was in *Sweetwater*.

**LOGIC, LET ME INTRODUCE YOU TO THIS WINDOW** Jack says they've launched a survey balloon, something never subsequently done. How many jackets and shirts does Daniel own? Not many, seemingly, since we keep seeing the same ones (see, for instance, 'Holiday' and 'Fair Game'). Both Jack and Sam gets close to the DHD but don't notice that it's broken. As she's preparing to step onto the ramp, Catherine's arms are hooked through Jack's and Daniel's. In one shot, however, they aren't. A voice says 'Shut it down' as SG-1 return, but the wormhole is already disengaged. What, exactly, can the military do to a civilian if he/she reveals classified materials? It's perhaps best not to ask. The hole through which the DHD falls is remarkably symmetrical. Catherine and her father had Scandinavian accents in the movie. If Catherine was 21 in 1945, that would make her just four in 1928 when the events of the movie took place. Ernest says that when he left Earth, there were 90 elements. In fact, in 1945 there were 96 known.

**QUOTE/UNQUOTE** Catherine: 'You speak?' Teal'c: 'When it is appropriate.'

Ernest's first words to another human in 50 years: 'It's about time!'

Jack, on the communication device: 'Some fancy light-show that might be the key to our existence. Or something.'

**NOTES** 'You've been completely alone here?' What a beautiful piece of work; a real gem out of left-field with a humanity and a sympathetic handling of the subject matter that is never mawkish or trite. A keystone to the future development of the series, and the best episode of the first year by some considerable distance.

Jack returned the amulet that Catherine gave to Daniel when he got back from Abydos. (He seemingly told her that Daniel hadn't died, see *Stargate*). He knows at least basic chemistry (recognising the atomic structure of hydrogen), and describes Hammond as 'a teddy bear'. General West is mentioned. No date in 1945 is given for Ernest's departure but it must have been after June 26th (the day the United Nations was formed). Ernest's planet has oceans (and, seemingly, some form of vegetation to produce food).

**CAST AND CREW COMMENTS** 'I'd say we were about 50/50 in the first season,' noted Robert Cooper. 'The show was finding its feet and we took some risks. I still look back fondly on "The Torment of Tantalus".'

**DID YOU KNOW?** Regarded as a bona-fide genius by many of his colleagues, award-winning designer Richard Hudolin was the first person headhunted to join the production team before the series was even developed in December 1996. 'I worked non-stop with the art department for about seven memorable weeks, and together we came up with a blueprint for the SGC,' he said.

# 12 BLOODLINES

US Transmission Date: 10 Oct 1997

UK Transmission Date: 17 Jun 1998
Story: Mark Saraceni
Teleplay: Jeff King
Director: Mario Azzopardi
Cast: Tony Amendola (Bra'tac), Teryl Rothery (Dr Janet Fraiser), Salli Richardson (Drey'auc), Neil Denis (Rya'c), Brian Jensen (Head Priest), Bob Wilde (Priest)

**SEASON 1**

When Teal'c joined SG-1, he kept secret the family he left behind. However, his son Rya'c has reached the age at which he'll receive a Gou'ald larva. SG-1 travel to Chulak and, with help from Teal'c's mentor, Bra'tac, battle Jaffa warriors and priests before finding Rya'c and his mother, Drey'auc. However, the boy needs a Gou'ald to survive. And the only one available is Teal'c's.

**ORIGINS OF THE SPECIES** Teal'c notes that the prim'ta (ceremony of implantation) occurs when a young Jaffa reaches a specific age. It's never revealed what. There has recently been an unsuccessful attempt to remove Teal'c symbiont. He notes there are many hundreds of Goa'uld larvae on Chulak. It's one of the few worlds with such an abundance. (Is Sha're creating them? See 'Hathor'.) A Jaffa cannot live without his symbiont for more than a couple of hours.

Bra'tac, Teal'c's Jaffa Master, knows that the Goa'uld are false gods. He is 133. (It's never made clear if Earth and Chulak years are comparable, though the fact that he's 135 in 'Into the Fire' suggests they're close.)

**IN THE INTERESTS OF NATIONAL SECURITY** Hammond initially refuses to let Teal'c go back to Chulak as his knowledge of the SGC makes him a security risk.

**POSSIBLE INFLUENCES** *The Searchers*. Daniel describes the Jaffa/symbiont existence as 'A Faustian bargain,' an allusion to *The Tragical History of Dr Faustus* by Christopher Marlowe (1564-93).

**'YOU MIGHT REMEMBER ME FROM...'** Tony Amendola played Sorrel in *Kindred: The Embraced*, Carl Jasper in *Cradle Will Rock* and Sanchez in *Blow*. He also appeared in *Seinfeld* and *She-Wolf of London*. Salli Richardson was in *Sioux City*. Brian Jensen appeared in *Screwed* and *Hope Island*. Bob Wilde was in *Blacktop*. Neil Denis appeared in *Spooky House* and *Bug and Hairy*.

**LOGIC, LET ME INTRODUCE YOU TO THIS WINDOW** When SG-1 leave the Gate on Chulak, Michael Shanks narrowly avoids colliding with one of the standing stones. Is the prim'-ta only for Jaffa boys? Teal'c implies so, yet we've seen female Jaffa. Why is Bra'tac so offended that Sam and Daniel took a larva from the temple? At the end, the glyphs on the DHD are not lit while the Gate is open. How does one keep track of time on another planet? Teal'c knows exactly when his son's ceremony will be, though presumably the day and year cycles would vary. A Jaffa does not communicate with the Goa'uld it carries. Yet they seem able to "ask" the larva to emerge when needed. Dr Fraiser's hair is surely too long for a serving military officer? So how, exactly, *did* Bra'tac get away with aiding in SG-1's escape?

**GOA'ULD LEXICON** 'Has'sak' means 'fool'. A 'kresh'ta' is an outcast from Jaffa society.

**QUOTE/UNQUOTE** Drey'auc: 'Come, carry your son back to the hovel that has become his home.'

Jack: 'Let's just say that nobody believes in anyone with glowing eyes and a snake in his head.'

**NOTES** 'A warrior becomes vulnerable if his family is held hostage to his enemy.' Halfway towards being a really decent episode, with a smashing cameo by Tony Amendola, spoiled by plot-holes (the ending is particularly risible) and by both Sam and Daniel being very out-of-character throughout.

Jack describes his leader, Hammond, as 'a good man ... from Texas' to Bra'tac (see 'The Serpent's Lair', 'Into the Fire'). Carter hasn't been to church for 'a while'. Leather miniskirts seem to be very big with Jaffa wives.

**DID YOU KNOW?** Tony Amendola's first convention was real eye-opener for the experienced actor. 'Because they're sci-fi buffs, they're generally extremely bright people. As warm, as wonderful, and as odd as anyone you encounter.'

## 13  FIRE AND WATER

US Transmission Date: 17 Oct 1997
UK Transmission Date: 24 Jun 1998
Story: Brad Wright, Katharyn Powers
Teleplay: Katharyn Powers
Director: Allan Eastman
Cast: Teryl Rothery (Dr Janet Fraiser), Gerard Plunkett (Nem), Gary Jones (Technician), Eric Schneider (Doctor MacKenzie)

> SG-1 return from P3X866 minus Daniel whom, they say, is dead. But, as his friends mourn him, Daniel is, in reality, a captive of an amphibious humanoid called Nem who is seeking information about his love, Omoroka, who was on Earth 4,000 years ago. Daniel struggles to recall Babylonian history and agrees to have his brain manipulated, to discover secrets locked within it. SG-1, meanwhile, all have the feeling that Daniel isn't really dead.

**THE WIT AND WISDOM OF JACK O'NEILL** After the squid-like Nem leaves, Jack asks Daniel to tell his story 'over sushi.'

**ORIGINS OF THE SPECIES** Daniel knows little Babylonian mythology but remembers an account by Berossus, a contemporary of Alexander the Great, of a conquering king named Belos, who battled Omoroka and 'cut her asunder'. Although Daniel identifies Omoroka as one of the Oannes (sea gods), she actually wasn't.[24] Nem

• • • • • • • • • • • • • • • • • • • • • • • • • • • • • • • • • • • • • • • • • • • • • •

24 Berossus was a Chaldean priest c.300BC who wrote of how Sumerian civilisation was founded by the Oannes. One of the Annedoti (repulsive ones) who came from the stars, lived in the sea: "The whole body of

uses Akkadian cuneiform writing to communicate.

**SEX AND DRUGS AND ROCK 'N' ROLL** Having false memories implanted into their brains, SG-1 suffer from low levels of Serotonin, a neurotransmitter that affects moods. At Daniel's wake, there are a lot of wine bottles on the table. Sam asks Jack for a beer.

**IN THE INTERESTS OF NATIONAL SECURITY** Jack, Sam and Teal'c are given the job of clearing out Daniel's (rather lovely) apartment so nothing that may reveal the existence of the Stargate will be left behind.

**POSSIBLE INFLUENCES** A story about perception, conditioned responses and false-memory, this shares lots of similarities with *The X-Files*. Daniel mentions a historical event being 'pre-flood', which suggests that he believes, historically at least, in Judaeo-Christian chronology. Or, he may simply have meant pre-the end of the last Ice Age when, scholars believe, the Mediterranean spilled over into the inhabited basin.

**BEHIND THE CAMERA** Allan Eastman also directed *Champagne Charlie* and episodes of *Star Trek: Voyager*, *The Littlest Hobo* and *Earth: Final Conflict*. Producer John Smith worked on *Time Runners*, *Street Justice* and *Two*.

**LOGIC, LET ME INTRODUCE YOU TO THIS WINDOW** Nem's energy blast on the beach seems to miss Daniel entirely before hitting the others. Why does Sam shout 'Help him!' when all of SG-1 are apparently under threat? The General calls for a medical team because SG-1 are early. In 'Solitudes,' he doesn't do this in an identical situation. When Nem writes on the sand, Daniel pushes up his helmet. Later, he does so again. When does Daniel learn Nem's name and Nem learn Sha're's? Daniel has stubble whilst trapped by Nem, but when he re-emerges from the water at the end, he's clean shaven. Sam opens Daniel's Abydos journal in the middle but reads about the first visit (see 'Stargate'). She then turns only a page or two and reads a section that was written after he returned to Earth ('Children of the Gods'). Janet's hair-length varies dramatically between scenes.

**QUOTE/UNQUOTE** Jack: 'Daniel Jackson made this place happen ... He was our voice. Our conscience.'
Daniel: 'Most of our history is buried in time.'

**NOTES** 'Daniel's dead, sir.' A decent premise; the SG-team suffering post traumatic stress from a battle they didn't, really, fight. The dramatic atmosphere is spoiled somewhat by Daniel's true status being revealed far too early and the horribly untidy solution which undercuts the previous tension. But otherwise, impressive stuff.

• • • • • • • • • • • • • • • • • • • • • • • • • • • • • • • • • • • • • • • • • • • • • • •

the animal was like that of a fish; and had under the fish's head another head, and also feet below, subjoined to the fish's tail." According to legend the Oannes (later renamed Dogon) came from Sirius, and the myth has latterly become the basis for a theory that the Dogon people were taught by aliens (see, for example, Robert Temple's *The Sirius Mystery*). Most Mesopotamian myths place these events c.2100BC during the Third Dynasty of Ur. However, some scholars suggest that Belos (aka: Marduk, see 'Thor's Hammer', 'The Tomb'), may have been a much later (and quasi-historical) figure, during the Neo-Babylonian empire of King Nebuchadrezzar (605-562BC).

Jack's a decent hockey player. Sam had experience of hypnosis with an undergrad Psych-group. Daniel keeps tropical fish.

**DID YOU KNOW?** Amanda Tapping and Richard Dean Anderson share a love of, and an almost encyclopaedic knowledge about, *The Simpsons* which can occasionally reduce the set to hysterics. Her Ralph Wiggum impression is, according to observers, uncannily accurate.

## 14   HATHOR

US Transmission Date: 24 Oct 1997
UK Transmission Date: 1 Jul 1998
Story: David Bennett Carren, J Larry Carroll
Teleplay: Jonathan Glassner
Director: Brad Turner
Cast: Teryl Rothery (Dr Janet Fraiser), Suanne Braun (Hathor), Dave Hurtubise (Kleinhouse), Amanda O'Leary (Cole), Bob Frazer (Airman), Ikkee Battle (SP Guard), Tracy Westerholm (Female Solider)

> Archaeologists accidentally release Hathor, a Goa'uld who has taken the persona of a power-ful Egyptian goddess. Hathor is drawn to the Stargate and uses her physical charms to seduce the men of the SGC and enlist them in her deranged plans for world domination. Carter, and the base's women, have other ideas.

**THE WIT AND WISDOM OF JACK O'NEILL** 'I have a hard time believing this woman down on 73rd who walks around talking about these little *devil people* that live in her hair. Even though she could use a little conditioner.' And: 'Is mental illness contagious?'

**ORIGINS OF THE SPECIES** In stasis for 2,000 years at Palenque[25] in the Chiapas mountains in Mexico, Hathor was, according to *The Book of the Dead*, both wife and daughter to Ra and 'the mother of all Pharaohs'.[26] The Goa'uld larvae come from Hathor, and others like her (Goa'uld queens, presumably). She needs DNA ('code of life') from a host species to make the symbionts compatible (and thus, it is implied, she has sex with Daniel). Nice work if you can get it. An academic's webpage (*Hathor - the Original Goddess of Love*) suggests the sex goddesses of various cultures were all, in fact, the same woman. Those mentioned include Aphrodite,[27] Ishtar,[28] Astarte[29] and Ceres.[30]

25 Palenque is where the notorious tomb-lid, that controversial author Erich Von Daniken claims shows a man piloting a spaceship, was discovered. The figure also, seemingly, wears a kilt and carries a bagpipe-like device, so one could also claim it proves the Scots discovered America.

26 Egyptian queens often commissioned works of art portraying themselves in the image of Hathor. An stun-ning example is Nefertiti (the wife of Pharaoh Akhenaten) in her temple at Abu Simbel.

27 The Greek goddess of love and promiscuity, wife of Hephaistos, lover of Ares and mother of Erōs and Hermaphrodite, who sprang from the foam of the sea where Uranos' severed genitals fell.

28 Akkadian goddess of sex and war. Her descent and return from the underworld metaphorically portrays the disruption and restoration of fertility.

Chulak has obviously been a Goa'uld stronghold for millennia since Hathor knows its Stargate address.

**SEX AND DRUGS AND ROCK 'N' ROLL** Daniel, on Hathor: 'The goddess of fertility, inebriety and music.' Jack: 'Sex, drugs and rock 'n' roll?'

After Hathor performs her prestidigitation on the men, Fraiser suggests this may be nothing more sinister than pheromones and sodium pentothal (a barbiturate anaesthetic).

**THE CONSPIRACY STARTS AT CLOSING TIME** The CIA are mentioned in the series for the first time.

**POSSIBLE INFLUENCES** Hammer's *Blood from the Mummy's Tomb*. Sam refers to 'women-behind-bars movies' and quotes from 'Ain't Gonna Cry' by Bryan Adams ('mama told me there'd be days like these'). Also, *Sgt. Rock* ('this man's army'). Jack alludes to the maxim 'my enemy's enemy is my friend.'

**'YOU MIGHT REMEMBER ME FROM...'** Suanne Braun played Jill Dupree in *Silk Stalkings*. David Hurtubise was Professor Wagg in *Doctor Who*. Amanda O'Leary played Ms Chang in *Zenon: Girl from the 21st Century*. Bob Frazer was in *Zacharia Farted*. Tracy Westerholm appeared in *Xtro II: The Second Encounter*. She is one of Amanda Tapping's regular stand-ins.

**BEHIND THE CAMERA** David Carren wrote for *Martial Law*, *Walker, Texas Ranger*, *Diagnoses Murder* and *Buck Rogers in the 25th Century*. Larry Carroll's CV includes episodes of *Space Precinct*, *Beauty and the Beast* and *Star Trek: The Next Generation*.

**LOGIC, LET ME INTRODUCE YOU TO THIS WINDOW** How did Kleinhouse's 'associates' find Daniel so easily when he's working for a covert military organisation? 'The Curse' suggests that, as far as the rest of the academic community is concerned, he's dropped-off the face of the planet. In 'Bloodlines,' Bra'tac indicated that the larva taken from the temple was not ready for implantation. So how is Hathor's ready so quickly? No-one comments on the fact that Daniel obviously told Hathor all about Ra, even though he'd been specifically ordered not to by Hammond. Who says 'Unauthorised Gate activation. All hands to the Gateroom,' as Hathor is leaving? It doesn't sound like a recording, but there's no-one in the control room. Why does Sam sweep the ceiling of the VIP room with her rifle when she enters it? Where is Daniel when Hathor turns Jack into a Jaffa? Hathor's larvae looks different from those previously seen. The URL for the website about Hathor starts with *file:///*. Where did Hathor get the raincoat? How did she get to the SGC from Mexico? Janet Fraiser is a captain in the Air Force yet says she hasn't handled a weapon since basic training. Aren't all active personnel (even medical staff) required to take occasional refreshers on something as important as how to fire a gun? Hathor emerges from her bathtub as dry as a bone - impressive, even for a god. What is

29 In Egyptian mythology one of Seth's two wives, the daughter of Ptah. Usually depicted as warrior goddess, naked and riding a horse. Also, the name of a Syrian goddess of fertility.

30 The Roman goddess of agriculture and the equivalent of the Greek's Demeter.

it that causes the water in Hathor's bath to ignite? After all that he's seen, why is Jack so hard to convince that Hathor isn't what she claims to be?

**QUOTE/UNQUOTE** Hathor, on Hammond: 'You, with the crown of marble.'

Sam, after she's clubbed Hammond unconscious: 'Yeah, my career is *over*.'

**NOTES** 'Fascinating lady, isn't she?' This one gives Amanda Tapping and Teryl Rothery the chance to prowl around like jealous cats in a story in which the Stargate women must prevent their men from making fools of themselves. 'Statement' rears an ugly head (not for the first time this season). Lots of good moments, however, (Suanne Braun is disturbingly good) and very popular with the male end of *Stargate* fandom.

Jack is Special Forces-trained to resist mind control. Daniel is still reasonably well known in archaeology circles, having been laughed out of academia for his preposterous ideas on ancient civilisations like the Egyptians and the Mayans being linked. (Compare this with, for example, 'The Curse', and the reasons given there for Daniel's exile from the archaeological community.) Teal'c has never met a good Goa'uld (see 'Brief Candle'). Fraiser's ex-husband was an army veteran (and, seemingly, a sexist git).

**CAST AND CREW COMMENTS** Jonathan Glassner has noted that both the character of Hathor and this episode were not highly regarded amongst the crew and cast and they were constantly surprised by the subsequent popularity of both amongst fans. He guesses this may be due to feminist elements in the script.

**DID YOU KNOW?** Glassner had the idea for the opening sequence when watching a TV documentary on archaeologists finding an intact Egyptian crypt.

## 15 SINGULARITY

US Transmission Date: 31 Oct 1997
UK Transmission Date: 8 Jul 1998
Writer: Robert C Cooper
Director: Mario Azzopardi
Cast: Teryl Rothery (Dr Janet Fraiser), Katie Stuart (Cassandra), Gary Jones (Technician), Kevin McNulty (Doctor Warner)

> SG-1 travel to P8X987, where another SG-team has been preparing to observe a black hole. But a strange disease has wiped out everyone except a young girl named Cassandra. Jack and Teal'c remain on the planet to observe the phenomenon whilst Sam and Daniel return to Earth with the girl. Sam discovers that chest pains Cassandra is experiencing are caused by a metallic device near the child's heart. The Goa'uld planted the device as part of a scheme to destroy the Earth's Stargate.

**ORIGINS OF THE SPECIES** Hanka (PX8987) is described as 'project 69'. Nirrti, the Goa'uld responsible for the trap, is an enemy of Apophis. In Hindu mythology, Nirrti means 'destruction', and was the goddess of death.

**THE ELEMENT WITHIN HER** There's a first reference to the name of the element from which the Stargate is made, Naqahdah,[31] and the first indication that some creatures have this in their bloodstream. (Cassandra has traces of it which is how Sam deduces that she's a walking booby-trap.) A combination of potassium and Naqahdah causes an intense nuclear reaction with high levels of gamma and particle radiation.

**SEX AND DRUGS AND ROCK 'N' ROLL** This episode sees the first reference to Daniel's allergies since 'The Broca Divide' (and the last for a long time).

**POSSIBLE INFLUENCES** *Aliens.* Daniel refers to The Trojan Horse. Also, *The Addams Family* ('It's showtime!').

**'YOU MIGHT REMEMBER ME FROM...'** Katie Stuart was in *Epicentre*.

**LOGIC, LET ME INTRODUCE YOU TO THIS WINDOW** Teal'c refers to Nirrti as 'he' though its host is female in 'Fair Game'. How did Sam decorate Cassie's room so quickly? Wouldn't Sam have been taught basic CPR in the Air Force (see 'In the Line of Duty')? How can Teal'c tell that the pyramid ship belongs to Nirrti based on observation through the telescope? Both Janet and Sam appear to have the stethoscope on backwards. Sam takes Cassie down 30 floors in the nuclear facility, but the elevator door has a 2 as the first number on it when they exit. If the nuclear facility is abandoned, why are there lights still on at the lower levels? Why is it Fraiser who get to keep Cassandra and not Sam, who has bonded with her so successfully?

**QUOTE/UNQUOTE** Cassandra on her cover-story: 'The Stargate is a secret and I was born in a place called Toronto.'

**NOTES** 'They're all dead.' This attempts to shoehorn Tapping into a Sigourney Weaver role of Earth mother and simultaneous alien killing machine, which she pulls off pretty well. It's predictable and (very) mawkish, even if the acting is impressive and the plot is well-structured.

Jack seems to know a fair bit about astronomy. (As Sam notes, the telescope on his roof, seen in 'Children of the Gods', isn't *just* to spy on his neighbours.) Sam has no artistic talent whatsoever. The, presumably now deceased, commander of SG-7 was John Smith (named after the producer N John Smith) and a Douglas McLean memorial observatory had been set up on Hanka (in tribute to *SG-1*'s art director).

---

31 Naqada was one of the largest pre-dynastic sites in Egypt, twenty miles north of Luxor. The historical name for the town was Nubt. Later it was eclipsed by Abydos (see 'Children of the Gods'). The mythical Seth was supposedly born in the Naqada region. In the *Stargate* movie, the main township on Abydos is called Nagadah. (At least, it is on the soundtrack CD sleeve notes.) There's also a border town in North Western Iran called Naqadeh, but nothing remotely interesting seems to have happened there prior to the Iraqi's bombing it flat in 1981.

**CAST AND CREW COMMENTS** 'Teal'c is a rebel in a society that has no room for rebels,' noted Christopher Judge.

**DID YOU KNOW?** A word about the title-sequence. When episodes air on Showtime in the US, they feature what has become known as the 'Big-Headed Cross-Eyed Pharaoh' sequence (as used on the opening of the movie). When they are subsequently rebroadcast in syndication a 'clips' sequence is used instead, which will be familiar to readers who have DVDs and videos of the series. This sequence is updated each year using different clips from recent episodes. This is often (although not exclusively) the sequence used on overseas broadcasts. (Sky One in Britain has always used the 'Big-Headed Pharaoh'). The MGM DVDs of seasons two and three, still use the season *one* title-sequence (featuring clips predominantly from 'The Torment of Tantalus' and 'Children of the Gods'). The season four and five DVDs, just to confuse matters, use the 'Big-Headed Pharaoh'.

# 16 COR-AI

US Transmission Date: 23 Jan 1998
UK Transmission Date: 15 Jul 1998
Writer: Tom J Astle
Director: Mario Azzopardi
Cast: Peter Williams (Apophis), David McNally (Hanno), Paulina Gillis (Byrsa Woman), Christina Jastrzembska (Female Elder), Michasa Armstrong (Shak'l), Kirby Morrow (Militia Man Warrior), Devon Finn (Young Hanno)

> Arriving on P3X1279, Teal'c recognises it as Chartago, home to the Bysra and one of the Goa'ulds favourite planets from which to harvest humans for assimilation. One of Teal'c's previous visits is remembered by Hanno, who accuses Teal'c of killing his father. Teal'c is put on trial for crimes that he admits. Whilst Jack, Daniel and Sam try to persuade Hanno that Teal'c has changed, the Jaffa seem resigned to his sentence of death.

**ORIGINS OF THE SPECIES** The Bysra seem to be a combination of two cultures; Greek and Roman judging by the derivation of their term for the Stargate '*Cirque Cacona*' meaning 'Circle of Woes'. '*Peccave*', the taking of a confession, is from the Latin meaning 'I have sinned.'

**THE CONSPIRACY STARTS AT CLOSING TIME** The US isn't in the business of influencing other people's affairs, says Hammond. 'Since when?' asks Jack. Good point. Hammond indicates that this administration is committed to such a policy.

**YOUR FUNERAL, MY TRIAL** Daniel notes that the concept of 'innocent until proven guilty,' is actually quite rare throughout history. In most cultures the practice was quite the opposite.

**POSSIBLE INFLUENCES** *Star Trek: The Next Generation*'s 'Encounter at

Farpoint', *The Princess Bride* and *Judgment at Nuremberg. Reader's Digest* is mentioned.

**'YOU MIGHT REMEMBER ME FROM...'** David McNally played Bobby in *1132 Pleasant Street*. Paulina Gillis was Maria in *Due South*. Christina Jastrzembska was Rachel in *The Spiral Staircase*. Kirby Morrow appeared in *Bones, Jerry's Day* and *MVP*.

**BEHIND THE CAMERA** Tom Astle was a producer on *Coach*. Casting Director Mary Jo Slater worked on *Jungle Juice, Star Trek VI: The Undiscovered Country, The Watcher, Let's Talk About Sex* and *Marshal Law*.

**QUOTE/UNQUOTE** Jack, after Daniel suggests the local population are returning from some communal ceremony: 'Why does it always have to be a religious thing with you? Maybe they're coming from a Swap-Meet?'

**NOTES** 'This Jaffa killed my father.' This one has aged better than many of its contemporaries. An interesting look at the complexities of war crimes. (Hammond suggests Teal'c's history is likely to be full of such moral ambiguities as this.) Daniel's impassioned performance at the Cor-Ai is excellent though, once again, good elements are badly-served by a disappointingly weak and obvious climax. They really hadn't got the pacing of a 45-minute episode right at this point.

Daniel admits that he wanted to hate Teal'c for his part in Sha're's loss (see 'Children of the Gods', 'Forever in a Day', 'Absolute Power').

**CAST AND CREW COMMENTS** 'You saw what an honourable and honest character Teal'c is,' noted Christopher Judge. 'The notion of being accountable for things in your life, no matter what the repercussions are; I think that's the pure essence of Teal'c.'

**DID YOU KNOW?** Many *Stargate SG-1* fans refer to themselves as 'Gaters'. 'I enjoy meeting the fans,' noted Peter Williams. 'In fact my appreciation for the gig has grown since I've done conventions, because the fans mirror the show back to you.'

# 17 ENIGMA

US Transmission Date: 30 Jan 1998
UK Transmission Date: 22 Jul 1998
Writer: Katharyn Powers
Director: William Gereghty
Cast: Tobin Bell (Omoc), Garwin Sanford (Narim), Tom McBeath (Colonel Harry Maybourne), Gary Jones (Technician), Gerard Plunkett (Tuplo), Frida Betrani (Lya), Woody Jeffreys (Guard), Tracy Westerholm (Airwoman)

SG-1 arrive on Tollan and find an erupting volcano and several bodies. The ten survivors are rescued, but the Tollan seem ungrateful. Their leader, Omoc, dismisses humans as primitive and refuses to answer questions about his planet's technology. Another Tollan, Narim, is more friendly, particularly towards Sam. But, with military intelligence keen on exploiting the refugees, SG-1 must risk court-martial to find a solution.

**SAM'S TRAUMATIC LOVE-LIFE**  Carter gets her first alien boyfriend in Narim, the handsome (if a bit wet) Tollan. He's got a nice poetic turn of phrase ('What your mind doesn't know, your heart fills in,') and they share a lengthy kiss. But he's only after her pussy - Schrödinger - really. She gives him the cat as a farewell gift (see 'Pretense').

**ORIGINS OF THE SPECIES**  The Tollan[32] are an advanced culture. Daniel believes that humanity would have colonised space by the late 20th Century if it hadn't been for the Dark Ages - 800 years where science was heresy. (Of course, he's over-looking the fact that the Dark Ages applied only to Europe. If his theory was correct we should have been seeing a Chinese space programme in the mid 1850s.) Daniel speculates that the Tollan didn't have such an era and thus developed more quickly than civilisations on Earth. (In the past, however, they did have their own versions of some Earth religious icons - including angels, called 'Shermal'.) The nearest planet to Tollan was called Sereta. The Tollan gave their neighbours access to their technology, which the Seretans promptly used to destroy themselves. The effects of this disaster were also felt on Tollan itself, sowing the seed for the planet's eventual fate. The last Tollan team stayed behind to seal the Gate before going to a planet outside the Gate system (see 'Pretense'). The Tollan have the ability to walk through solid objects and possess a device that can 'record' emotions. Narim claims that they have surpassed quantum physics. They are aware of the Goa'uld but don't interact with them. There have been no animals on Tollan for generations. They are offered sanctuary in the Land of Light by Tuplo (see 'The Broca Divide'), which Omoc rejects. And, subsequently, on the planet of the Nox, which they gladly accept.

**THE CONSPIRACY STARTS AT CLOSING TIME**  Further to the current administration's political leanings (see 'Cor-Ai'), Daniel says, angrily, that he voted for this President. If that isn't proof of a Democratic White House, what is? Maybe *SG-1* takes place in *The West Wing* universe?

**IN THE INTERESTS OF NATIONAL SECURITY**  This episode sees the debut of the NID's Colonel Harry Maybourne. He replaced Kennedy (see 'The Enemy Within'), who was promoted. Sam describes the NID as specialising in chronic paranoia.

**POSSIBLE INFLUENCES**  *The Day the Earth Stood Still*. Daniel mentions the volcanic disaster of Pompeii (79AD). Also, the *Star Trek*-y silver Tollan outfits, *Doctor Who* ('we have that custom too', plus the Tollan/Sereta situation is similar to the Time Lords' relationship with the Minyans in *Doctor Who*'s 'Underworld'), Austrian physicist Erwin Schrödinger (1887-1961) and his famous theory involving a cat, and Albert Einstein (1879-1955).

**'YOU MIGHT REMEMBER ME FROM...'**  Tobin Bell played David Ferrie in *Ruby* and appeared in *Goodfellas*, *Serial Killer* and *Malice*. Woody Jeffreys was in *Valentine*. Tom McBeath's movies include *They Nest*, *In Cold Blood*, *Cadence* and *Along Came a Spider*.

---

32 Named after the legendary Toltec city in which Quetzalcoatl was worshipped.

Garwin Sanford was in *Get Carter*, *Shutterspeed* and *The Fly II*.

**LOGIC, LET ME INTRODUCE YOU TO THIS WINDOW** During most of the scene with Maybourne in the briefing room, Daniel's left arm is straight on the table. In one shot, however, it's bent at an angle. Enough time has elapsed before the briefing for SG-1 to get cleaned up, yet some of the Tollan are only just being wheeled into the infirmary. How does Lya operate the Gate? Someone has a Monty Burns moment and *releases the hounds* on the Tollan. Daniel gives Omoc his right hand, with his notebook in his left. In the next shot, as they step through the wall, Daniel's left hand is in Omoc's right, and the notebook is gone.

**QUOTE/UNQUOTE** Sam, on Tollan air-quality: 'Seems to be in pockets ranging from 1500 degrees down to 200.' Jack: 'Sounds like LA.'

Jack, on the Nox: 'God, I *love* those people.'

**NOTES** 'Don't help us.' A game of two halves, somewhat. The Tollan are beautifully aloof, but their impact is ruined by some one-dimensional politics for the under fives, a pointless 'Sam's traumatic love-life' subplot and a slow-moving story which takes half an hour to get going. A terrific last few minutes help.

Daniel describes Antaeus (see 'The Nox') as 'the little guy with the funny hair'.

**CAST AND CREW COMMENTS** What's it like to work with Richard Dean Anderson (second edition)? 'He's got a great sense of humour,' noted Amanda Tapping. 'He's very generous. Having had the amount of experience he has, he really looks out for us. He's a lovely man.'

**DID YOU KNOW?** This episode sees the debut of the UAV (Unmanned Aerial Vehicle).

# 18 SOLITUDES

US Transmission Date: 6 Feb 1998
UK Transmission Date: 29 Jul 1998
Writer: Brad Wright
Director: Martin Wood
Cast: Gary Jones (Technician), Dan Shea (Sgt Siler)

The Stargate malfunctions whilst SG-1 are evacuating from a firefight on P4A771. Teal'c and Daniel make it back home, but Jack and Sam find themselves trapped near a Stargate in a barren icy landscape, with O'Neill suffering from a broken leg. As a desperate race to repair the Stargate gets underway at the SGC, Teal'c and Daniel struggle to work out what went wrong and where their comrades might be.

**THE TORTURED SKELETON OF JACK O'NEILL** Jack has broken eight bones prior to this. He fractured his skull in a parachute accident near the Iran/Iraq border during the 1980s. How did he manage that?, Sam asks. 'I hit the ground,' he replies. As the mission was undercover, he had to make his own way to safety. It took him five days and he made it only through his desire to see Sara again (see 'Cold Lazarus').

**THE CONSPIRACY STARTS AT CLOSING TIME** Sam notes that the Stargate creates an artificial wormhole transferring an energised matter-stream in one direction along an extradimensional conduit. Siler puts it more simply, describing the Gate as 'a giant superconductor'.

The Stargate used to shake when in use (as seen in a couple of early episodes). Hammond notes that frequency dampeners have been installed to counteract this anomaly.

The second Gate's location was in the Ross Ice Shelf of the Antarctic, 50 miles from McMurdo Base.

**POSSIBLE INFLUENCES** *The Wizard of Oz* ('I don't think we're in Kansas anymore'), plus name-checks for *To Die For* and Elvis Presley's 'It's Now or Never' and allusions to The Rolling Stones' '2,000 Light Years from Home' and *Love and Death* (Sam cooking snow).

**BEHIND THE CAMERA** Martin Wood directed *The Impossible Elephant*, *Teenage Space Vampires* and *The Invisible Man*. Musical composer Joel Goldsmith worked on *Diamonds*, *Kull the Conqueror*, *Shiloh*, *Star Trek: First Contact* and *Joshua Tree*.

**LOGIC, LET ME INTRODUCE YOU TO THIS WINDOW** Daniel asks how many Earth-based cultures the SGC have encountered from periods both before and after the Stargate was buried. The presence of a second Gate which was, presumably, frozen long before the first was buried at Giza may explain some of the former cases, but it doesn't explain the latter: see 'Demons'. Longitude and latitude co-ordinates cover a wide geographical area. Even though the SGC pinpoints the second Stargate's location more accurately than just seismic data, it still wouldn't be easy to find Jack and Sam down in that particular crevice. After Castleman is injured, the medical team is called to the 'Embarkation Room' (the first time it's been called this since 'Children of the Gods').

**QUOTE/UNQUOTE** Jack, on his injury: 'You wouldn't think jagged bone digging into raw nerves would hurt... but it does.'

Jack, when he and Sam are sharing a sleeping bag and she feels something hard pressing against her: 'It's my sidearm, I swear.'

**NOTES** 'I'll be damned if I'm going to die on some Godforsaken block of ice a million light years from home.' As a character-building exercise, 'Solitudes' works magnificently, allowing Anderson and Tapping the opportunity to go for something more subtle than groin-thrusting gung-ho. One of the best episodes of the season and a pointer to party-times ahead.

Jack says he can't cook. His only regret, he notes, is 'dying'. Dr Warner is mentioned. For the second time on the show, Amanda Tapping injured herself when attempting a minor stunt, in this case, a bruised bottom as Carter slides down the ice shelf.

**CAST AND CREW COMMENTS** 'I would have crawled over broken glass to get this job,' makeup director Jan Newman told Rhonda Krafchin. As Richard Dean Anderson's personal makeup artist on *MacGyver*, Newman had a chance to observe the actor's peculiarities. 'He was always active, really into getting cuts and scrapes.'

**DID YOU KNOW?** This episode marks the debut of the popular Sergeant Siler played by Dan Shea. Dan originally wanted to play professional ice hockey but, when injured, he auditioned for a beer commercial and became an actor and stand-up comedian instead. 'Sadly, I had no comic timing, so my future was limited,' he noted. Hired as Richard Dean Anderson's stand-in on *MacGyver*, he did some stunt-work on the show and, in 1997, followed Anderson to *SG-1*. As stunt co-ordinator, he has choreographed hundreds of stunts as well as performing a huge number himself.

# 19 TIN MAN

US Transmission Date: 13 Feb 1998
UK Transmission Date: 5 Aug 1998[33]
Writer: Jeff King
Director: Jimmy Kaufman
Cast: Teryl Rothery (Dr Janet Fraiser), Jay Brazeau (Harlan), Dan Shea (O'Neill Alternate)

On PX3989, SG-1 are rendered unconscious and awake to find themselves in an underground facility with Harlan, a decidedly odd individual, who says he has improved them. When they return to Earth, SG-1 discover that they've had their bodies replaced. Worse, they will die unless they return.

**THE WIT AND WISDOM OF JACK O'NEILL** To his duplicate, on their colleagues: 'They're debating the meaning of life. The Daniels say this is all fascinating. The Carters are arguing already.'

**ORIGINS OF THE SPECIES** Altair's biosphere could no longer support life over 11,000 years ago. About 1,000 scientists were chosen to be transferred into synthetic duplicate bodies. The process killed some - including Hubble, the process's 'creator'. Harlan is the last survivor.

**MILITARY INTELLIGENCE?** Does Daniel really think Military Intelligence are going to let the duplicates continue as SG-1, Jack asks.

**IN THE INTERESTS OF NATIONAL SECURITY** Jack is concerned that his duplicate may be a security risk and even considers sending a bomb through the Stargate.

**POSSIBLE INFLUENCES** Some elements are similar to the *Star Trek* episode 'What Are Little Girls Made Of?' and to *Westworld*. The meeting of the duplicate SG-1 and their counterparts may have been inspired by that bit in *Yellow Submarine* where the Beatles meet Sergeant Peppers' Lonely Hearts Club Band. The title is another

33 The UK listings magazine *Radio Times* erroneously credited the episode shown on this date as 'Solitudes'.

reference to *The Wizard of Oz*. It was also the name of a *Star Trek: The Next Generation* episode. Jack refers to the African hymn 'Kumbaya'. Also, *The Simpsons* ('Your point being...?') and *On Her Majesty's Secret Service* ('We have all the time in the world'). The Altairian 'creator' is named after US astronomer Edwin Hubble (1889-1953), noted for his investigations of nebulae and the recession of the galaxies. Harlan may be named after noted SF author Harlan Ellison.

**'YOU MIGHT REMEMBER ME FROM...'** Jay Brazeau played Bobby Long in *Double Jeopardy* and appeared in *Johnny's Girl* and *Insomnia*.

**BEHIND THE CAMERA** Jimmy Kaufman was an assistant director on *Scanners* and *Children of a Lesser God*. His directing work includes *Nightmare Man*, *Red Rain*, *Sirens* and *Due South*.

**LOGIC, LET ME INTRODUCE YOU TO THIS WINDOW** When duplicate Jack jumps from the first storey balcony, the viewer gets a good look at Dan Shea's face as he performs the stunt. Why did Teal'c take so long to realise his Goa'uld was gone? 11,000 years doesn't equal 99,270,000 hours. It's approximately 96,426,000 (including leap years). Jack uses the stethoscope backwards. Harlan's replication process doesn't reproduce clothing but does, seemingly, copy watches and GDOs. Were the real SG-1 stuck on those platforms the whole time? Jack had obviously talked to Harlan at some point, because he asked why it took so long for Harlan to get back. He also knew how to work the door. Didn't Jack see the copy when he removed his gag? Why, therefore, was he surprised to find out about the synthetics?

**QUOTE/UNQUOTE** Jack, on Harlan: 'Perceptive little runt.'
Jack: 'Kumbaya.' Harlan: 'Com'traya.' Jack: 'Whatever.'

**NOTES** 'This is what you are now.' The absolute nadir of the first season's painfully obvious checklist of clichéd SF conceits. ('We haven't done androids yet. Okay, that's episode 19 sorted.') This is a dreadful waste of talent. Jay Brazeau is particularly annoying.

Sam has a mole somewhere embarrassing. Hammond's wife died from cancer four years ago. He has two granddaughters, named Tessa and Kayla (see 'Crystal Skull', 'Chain Reaction').

**AN OFFICER AND A GENTLEMAN** Don Davis credits his military background with informing his character. 'I dealt with field-grade officers,' says the former captain with the Fifth Infantry division. 'In doing so, I realised that they're people just like everyone else. Poets, artists, dreamers, men and women who are writing that great unfinished novel. That's the direction I've tried to take my character. To bring some humanity and show the audience another side of Hammond's personality.'

**DID YOU KNOW?** For the stunt where O'Neill had to jump onto a pile of boxes, Dan Shea remembers: 'Unfortunately, someone forgot to *empty* the boxes, so it was like I hit a concrete pavement.' The interiors of Harlan's base were filmed at an abandoned power station in Vancouver, subsequently also used for locations in 'Watergate' and 'Beneath the Surface'.

# 20 THERE BUT FOR THE GRACE OF GOD

US Transmission Date: 20 Feb 1998
UK Transmission Date: 12 Aug 1998
Story: David Kemper
Teleplay: Robert C Cooper
Director: David Warry-Smith
Cast: Elizabeth Hoffman (Catherine Langford), Gary Jones (Technician[34]), Laara Sadiq (Technician #2), Stuart O'Connell (Marine), Michael Kopsa (News Anchor), Shawn Stewart (Jaffa)

> On P3R233, a world apparently destroyed by the Goa'uld, Daniel discovers a shimmering mirror which transports him to an alternate reality. An Earth were he never joined the SGC and which is facing destruction.

**THE WIT AND WISDOM OF ALTERNATE JACK O'NEILL** 'The Jack O'Neill I know would do it,' says Daniel, trying to persuade Jack to help him return to his own reality. 'Apparently you and I have never met,' is the icy reply.

**SAM'S TRAUMATIC ALTERNATE REALITY** In this reality, Sam and Jack are engaged (see 'Politics', 'Point of View').

**MIRROR, MIRROR** Sam notes that the parallel-universe theory states there are (at any time) an infinite number of alternate realities. Some are very different, others almost identical. Daniel *is* known in the alternate universe as a linguist and ancient Egyptian historian. (His theories are still considered radical.) Catherine *did* try to recruit him to the Stargate programme, but that, presumably, was the point in history where the timelines separate. (Daniel was, apparently, rather rude.) Catherine's team ultimately deciphered the Stargate and Jack still went to Abydos (and probably blew it up). But they never went to Chulak. General Jack O'Neill runs the SGC aided by Colonel Hammond, Dr Sam Carter (who is a PhD in astrophysics and not a member of the military) and Catherine.

Daniel was living in Egypt in 1997 and is probably dead, killed in the first wave of Goa'uld attacks. 1.5 billion people have died worldwide. The map shows that destroyed areas include most of England, France, Belgium, Holland, Spain, Portugal and North Africa and parts of Ireland, Germany, Italy, Central Europe, Scandinavia and Russia. The Goa'uld attack on the US East Coast begins with carnage in Washington DC and Philadelphia. Air Force One (the President's plane) is destroyed by a Goa'uld mothership whilst on its way to the SGC. Here, Teal'c is still the First Prime of Apophis.

**ORIGINS OF THE SPECIES** Teal'c recognises the symbol 'Korush'nai'

34 Character named Harriman in dialogue. However, see '2010'.

(meaning 'turn back') placed on P3R233. This indicates that the world was ravaged by the Goa'uld and left radioactive. The planet's people were clearly advanced and had visited Earth through the Stargate at various times. (Artefacts found include a Turkinese mask and a clay cone from Nagash with cuneiform symbols.) In the alternate reality they discovered the Goa'uld origin address, but were still destroyed.

**IN THE INTERESTS OF NATIONAL SECURITY** A 'Genesis List' of world leaders, scientists and doctors is being sent to the beta site in the alternate reality.

**POSSIBLE INFLUENCES** It's probably coincidental, but this episode bears many similarities to Don Houghton's 1970 *Doctor Who* classic 'Inferno', in which a character slips into a parallel, military-run Earth which is about to be destroyed. Also, *Star Trek*'s mirror universe stories, John Wyndham's *Random Quest*, DC's *Crisis of Infinite Earths*, *Seconds*, *Sliders*, an evacuation craft called *Voyager*, Einstein's theory of relativity (1905) and *Let's Make a Deal* ('What's behind curtain number two?'). The title is from a quotation attributed to penal reformer John Bradford (1510-55). It's also the name of a *MacGyver* episode.

**'YOU MIGHT REMEMBER ME FROM...'** Mike Kopsa was in *Chain of Fools*. Stuart O'Connell appeared in *Futuresport*. Shawn Stuart was in *Andromeda*.

**BEHIND THE CAMERA** David Warry-Smith directed episodes of *Earth: Final Conflict*, *Xena: Warrior Princess*, *The Outer Limits* and *Due South*. David Kemper has written for *Farscape*, *SeaQuest DSV* and *Swamp Thing*.

**LOGIC, LET ME INTRODUCE YOU TO THIS WINDOW** Catherine's file on Daniel reads 'Currrent Status'. Perhaps that's how it's spelled in this reality? When Daniel travels through the mirror, he stays on the same side on which he started. In 'Point of View', when Sam and Kawalsky undergo the same process, they reappear on the opposite side (where their reflections would be). It's convenient that a computer's available so that Jack can show Teal'c Daniel's videotape. Daniel says that the only unique symbol is 'the point of origin for 233'. But when he dials out, he uses the common glyph Pisces as the seventh symbol. Daniel rests his video-camera on the table before putting the artefacts into his backpack. When he reaches for the mirror control, the camera has disappeared. While dialling the beta-site, the technician says chevron one is encoded, but chevron seven is shown locking. When Daniel touches the mirror, he's not holding the sheet containing the Goa'uld homeworld address. Through the mirror, he collapses, his right hand is tucked under his left armpit. But in the next shot, Sam takes the paper from his right hand, which is now at his side.

**QUOTE/UNQUOTE** Daniel: 'I'd say we've pissed the Goa'uld off just as much as you have.'

**NOTES** 'I feel like the victim of the biggest practical joke ever.' An excellent (albeit highly derivative) script, but it's a bit like *Independence Day* would have been if that movie had never left the President's bunker. Once again -

as so often this season - a lack of money hampers the production of something that could have been so much more.

Under normal circumstances, a wormhole can be kept established only for around thirty eight minutes maximum. Daniel tells Catherine about helping her other self find Ernest ('The Torment of Tantalus').

**CRITIQUE** 'Parallel universe stories are usually pretty good, if only because they allow the writers to make the characters different for a week, kill some regulars and do things that would mean the end of the normal show,' wrote Paul Spragg.

**CAST AND CREW COMMENTS** 'My character's a computer nerd,' noted Gary Jones. 'But he got to fire a machine gun, which was pretty cool. One of the crew handed me an automatic weapon and asked "Have you ever fired one of these before?" I said "Are you kidding?" We went out into the parking lot, he stuck a pair of heavy-duty earmuffs on me, put a blank clip in the gun and said "Fire away!"'

**DID YOU KNOW?** 'An ongoing battle I've had from day one working in the TV industry is this idea of dumbing things down for the viewer,' said Richard Dean Anderson. 'If only I'd been in the position to say "You're fired!" the first time I heard someone say that. How dare anyone even consider taking an intelligent idea and tearing away the wit in order to make it easier for people to understand? That's an insult to me as an actor, and certainly to the audience.'

# 21 POLITICS

US Transmission Date: 27 Feb 1998
UK Transmission Date: 19 Aug 1998
Writer: Brad Wright[35]
Director: Martin Wood
Cast: Robert Wisden (Samuels), Ronnie Cox (Senator Kinsey),
Peter Williams (Apophis)[36]

> Daniel warns that it's only a matter of time before the Goa'uld launch an attack, but the Stargate programme faces a more immediate threat; an influential US Senator who sees it as wasteful and with dubious goals. As he reviews previous missions with Hammond and SG-1, he seems determined to shut down the project.

**THE WIT AND WISDOM OF JACK O'NEILL** After Kinsey's initial anti-Stargate rant: 'Well, as long as you've got an open mind...' And: 'Politics isn't my strong suit, but doesn't President outrank Senator?'

---

35 Unusually, for a 'clip-show', individual writers of episodes used for flashbacks - Robert Cooper, Katharyn Powers, Jonathan Glassner and Hart Hanson - are credited on-screen.
36 Seen only in flashbacks from 'The Nox'.

**ORIGINS OF THE SPECIES** The 'Beware the destroyers' message concerning the Goa'uld from the people of P3R233 is repeated ('There But For the Grace of God'). The Goa'uld have enslaved 'a galaxy of worlds' notes Teal'c. Daniel believes Goa'uld society is feudal, though Sam mentions that their technology can generate force-fields around individuals ('The Nox') or ships. This episode sees the first use of the term 'death glider', referring to the Jaffa-piloted craft seen in 'Children of the Gods'.

**THE CONSPIRACY STARTS AT CLOSING TIME** Kinsey is Chairman of the Appropriations Committee and is, in effect, the man who oversees the SGC's $7.4 million annual budget. The Pentagon refers to the Stargate programme as 'Area 52'.

**MILITARY INTELLIGENCE?** Samuels has been promoted to Lieutenant Colonel at Stargate Mission Analysis at The Pentagon. Illness robbed Kinsey of the chance to serve in the military.

**POSSIBLE INFLUENCES** *The Wizard of Oz* ('... *You* were there. And *you* were there,' 'There's no place like home'), *Independence Day* ('We'll just upload a computer virus into the mothership' - a possibly deliberate snipe by the production team at Devlin and Emmerich), I Timothy 6:12 ('Fight the good fight'), Kinsey refers to Pandora's Box and quotes from the Pledge of Allegiance ('One nation, under God').

**'YOU MIGHT REMEMBER ME FROM...'** Ronnie Cox's movies include *Total Recall*, *Deliverance*, *Crazy As Hell*, *Robocop* and *Beverly Hills Cop II*.

**LOGIC, LET ME INTRODUCE YOU TO THIS WINDOW** According to the reports, the initial mission to Chulak took place on February 10. But the scenes at Jack's house in 'Children of the Gods' certainly don't look like February in Colorado.

**QUOTE/UNQUOTE** Jack: 'Engaged?' Sam: 'It *is* theoretically possible.' Jack: 'It's against regulations!'

Kinsey: 'I've spent a career listening to doomsayers in uniform. Let us build our billion-dollar machine and we will save America from the Barbarians at the gate.'

**NOTES** 'I gave the President my word I would give you a fair hearing.' This takes the form of a metaphor for the annual begging sessions between series and networks. We get 20 minutes of talky drama that's actually quite involving. Then, the money runs out and they resort to that end-of-season standby, the clip-show, in the hope that no-one will notice. Oops, too late. Best bit: Jack's and Sam's reaction when Daniel tells them that, in the alternate reality, they were engaged.

Jack mentions P4A771 (see 'Solitudes'). SG-2 recently made contact with the Argosians ('Brief Candle'). They're adjusting well to long-life. Kynthia is mentioned and Jack says he's thinking of retiring there (see 'A Hundred Days', 'Shades of Grey', '2010'). Jack's report on the Chulak mission was written on 23 February (almost a fortnight after the mission). Hammond's report on events of 'The Broca Divide' was in March.

For some reason, the deaths of SG-1 that were cut from 'The Nox' by Channel 4 were left uncut here in the flashbacks.

**DID YOU KNOW?** Martin Wood usually appears in the episodes he directs - he is often seen accompanying Sgt Siler, who, more often than not, carries a huge wrench (presumably to fix some part of the Gate).

## 22 WITHIN THE JERPENT'J GRAJP

US Transmission Date: 6 Mar 1998
UK Transmission Date: 26 Aug 1998
Story: James Crocker
Teleplay: Jonathan Glassner
Director: David Warry-Smith
Cast: Peter Williams (Apophis), Alexis Cruz (Skaara), Brent Stait (Louis Ferretti), Gary Jones (Technician), Michael Richard Dobson (Jaffa)

> The Stargate is being closed but SG-1 defy orders and make an unauthorised trip to what they believe to be the Goa'uld homeworld. Instead, they find themselves on a ship full of Jaffa. As Sam and Daniel wire the ship with explosives, Jack and Teal'c discover that Skaara is on board. But, is his human spirit still alive or has it been consumed by his Goa'uld parasite, Klorel?

**ORIGINS OF THE SPECIES** Teal'c says that the fastest Goa'uld ships can travel at ten times the speed of light, though this one (and presumably, Apophis's, which is accompanying it) can go much faster than that (if Sam's calculations about the length of time taken to get to Earth weren't merely ill-informed guesswork). Jack proves that what he and Daniel have suspected since 'Children of the Gods' (something of the host survives Goa'uld implantation) is true when Klorel lets Skaara speak (see 'Pretense').

Goa'uld zat'n'ktel guns (nicknamed zats) discharge an energy bolt, causing the person shot great pain. A second shot will kill most subjects. A third hit disintegrates the body.

**THE CONSPIRACY STARTS AT CLOSING TIME** Hammond says he was one month away from retirement before 'we started the SGC' (presumably meaning the reactivation in 'Children of the Gods', since there is no evidence that Hammond was involved in General West's command).

**POSSIBLE INFLUENCES** *The Prisoner* (the hovering communication device), the movies of John Woo (Daniel, with two pistols).

**'YOU MIGHT REMEMBER ME FROM...'** Michael Dobson was the voice of Leonardo in *Ninja Turtles: The Next Mutation*.

**BEHIND THE CAMERA** James Crocker worked on *Star Trek: Deep Space Nine*, *The Twilight Zone* and *Max Headroom*.

**EPIC DOUBLE ENTENDRE** Teal'c must suffer the most painful death a Jaffa can know, says Apophis. 'Removal of his prim'ta.' Ouch.

**LOGIC, LET ME INTRODUCE YOU TO THIS WINDOW** Apophis refers to Klorel as 'my son'. Yet in 'Children of the Gods', Skaara was clearly taken by another pair of Goa'uld to bear *their* offspring. Does 'prim'ta' mean the ceremony of implantation (as in 'Bloodlines') or the larval Goa'uld (as suggested here) or both? SG-1 leave the sarcophagus room and walk down a corridor along the left wall. Assuming they ducked into the nearest room when someone approached, the glider bay is, therefore, on that side of the ship. But the procession of Jaffa and sarcophagus travel in the opposite direction. When storming the peltak, how do Daniel and Sam avoid shooting Teal'c? Daniel has two handguns as they attack the peltak. One slides away when Klorel grabs him. What happened to the other one? Was Jack the only one who could have shot Klorel to save Daniel, or was this dramatic licence? A woman with dark hair and an orange dress to the left of the sarcophagus during Apophis' message, has no head tattoo. Who is she? The President is said to be mobilising the armed forces (including National Guards) in preparation for the Goa'uld attack. But this is, seemingly, done without alerting the public to the existence of extra-terrestrials. Not very likely, is it?

**GOA'ULD LEXICON** 'Remoc' means 'arrival'.

**QUOTE/UNQUOTE** Jack, on the Jaffa: 'I always get a happy, tingly feeling when I see those guys.'

**NOTES** 'Don't you think we should see if we can stop the same slaughter from happening here?' Something of an effects overload, with a very good cliffhanger (an *SG-1* trademark). This is obviously where most of the season's money went. Good performances (particularly from Shanks). There's a feeling of synchronicity as many of the more insignificant aspects of the first season are shaken off.

Daniel mentions Kendra's fight for control of her mind with her symbiont ('Thor's Hammer'). In the alternate reality, he notes that Sara, Carter's family and, even, he himself were all dead. A recovered Ferretti (see 'Children of the Gods') is now leading SG-2.

**CRITIQUE** In a contemporary review, this author noted: 'It's always difficult to escape the fact that there are few real characters outside the regulars, though Richard Dean Anderson gets his usual share of pithy quips. Otherwise, you get what you normally get, mean aliens and cheap gun battles. I have a lot of time for this series, but I just wish once in a while it would *surprise* me.' Thankfully, the surprises were coming.

**CAST AND CREW COMMENTS** 'She says a lot of scientific technobabble,' Amanda Tapping freely acknowledges regarding Carter. Amanda was so concerned about this that, on getting the part, she made a point of going on the internet to research astrophysics and reading Stephen Hawking's *A Brief History of Time* so that she would, at least, have a vague idea about what some of her lines actually meant.

**DID YOU KNOW?** Jack's 'Think you get Showtime?', regarding the Goa'uld communications device was edited for syndication repeats to 'Goa'uld-TV!'

# STARGATE SG-1 SEASON 2 (1998-1999)

'You know that "Meaning of life" stuff?
I think we're gonna be all right.'

# STARGATE SG-1™ SEASON 2 (1998-1999)

Double Secret Productions/Gekko Film Corp/
Metro-Goldwyn-Meyer

Developed for Television by Brad Wright, Jonathan Glassner

Executive Producer: Brad Wright, Jonathan Glassner

Co-Executive Producer: Michael Greenburg, Richard Dean Anderson

Producer: N John Smith

Co-Producer: Robert C Cooper (33-44)

Post Production Consultant: R Michael Eliot

Senior Advisor: Terry Curtis Fox (23-29)

Executive Story Editor: Robert C Cooper (23-32)

Story Editor: Tor Alexander Valenza (34-44)

Regular Cast: Richard Dean Anderson (Jack O'Neill), Michael Shanks
(Daniel Jackson), Amanda Tapping (Samantha Carter), Christopher Judge
(Teal'c), Don S Davis (General George Hammond)

SEASON 2

# 23 THE SERPENT'S LAIR

US Transmission Date: 26 Jun 1998
UK Transmission Date: 2 Sep 1998
Writer: Brad Wright
Director: Jonathan Glassner
Cast: Robert Wisden (Samuels), Peter Williams (Apophis), Gary Jones (Technician), Alexis Cruz (Skaara/Klorel), Tony Amendola (Bra'tac), Laara Sadiq (Technician), Douglas H Arthurs (Kah'l), Michael Brynjolfson (Jaffa), Phillip Mitchell (Jaffa #2), Bernie Neufeld (General's Aide)

As two Goa'uld warships head toward Earth, SG-1 are on a suicide mission, planting C4 to stop the attack. Aided by Teal'c's mentor, Bra'tac, they realise that their deaths may be the only way to save their planet.

**THE WIT AND WISDOM OF JACK O'NEILL** One of the series' finest moments. Jack, paraphrases George Patton: 'I think it's time for a new plan.' Bra'tac: 'We offer to lay down our lives for your world, human. You cannot ask more.' Jack: 'No, I think a better idea is to get the other guys to lay down *their* lives for *their* worlds first.'

**THE CONSPIRACY STARTS AT CLOSING TIME** SG-5 found a small amount of Naqahdah ore two months ago.

**MILITARY INTELLIGENCE?** Samuels and Maybourne have developed a new super-weapon for pre-emptive use against the Goa'uld at Area 51.[37] An MK 12-A warhead enriched with Naqahdah, it's the equivalent of a 1,000 megaton weapon. Two are launched from Vandenberg Air Force Base. They're ineffective.

**POSSIBLE INFLUENCES** Visually, *Star Wars*, *Moonraker*, *Return of the Jedi*. The real Space Shuttle Endeavour plays a prominent off-screen role. Also, *Space Ghost* ('Space monkey!').

**'YOU MIGHT REMEMBER ME FROM...'** Douglas Arthurs was in *Acts of War*. Phillip Mitchell appeared in *Dirty Little Secret*.

**LOGIC, LET ME INTRODUCE YOU TO THIS WINDOW** Bra'tac says the peltak is two decks above the level of the Gateroom. But Daniel manages to get from the peltak to the Gate in about 75 seconds. The dialling sequence that Daniel uses for P3X984 appears to start with Orion, but in 'There But For the Grace of God' the same planet's sequence began with Eridanus. NASA confirms that the ships weren't destroyed by Samuels' missiles, but

37 Area 51 (aka Groom Lake or 'Dreamland'): A slightly-less-secret-than-it-used-to-be military facility near Las Vegas, Nevada built in the 50s as a base for America's U-2 spyplanes. Now home for numerous 'black ops' aircraft programmes (including the F-117 stealth fighter), the site, and its surrounding area, are also associated - to varying levels of credibility - with UFOs and conspiracy theories, and are a key-element in the back-story of TV series like *The X-Files* and *Roswell*.

Hammond informs the President that an Electromagnetic Pulse took out all satellite communications. What was NASA using to detect the ships' presence? How do the Endeavour crew know that whoever's in the death gliders are friendly? We hear them say 'Houston, we have them in sight' as if they're specifically looking for SG-1, but Daniel couldn't have known they would use that method of escape. Klorel says that he's Apophis's son, noting: 'He seeded the Queen-mother.' As 'Hathor' makes clear, that results in lots of larvae. Apophis couldn't treat all of them as his heirs. Jack picked up the grenades when Bra'tac gave SG-1 their weapons, and he is the one who has them when they destroy the shield generators on Apophis's ship. So why did he ask Sam how many were left? Those 'reports from all over the country' of lights in the sky comes in *remarkably* quickly.

**GOA'ULD LEXICON** 'Chal'til' means 'untrained warrior.' 'Ral-tora-kee' is a Jaffa wish of good luck.

**QUOTE/UNQUOTE** Jack: 'I suppose now is the time for me to say something profound... Nothing comes to mind. Let's do it.'

Bra'tac: 'You are not a god. You're a parasite within a child. I despise you.'

**NOTES** 'This wasn't such a bad day after all.' What a great piece of reformatting. Overnight (well, over the summer) *SG-1* becomes a different series, and you can tell that the actors are delighted about it. A fabulous mini-action movie and the first signs of an emerging greatness in the production. Best bits: Jack's and Daniel's embarrassed description of space shuttles and Bra'tac's first meeting with Hammond 'of Texas'.

Major Castleman is mentioned ('Solitudes'). Bra'tac tells Teal'c that Rya'c is growing and will be a great warrior. Goa'uld 'shock grenades' cause temporary blindness.

**CAST AND CREW COMMENTS** The script had Klorel dying along with every-one else on Apophis's ship but, after the episode was completed, the production team saw the positive fan reaction to the return of the character in 'Within the Serpent's Grasp'. 'And we'd just killed him,' Brad Wright noted. Fortunately, Jonathan Glassner had the idea to superimpose a shot of Alexis Cruz from earlier in the episode into the sequence of Apophis being ringed away. 'So we cut and paste Klorel, stick him next to Apophis and he escapes too,' Wright adds. 'That wasn't the way it was written, or even how it was shot. But that's the way it was edited.'

**DID YOU KNOW?** When Klorel emerges from the sarcophagus, he says 'Mak tak Tauri' ('Kill the humans'). It sounds *very* like 'ratatouille'. For reasons far too complicated to go into here, this word is a catchphrase on Sky Sports' excellent Saturday morning magazine/comedy show *Soccer AM* in the UK and, as a consequence, this clip has featured on several occasions.

# 24  IN THE LINE OF DUTY

US Transmission Date: 3 Jul 1998

SEASON 2

UK Transmission Date: 9 Sep 1998
Writer: Robert C. Cooper
Director: Martin Wood
Cast: Teryl Rothery (Dr Janet Fraiser) Tracy Westerholm (Technician #2), Katie Stuart (Cassandra), Woody Jeffreys (SF Guard), Laara Sadiq (Technician), Peter Lacroix (The Ashrak), Judy Norton (Talia), Joe Pascual (Medical Technician), Nicole Rudell (Nurse), Benz Antoine (Driver), Jim Thorburn (SF Guard 2), David Allan Pearson (Quinta), Ian Robison (Security Officer), Reg Tupper (Doctor)

> During a rescue mission to Nasya, Sam's body is taken over by a Goa'uld hiding in the mortally wounded body of a Nasyan. Cassandra recognises the Goa'uld presence and Carter is confined. However, the Goa'uld tells Teal'c that he is Jolinar of Malkshur, one of the Tok'ra, and he's being pursued by the Ashrak, an assassin intent on killing him.

**ORIGINS OF THE SPECIES** A first reference to the legendary Tok'ra, a small alliance of Goa'uld who oppose the System Lords. It's alleged that they take hosts who are about to die, and coexist in a relationship that may be rewarding for both symbiont and host (see 'The Tok'ra'). Teal'c believes that the Goa'uld's greatest weakness is their arrogance. They sometimes reveal their strategies unwittingly whilst trying to appear more powerful than they actually are. There has been no Goa'uld interference with the benign Nasyans for over three centuries.

**THE CONSPIRACY STARTS AT CLOSING TIME** Three new SG-teams (designated SG-10 to 12) have recently been created.

**IN THE INTERESTS OF NATIONAL SECURITY** Jack believes that the Goa'uld have a specific agenda against the SGC because 'we just kicked the crap out of Apophis'.

**POSSIBLE INFLUENCES** Allusions to *The Hitch-Hiker's Guide to the Galaxy* ('Don't panic') and US President(s) John Adams (1735-1826, 1767-1848). *The X-Files'* shape shifting alien bounty hunter may have been an influence on the Ashrak.

**'YOU MIGHT REMEMBER ME FROM...'** Peter LaCroix was in *Noroc* and *The Silencer*. Reg Tupper appeared in *Scary Movie*. Judy Norton-Taylor played Mary Ellen in *Homecoming*. Ian Robison appeared in *Replicant*. Joe Pascual was in *Head over Heels*. Ben Antoine appeared in *Heist, Sanctimony* and *Spooky House*.

**LOGIC, LET ME INTRODUCE YOU TO THIS WINDOW** Sam shouts: 'This man's alive!'. Then she starts giving him CPR, so he can't be *that* alive. Why can't Jolinar sense the Ashrak under the bandages? Why does the Ashrak use a device to detect Jolinar? Cassandra could detect Jolinar by being near Sam, so why can't he? Why isn't the alarm on the palm-reader at the Gate linked to elsewhere in the base? How did the Ashrak disable the cell beams? Teal'c says Jolinar once tried to overthrow a System Lord but was defeated. In 'The Tok'ra' we're told that they work by infiltration. When Teal'c runs the keycard through the reader, the magnetic strip is facing the wrong way. Fraiser wants to 'cardiovert at 40 joules' but the pulse monitor appears normal. She glances at the chart for the patient in Room 12 and immediately pulls off the bandages, indicating that she suspects it's Jacobs. Why? How does one differentiate between two separate brainwaves on an EEG? In addition to being chief medical officer at the SGC, Janet has an office at the USAF Academy Hospital nearby. Where does she get the time to do both jobs *and* bring up Cassandra (see 'Singularity')?

**GOA'ULD LEXICON** 'Tok'ra' is said to mean 'resistance' (see 'The Tok'ra'). 'Harakash' is the Goa'uld term for the System Lords. 'Ashrak' means 'hunter'.

**QUOTE/UNQUOTE** Teal'c: 'When you speak to her, do not see [her as] your friend?' Jack: 'How do you do that?'
   Teal'c, having shot Daniel with a zat: 'Are you injured?' Daniel: 'Dumb question.'

**NOTES** 'We may have a Goa'uld out there on a mission to kill Carter.' Great opening sequence, and the rest of the episode ain't too shoddy. Tapping puts in a fine performance with just the right degree of anger. Apart from a pointless little subplot with Cassandra, this is damn-near perfect.
   There are references to Kawalsky, Maybourne and Bra'tac. Jolinar claims to know where Sha're is.

**DID YOU KNOW?** SG-1 is proactive in giving fans a look behind-the-scenes. Season two in the US, for instance, opened with a 30 minute *Making Of* documentary, fronted by Chris Judge and Amanda Tapping, which took viewers on location and into the studio with the cast and crew. (This was broadcast immediately prior to 'The Serpent's Lair'.) Subsequently, the production has made numerous featurettes, many for use as extras on DVD releases. These include a series of short introductory pieces in which Don Davis and Teryl Rothery, in-character, allow viewers access to *Secret Files of the SGC*. (This became a regular feature of the fourth season DVDs.) Other bonuses include a Teryl Rothery video-diary on the making of 'Rite of Passage' and similar Don Davis and Amanda Tapping pieces on the sets of 'Threshold' and 'Red Sky' respectively; three *Timeline to the Future* documentaries, introduced by Richard Dean Anderson and Brad Wright; and numerous season four and five DVD commentaries provided by Peter DeLuise, Martin Wood, James Tichenor, Jim Menard, Robert Cooper, Michael Shanks, Amanda Tapping, Chris Judge and others, which give fascinating insights into the creative genesis of the episodes.

## 25 PRIJONERJ

US Transmission Date: 10 Jul 1998
UK Transmission Date: 16 Sep 1998
Writer: Terry Curtis Fox
Director: David Warry-Smith
Cast: Bonnie Bartlett (Linea), Mark Acheson (Vishnor), Andrew Wheeler (Major Stan Kovacek), Colin Lawrence (Major Warren), Laara Sadiq (Technician), Michael Puttonen

(Simian), Colleen Winton (Dr Greene), David Bloom (Scavenger), Kim Kondrashoff (Roshure)

SG-1 inadvertently help a man who turns out to be accused of murder. By aiding him, SG-1 are considered complicit in his crime. They are sent through a Stargate to Hadante, a penal world. The most powerful person on Hadante seems to be Linea, a diminutive woman who terrifies the other prisoners. SG-1 strike a deal with Linea: if she helps to power the Stargate, they will help her to escape. It seems a fair trade, but why was Linea there in the first place?

**ORIGINS OF THE SPECIES** The people of P3X775 are xenophobic, arrogant and have a zero tolerance for crime. The planet is made up of island states. SG-3 are scheduled for a reconnaissance visit to P2A509.

**THE CONSPIRACY STARTS AT CLOSING TIME** Sam notes that power will free up the superconducting ring of the Stargate and dialling manually has worked before ('The Torment of Tantalus'). Linea has perfected a form of organically-based cold fusion which Sam believes could eliminate pollution of Earth.

**MILITARY INTELLIGENCE?** SG-9, led by Major Kovacek, is the SGC's diplomatic corp.

**POSSIBLE INFLUENCES** Visually, *Superman II*. Conceptually, *Alien³*, *Cool Hand Luke* (and loads of other prison movies). Daniel mentions Botany Bay, the British penal colony in Australia that subsequently became Sydney (or, is this a subtle reference to *Star Trek II: The Wrath of Khan*?; after all, it's subsequently established that Daniel's a fanboy - see '1969').

**'YOU MIGHT REMEMBER ME FROM...'** Bonnie Bartlett played Ellen Craig in *St Elsewhere* and Grace in *Little House on the Prairie* and appeared in *Salem's Lot* and *Primary Colors*. Mark Acheson was Jules in *The Proposal*. Michael Puttonen appeared in *Look Who's Talking Now*. Andrew Wheeler was in *Big Bully*. Colleen Winton played Suzanne Preston in *Daughters*. Kim Kondrashoff was in *Titanic*.

**BEHIND THE CAMERA** Terry Curtis Fox previously wrote for *JAG* and *Hill Street Blues*. Editor Brad Rines worked on *Robocop*, *Sea Hunt* and *Jeremiah*.

**LOGIC, LET ME INTRODUCE YOU TO THIS WINDOW** The Taldor removes all SG-1's weapons and equipment, yet Linea managed to keep her palm device. Is Linea from P3X775 originally, or was she already a traveller when she created the plague? It's unclear from what she and Simian say, but she certainly seems to know a lot about other planets. SG-1 get a clear view of the address Linea goes to, so why don't they follow her once they get the system running again? Doesn't Makepeace, rather than Major Warren, lead SG-3? The Taldor are supposedly superior to Earth technologically, yet the prisoners on Hadante act as if they come from a primitive society. Maybe jail does that to you?

**QUOTE/UNQUOTE** Jack: 'Teal'c, look scary and take point.'

Linea: 'There are many forms of power. Some more subtle than others.'

**NOTES** 'Well, this sucks!' A terrific episode that deals with issues of crime and responsibility without presenting any obvious or patronising messages (see also 'Cor-Ai' and compare and contrast with 'Emancipation'). Proof that *SG-1* can be a really intelligent humanist vehicle when it's not too busy shooting at the enemy.

Jack suggests that he's been in prison before (see 'A Matter of Time'). Daniel hasn't. Hammond goes through the Stargate for the first time.

**CAST AND CREW COMMENTS** Lynn Smith joined the show as locations manager in season two. Whether a story requires a Starbucks coffee shop or an alien landscape, she and her assistant Jamie Lake have to find the spot. 'I get a script and highlight all the locations, interiors and exteriors,' she noted. 'Our writers live locally, so they'll sometimes write around a particular place they know in the area, such as a motel or a café. Of course, that's not always the location they end up getting.'

**DID YOU KNOW?** Amanda Tapping appreciates the physical aspect of working on a series that features spectacular action. 'I love the fact they let me do a lot of my own stunts,' she said. 'The only thing they won't let me do is fall from heights, but all the fights I do myself. I met up with an ex-Navy Seal, who showed me how to handle a gun.'

# 26 THE GAMEKEEPER

US Transmission Date: 17 Jul 1998
UK Transmission Date: 23 Sep 1998
Story: Jonathan Glassner, Brad Wright
Teleplay: Jonathan Glassner
Director: Martin Wood
Cast: Dwight Schultz (The Keeper), Jay Acovone (Charles Kawalsky), Teryl Rothery (Dr Janet Fraiser), Laara Sadiq (Technician), Michael Rogers (John Michaels), Lisa Bunting (Claire Jackson), Robert Duncan (Melburn Jackson), Diane Brown (Docent), Gillian Barber (Resident #1), Cathy Weseluck (Resident #2)

> On P7J989, SG-1 discover a beautiful garden and a dome of metallic chambers, each containing an lifeless person. Ensnared in four of the chambers, they find themselves reliving pivotal moments in their lives in the hope of changing the outcome. A shadowy figure called the Keeper explains that they're part of a game feeding memories into a virtual reality created for the amusement of his residents.

**ORIGINS OF THE SPECIES** Teal'c says the Goa'uld have experimented with time manipulation.

P7J989 was all-but destroyed by a chemical disaster 1022 years ago.

**IN THE INTERESTS OF NATIONAL SECURITY** In 1982, Captain Jack O'Neill was on a team, with Kawalsky and a soldier named Thomas, led by Colonel John Michaels. They attempted the covert rescue of a Soviet agent named Boris from a house in East Germany. The mission - Operation East Fly - was a disaster and Michaels was killed.

**POSSIBLE INFLUENCES** The *Red Dwarf* episode 'Better than Life' shares many similarities (as does *The Matrix* although, interestingly, 'The Gamekeeper' came first) and *Lost in Space*'s 'The Keeper'. Bearing in mind that the main guest star played the holo-addicted Reg Barclay, it's hard not to see this as a *Next Generation* holodeck-gone-wrong story. The specific *Star Trek* episode that it most resembles, how-ever, is *Voyager*'s 'The Thaw'. Also, *An American Werewolf in London* (a dream within a dream) and Genesis ('Where there's a garden, there's snakes').

**'YOU MIGHT REMEMBER ME FROM...'** Dwight Schultz will be familiar to readers as Reg Barclay in the various *Star Trek* series and as Murdoch in *The A-Team*. Lisa Bunting was in *The Incubus*. Michael Rogers appeared in *Mission: Impossible*. Robert Duncan played Mabus in *First Wave*. Gilliam Barber's movies include *Cats and Dogs*, *The Guilty* and *Maternal Instincts*. Cathy Weseluck was a voice artist on *Barbie in the Nutcracker* and *CyberSix*.

**LOGIC, LET ME INTRODUCE YOU TO THIS WINDOW** The stones that fall on Daniel's parents are painfully fake. Does Teal'c look like Thomas and, if not, why bother to give him hair in the simulation? After 1022 years in the machines, the Residents appear to have no prob-lems moving around and adjusting to the real environment. There's no MALP visible when SG-1 arrive, though they had been looking at live-feed from it. Kawalsky was, seemingly, a captain in 1982, yet he was only a lieutenant a decade later (see 'Stargate'). Despite what Sam says, there *are* no 'logical' theories on time travel.

**QUOTE/UNQUOTE** Daniel: 'Imagine if you were locked in a room for a thousand years with only a VCR, a TV and five movies. How long could you watch those five movies before you were bored silly?'

**NOTES** 'Why should I go through this again?' A thoroughly rotten 'message' episode which starts badly and gets worse with the intro-duction of Dwight Schultz sporting a silly hat and an even sillier Peter Sellars-like Germanic accent. It could still, just, have worked if the episode's plot hadn't disappeared around the 25 minute mark. The rest is, merely, a series of depressing runarounds.

Daniel's parents, Claire and Melburn, were both archaeologists. They died in New York's Museum of Art when an exhibit fell of them when Daniel was a child. Kawalsky played street hockey with Jack. O'Neill promised to look after the dying Michaels' wife, Barbara.

**DID YOU KNOW?** The site chosen for the Gamekeeper's garden by Lynn Smith was the beautiful Bloedel Conservatory in Vancouver's Queen Elizabeth Park. 'Once we have the location,' Lynn noted, 'Richard Hudolin and art director Bridget McGuire come in and work magic. Then the set decorators will dress the place up with all kinds of cool stuff. They can take a location that's very plain or desolate and fix it up in such a way as to make you go, "Wow!"'

# 27 NEED

US Transmission Date: 24 Jul 1998
UK Transmission Date: 30 Sep 1998
Story: Robert C Cooper, Damian Kindler
Teleplay: Robert C Cooper
Director: David Warry-Smith
Cast: Heather Hanson (Shyla), Teryl Rothery (Dr Janet Fraiser), Gary Jones (Technician), George Touliatos (Pyrus), Andrew Guy (Jaffa #1), Michael Philip (Jaffa #2), Jason Calder (SF Guard), Roy Prendergast (Guard)[38]

Exploring on P3R636, Daniel saves a young woman from suicide. She is Shyla, the daughter of Pyrus The Godslayer. SG-1 are enslaved and forced to work in the Naqahdah mines, but when Daniel falls ill, the Princess uses a Goa'uld sarcophagus to cure him. Shyla explains that Pyrus has lived for 700 years but is now dying. She wants Daniel as her king.

**THE WIT AND WISDOM OF JACK O'NEILL** On conditions in the mine: 'I've seen a lot of union violations around here. I should probably speak to your supervisor.'

**SAM'S TRAUMATIC LOVE-LIFE** Daniel suggests, rather cruelly, that Sam has never known true love.

**ORIGINS OF THE SPECIES** The Goa'uld enslaved P3R636, but 700 years ago Pyrus killed the (nameless) Goa'uld who ruled. He continues to mine raw Naqahdah and send it through the Stargate to an unknown destination - presumably the System Lords.

The use of a sarcophagus when one is already healthy has significant side-effects: it heals abnormalities such as vision problems but causes addiction, altered mental state and arrogance, typical of the Goa'uld mentality.

**SEX AND DRUGS AND ROCK 'N' ROLL** The effect of the sarcophagus seem to be beneficial but, as Sam notes, it sends Daniel's endorphin levels to outrageous heights. The Tok'ra will not use the sarcophagus as, they believe, it damages their kah'lesh (soul).

**POSSIBLE INFLUENCES** Allusions to *Snow White and the Seven Dwarves* ('Hi-ho, hi-ho'), *Quantum Leap* ('Oh boy'), the *Star Wars* movies ('You're going Dark-Side on us'), *The Man Who Would Be King*, The Doors' 'Celebration of the Lizard' ('I can do anything!') and *The Godfather* ('You've never shown me any respect').

**'YOU MIGHT REMEMBER ME FROM...'** Heather Hanson was in *After School Special* and *Bordello of Blood*. Roy Prendergast was in *Spanking Amy*, *A Strange Smell* and *JFK*. George Touliatos appeared in *Jitters*, *The Final Cut*, *Divided Loyalties* and *Forever Knight*.

**BEHIND THE CAMERA** Damien Kindler wrote episodes of *Beast Master* and *PSI-Factor: Chronicles of the Paranormal*. Camera Operator Andy Wilson

38 Uncredited.

SEASON 2

worked on *We're No Angels*, *Cadence* and *Jennifer Eight*.

**LOGIC, LET ME INTRODUCE YOU TO THIS WINDOW** Presumably the uniforms worn by the guards were those of the ruling Goa'uld's Jaffa 700 years ago? They don't look that old. Did Shyla give Daniel a bath, or does the sarcophagus remove dirt as well? Why doesn't Daniel tell Shyla about Sha're? Why wasn't there a guard at the table in the hall when Daniel escapes? Daniel's system is badly affected, he has a fever and his chemicals are unbalanced. But he's left in sickbay in ordinary clothes and without an IV. A ribbon device destroys a sarcophagus, but a staff blast only short-circuits it? Though the two weapons use different energy sources, staff blasts are usually quite destructive. Jack tells Daniel he knows what withdrawl is like. Is this a reference to his own 'private hell' (Charlie's death), or has Jack suffered from, say, alcoholism in the past? Was there anyone on the other side of the Stargate still receiving the Naqahdah shipments after all this time?

**QUOTE/UNQUOTE** Jack: 'We had a nice time, Sir. Carter picked up some Naqahdah. Teal'c made some new friends as usual. Daniel got engaged. I'm gonna hit the showers.'

**NOTES** 'Look at yourself. It's like you need a fix.' After a slow and awkward beginning, this turns into one of the best episodes of the season. The addiction metaphor is well handled, with Shanks acting his cotton socks off as Daniel becomes manic, ranting and pumped full of junk. A *just say no* story without any soapbox soundbites or feeble gestures.

Sam (or more accurately, the essence of Jolinar within her) can sense when a Goa'uld is nearby. She says she even gets a weird feeling around Teal'c. ('Hey, who doesn't?' asks Jack.) Daniel says he always felt out of place on Earth. SG-1's next mission is to P3H826. SG-3 recovered a quantity of Naqahdah last year (presumably in addition to that returned by SG-5 mentioned in 'The Serpent's Lair').

**CAST AND CREW COMMENTS** 'It's always a little dangerous to have a device that brings people back from the dead,' Robert Cooper noted. 'In one respect the audience always knows your heroes are in jeopardy and at the same time they are probably going to show up next week, but you don't want to always have that magic pill that will bring everybody back to life. So we took that device and gave it a negative connotation: yes, it does do this, which is kind of neat, but it's at a price...'

**DID YOU KNOW?** There were only seven Serpent Guard helmets made (eight including Apophis's gold version). Two of the grey ones feature the mechanism allowing them to open and close.

# 28 THOR'S CHARIOT

US Transmission Date: 31 Jul 1998
UK Transmission Date: 7 Oct 1998
Writer: Katharyn Powers

Director: William Gereghty
Cast: Tamsin Kelsey (Gairwyn), Mark Gibbon (Thor), Laara Sadiq (Technician), Douglas H Arthurs (Heru'ur), Michael Tiernan (Horus Guard), Andrew Kavadas (Olaf)

SG-1 return to Cimmeria after learning that Heru'ur has invaded. They feel responsible since, on their previous visit that they destroyed Thor's Hammer. As Teal'c and Jack come face to face with the enemy, Daniel, Sam and Gairwyn search for the Hall of Thor's Might.

**ORIGINS OF THE SPECIES** The Goa'uld send advance scouts through the Gate. If they don't return, it's a deterrent to invasion. Horus guards are the bodyguard of the Ra family, in this case protecting Heru'ur, the son of Ra and Hathor. ('Nice pedigree,' notes Jack.) Teal'c says that Heru'ur is a very powerful and much feared System Lord.

*Biliskner*, which Thor describes as his ship, was, in Norse mythology, the name of Thor's palace. Sam describes Thor as 'a Roswell[39] grey' and believes that the Asgard have visited Earth many times, contributing to the post-war UFO mythos. Thor, via Gairwyn, confirms this. He says that the Asgard and the Goa'uld are 'at war'. ('Fair Game' makes clear that this isn't entirely accurate. The Asgard are, however, an extremely powerful and benevolent race.) Gairwyn mentions 'Ragnarok', the Norse version of Armageddon.[40]

P53629 is located in a corridor of space that the Goa'uld use to reach Earth. A 'seeker project' is being developed that can track the footprint of a Goa'uld ship even if it's travelling at lightspeed.

**THE CONSPIRACY STARTS AT CLOSING TIME** Sam discovers that she has the power to use the Goa'uld ribbon device and, seemingly, other Goa'uld technology (presumably as a side-effect of the Naqahdah Jolinar left within her, see 'In the Line of Duty').

**POSSIBLE INFLUENCES** The Hall of Thor's Might sequence is pure *Indiana Jones and the Last Crusade*. Sam gives a precise essay on pi (3.14159) and the ratio of the circumference of a circle to its diameter ($2\pi r$) for Daniel. (Well, he's an archaeologist, not a mathematician.)

**'YOU MIGHT REMEMBER ME FROM...'** Andrew Kavades appeared in *Fear of Flying* and *Babylon 5: The Legend of the Rangers*. Michael Tiernan was in *Carpool*.

**LOGIC, LET ME INTRODUCE YOU TO THIS WINDOW** One of Heru'ur's Jaffa can't pronounce 'Chaapa'ai' properly. The landscape around the Gate seems completely different from that seen in 'Thor's Hammer'. Did SG-1 really leave Earth's Stargate address with Gairwyn or Kendra? The fact that Sam says she got iridium incorporated in the Sagan Box suggests that she was involved in its development. Yet, in 'Thor's Hammer', the impression given is that it was Daniel's idea. How did Heru'ur discover that Cimmeria

39 A dustbowl town-in-the-arse-end-of-nowhere, New Mexico. Allegedly the site of an infamous UFO cover-up by the military, following a crash in nearby Corona, in July 1947. See *High Times: An Unofficial and Unauthorised Guide to Roswell* (Virgin Books) by this author for further details.
40 The Viking poem Voluspa ('Prophecy of the Seeress' c.1000AD) describes Ragnarok thus: "The sons of Muspell shatter Bifrost whilst the Giants arrive with Loki, the Trickster, as their steersman. Fenrir, the wolf, devours Odin. Thor slays the World Serpent but is destroyed by its poison. Midgard is set-ablaze and the sky falls."

SEASON 2

was now vulnerable? Lucky guess? Any Jaffa scouts sent to Cimmeria should still have been sent to the labyrinth. (The Gate obelisk was intact at the end of 'Thor's Hammer'.) Presumably the Cimmerians never got round to sealing the labyrinth like Gairwyn promised. Daniel isn't wearing his hat in Thor's Hall but he is when he and Sam are transported back to the obelisk in the forest. Olaf leaves his axe embedded in the Jaffa's chest, but has it later in the caves. There's a distinct conceptual difference between the representation of 14 and the digits one and four. When did Kendra get a family?

**GOA'ULD LEXICON** 'Ha'tak' is the name of a class of Goa'uld pyramid warship.

**QUOTE/UNQUOTE** Teal'c: 'Things will not calm down, Daniel Jackson. They will, in fact, calm up.'

Jack: 'You all know I take great pride in my title as Mr Positive. However, we did destroy their de-Goa'ulding thing. Might not they look unkindly on that?'

**NOTES** 'There's a time and a place for mythology.' A really cool sequel to 'Thor's Hammer' which introduces a whole bushel of new toys for the production team to play with (e.g. Sam's new-found abilities, Thor and the Asgard's real power). A terrific example of the series' new-found reliance on action, humour and suspense in equal doses.

Daniel is acrophobic (he has a fear of heights). He seems conversant with aspects of Sioux Indian culture.

**CAST AND CREW COMMENTS** 'In 'Thor's Hammer' we found ourselves with the problem of Teal'c being trapped. We destroyed that trap in order to save Teal'c but in doing so we opened up the door for the Goa'uld to conquer that planet. And that's exactly what happens,' said Jonathan Glassner. 'We'll probably revisit that world again because an even bigger door has been opened when we meet Thor.'

**DID YOU KNOW?** The voice of Thor in his true form is provided by Michael Shanks.

# 29 MESSAGE IN A BOTTLE

US Transmission Date: 7 Aug 1998
UK Transmission Date: 14 Oct 1998
Story: Michael Greenburg, Jarrad Paul
Teleplay: Brad Wright
Director: David Warry-Smith
Cast: Teryl Rothery (Dr Janet Fraiser), Gary Jones (Technician), Dan Shea (Sgt Siler), Tobias Mehler (Lt Graham Simmons), Kevin Conway (SG Leader)

On a now-dead world, SG-1 find an orb sending electromagnetic signals. Believing them to be messages from a lost civilisation, they bring it back to Earth. When the orb begins to heat up, it is decided to return it to P5C353. The orb, however, seems to have other ideas, shooting a metallic shaft through Jack's shoulder.

**SAM'S TRAUMATIC LOVE-LIFE** Young Graham Simmons appears to have a (nervous) crush on Sam, so you just know he's not going to have an easy time.

**ORIGINS OF THE SPECIES** The moonlike P5C353 (Tal'lak) supported life 100,000 years ago. The civilisation, facing a great cataclysm, left behind an orb containing the virus-like inhabitants. The orb is made from a non-terrestrial alloy several hundred times stronger than steel. It maintains an interior temperature of 33 degrees Fahrenheit, generates an electromagnetic field and emits small amounts of alpha, gamma and delta radiation, using a power source that lasts for thousands of years. The organism infects everything it touches (including fabric and concrete), metabolising its subatomic structure as a virus would with tissue. Janet believes it's a form of necrotising fasciitis. It reproduces exponentially, needs oxygen but goes dormant in an anaerobic environment and feeds on energy.

SG-1 are scheduled to visit P4G881 - a primordial world with no civilisation. They agree to send the orb and the organism through the Stargate to this uninhabited world. When a Goa'uld's world is conquered, he will sometimes leave behind a boobytrap to destroy the conqueror.

**SEX AND DRUGS AND ROCK 'N' ROLL** A briefly-glimpsed book in the lab has the title *Clinical Anaesthesia*. Janet gives Jack a broad-spectrum antibiotic (a tetracycline) to fight the infection caused by the organism, which seems to work prophyactically.

**MILITARY INTELLIGENCE?** The NID (and Maybourne in particular) want to study the orb.

**IN THE INTERESTS OF NATIONAL SECURITY** The General's security code to override the auto self-destruct sequence is 'HAMMONDG 445-243-978-0 81452667'. A 'Wildfire directive' means complete isolation for the base.

**POSSIBLE INFLUENCES** The *Star Trek: The Next Generation* episode 'The Inner Light', *The Satan Bug*, *The Andromeda Strain* (the Wildfire directive), *Outbreak* and *The X-Files* movie. The title was a single by The Police. Jack alludes to The Rolling Stones' 'Wild Horses'. There's a couple of nods to the Apollo 11 moon landings (notably Jack's 'One small step, one giant leap') and a misquote from Genesis 1:28 ('Go forth ... and multiply').

**'YOU MIGHT REMEMBER ME FROM...'** Tobias Mehler was Harvey in *Sabrina, The Teenage Witch* and appeared in *Avalanche Alley*.

**BEHIND THE CAMERA** Jarred Paul is best known as an actor, playing Adam Rafkin in *Action* and appearing in *Buffy*, *Liar Liar*, *Home Improvement* and *Cybill*. He's Michael Greenburg's godson.

**LOGIC, LET ME INTRODUCE YOU TO THIS WINDOW** In the opening shot, we don't see the transport vehicle near SG-1. Why does Simmons, who had little contact with the orb, become infected when, for instance, Daniel doesn't? What's the milky ooze that attacks Sam in the elevator? The dialling sequence for P4G881 starts Aries, then Orion. But the computer shows Scorpio, Crater and Triangulum - the start of the Chulak sequence. Did all the organisms leave? If so, how did the ones in the computers, wiring, elevators and Jack get back to the orb so quickly? The SGC mainframe can, seemingly, reboot itself in less than 30 seconds. The technician starts dialling before the computer reboots.

**QUOTE/UNQUOTE** Daniel: 'They could be saying "Take me to your leader", for all I know.'
Teal'c: 'Undomesticated equines could not remove me.'

**NOTES** 'We've brought things back from all over the galaxy. One of them's finally snapped us in the ass.' Overcomplicated but, fundamentally, an essay on communication (in all its forms). *SG-1* usually works best when it's following the BBC's motto of nation speaking peace unto nation, and this episode, like 'The Fifth Race' and 'Cold Lazarus', takes the metaphor quite literally. Again, Anderson shines in a vehicle designed to show that he's far more of an actor than often given credit for.

Sam notes that the orb contains two elements that weren't previously known to exist (see 'The Torment of Tantalus'). The spacesuits that SG-1 wear in this episode are real NASA ones used for training and exhibitions.

**DID YOU KNOW?** The symbols on the SGC Stargate represent, in order: Earth, Crater, Virgo, Boötes, Centaurus, Libra, Serpens Caput, Norma, Scorpio, Corona Australis, Scutum, Sagittarius, Aquila, Microscopium, Capricorn, Piscis Austrinus, Equuleus, Aquarius, Pegasus, Sculptor, Pisces, Andromeda, Triangulum, Aries, Perseus, Cetus, Taurus, Auriga, Eridanus, Orion, Canis Minor, Monoceros, Gemini, Hydra, Lynx, Cancer, Sextans, Leo Minor and Leo.

# 30 FAMILY

US Transmission Date: 14 Aug 1998
UK Transmission Date: 21 Oct 1998
Writer: Katharyn Powers
Director: William Gereghty
Cast: Peter Williams (Apophis), Teryl Rothery (Dr Janet Fraiser), Tony Amendola (Bra'tac), Brook Parker (Drey'auc[41]), Neil Denis (Rya'c), Laara Sadiq (Female Technician), Peter Bryant (Fro'tak), Jan Frandsen (Dj'nor)

Bra'tac arrives with shocking news. Apophis is alive and has kidnapped Rya'c. SG-1 return to Chulak but find it much changed. Drey'auc has remarried, to Fro'tak, and Rya'c's been brainwashed by Apophis, denouncing his father as a traitor. Fro'tak attempts to betray SG-1, but the

---

41 Character previously played by Salli Richardson in 'Bloodlines'.

team successfully rescue Rya'c. Jack, however, feels it was too easy.

### ORIGINS OF THE SPECIES
Both Fro'tak and Teal'c were Bra'tac's wards during their Bashaak training. Fro'tak, from the High Cliffs, works in the Hall of Recordings in the west wing of Apophis's palace and has high status in Jaffa hierarchy (as evidenced by him having a gold, rather than a black, symbol on his forehead). Dray'auc is from the Cord'ai Plains. Rya'c loves his mother's satta cakes.

### THE CONSPIRACY STARTS AT CLOSING TIME
Two individually harmless organisms contained in hollow teeth in Rya'c's mouth, when combined, would make anthrax 'look like the cold virus,' and, if released into the atmosphere, could destroy all life on earth.

### 'YOU MIGHT REMEMBER ME FROM...'
Peter Bryant played Bling in *Dark Angel* and was in *Scary Movie* and *Jumanji*. Brook Parker was Rainbow in *The Last Patrol* and Cecile in *Strange Days*.

### LOGIC, LET ME INTRODUCE YOU TO THIS WINDOW
Sam spent two years at the Pentagon 'trying to make the Stargate work' (as previously mentioned in 'Children of the Gods'). Presumably this was during the period that Catherine and her people were trying to do the same (see *Stargate*), prior to Daniel's arrival. So, what did Sam do in the year between the Abydos trip (which, she says, she should have been assigned to) and her joining SG-1? Teal'c hides behind one of the standing stones, leans against it and it moves. Bra'tak swears he did not know of Drey'auc's remarriage. Why not, given that he was supposed to be training Rya'c? When Bra'tak arrives, the computer registers his iris-code before the wormhole is established. Daniel speculates that Apophis and Klorel 'must have used those ring things to get to the Gate just after I did.' But in 'The Serpent's Lair', Daniel escaped through the Gate, it was the rest of SG-1 (and Bra'tac) who used the rings. Though Apophis's forces are dangerously low, he's still prepared to sacrifice seven Jaffa to deliver Rya'c back to Earth (five escorted the boy, two guarded the Stargate). Janet gives Rya'c a sedative intra-muscularly but he collapses almost immediately. A Jaffa's symbiont can heal most anything, including broken bones. But not, seemingly, broken *teeth*. How were Rya'c's teeth extracted *without* releasing the virus? Since Drey'auc had her marriage to Teal'c 'removed', is she still married to him under Chulak law?

### GOA'ULD LEXICON
'Kel Mar Tokeem' means, literally, 'Revenge by the wearer of the horns.' (Daniel indicates that this is a Jaffa term for a cuckold, however it seems to be in wider use than simply by spurned husbands. Teal'c spits it at Cronus in 'Fair Game', for instance, so it may be a general curse to a hated enemy.) 'Shesh'ta' is a Goa'uld unit of currency. (Apophis offers two million for Teal'c.) 'Ha'taaka' seems to mean 'Vile one'.

### QUOTE/UNQUOTE
Jack: 'You've got a price on your head. You're doing your job.'

### NOTES
'I take it this isn't a social call?' A slow and disappointing remake of 'Bloodlines' rather than, as intended, a sequel to it. Poorly-plot-

ted and ordinary, with really obvious twists. Unlike, say, *Buffy*, *SG-1*'s metaphors don't always work. This is a good example.

Jack repeats that he's 'of the windy city' (see 'Children of the Gods', 'The Fifth Man'). Mention is made of Cassandra and the events of 'Singularity', and of SG-1's belief that Apophis and Klorel are dead ('Within the Serpent's Grasp'). After his defeat by SG-1, Apophis returned to Chulak in shame. His forces are now very limited. (Nearly all the guards loyal to Apophis died in Earth's orbit.) He's trying to rebuild before other System Lords move against him. Dray'auc and Rya'c are sent to live in the Land of Light (see 'The Broca Divide'). Jack penetrates Heru'ur's energy barrier with a knife. The shield's deflection capability is, according to Sam, directly proportional to the kinetic energy directed at it. Carter theorised this after SG-1's attack on Apophis ('The Nox').

**DID YOU KNOW?** Asked what future storylines he would like to see for his character, Chris Judge is emphatic. 'I want more sex! Everyone else on the show has the occasional dalliance, so Teal'c needs to get some!'

# 31 SECRETS

US Transmission Date: 21 Aug 1998
UK Transmission Date: 28 Oct 1998
Writer: Terry Curtis Fox
Director: Duane Clark
Cast: Chris Owens (Armin Selig), Vaitiare Bandera (Sha're), Peter Williams (Apophis), Douglas H Arthurs (Heru'ur), Carmen Argenziano (Jacob Carter), Erick Avari (Kasuf), Michael Tiernan (Ryn'tak)

> Daniel returns to Abydos a year after leaving, to fulfil the promise he made to Kasuf. He learns that Sha're is also there, and is pregnant. The father is Apophis, who plans to use the baby as his new host. Jack and Sam, meanwhile, are in Washington to receive a bravery medal. Jack is approached by a reporter who knows about the Stargate programme and intends to publish. Sam discovers that her father has cancer.

**THE WIT AND WISDOM OF JACK O'NEILL** When Selig threatens to expose the Stargate project publicly: 'I wanna make sure you get one thing right. It's "O'Neill", with two 'l's. There's another Colonel O'Neil with only one 'l'. He has no sense of humour at all.'

**ORIGINS OF THE SPECIES** Abydos has seasons that seem roughly to correspond to those on Earth. Sha're's symbiont sleeps whilst she is pregnant so as not to harm the child. When free of Armunet's influence, Sha're retains many of the Goa'uld's memories.

**THE CONSPIRACY STARTS AT CLOSING TIME** Selig knows that the two brilliant flashes in the night sky a few months ago were really two exploding alien spacecraft (see 'The Serpent's Lair'). It's not revealed where he got his information from (though Kinsey does, indeed, seem a likely source). Also unrevealed are the identities of the two men who kill Selig. (Hammond genuinely seems to believe it's a hit-and-run accident. Jack's more sceptical.)

**IN THE INTERESTS OF NATIONAL SECURITY** The official cover-story for the Stargate programme is 'analysis of deep-space radar telemetry.'

**POSSIBLE INFLUENCES** Given the involvement of Chris Owens, it's no surprise that the Selig-subplot is *pure X-Files*. The scene in which Jack meets Selig has location, visual and dialogue links to Jim Garrison meeting Mr X in *JFK*. Also, *Inseminoid* and *The Manchurian Candidate*.

**'YOU MIGHT REMEMBER ME FROM...'** Carmen Argenziano's CV includes *Swordfish*, *Gone in Sixty Seconds*, *A Murder of Crows*, *The Godfather Part II*, *Melrose Place*, *The West Wing*, *Caged Heat*, *The Jesus Trip*, *Kojak* and *The Rockford Files*. Chris Owens played Jeffrey Spender in *The X-Files*. He also appeared in *My Louisiana Sky* and *Disturbing Behavior*.

**BEHIND THE CAMERA** Duane Clark worked on *Highlander* and *Boston Public*. Special effects supervisor Wray Douglas's movies include *Heaven's Fire*.

**LOGIC, LET ME INTRODUCE YOU TO THIS WINDOW** Sha're's baby has no umbilical cord, seemingly. Why doesn't Daniel think of using the recently restored Thor's Hammer to free Sha're from Amaunet? How does Teal'c know Sha're's baby will be born within days? How does Heru'ur know that the baby has *already* been born when he arrives? Jack is drinking in a bar in uniform whilst on official duty? *Excellent!* How does Sam know not to shoot Teal'c, since he's in armour when she and Jack arrive? Where did Amaunet get the dress, makeup and crown from? Teal'c makes no mention of the Harsesis (see 'Maternal Instinct'). We see video of Kasuf peering into the MALP, but there's no sign of a MALP in the Abydos gateroom. When Sam and Jack dial Abydos, the seventh chevron lights up with the first chevron and again with the sixth. When Apophis dials, something similar happens. How old is Sam? She was close to joining NASA when the Challenger disaster happened in 1986. Assuming she'd graduated from college, that would mean she's in her late 30s. One of Heru'ur's Jaffa refers to the Stargate as 'the Stargate' and not 'the Chaapa'ai.' Jack says that *if* Senator Kinsey knows about the Stargate 'so do a dozen sycophants'. But he *does* know about it (see 'Politics').

**QUOTE/UNQUOTE** Jack, meeting Jacob: 'I've heard *nothing* about you, sir!'

Hammond: 'Civilians sign nondisclosure statements. Technically, they're liable to prosecution under the espionage act.' Jack: 'So, what do we do, sue 'em?'

**NOTES** 'It'll read like science fiction, Armin.' Nice. A clever juxtaposition of two engaging (if completely separate) storylines, which gives the series a couple of new layers of darkness (specifically, the conspiracy hints *and* the fate of Sha're).

Jack says he always gets lost in Washington. Daniel refers to Kasuf by the Abydonian term 'good father'. Sam's father, Jacob, is a two-star Air Force general who served with Hammond during the cold war. Sam has wanted to be an astronaut since she was a child. Jacob says he made a call to Bollinger, the head of NASA, and can get her into the shuttle programme. Hammond seems to be a boxing fan.

Filming locations include the Vancouver Art Gallery (also used in 'Foothold').

CRITIQUE 'Keeping one storyline going is a good trick,' noted *Xposé*. 'To keep three running simultaneously is remarkable. It was way past time the Sha're plotline was continued and this certainly doesn't disappoint.'

CAST AND CREW COMMENTS Doesn't dressing in camouflage gear and uniforms week after week cramp Amanda Tapping's femininity? 'Initially I was so pumped by the idea - no high heels, no pantyhose,' she noted. 'But after a while I'm thinking, "Give me a skirt!" I don't always feel attractive in all that. I never thought I'd say it, but I'd actually love to see Carter in a dress.'

DID YOU KNOW? 'Carmen is lovely,' Amanda Tapping says about her screen dad. 'Whenever I'm in Los Angeles I spend time with him and his family. He's become very protective of me.'

## 32  BANE

US Transmission Date: 25 Sep 1998
UK Transmission Date: 4 Nov 1998
Writer: Robert C Cooper
Director: David Warry-Smith
Cast: Teryl Rothery (Dr Janet Fraiser), Tom McBeath (Colonel Harry Mayborne), Scott Hylands (Timothy Harlow), Colleen Rennison (Ally), Alonso Oyarzun (Punk Leader), Richard Leacock (Sergeant)

On BP63Q1, SG-1 are attacked by giant insects and Teal'c is infected. When they return to Earth, a transformation begins as the venom rewrites Teal'c's DNA. His condition interests Mayborne, who sees biological uses in the venom. Teal'c escapes, leaving behind his Goa'uld larva, and is befriended by Ally, a young girl. The SGC try to devise a vaccine, but will they find Teal'c in time?

THE WIT AND WISDOM OF JACK O'NEILL On Mayborne: 'General Hammond. Request permission to beat the crap out of this man?'

ORIGINS OF THE SPECIES The insects bypass normal breeding by genetically transforming their victims into offspring. BP63Q1's inhabitants were human - possibly from Earth.

Teal'c says he received his forehead emblem by having the skin cut with an Orak knife and then molten gold poured into the wound. Larval Goa'uld can, seemingly, be temporarily maintained outside a host by simulating conditions within the body, including temperature, nutrient balance and electrical current.

SEX AND DRUGS AND ROCK 'N' ROLL Sam suggests using the painkiller novocain on Teal'c after he's infected.

MILITARY INTELLIGENCE? Mayborne notes that the SGC's mandate is 'search and retrieval'. His is 'research and development', which he carries out from Area 51 (see 'The Serpent's Lair').

**IN THE INTERESTS OF NATIONAL SECURITY** Dr Timothy Harlowe's one of the world's top geneticists and worked with Sam at the Pentagon. He has full security clearance.

**POSSIBLE INFLUENCES** *E.T. The Extraterrestrial*, *The Fly*, Kafka's *Metamorphosis*, *Star Trek*'s 'The City on the Edge of Forever' and 'Operation Annihilate' and the *MacGyver* episode 'Nightmares'. (MacGyver escapes from foreign agents after being injected with a hallucinogen that will kill him in six hours. He's then helped by a street-wise girl, living in a abandoned building.) *The Godfather*, *The Fugitive* ('you a Kimble?'), *ER* (Jack seems to be a fan), *Alien* and James Bond are mentioned.

**'YOU MIGHT REMEMBER ME FROM...'** Colleen Rennison played Miranda in *Poltergeist: The Legacy* and was in *The Waiting Room*. Scott Hylands appeared in *Cannon*, *Harry O*, *Ignition*, *The Oasis* and *Earthquake*. Alonso Ovarzan was in *Lone Hero*.

**LOGIC, LET ME INTRODUCE YOU TO THIS WINDOW** Vehicles and people can be seen in the distance whilst the team is on the supposedly uninhabited BP63Q1. When SG-1 return from their mission to retrieve an insect, one follows them through the Gate. If the plan was to let it, then why does Jack tell the SGC to 'lock [the Gate] up' before the insect appears? Sam's lipstick changes shade during the episode. Curiously, Jack, Sam and Daniel return to BP63Q1 without any additional protection, like hazard suits. Maybourne questions Ally and then leaves without having someone keep an eye on her. Or, for that matter, giving her a hiding to remember when the cheeky minx talks to him in a way that only Jack O'Neill can usually get away with.

**QUOTE/UNQUOTE** Teal'c: 'I do not want to become something other than who I am.'
    Ally: 'You look like you could use a couple more days in rehab.'

**NOTES** 'It appears that the alien insect's venom is rewriting Teal'c genetic material.' Potentially dreadful (mix one cute lippy kid, a terminally injured alien and the military... you see where I'm going with this?). But 'Bane' develops into a cracking episode, thanks to a dry and sarcastic wit throughout. (Jack and Maybourne playing mind-games with each other.)
    The SGC has canine units (see 'Enigma'). SG-1's signal code on the GDO is 70629570282002. Jack's own personal code is 32-333-0. Ally's father, a policeman, was shot and killed some time ago.

**CRITIQUE** 'The idea of shady military types exploiting an infected victim isn't new,' noted *DreamWatch*'s review. 'And the brat that befriends Teal'c during his infection is as annoying as they come!'

**CAST AND CREW COMMENTS** 'There's a stigma surrounding syndicated, science-fiction, cable genre shows,' noted Robert Cooper. 'There's a certain kind of fan that likes science-fiction we certainly cater to. But I find among my own personal acquaintances, people who don't necessarily watch that kind of show [are] surprised at how good it is.'

**DID YOU KNOW?** 'One of the great things about Teal'c is that he's popular with children,' said Chris Judge. 'Both *Stargate* and my character allow me to become involved in causes I don't know if I'd be involved in otherwise. It's certainly one of the most rewarding things about the job.'

# 33 THE TOK'RA (PART I)

US Transmission Date: 2 Oct 1998
UK Transmission Date: 11 Nov 1998
Writer: Jonathan Glassner
Director: Brad Turner
Cast: Steve Makaj (Colonel Makepeace), Laara Sadiq (Technician Davis), Carmen Argenziano (Jacob Carter), Sarah Douglas (Garshaw), JR Bourne (Martouf), Winston Rekert (Cordesh), Joy Coghill (Selmak), Tosca Baggoo (Tok'ra Council Woman), Roger Haskett (Doctor), Stephen Tibbetts (Guard)

> Sam has a vivid dream, in which she sees through the eyes of Jolinar. Though her father is dying of cancer, Carter knows she must go on the mission with SG-1 to find the Tok'ra on P34353J. They meet the Goa'uld rebels and there's talk of an alliance. But the trust is fragile.

**SAM'S TRAUMATIC LOVE-LIFE** Sam's second alien boyfriend, Martouf, appears. Jolinar always had female hosts before the final one (see 'In the Line of Duty'). Lantash, Martouf's host, was Jolinar's 'mate' for almost 100 years. Jolinar's previous host, Rosha, had eyes like the oceans of Marloon and hair the colour of sand on Abydos (so, sort-of dirty yellow, then?). Sam is uncomfortable with the thought of becoming a host again - primarily because she finds it hard to separate Jolinar's memories and emotions from her own. She feels the things that Jolinar felt, such as Jolinar's love for Martouf.

**ORIGINS OF THE SPECIES** The stated goal of the Tok'ra is the destruction of the System Lords and a change in the ways of the Empire. They are hunted and despised by the Goa'uld. ('My kind of guys', notes Jack.) When the Tok'ra arrive on a planet, they go into hiding deep underground. They possess the technology to 'grow' and collapse crystalline tunnels. The symbiotic relationship between the Tok'ra and their host is what makes them different from the Goa'uld. They will not use the sarcophagus to prolong life, as it drains the 'good' from them. (Daniel agrees, an allusion to 'Need'.)

**POSSIBLE INFLUENCES** *The Wizard of Oz* ('Where's that yellowbrick road when you need it, Dorothy?'). There's an oblique reference to Frank Herbert's *Dune*.

**'YOU MIGHT REMEMBER ME FROM...'** Sarah Douglas appeared in *Bergerac*, *The Professionals* and *Space: 1999* in her native England before moving the US to play Pamela

Lynch in *Falcon Crest* and Ursa in *Superman II*. She was also in *Voodoo* and *Matlock*. JR Bourne appeared in *Josie and the Pussycats*, *Jungleground* and *Madison*. Winston Rekert was in *Adderly*, *High Stakes* and *Suzanne* and worked as a producer on *Neon Rider*. Tosca Baggoo appeared in *The Stepsister*. Joy Coghill appeared in *My Life as a Dog* and *Silence*.

**LOGIC, LET ME INTRODUCE YOU TO THIS WINDOW** Where have the Tok'ra been getting hosts from? Sam describes multiple personality disorder as schizophrenia. It isn't. The team is under guard in the Tok'ra complex, but no-one notices Jack following Cordesh.

**GOA'ULD LEXICON** The literal translation of 'Tok'ra' is 'against Ra'.

**QUOTE/UNQUOTE** Daniel: 'We're here to see the Tok'ra.' Jack: 'Assuming, of course, you *are* the Tok'ra?' Cordesh: 'And if we're not?' Jack: 'Well, I guess we all start shooting. There's blood, death, hard feelings. It'd suck.'

Martouf: 'We love as one, and we mourn as one.'

**NOTES** 'I do not believe you can be of any service to us.' A really good episode which sets up a road full of new lore for the show. The Jacob Carter subplot at first seems forced and tacked on but it's paid off well in the next episode. Only the Sam/Martouf scenes appear out of place.

Jacob's lymphoma has spread to his liver and he's near death. He moved into a Colorado Springs apartment to be close to Sam during his final days. But Jacob is stubborn, and refuses to allow his daughter to watch him fight a losing battle. The Tok'ra had operatives who died on the ships of Apophis and Klorel ('The Serpent's Lair').

**DID YOU KNOW?** Kawoosh! Productions is named after the description the scripts give to the plume that comes out of the Gate when a wormhole is established.

# 34 THE TOK'RA (PART II)

US Transmission Date: 9 Oct 1998
UK Transmission Date: 18 Nov 1998
Writer: Jonathan Glassner
Director: Brad Turner
Cast: Steve Makaj (Colonel Makepeace), Laara Sadiq (Technician Davis), Carmen Argenziano (Jacob Carter), Sarah Douglas (Garshaw), JR Bourne (Martouf), Winston Rekert (Cordesh), Joy Coghill (Selmak), Tosca Baggoo (Tok'ra Council Woman), Roger Haskett (Doctor), Stephen Tibbetts (Guard)

> Garshaw, disturbed that none of the humans will act as host for Selmak, turns down SG-1's request for an alliance. Sam suggests that her father would make an ideal candidate. But when she and Jack return through Stargate with Jacob, the Goa'uld launch an attack on the Tok'ra. The bonding will be difficult, but with Goa'uld death gliders bombing the tunnels, it requires some urgency.

**ORIGINS OF THE SPECIES** On their previous planet, the Tok'ra kept their Stargate within their complex (presumably underground), as seen in Sam's vision. They use Goa'uld transport rings. Selmak is small, pink and very larval-like. Are there varieties of symbiont colouring, or does the mature symbiote lose some of its form and shape when it inhabits a host? Selmak is amongst the oldest, wisest and best educated of the Tok'ra and, apparently, has a wonderful sense of humour. The symbiont has the ability to cure many human illnesses, including cancer. But even it has limitations. It cannot, for instance, cure a disease if it is too far progressed. A Tok'ra (and, therefore, a Goa'uld) cannot blend with a new host, cure its diseases and then leave (this is contradicted in 'Frozen' and 'Abyss'). Blending is intended to be permanent. The Tok'ra do not enter their hosts through the back of the neck, as Goa'uld parasites do. This leaves a scar that many find unsettling. Instead, they enter through the mouth (as Jolinar did to Sam during 'In the Line of Duty'). The Goa'uld don't do this because they do not wish to remember the horror on their host's face every time they look into a mirror.

**ANOTHER GIRL, ANOTHER PLANET** When Jacob says that P34353J looks like Earth, Sam notes that the Stargate was probably built specifically to transport humans (or something close to humans in psychology) around the galaxy. Therefore it seems to go mostly to places where the environment supports human life.

Sam says that she and SG-1 travel through the Stargate once or twice a week. 'Beats the hell out of a shuttle on the back of a rocket,' notes Jacob.

**LOGIC, LET ME INTRODUCE YOU TO THIS WINDOW** How did Cordesh leave his former host without killing him? And how did he get into the Council woman, since she already had a symbiont? The Gate chevrons are lit when the Technician says 'Still no SG-1 signal, Sir.' What sort of long-range communications do the Tok'ra use to their undercover operatives (of whom, as subsequent episodes reveal, there are many), if they don't use the unsecure 'teleball' devices?

**GOA'ULD LEXICON** A direct translation of 'Chel'nok' is 'very cool'.

**QUOTE/UNQUOTE** Jacob: 'You don't look so good.' Selmak: 'You are no vision of beauty yourself!'

**NOTES** 'My only other choice is death. That's not acceptable.' A fantastic performance by Carmen Argenziano is the highlight of this breathless, highly-charged episode which wraps up the two-parter nicely. Excellent action-sequences, some homely psychological stuff about fate and destiny and a happy ending.

The one thing the Tok'ra need most, Earth can provide; men and women dying of terminal illnesses who are willing to become hosts. Jacob, who wakes up with 'a headache the size of Kuwait' and his cancer and arthritis cured, will serve as liaison between the Tok'ra and Earth.

**CRITIQUE** 'One part too long,' noted *DreamWatch*. 'The whole thing drags to the point of frustration and the main intention of the story was painfully obvious from the beginning.'

**DID YOU KNOW?** There are only two working Staff Weapons (i.e. those that actually open up and appear to fire). Others are usually solid although foam lightweight replicas are also used for some scenes. (In one of the *Making Of...* documentaries, Richard Dean Anderson, during the location filming for 'Children of the Gods', wobbles one for the cameras).

## 35  *SPIRITS*

US Transmission Date: 23 Oct 1998
UK Transmission Date: 25 Nov 1998
Writer: Tor Alexander Valenza
Director: Martin Wood
Cast: Rodney A Grant (Tonane), Alex Zahara (Xe'ls), Christina Cox (T'akaya), Kevin McNulty (Dr Warner), Roger R Cross (Connor), Laara Sadiq (Female Technician), Chief Leonard George (Elder #1), Byron Chief Moon (Elder #2), Jason Calders (Alien #1)

SG-11 haven't returned from PXY887, where they discovered a mineral, Trinium, one hundred times lighter and stronger than steel. The inhabitants of the planet fire an arrow through the Stargate, injuring Jack. SG-1, led by Sam, travel to negotiate a mining treaty. They meet Tonane, a plainspoken Salish Indian, who explains that SG-11 were taken by the spirits. Tonane returns to Earth with SG-1 to look at alternative mining methods. But strange things begin to happen as the spirits reveal themselves.

**THE WIT AND WISDOM OF JACK O'NEILL** How does Jack know that Daniel is Daniel when shapeshifters are around? '*Because,*' says an irritated Jackson. 'Oh, yeah...' notes Jack.

**ORIGINS OF THE SPECIES** Teal'c says the Jaffa don't believe in ghosts.
On PXY887, the natives live in a style akin to the Central Coast Salish Indians. They call Trinium 'Ke'.

**THE CONSPIRACY STARTS AT CLOSING TIME** SG-11, led by Captain Connor, is the SGC's engineering unit.

**IN THE INTERESTS OF NATIONAL SECURITY** The NID proposes a sneaky way of obtaining Trinium. Wait until the Salish migrate south for the winter and then send an SG team in to extract what they need. 'You mean *steal it*?' asks Jack.

**POSSIBLE INFLUENCES** Sam alludes to *Little Red Riding Hood* when seeing T'akaya ('My, what big eyes you have').

**'YOU MIGHT REMEMBER ME FROM...'** Alex Xahara played Johanssen in *Dark Angel* and appeared in *Turbulence 3: Heavy Metal*. Rodney Grant was in *Wild Wild West*, *The Killing Grounds*, *Legend*, *The Doors* and *Dances With Wolves*. Christina Cox played Jeanne d'Arc in *Forever Knight* and was in *Better Than Chocolate*. Byron Chief Moon appeared in *Alaska, Samurai Cowboy* and *The Outer Limits*.

**LOGIC, LET ME INTRODUCE YOU TO THIS WINDOW** The Salish, or Flathead (so named for the hairstyles they wore), tribes are originally from Montana, and most of them still live there. Their literature mostly has the coyote as their heroic guardian spirit, not the wolf. When Tonane and Jack talk in the infirmary, the alarm noise has stopped though the light is still flashing. Tonane's village is 'a couple days' walk' from SG-11's camp but SG-1 seem to get back pretty quickly. The aliens call humans 'Earthlings' for some obscure reason. T'akaya zaps members of the SGC just by looking at them in wolf form, so why do the spirits need to wave their arms at other times? SG-11's return is announced before the wormhole is established. How did the spirits 'drive away' the Goa'uld? (Not just *any* Goa'uld either, but someone from Apophis' line, seemingly.) Daniel suggests that Indians from a mere handful of generations ago were taken to populate PXY887. How, when Earth's two Stargates have been buried for 10,000 years in the case of the one in Giza (see 'Children of the Gods') and, probably, *millions* of years for the one in Antarctica (see 'Solitudes', 'Red Sky')? When the duplicate Warren falls to the ground, he's face down. Yet when the body morphs into Xe'ls, he's face up. The same thing happens with the spirit impersonating Hammond, who morphs with his back turned away from camera and re-emerges looking in the opposite direction.

**QUOTE/UNQUOTE** Jack: 'Aliens are always poking me full of holes.'

**NOTES** 'You can't see the wind... but you know it's there.' Yet another example of America inflicting its enormous guilt complex over the mistreatment of its indigenous natives on the rest of the world (something that just about every US series from *Buffy* to *The West Wing* and *The X-Files* to *The Simpsons* have done). A very heavy-handed metaphor follows and, though it's not without some redeeming features (Rodney Grant's good, and Anderson's performance is full of piss and anger), it's still pretty grim viewing.

**DID YOU KNOW?** Lots of the guns carried by extras - in particular the MP5s seen carried by SGC guards - are actually Marui airsoft plastic replicas.

# 36  TOUCHSTONE

US Transmission Date: 30 Oct 1998
UK Transmission Date: 2 Dec 1998
Writer: Sam Egan
Director: Brad Turner
Cast: Tom McBeath (Colonel Harry Mayborne), Eric Breker (Reynolds), Matthew Walker (Roham), Jerry Wasserman (Whitlow), Tiffany Knight (La Moor), Conan Graham (NID Man)

When a group posing as SG-1 steals the climate-controlling Touchstone from Madrona, the planet's weather deteriorates. SG-1 find that Earth's second Stargate, officially decommissioned, was reactivated on high level orders and used to steal the Touchstone. They must try to find the device and discover the hidden agenda behind the Touchstone's theft.

**THE WIT AND WISDOM OF JACK O'NEILL** To the Madronians: 'We came here in peace. We expect to leave in one... Piece.' And, on how to find the second Gate: 'Let's put out an APB for a huge, honkin' two-storey metal ring with 39 little pictures engraved on it.'

**ORIGINS OF THE SPECIES** It's five weeks since SG-1 last visited PX7941 (Madrona). The inhabitants are able to create their own climate via the Touchstone. It was, Daniel suspects, probably made by the (much more advanced) alien race who terraformed the planet and made it habitable for the Madronians.

**THE CONSPIRACY STARTS AT CLOSING TIME** When the Stargate programme began (presumably, the formation of the SG teams in 'Children of the Gods' rather than West's command, which preceded it) there was, Hammond notes, a 'philosophical skirmish' about its mandate. Some interested parties wanted to make sure that all discoveries of a scientific or military nature were brought back to Earth regardless of considerations like interplanetary diplomacy. The General felt there was someone behind the scenes - possibly non-military but political, very powerful and, seemingly, well-shielded - who was pulling the strings (see 'Shades of Grey', 'Chain Reaction', 'Desperate Measures').

Sam discovers that the computer logged a transitory glitch when SG-2 returned from a recent mission. A tremendous energy spike was hidden by the fact that someone used the second Stargate a split second after the SGC Gate was activated. This may mean that the rogue team has an operative inside the SGC, feeding them information on the Stargate's usage down to a split second. If Maybourne *is* involved, though, he may have legitimate access to this kind of information.

**MILITARY INTELLIGENCE?** The NID landing site used to store the second Gate (which doesn't, officially, exist) is in Southern Utah, west of Parowan. Hammond gets details on it from the mysterious Whitlow. It's not revealed who he works for (a shadowy part of the Air Force judging from the NID's request for a C-5 landing on his desk) but, George notes, he has fingers in every agency including Military Intelligence, the NSA and the CIA. He owed Hammond a favour which has now, seemingly, been repaid.

**IN THE INTERESTS OF NATIONAL SECURITY** The second Gate ('Solitudes') ended up at Nellis Air Base, part of Groom Lake (see 'The Serpent's Lair'). This is also where any artefacts 'officially' brought through the Stargate are taken. Medical research is being undertaken on a potential cure for Alzheimer's disease that SG-5 procured. A research group are studying the 'Heliopolis' records that Daniel discovered on Ernest's planet ('The Torment of Tantalus'). This is also where the Goa'uld death gliders in which SG-1 escaped from Apophis's ship ('The Serpent's Lair') are stored. Maybourne hints that the second Gate's move across country was authorised by someone, and it's being used in a civilian operation. In his conversation with Hammond, Whitlow also suggests this - otherwise, he believes, he'd know about it.

SEASON 2

**POSSIBLE INFLUENCES** As with all NID subplots, there's a lot of *The X-Files* going on here (particularly Whitlow's 'Deep Throat'-like character). Also *Hanger 18*, *Roswell*, *Capricorn One*, *Aliens* and thematic links to *Flash Gordon* and the *Blake's 7* episode 'Star One'. *The Weather Channel* and *C-SPAN* (Jack's favourite, apparently) are mentioned. There's an oblique reference to Bob Hope's 'Thanks for the Memory'.

**STORMY WEATHER** Reports put down the severe climactic changes caused by the brief use of the Touchstone on Earth to the El Niño effect. Storms rage all over America, with flooding in such unlikely places as Phoenix, Palm Springs and Florida. Record rainfall is also recorded in Albuquerque, and violent hail showers in the Panhandle. The Touchstone may have been configured specifically for Madrona's atmospheric conditions (making it impossible to use correctly on Earth).

**'YOU MIGHT REMEMBER ME FROM...'** Eric Breker was in *Dudley Do-Right*. Tiffany Knight appeared in *First Wave*. Matthew Walker was in *The Amy Fisher Story*, *Misbegotten* and *Casual Sex?* Jerry Wasserman played Doctor Warren in *M.A.N.T.I.S* and appeared in *Golf Punks* and *Christina's House*.

**BEHIND THE CAMERA** Sam Egan wrote for *Northern Exposure*, *Snoops*, *Quincy*, *Manimal* and *The Incredible Hulk*. Sound Mixer Sina Oormchi worked on *Hollywood Off-Ramp*, *The Final Cut* and *Revisited*.

**LOGIC, LET ME INTRODUCE YOU TO THIS WINDOW** How did someone reproduce the plastic Gate in such detail, whilst it was en-route from Antarctica? Or, is Maybourne lying? The latter seems likely given what we know about Dirty Harry, but he seems sincere when he tells Jack that the Gate in the crate at Area 51 was the one delivered from the Antarctic. 900 years after being terraformed, yet it'll take only 72 hours to ruin Madrona permanently? Doesn't the MALP have infrared or thermal sensors? SG-1 don't secure the NID men's weapons before Jack walks between them. The door to the bioresearch lab has a card reader, but the Major taps at it as if it were a numeric keypad. Why do Jack and Daniel go back to Madrona to send the probe through to the second Gate? They could do that from any planet, and they wouldn't have to do so in a blizzard. Roham aligns all the rings on the Touchstone (starting it glowing) but when he enters the building, they aren't in that position any longer. There's no evidence of a power source to the second Gate, and there's definitely no connection between the DHD (in the truck) and it.

Teal'c says that SG-2 have visited a planet 'galaxies away'. This highlights an inconsistency concerning which area of space in being covered. In the movie, Abydos was in another galaxy, but that seems to have changed in *SG-1*, where Abydos is so close to Earth it doesn't require recalculation for planetary shift. However, 'The Fifth Race' suggests that *all* 7-digit Stargates are in the Milky Way and that to get further afield (like Othana) needs an 8-digit address. In 'Shades of Grey', Newman says he was one of the men who escaped through the second Gate. But none of the four men here looks anything like him. Hammond suggests that Maybourne has only recently been transferred to Nellis. However, it was mentioned that he was working there during 'Bane'.

**QUOTE/UNQUOTE** Hammond: 'I need some documents hand-delivered to the Groom Lake Facility.' Jack: 'Are [they] sensitive enough to warrant a three-man team with a Jaffa escort?'

Reynolds: 'There are no alien lifeforms at Area 51.' Jack, looking at Teal'c: 'Present company excluded, of course.'

Maybourne: 'Strange things happen in high places. People get reassigned, so does property. Artefacts get misplaced. Orders change. Every day's a new day.'

**NOTES** 'Let me give you a life-lesson on thieves. They're not really in touch with their feminine side.' Initially a seemingly obvious 'someone's impersonating our heroes' plot which suddenly gets nefarious and *very The X-Files*-like back on Earth. 'Touchstone' is an important building-block in establishing what a dark and sinister world SG-1 inhabits behind the facade of humanistic rhetoric. Gorgeously well-done, and with an ending that was crying out for a sequel (see 'Shades of Grey').

In Teal'c's culture, he would be within his rights to dismember Maybourne for what he did to Teal'c in 'Bane'. Hammond has been in the service for 30 years (actually, probably slightly more; see '1969'). The Stargate appears to destroy the top of the crate in which it was stored when activated by the NID men. This confirms the principle that the initial kawoosh of the wormhole's event horizon vaporises anything in its path (see, for instance, 'Prisoners' and 'Secrets').

**CRITIQUE** 'Without a doubt *Stargate SG-1* is a formidable series,' wrote Jeff Watson. 'Consistently offering intelligent scripts, detailed characterisation and incredible special effects, making for an entertaining experience few can match. 'Touchstone' is a tense and intriguing episode, full of unanswered questions and with a disconcerting scent of conspiracy.'

**CAST AND CREW COMMENTS** 'I bring my own sense of humour to [the show],' noted Richard Dean Anderson. 'Cynical, sarcastic, wry and naughty - irreverent, like you Brits.'

**DID YOU KNOW?** When she read the pilot script, Amanda Tapping got the impression that her character was going to be more an intellectual and less "one of the guys". '[It's] turned into this great physical show for me, which is something I hadn't imagined, and a great gift, particularly for a woman,' she told the *Sci-Fi Entertainment* website. 'In the midst of the testosterone fest, I'm your happy estrogen bubble.'

# 37 THE FIFTH RACE

US Transmission Date: 22 Jan 1999
UK Transmission Date: 9 Dec 1998
Writer: Robert C Cooper
Director: David Warry-Smith
Cast: Teryl Rothery (Dr Janet Fraiser), Dan Shea (Sgt Siler), Tobias Mehler (Lt Graham Simmons), David Adams (Expert)

SG-1 travel to P3R272 in an attempt to decode an alien language discovered by a probe. Jack peers through a viewer and is caught momentarily in its grasp. Afterwards, alien words start to puncture his speech and his brain is overwhelmed with a vast but indecipherable knowledge. Daniel believes that Jack now possesses the knowledge of the Ancients, the race who built the Stargates, but realises the knowledge is too complex for a human mind.

**SENSES WORKING OVERTIME** Jack's scribbled equation is in base-8, rather than base-10, suggesting that it was created by a race with four fingers. Sam believes that the formula is a revolutionary method of calculating the distance between planetary bodies. The Ancients, Daniel says, may be the Ancient Ones, the Gods of Roman mythology who taught them to speak Latin and build roads. (The Ancients language is a derivation of Medieval Latin.)

Jack travels to the Asgard planet Othana, in the Ieda galaxy. The Ancients moved from 'our region of space' millennia ago, according to Thor. This may refer to the Asgard's galaxy, or the portion of the universe that includes both Earth and Othana. The Asgard have studied humanity closely, as implied in 'Thor's Chariot', and believe that our race has 'great potential.' There was once an alliance of the four great races in the galaxy (see 'The Torment of Tantalus'), the Asgard, the Nox ('Met them!' notes Jack, proudly), the Furlings ('Don't know them!') and the Ancients. The Asgard consider humanity on its way to becoming the fifth race.

**THE CONSPIRACY STARTS AT CLOSING TIME** It takes the SGC computer days to calculate a new Stargate location based on planetary shift over thousands of years, using addresses found on the Abydos cartouche. The SGC (or the NID) have been studying the dial-home device found with the second Stargate in Antarctica ('Solitudes'). To place a Gate on the binary-star planet P9Q281, the Ancients must have developed significant heat-resistant technology. The dialling programme that Jack put into the computer to reach Othana requires eight chevrons. Sam presumes the eighth is necessary to calculate a distance factor, like dialling an area code on a telephone.

**POSSIBLE INFLUENCES** Includes a very *Close Encounters of the Third Kind* ending. Jack's 'speaking in tongues' echoes the spiritual gift of *glossolalia* as described in Acts 2:4. Also, McLuhanism.[42]

**LOGIC, LET ME INTRODUCE YOU TO THIS WINDOW** Nobody seems concerned that Jack might not be Jack when he returns both from P3R272 (despite how oddly he's behaving) and, more specifically, from Othana. Wouldn't the new locations Jack that puts into the computer need to be adjusted for stellar expansion, since the Ancients created their database long ago? Ernest's planet ('The Torment of Tantalus') is now listed as PB2908 (rather than P3X972). SG-1 got images of the symbols from a probe, but there's none visible when they arrive. Daniel speaks 23 languages (including Latin), but he doesn't know 'locas' means 'location' without looking it up? The video that Daniel shows Jack doesn't match what we saw in the control room. Why did Jack's subconscious seek the Asgard planet when it was the Ancients' database? If the Ancients built the Stargates

---

42 The philosophy of Canadian media-guru Marshall McLuhan (1911-80), author of *The Medium is the Message*, that the way people communicate with each other is more important than what they actually communicate.

then, presumably, they were on Earth well before the Goa'uld (pre 8,000BC at least, when the Giza Stargate was buried). Yet the Romans, with whom the Ancients seem to have had most contact, came *long* after this.

**THE ANCIENTS' LEXICON** Jack provides a plethora of Ancients words: 'Cruvus' means 'wrong'. 'Cosars' are 'legs'. 'Falatus' is 'ability'. 'Fron' means 'head'. 'Farit' is 'finished'. 'Etium' means 'to understand'. 'Euge' is 'good'. 'Nou ani anquietas' means 'We are the Ancients'. 'Ego indio navo locas' means 'I need new location'. 'Ego deserdi asoundo' is 'I desire help'. 'Comdo' means 'please'. According to Daniel, the circle of symbols translates as 'the place of our legacy' (or, possibly, 'a piece of our leg', though, he confesses, the former makes more sense).

**QUOTE/UNQUOTE** Janet: 'Do you think this is going to help?' Daniel: 'I really don't know.' Jack writes something. Daniel (reading Jack's note): 'Shut up and go away!'

Jack's mission statement: 'You folks should understand that we're out there, now. And we might not be ready for a lot of this stuff but we're doing the best we can. We are a very curious race.'

Jack, to Daniel: 'You know that "meaning of life" stuff? I think we're gonna be all right.'

**NOTES** 'What the hell is going on with me?' An episode touched with a sense of *magnificence*. A vital cornerstone in *SG-1*'s *raison d'être*: the human face of military-SF. *SG-1* sometimes has an almost fatal aloofness in form and subject matter, but the ability to stand back and provide a caustic observational eye (and a willingness not to take itself too seriously) is often its salvation. Some episodes render *SG-1* a touch gauche next to, for instance, *The X-Files'* groundbreaking and urbane recontextualisations, and positively anaemic compared with the sophisticated metaphors of *Buffy the Vampire Slayer*. Then you get an episode like 'The Fifth Race' that simply says "*This* is what we stand for". A hymn to the best in humanity and an observation that when we stop talking we *start* to communicate. Proof, if any were needed, that Richard Dean Anderson (whom many still believe has trouble rubbing two emotions together) is an actor of outstanding depth. The best episode of the series by a *very* long way.

Major Castleman is mentioned again ('Solitudes', 'The Serpent's Lair', 'Fair Game') and accompanies Sam and Teal'c on SG-1's mission to P9Q281.

**CRITIQUE** Paul Spragg praised Richard Dean Anderson 'brilliantly delivering his lines so that the "foreign" words make sense in context... It's really Anderson's episode, as O'Neill becomes increasingly frustrated by his inability to communicate.'

**CAST AND CREW COMMENTS** The 2D computer generated morph effect used for the sequence where Jack's head is clamped by the Ancients' device remains a favourite of James Tichenor, although he points out if you look closely, it's possible to see where two shots of the effect were joined together.

**DID YOU KNOW?** When Teal'c hits Jack during their sparring match, Chris Judge really did catch Anderson with a fearsome uppercut, putting him on the floor. Ever the professional, Rick managed to continue with the scene but his line 'Is my nose bleeding?' was genuine.

## 38 A MATTER OF TIME

US Transmission Date: 29 Jan 1999
UK Transmission Date: 16 Dec 1998
Story: Misha Rashovich
Teleplay: Brad Wright
Director: Jimmy Kaufman
Cast: Teryl Rothery (Dr Janet Fraiser), Dan Shea (Sgt Siler), Tobias Mehler (Lt Graham Simmons), Colin Cunningham (Major Davis), Biski Gugushe (SF Guard), Marshall Teague (Colonel Cromwell), Kurt Max Runte (Major Boyd), Jim Thorburn (Watts)

Whilst attempting to save SG-10 from a black hole on P3X451, Sam activates the Stargate and exposes the SGC to the gravitational pull. Even without power, the gravity continues to draw them closer to the swirling wormhole. With the space/time continuum warped, the SGC loses contact with the outside world, and the Pentagon sends Special Forces Colonel Frank Cromwell to investigate.

**ORIGINS OF THE SPECIES** The indigenous life on P3X451 is recently extinct. When the bomb detonates, the wormhole jumps to P2A870.

**THE CONSPIRACY STARTS AT CLOSING TIME** SG-10 was commanded by Major Henry (Hank) Boyd, whom Jack recommended for the post. His GDO authorisation code is 10245-3B. Daniel is off-world with SG-6 at an archaeological dig on PX3808.

This episode sees the debut of the very popular Major Davis, the liaison officer between the Office of the Joint Chiefs at the Pentagon and the SGC.

**MILITARY INTELLIGENCE?** Some years ago, whilst under the command of Frank Cromwell, Jack was part of a Special Ops mission. He was shot and presumed dead. Jack spent four months in a stinking Iraqi prison (see 'Prisoners'). He never forgave Cromwell for leaving him.

**YE CANNAE CHANGE THE LAWS OF PHYSICS** Sam's theory states that a wormhole is an interdimensional conduit and can form only between two open Gates. Wormholes are not always present, needing to be accessed. The wormhole theory indicates that the Gate should act as a doorway that you step through whole. This contradicts the movie and some early episodes which show the monitors indicating that the travellers are dematerialised, transmitted, then rematerialised like *Star Trek*'s transporters. Time dilation causes time to pass more slowly within the facility than it does outside. There's a theoretical limit to the length of time that a wormhole can be maintained. (This had previously been mentioned in 'There But For the Grace of God', though that was in an alternate reality.) The SGC's Stargate is powered by capacitors (basically, giant batteries). The original SGC iris, destroyed by the gravity, is replaced with a new trinium-strengthened iris (see 'Spirits').

**POSSIBLE INFLUENCES** The 'insane computer' subgenre takes in half-a-dozen *Star Trek* episodes (mostly those written by Gene Roddenberry). And *The Movie* for that matter. Plus, *Doctor Who*'s 'The Green Death', 'The Ice Warriors' and 'The Face of Evil', *Colossus: The Forbin Project, 2001: A Space Odyssey, The Avengers*' 'The House That Jack Built', *The Prisoner*'s 'A, B and C', and numerous other examples.

**'YOU MIGHT REMEMBER ME FROM...'** Colin Cunningham appeared in *AntiTrust*, *The Sixth Day, Stealing Sinatra, Cold Squad* and *The X-Files*. He wrote and produced the movie *Zacharina Farted*. Marshall Teague was in *Armageddon, The Rock* and *Days of Our Lives*. Kurt Max Runte played Danny in *A Perfect Execution* and Ta'Lon in *Babylon 5*.

**LOGIC, LET ME INTRODUCE YOU TO THIS WINDOW** If this is their first mission, what have SG-10 been doing since they were commissioned months ago ('In the Line of Duty')? An outgoing wormhole drawing energy from a black hole is contrary to the laws of physics. If only a fraction of a second has gone by in the video from SG-10, how does the monitor show shots of Major Boyd both with his head turned away and directly facing the camera? How can people move up and down the mountain shifting so easily through different rates of time? How do the elevators work properly? Why is the MALP still responding to commands? Shouldn't it be suffering from the change in signal speed? If the ropes and everything else go horizontal outside the open control room window, how can Sam and co. stand upright in the room itself? Why would the SGC computer accept Cromwell's self-destruct authorisation code? After the stock footage of an aeroplane heading to DC, we get another stock shot of the mountain entrance, without all the extra vehicles that pulled up when Cromwell's men arrived. Jack leaves the infirmary on Level 21 and runs into Cromwell and Janet. She walks down the hall to the stairs to the control room (Level 28). EVAC shows up on the monitor before the General gives the command. With the threat of the SGC's destruction, Hammond suggested setting up a new Stargate programme at Nellis (see 'Touchstone'). Wasn't the second Stargate to be reassigned to the SGC? Wouldn't the gravitational forces in a binary star system preclude the formation of *any* stable planets? Jack is strong enough to pull himself free of the gravitational force of a black hole, seemingly. Sam calculates that time is passing something like 600 times more slowly within the facility than outside. Subsequently Daniel tells Jack that, since yesterday, a fortnight has passed. Shouldn't that be something like *18 months* if the 600% is accurate?

**QUOTE/UNQUOTE** Jack: 'We are witnessing good men dying in slow motion, Captain.'

Cromwell: 'The Pentagon suspects alien hostiles.' Jack: 'And they sent *you*?'

Hammond: 'Relativity gives me a headache.'

**NOTES** 'We're experiencing a paradox the Stargate was never designed for.' A ludicrous premise scientifically (see **Logic**), but the episode gets away with it by papering over the cracks with humour, the excellent effects-driven opening and a pyrotechnic overload at the end. Best bit: Sam using a doughnut to simulate a Stargate during her little lecture to Hammond about relativity.

Teal'c knows nothing about quantum gravity. General Cohen is named after MGM executive Hank Cohen.

**CAST AND CREW COMMENTS** 'A fan asked me what a "naked singularity" was,' noted Amanda Tapping. 'I felt like saying "Sam Carter on a Saturday night."'

**DID YOU KNOW?** 'That one really screwed my head,' noted James Tichenor. 'We had to shoot a scene in which Richard and Marshall Teague lower themselves into the Gateroom horizontally. We went through this quite maddening thought process to decide how to shoot all the elements. I remember we did this pseudo-do-motion control shot that required us to build a duplicate of our Gateroom set that was turned on a 90-degree angle. We had our actors suspended from wires in front of a huge green-screen also at a 90-degree angle.'

## 39 SERPENT'S SONG

US Transmission Date: 5 Feb 1999
UK Transmission Date: 6 Jan 1999
Writer: Katharyn Powers
Director: Peter DeLuise
Cast: Peter Williams (Apophis), Teryl Rothery (Dr Janet Fraiser), Dan Shea (Sgt Siler), Peter Lacroix (The Ashrak)[43], Tobias Mehler (Lt Graham Simmons), JR Bourne (Martouf)

> Outcast by his own kind, Apophis throws himself on the mercy of SG-1, who grant him sanctuary. Apophis is dying and promises information on the Goa'uld in return for a new host. He's being pursued by Sokar. Conquered by Apophis in Egypt, Sokar has come to wreak his revenge and will kill anything standing between him and his adversary.

**THE WIT AND WISDOM OF JACK O'NEILL** Jack: 'What do you want?' Apophis: 'To live.' Jack: 'Can't help you. That's between you and your god. Oh, wait a minute...!'

**SAM'S TRAUMATIC LOVE-LIFE** Martouf's first word on arrival is, significantly, 'Samantha'.

**ORIGINS OF THE SPECIES** Apophis's failed attack on Earth ('The Serpent's Lair') has weakened his place amongst the System Lords (first mentioned in 'Family'). Rival Goa'uld, such as Sokar, are taking advantage of this. The last of Apophis's loyal Jaffa died protecting him as he escaped from Sokar. As subsequent episodes make clear, there are many on Chulak who still worship Apophis, though Teal'c would have him believe that the entire planet has turned against him. Apophis senses that Sam hosted a Goa'uld ('In the Line of Duty'). This supports the notion (raised, by Sam, in 'Need') that one Goa'uld

----

43 Seen only in flashback from 'In the Line of Duty'.

can sense another. Apophis's host was a scribe in the Temple of Amon[44] at Karnak[45]. Which, presumably, means he was a worshiper of Ra. How ironic.

The Unas race served as original hosts for the Goa'uld before humans were discovered by Ra (see 'Thor's Hammer'). They lived with humans on Earth under the rule of Sokar, a Goa'uld who once ruled the System Lords. He was conquered by an alliance of others, including Ra and Apophis (said to be mortal enemies in 'Children of the Gods', so Sokar must have been bad if they worked together to defeat him). Daniel says Sokar was the original god of the dead and may have ruled the entire planet at one time. He was the most feared deity in ancient Egypt. His lands around Memphis were 'covered by darkness and serpents', and his throwing of enemies into a lake of fire in his portion of Tuat, or the Outerworld, may be the basis for the Judaeo-Christian Satan (see 'Jolinar's Memories'). He is said to be presently at war with Heru'ur.

The Tok'ra are allies of the Tollan. Martouf gives Sam a Tollan communications device (as used to contact the Nox in 'Enigma'). Since the Tollan have a strict law forbidding the sharing of any technology with less advanced beings (see 'Pretense', 'Shades of Grey') they must, therefore, regard the Tok'ra as their technological equals. Daniel reads out funerary spells to Apophis's host. These spells were an important part of Egyptian death rituals but scholars don't really know if they were recited before death, only that they were written down and buried with the deceased.

**SEX AND DRUGS AND ROCK 'N' ROLL** Apophis experiences withdrawal symptoms from the sarcophagus, similar to those that Daniel suffered in 'Need'. Janet uses morphine sulphate to ease Apophis's agony from his injuries.

**THE CONSPIRACY STARTS AT CLOSING TIME** Sam remembers the pain when the Ashrak killed Jolinar. She believes the same device was used on Apophis.

**POSSIBLE INFLUENCES** *Saturday Night Live* ('Well, isn't that special?')

**BEHIND THE CAMERA** Having first appeared on TV, on his father Dom's show, as a two-year old, Peter DeLuise began his career as an actor. He played Dagwood in *SeaQuest DSV* and appeared in *The Shot*, *Storm of the Heart* and *Friends* before becoming a director on *Silk Stalkings*, *Southern Heart* and *Between the Sheets*.

**LOGIC, LET ME INTRODUCE YOU TO THIS WINDOW** Why do the SGC assume that the radio communication came from the Tok'ra when they specifically gave them the Sagan box for such an eventuality (and, indeed, that's exactly what Martouf uses later in the episode)? How did Apophis know how to contact the SGC? Why didn't Daniel remember the accelerated dialling program from the alternate reality before (see 'There But For the Grace of God')? When the death glider fires at Jack as he drives into the Stargate, the

44 One of the Ogdoad (see 'Children of the Gods'), Amon was a relatively minor fertility god until his name became linked with Ra to become Egypt's supreme deity during the monotheistic period of Theban hegemony (14th century BC). His name derives from the Libyan word for water, *aman*. As part of the Ogdoad, *Amun Kematef*, he was able to resurrect himself by taking the form of a snake shedding its skin.
45 The northern part of Thebes (the site of modern Luxor and The Valley of the Kings). The pre-eminent religious centre of Egyptian society and, briefly, the capital (c.2000BC).

blast must have impacted on the ground (despite its angle). Otherwise, it would have travelled through the Gate. When the Gate is sending Martouf home, chevron seven lights up and opens at the same time as chevron one. Where did the SGC get the black cloak with the appropriate symbol to cover Apophis's face after death? The shroud shows no sign of the apparatuses on Apophis's legs. In Egyptian mythology, Sokar was a relatively minor funerary god of the Necropolis and far from the Satanic deity that Daniel describes. (By the Old Kingdom, Sokar became associated with Osiris, whose murder allowed Sokar to expand his influence into Upper Egypt, and become 'the creator of Royal bones'.) Apophis may have heard Daniel's name from Amaunet but they've met only very briefly (twice) in 'Children of the Gods', so how does Apophis know that Daniel is Daniel? Similarly, Hammond says that he and Apophis have met. In fact, they encountered each other for about ten seconds in the Gateroom in 'Children of the Gods'. Did Apophis have an iris-like barrier guarding his Stargate before being captured by Sokar? (He said that Sokar used the same weapon on him.)

### GOA'ULD LEXICON

'Kel'mah' means 'sanctuary'.

### QUOTE/UNQUOTE

Daniel: 'He gambled we would show compassion to our worst enemy. He was right.'

Martouf: 'Overconfidence was *their* failing, O'Neill. I hope it has not also become yours.'

### NOTES

'Holy buckets!' One of the best action sequence openings of any episode leads into a thoughtful and intelligent look at the realities of how to treat enemies during wartime. Jack, Daniel and Teal'c, all with their own valid reasons to hate Apophis, come face to face with their nemesis and find the experience ... uncomfortable. It's different when you've got to look someone in the eye and pull the trigger, isn't it?

The longest sustained attack on an iris was 38 minutes - this seems to be the maximum time a wormhole can be maintained. (This *was* established in 'There But For the Grace of God', but only in the alternate reality. A limit was mentioned in 'A Matter of Time', but no specific figure given. See, also, 'Chain Reaction'). Sam says that Sokar is firing a particle accelerator at the wormhole. The space between the wormhole and the iris is enough to allow high energy subatomic particles to reintegrate, but moving at near-light velocities. Modulating the particle stream can create an image, and intense heat, notes Sam. And lots of other scientific gobbledegook that Martouf alone seems to understand.

### CAST AND CREW COMMENTS

'Serpent's Song' was 'an interesting challenge,' remembered Peter DeLuise. 'The biggest hurdle was that Apophis spends most of the story strapped to a bed. That had the potential to become extremely boring. I had Peter Williams wear a bondage straightjacket because his character is similar to Hannibal Lecter.'

'I spent most of the episode wearing full facial makeup including contact lenses and false teeth,' added Williams. 'It was quite fun in a perverse sort of way.'

### DID YOU KNOW?

Peter DeLuise, like Martin Wood, usually finds a way to appear in front of the camera on the episodes he directs (*ala* Alfred Hitchcock). He's played a variety of guards and technicians, a Tok'ra and even the younger, uniformed, version of the character Urgo, played by his father (see 'Urgo').

# 40 HOLIDAY

US Transmission Date: 12 Feb 1999
UK Transmission Date: 13 Jan 1999
Writer: Tor Alexander Valenza
Director: David Warry-Smith
Cast: Teryl Rothery (Dr Janet Fraiser), Michael Shanks (Ma'chello)[46], Alvin Sanders (Fred), Melanie Skehar (Waitress), Darryl Scheelar (Cop)

When SG-1 stumble on the chamber of former Goa'uld enemy Ma'chello, Daniel falls victim to his powerful body-swapping invention and finds himself trapped in the body of a dying man. Ma'chello flees the SGC and gets a taste of life on Earth. In an attempt to help their friend, Jack and Teal'c bring the contraption to the SGC, but accidentally trigger it and find themselves in each other's body. With hilarious consequences.

**ORIGINS OF THE SPECIES** Ma'chello has been a fugitive from the System Lords since before Teal'c was born, developing advanced technology to battle the Goa'uld. After fighting them for 50 years, Ma'chello was betrayed by his wife. He lost his world: two billion of his people died rather than turn him over to the Goa'uld. He was eventually captured, tortured and marked to become a host so that his knowledge could be retained. Before implantation, Ma'chello killed several Jaffa and escaped. One of Teal'c's first assignments as First Prime of Apophis was to hunt Ma'chello.

**POSSIBLE INFLUENCES** The title is a song by Madonna. Allusions to The Beatles' 'I Feel Fine', *Spartacus* and Iraqi dictator Saddam Hussain.

**'YOU MIGHT REMEMBER ME FROM...'** Alvin Sanders was in *Cats and Dogs* and *Romeo Must Die*. Melanie Skehar appeared in *Puddle Cruiser*.

**LOGIC, LET ME INTRODUCE YOU TO THIS WINDOW** Why do Jack and Teal'c lift the device by its *handles*? That's a schoolboy error. The network of neurons is 'remapped' by the machine, apparently. So that's a metaphysical change forced on physical cells with synapses between axons and dendrites. Can we say *ridiculous* at this point? 'It's not in any dialect that I understand,' says Sam. Since when would anyone expect her to know *any* dialects, as she's not a expert on pronunciation? Daniel knows that Ma'chello's code is a mixture of Greek and Latin, but the icons we see on the device are neither. The SGC doesn't have the necessary technology to reprogramme the device, but shouldn't Ma'chello have it on his planet? Teal'c (in Jack's body) calls Daniel 'Doctor Jackson,' rather than 'Daniel Jackson'. In the infirmary, Daniel (in Ma'chello) wears an oxygen mask in the background and in the first shot of him in bed, but has a nasal canula fitted later. Janet says Ma'chello is in 'defib', but the monitor shows him flatlining. Daniel appears to have moved to a new apartment. Security, presumably? Why must Teal'c have a shaved head, no matter what body he's in? Other Jaffa (Bra'tak, for instance) have hair.

When did Ma'chello discover that Daniel was an archaeologist? Where are Jack and Teal'c whilst Daniel's in a coma? Chevron seven lights at same time as the wormhole engages.

**GOA'ULD LEXICON** 'Kelno'reem' is a Jaffa meditative state, aligning the host and symbiont consciousnesses. It is, notes Teal'c, similar to hibernation and far deeper and more complex than most human meditative states.

**QUOTE/UNQUOTE** Daniel, to Sam: 'It's nice to know you don't just like me for my looks.'

**NOTES** 'It could lead to my death. Rather, *your* death.' After such a great run of episodes, what a disappointment. This is a right *load*, full of painfully obvious SF clichés and rotten characterisation, a real throwback to the one-dimensional stories of the first season. Shanks, at least, gets to flex his acting muscles, and Anderson does a pretty good Teal'c. But Chris Judge just can't pull of O'Neill's mannerisms at all.

Daniel drives. He lives in an apartment at 1152 Mainland Street and doesn't have a sister (and, if he did, he wouldn't let Jack anywhere near her). Cassandra (see 'Singularity') is 12. (She's turned 13 by '1969'.)

**CAST AND CREW COMMENTS** 'From a production standpoint in season two we learned there were a lot of stories we could tell on Earth, bringing the adventure to us,' Brad Wright noted. 'Our show is set today, and the people who are experiencing all these fantastic things are us. In most other science fiction they can just press the "Deckion Generator". We have to use our - 20th Century - wits to get out of a situation.'

'I've occasionally read some comments on the internet,' Wright continued. 'They say "it wasn't a very satisfying ending", because they don't realise we left it open on purpose, for later down the line.'

**DID YOU KNOW?** On the evening that Brad Wright and Jonathan Glassner were given the go-ahead to develop *SG-1*, they went to dinner to celebrate. In the course of this, Brad mentioned, 'We won't know if we're successful until we have a big convention.' By the end of the second season *Stargate SG-1* conventions were beginning to get very big indeed.

# 41   ONE FALSE STEP

US Transmission Date: 19 Feb 1999
UK Transmission Date: 20 Jan 1999
Writers: Michael Kaplan, John Sanborn
Director: William Corcoran
Cast: Teryl Rothery (Dr Janet Fraiser), Daniel Bacon (Technician), Colin Heath (Steve), David Cameron (Elder), Richard DeKlerk (Joe), Shaun Phillips (Jim)

> On PJ2445 the UAV crashes. Sent to recover the plane, SG-1 discovers that the planet's inhabitants are gentle, mute creatures. Shortly after SG-1's arrival, however, aliens begin to fall ill as

a plague sweeps through the village. Jack and Daniel act erratically and complain of headaches which disappear only when they are back at the SGC. It appears that SG-1 may have unwittingly unleashed something that threatens the survival of a civilisation.

**THE WIT AND WISDOM OF JACK O'NEILL** Daniel: 'I thought the alien on the video looked fairly docile. More curious than harmful.' Jack: 'I thought it looked bald, white and naked.' Daniel says he's bothered by Jack's 'inappropriate sarcasm'.

**ORIGINS OF THE SPECIES** The aliens of PJ2445 are utterly benign and passive. They appear to be communal and, although mute, have a symbiotic relationship with the plant-like organism that provides them with the low-vibration sound sustaining them.

**SEX AND DRUGS AND ROCK 'N' ROLL** Janet prescribes one milligram of epinephrine and lidocaine for the stricken alien.

**IN THE INTERESTS OF UNIVERSAL HEALTH** Janet is surprised that SG-teams haven't infected alien populations more often. She theorises that because humans have been transplanted from Earth to many planets throughout the galaxy, most of the contaminants carried by SG-teams are already out there. This episode includes Janet's second trip through the Stargate. (The first was in 'Singularity'.)

**POSSIBLE INFLUENCES** Visually, *The Man Who Fell To Earth* and *The Illustrated Man*. Conceptually, Ursula LeGuin's *The Word for World is Forest*, Andrei Tarovsky's *Solaris* and the *Doctor Who* stories 'The Ark' and 'Kinda'. There are possible allusions to *The Wonderful World of Disney* and Rod Serling's introductions to *The Twilight Zone* ('Witness, if you will, squat...') and *The Adventures of Rocky and Bulwinkle* ('Are they friendly spirits?')

**'YOU MIGHT REMEMBER ME FROM...'** Daniel Bacon was in *2gether*. Richard de Klerk appeared in *Mr. Rice's Secret*. Colin Heath was in *Voyage of the Unicorn*.

**BEHIND THE CAMERA** Bill Corcoran directed *Quints* and episodes of *First Wave* and *Wiseguy*.

**LOGIC, LET ME INTRODUCE YOU TO THIS WINDOW** When Daniel leaves his office, the video is running on his computer. When he, Jack and Sam return, it's off. Jack, Sam and Janet are in the infirmary when Daniel gets the idea to check the tape. Only Jack and Sam return with him to his office. But Janet is with them again when Sam takes the tape to the control room. It's obvious where the aliens' body-stockings end in some shots. Teal'c says 'The plants are growing' before they actually do so. Teal'c's certainly been involved in conversations in which the phrase 'keep an eye on [something]' has been used ('The Fifth Race', for example). So why his unfamiliarity with it when Daniel asks him to keep an eye on the plants? Just how exactly does the UAV's Terrain Radar System have anything to do with its long-range communications? These are two separate systems.

**QUOTE/UNQUOTE** Daniel: 'I've had more successful communications with dogs.'

Jack, to the aliens: 'Don't forget your sunblock.'

**NOTES** 'This is turning into an epidemic.' A charmingly bizarre little tale with some interesting things to say about humanity as potential carriers of deadly plagues to the furthermost reaches of the universe. Best bits: Daniel's impression of a UAV. Jack's and Daniel's 'little chat'.

Mythology is, according to Jack, 'rumours, lies and fairy tales'. He loves watching the UAV fly through the Stargate. ('That *never* gets old!') Sam isn't a botanist, she notes, though she does talk to her plants. Daniel's allergies ('Children of the Gods') are mentioned for the first time in a while. The Jaffa don't have an equivalent of *déjà vu*. When the subject of first impressions concerning aliens comes up, the Nox are alluded to. The UAV carries an automatic Terrain Radar System for long-range communications.

**CAST AND CREW COMMENTS** The series is 'a well-oiled, well-run, giant machine,' Peter DeLuise has noted. 'One of the things they do that's not common on other programmes is have rotating directors of photography. That's because this show is *big*. And Peter Woeste and Jim Menard kick major butt when it comes to lighting the series.'

**DID YOU KNOW?** This episode includes one particularly memorable stunt. As Dan Shea described it: 'An air-ram is like a diving board you stand on that shoots you up in the air. Generally, when you do these you fall onto a pad. But the director, Bill Corcoran, wanted to actually see us hit the ground.'

# 42 SHOW AND TELL

US Transmission Date: 26 Feb 1999
UK Transmission Date: 27 Jan 1999
Writer: Jonathan Glassner
Director: Peter DeLuise
Cast: Jeff Gulka (Charlie), Teryl Rothery (Dr Janet Fraiser), Carmen Argenziano (Jacob Carter), Daniel Bacon (Technician)

A young boy arrives through the Stargate and tells Jack that he's come with his mother, a member of the invisible Reetou. The boy, Charlie, says that the Goa'uld destroyed their planet and that a terrorist faction of the Reetou intend to kill all potential hosts for the Goa'uld, starting with humanity. SG-1 call the Tok'ra, and Jacob arrives bringing a laser device which can make the Reetou visible. But, it may be too late.

**ORIGINS OF THE SPECIES** The Reetou are from the planet Reetalia, which was recently destroyed by the Goa'uld. Charlie was created (either cloned or genetically engineered) by his mother to serve as an intermediary between the Reetou and humans, to warn of the coming attack. But due to his accelerated growth, the boy has several congenital defects in his major organs. They're failing and unless he receives expert medical help he will die. At the end he goes to become a Tok'ra host in the hope that this will save his life.

Goa'uld larva become agitated when in the presence of a Reetou. The Reetou are 180 degrees out of phase with everything else, their light and sound waves being virtually undetectable. The Reetou must interact with objects in our phase, however: Mother operated the Stargate's iris and Reetou weapons can kill. The rebel Reetou operate in five-member suicide squads that infiltrate a target and try to do as much damage as possible. (Jacob compares them to terrorist groups on Earth.) Each rebel carries at least one explosive device equivalent to a small nuclear weapon.

Sam and Daniel used the Tollan device given by Martouf ('Serpent's Song') to signal the Tok'ra.

**THE CONSPIRACY STARTS AT CLOSING TIME** Charlie is checked by Janet for two possible threats: a Naqahdah bomb ('Singularity') or biohazardous chemicals ('Family'). Mother is said to have been watching the SGC for weeks before Charlie's arrival. She followed SG-1 back from a mission and observed them, being particularly impressed with the way they dealt with the Tonane situation ('Spirits').

**MILITARY INTELLIGENCE?** Standard mission protocol calls for SG teams to report in at specified times when offworld. A wormhole activation is automatically designated as 'unauthorised incoming traveller' when a report or return trip is not scheduled.

**IN THE INTERESTS OF NATIONAL SECURITY** Palm scanners are installed in the SGC computer system, so that other Reetou infiltrators cannot open the iris as Mother did. The Goa'uld developed the Transphase Eradication Rod (TER), which is capable of detecting the unseen Reetou emanations. It can also fire a shot that will kill a Reetou. The Tok'ra possess a small number of these and give at least two to the SGC. Jacob promises more when they become available.

**POSSIBLE INFLUENCES** Owes a huge conceptual debt to *Aliens*, *Starship Troopers* and *Predator* and to *Doctor Who*'s 'The Ark in Space'. *Boys Don't Cry* is mentioned.

**'YOU MIGHT REMEMBER ME FROM...'** Jeff Gulka played Gibson Praise in *The X-Files*.

**LOGIC, LET ME INTRODUCE YOU TO THIS WINDOW** How did the Reetou create a human child? Assuming human DNA was needed, from whence did they acquire it? How can the technician know it's an unauthorised traveller after only one chevron is lit, especially when there are two outstanding SG teams? The infirmary is on Level 21. Unless Charlie and Mother weren't being kept there (and it certainly looks like the infirmary), then there's no way Daniel and Jack could end up at that room after sweeping Corridor A7 on Level 28. Why doesn't Charlie react to Teal'c's presence in the Gateroom? Why isn't Teal'c affected by Mother's presence while standing in the infirmary doorway? He and Jacob are affected by the Reetou on the staging planet at a much greater distance. And, how can the TERs illuminate the Reetou at such a distance? When Daniel and Sam send the signal to the Tok'ra, it looks like stock footage of Omoc's hands from 'Enigma'. How do the Reetou interact with things in our phase (see 'Crystal Skull', 'Wormhole X-Treme!')? How do the suicide squad of Reetou get through the Gate quickly enough to avoid detection by Jacob and his Tok'ra guard? Janet puts her stethoscope on backwards at least once when examining

Charlie. Why didn't Charlie mention that there were Reetou rebels in the room before Mother was killed? Even if he didn't spot them surely *she* did?

Janet: 'It's like mother nature put him together in a hurry and got everything a little wrong.'

'I am here to warn you.' Stagy and one paced, 'Show and Tell', whilst being as manipulative as 'Singularity', nevertheless has more emotional depth and much to offer in lush characterisation. (Anderson's always good with kids and, here, he gets one who can act.) The story again uses metaphor like a sledgehammer instead of a chisel, but with some nice effects and good acting the 'hardly a dry eye in the house' finale has some merit.

Janet Fraiser is sceptical about things like ESP and telekinesis. Jacob seems to be adjusting well to his new life as a Tok'ra. He still wears his wedding ring. It can be seen as he takes Charlie's hand. The SGC appears to have added at least two new Stargate teams during the last few months (SG-10, 11 and 12 were added in 'Prisoners'). SG-14 is one of the teams mentioned as being offworld. (SG-5 is the other.) SG-12 accompany SG-1 and Jacob on the mission to the Reetou staging planet. Rothman is mentioned (see 'Forever in a Day').

'Show and Tell' is a favourite of Don Davis, as he told the audience at the 2000 Gatecon convention: 'No parent can watch that episode and not be moved.'

Fans often wonder about the patches and badges worn by SG-1 - are they accurate? According to Master Sergeant Tom Giannazzo they are. Hammond wears Pilot wings, a Department of Defense badge and a Space Missile badge. Jack sports a Department of Defense badge, a Paratrooper badge, and a SCUBA bubble. Sam has a Space Missile badge.

# 43 1969

US Transmission Date: 5 Mar 1999
UK Transmission Date: 3 Feb 1999
Writer: Brad Wright
Director: Charles Correll
Cast: Alex Zahara (Michael), Aaron Pearl (Lt George Hammond), Amber Rothwell (Jenny), Pamela Perry (Cassandra), Glynis Davies (Catherine), Fred Henderson (Major Thornbird), Sean Campbell (Sergeant), Efosa Otuomagie (Security Police), Daniel Bacon (Technician)

> Through a cosmic accident, SG-1 are propelled back to 1969. Carrying a letter that Hammond gave her, Sam is searched by a Lieutenant, who is astonished by the letter's contents. As the team is transported for interrogation, the Lieutenant, a young George Hammond, helps them escape. Desperate to find the Stargate, SG-1 are picked up by a hippie couple. Sam discovers that Hammond's note includes the date of the next solar flare. They must get to the Stargate or

remain stuck in the past.

**THE WIT AND WISDOM OF JACK O'NEILL** 'This is a top secret facility. Anonymity does not go over big here.'

**SEX AND DRUGS AND ROCK 'N' ROLL** Hey, it's the sixties, what do you expect?
The concert to which Michael and Jenny are travelling in upstate New York to would seem to be Woodstock (which took place between 14 and 17 August 1969).

**THE TIME TRAVEL STARTS AT CLOSING TIME** Sam says that the wormhole will take them close to the sun at this time of year - within 70,000 miles. The computer's drift calculations have to be updated to take into account gravitational space-time warping. SG-1 are thrown back in time because a solar flare erupted on the sun the moment the team passed it while travelling through the wormhole. This caused the wormhole to slingshot around the sun - a theoretical means of time travel. For a few seconds, SG-1 appear to occupy both time periods simultaneously due to time dilation. Sam warns the team against changing anything in Earth history because of the Grandfather Paradox. This states that if you go back in time and kill your own grandfather (why anybody would want to do such a terrible thing never seems to enter the equation), you would never be born - and therefore be unable to go back in time to kill your grandfather.

**MILITARY INTELLIGENCE?** After the first Abydos mission, Hammond asked Sam to explore other applications for the Stargate, including time travel, obviously because he knew that the, as yet uncreated, SG-1 would be trapped in 1969 and need a way home.

**POSSIBLE INFLUENCES** *The Electric Kool Aid Acid Test, The Doors, Help!, 1969, Forrest Gump, The Wizard of Oz* ('Auntie Em?'), *Austin Powers: International Man of Mystery, Star Trek IV: The Voyage Home* and the *Star Trek* episodes 'Tomorrow is Yesterday' and 'Assignment: Earth'. The title also alludes to a classic song by Iggy Pop and the Stooges. Headlines from the *New Jersey Star* for 10 August 1969 include NIXON TO VACATION AT SUMMER WHITE HOUSE and SHARON TATE, FOUR OTHERS MURDERED. The latter refers to the gruesome Tate/La Bianca murders carried out by members of Charles Manson's 'Family' cult in Beverly Hills on 9 August. Both Jack and Daniel establish their SF-fanboy credentials with references to *Star Trek* and *Star Wars*. In their hippie disguises, Teal'c turns into Jimi Hendrix, Jack into Lou Reed and Daniel into an unholy and rather frightening cross between John Sebastian and Ray Manzarek. There's an oblique reference to the *Stargate* movie ('The doorway to heaven').

**'YOU MIGHT REMEMBER ME FROM...'** Aaron Pearl was in *Duets*. Pamela Perry appeared in *Bliss*. Glynis Davies played Buffy's Mom in *Scary Movie*. Fred Henderson was in *Friday 13th Part VIII: Jason Takes Manhatten.*

**LOGIC, LET ME INTRODUCE YOU TO THIS WINDOW** Hammond's note didn't specify time zones, so how did SG-1 know whether he meant Eastern Standard Time or, for instance, Mountain Time - two hours behind - which covers Colorado where the Stargate is in 1999? If the times in the note are when the flares were visible from Earth, wouldn't that mean SG-1 had missed if they went through the Gate at that point? SG-1 pick a side of the road to hitch from (and thus a direction to travel) before Daniel realises that they should head to New York. SG-1 bypass a fence and grounds and get into an armoury undetected whilst dressed like a bunch of hippies. We all knew they're good, but *that* good? How did the SGC know that SG-1 never made it to P2X555 (as opposed to making it there and encountering difficulties)? Trees and lush green hills *in New Mexico*? Since when? When was the missile silo replaced with separate flooring? Jack says that he isn't used to astronomy 'on this scale'. Yet in 'Singularity,' he operated a telescope after SG-10 were killed. When did Teal'c learn to drive? What stops zat-blasts from bleeding off the equipment boxes and onto the floor of the truck? The Major interrogating Jack is obviously unfamiliar with *Star Trek*, which had recently completed its three year run on US TV in August 1969. In order to go forward in time instead of back, Hammond had to locate flares on the opposite side of the sun. Not only would the line between Earth and P2X555 take the wormhole close to the sun again in 1969, but it would have to do so on the *opposite* side. During their drive across the US, SG-1 passes through Chicago, and the Sears Tower is shown briefly. Construction of this didn't begin until 1970. The military transport four probable Soviet spies all the way from Colorado to New Mexico *in a truck*. That's cruel and unusual treatment and probably against the Geneva Convention. Let's all hope we never see Teal'c's Afro-wig again. It's big and it's hairy and I be afeared of it. So, did Michael go to Vietnam or dodge the draft by crossing the border to Canada? Is the cut on Sam's hand the one she got in 'One False Step'? This is never made clear. Is it possible for a noncorporeal being (i.e. Daniel) to go bald (see 'Meridian')?

**QUOTE/UNQUOTE** Daniel: 'What's the plan?' Jack: 'Find the Stargate.' Daniel: '*That*'s the plan?' Jack: 'Elegant in its simplicity, don't you think?'

Teal'c: 'I am not at liberty to reveal my identity.' Michael: 'Far out!'

Jack: 'We came to Earth to hide among your people a long, long time ago.' Daniel: 'From a galaxy far, far away.'

**NOTES** 'Get us back before we left and it won't happen.' *SG-1* takes all the best bits of the time-travel genre, shakes 'em up in a bag, throws 'em on the floor and says 'Right, let's have a party'. '1969' is, excuse the vernacular, a groovy *romp*. Logically bollocks, of course, but funny, exciting and cheeky, a stylishly *informed* tribute to the kind of science fiction that the writers, and many of the audience, grew up on.

Jack is a big fan of the classic era Corvette. Daniel says that he was four and a half in 1969. German and Russian are two of the 23 languages he speaks. Given the chance to travel in time, Daniel would wish to visit Babylon and see the Great Wall of China built. Cassandra suggests that in the future he will go bald (but, see 'Meridian'). Hammond watched the Apollo 11 moon landing (on 21 July 1969) from his father's hospital bedside two days after Mr Hammond's first heart attack. The note that Hammond writes himself says: "*George. Help them. August 10th 9.15am. August 11th 6.03pm*". Heinrich Grüber (whose son Daniel impersonates) worked with Catherine's father. Catherine tells Daniel and Sam that she always knew there was a second device with which to control the ring: the DHD (see 'Watergate'). Catherine was living in New York in 1969. When Cassandra opens the future-Stargate to send SG-1 back to 1999, she uses a hand device to establish a wormhole automatically. This technology has been used by Apophis ('Children of the Gods') and Lya ('Enigma'). Cassie appears to be in her 60s. She is 12 in 1998, so SG-1 seem to be thrown forward to circa 2050.

**CAST AND CREW COMMENTS** 'That was our "amusing" entry for the second season,' noted Brad Wright. 'It doesn't take itself seriously and embraces the fun universe that *Stargate* can be.'

**DID YOU KNOW?** Vancouver's Gordon Southam Observatory doubles for the Washington location that Jack and Teal'c use to confirm the solar flares.

# 44 OUT OF MIND

US Transmission Date: 12 Mar 1999
UK Transmission Date: 10 Feb 1999
Story: Jonathan Glassner, Brad Wright
Teleplay: Jonathan Glassner
Director: Martin Wood
Cast: Teryl Rothery (Dr Janet Fraiser), Suanne Braun (Hathor), Dan Shea (Sgt Siler)[47], Tom Butler (Major General Trofsky), Samantha Ferris (Dr Raully)

> Awakening from cryogenic suspension, Jack finds himself in a futuristic version of the SGC. He is told he was frozen 79 years ago and that the rest of SG-1 are dead. Hooked up to a device which records his memories, Jack faces questioning about races able to defeat the Goa'uld, with whom the SGC are still at war. But is everything as it seems?

**ORIGINS OF THE SPECIES** Teal'c says that Horus guards and Serpent guards working together is a very unusual combination. Horus guards serve the family of Ra - including Hathor and Heru'ur. Serpent guards serve Apophis, Ra's worst enemy.

General Trofsky tells Raully to keep Sam more heavily drugged, because she has Naqahdah in her blood and would sense that they were Goa'uld. It's, presumably, the mineral that allows Sam to use Goa'uld technology (demonstrated in 'Thor's Chariot'; see, also, 'Absolute Power').

Hathor possesses cloaking technology, something no other Goa'uld has at this point. (Nirrti is subsequently revealed to possess this also. See 'Fair Game', 'Rite Of Passage'.) Was it, therefore, *she* who attacked the Reetou ('Show and Tell')? Hathor has been rebuilding her forces since escaping Earth. She has attracted a small army of Jaffa from the remote outposts of her enemies and acquired a Goa'uld mothership. Based on the detailed reproduction of the SGC that she has constructed, Hathor seems to have planned this deception for some time.

**SEX AND DRUGS AND ROCK 'N' ROLL** Hathor returns, looking as disturbingly alluring as ever and still with a big glowy thing where her bellybutton should be.

**MILITARY INTELLIGENCE?** SG-3 and SG-7 went through the Gate to the (nameless) planet on which SG-1 were attacked. They found Teal'c barely alive beside the Stargate.

**IN THE INTERESTS OF NATIONAL SECURITY** When it appears that Jack and the others are dead, Teal'c resigns from the SGC and returns to Chulak (see 'Into the Fire'). Hammond repeats that Teal'c represents a security risk ('The Enemy Within').

**POSSIBLE INFLUENCES** *The Matrix*, *Star Trek: The Next Generation*'s 'Future Imperfect', *Project X*, *Dark Star*, *Farscape* and *The Wizard of Oz* ('there's no place like home'). When Hathor asks Jack how to contact the Asgard, he alludes to the town of Roswell ('Little place in New Mexico').

**'YOU MIGHT REMEMBER ME FROM...'** Tom Butler was in *Legs Apart* and *Death Match*. Samantha Ferris appeared in *Along Came a Spider*.

**LOGIC, LET ME INTRODUCE YOU TO THIS WINDOW** Convenient, isn't it, that the technicians with whom Jack and Sam trade clothes are exactly the same sizes as them. Can you have 'memories' seen from a third-person point of view? Or, for that matter, 'memories' of events at which the person doing the remembering wasn't present? (Sam remembers Apophis and Klorel taking the transport rings off their ship; Daniel remembers Jack being turned into a Jaffa by Hathor.) The mature Goa'uld doesn't look anything like the one in 'Children of the Gods'. It takes Jack a long time to speak after coming out of the cryogenics, but Sam can do so after just seconds.

**QUOTE/UNQUOTE** Jack, on the memory device: 'These things have a nasty habit of going off when you least expect it. Try not to think too much.'

Jack, on Hathor: 'I was *so* hoping never to see you again.'

**NOTES** 'Everyone I ever knew is gone.' What a letdown. After a generally brilliant six months of TV with episodes full of innovation, imagination, wit and flair, how disappointing that it all ends up with yet another clip-show (see 'Politics').

According to Raully, the memory device was acquired from the Tok'ra. It stimulates the memory centre of the brain and amplifies it like a capacitor. It projects the memories holographically. Amongst the memories that Jack dredges up are the Nox's ability to revive their dead ('The Nox'), his meeting with the Asgard ('The Fifth Race') and the discovery of the Heliopolis ('The Torment of Tantalus').

**CAST AND CREW COMMENTS** 'The first season was all about developing the character and trying to figure out who she was,' noted Amanda Tapping. 'I had pretty much everything I wanted to achieve with Carter happen throughout season two and now I'm really looking forward to seeing what this year will bring. I'd still like to explore more of the relationships with the team members because they've sectioned us off a little.'

**DID YOU KNOW?** 'I've worked 18 hour days on *The X-Files*, *Millennium* and *The Outer Limits*,' Amanda Tapping remembered. 'Here my day is 14 hours long, which gives me just enough time to drive home, work on the script for the next day, go to sleep, get up and go back to the studio. Compared [with] other shows, I guess we're lucky.'

However, she's happy to put the effort in for the show's loyal fanbase: 'You don't really do television to please yourself. You do it to gain an audience, and once you've got that audience you have to stay loyal to them and treat them with respect. We don't want our scripts to be in any way condescending.'

# STARGATE SG-1
# SEASON 3 (1999-2000)

'You know that "We come in peace" business?

Bite me.'

# STARGATE SG-1™ SEASON 3 (1999-2000)

Double Secret Productions/Gekko Film Corp/
Metro-Goldwyn-Meyer

Developed for Television by Brad Wright, Jonathan Glassner

Executive Producer: Brad Wright, Jonathan Glassner

Co-Executive Producer: Michael Greenburg, Richard Dean Anderson

Producer: Robert C Cooper (45-55), N John Smith

Supervising Producer: Robert C Cooper (56-66)

Post Production Consultant: R Michael Eliot[48]

Senior Story Editor: Tor Alexander Valenza

Story Editor: Heather E Ash (49-66)

Regular Cast: Richard Dean Anderson (Jack O'Neill), Michael Shanks
(Daniel Jackson), Amanda Tapping (Samantha Carter), Christopher Judge
(Teal'c), Don S Davis (General George Hammond)

SEASON 3

48 Credited as Michael Eliot from 'Crystal Skull' onwards.

# 45   INTO THE FIRE

US Transmission Date: 25 Jun 1999
UK Transmission Date: 22 Sep 1999
Writer: Brad Wright
Director: Martin Wood
Cast: Gary Jones (Technician), Steve Makaj (Colonel Makepeace), Tony Amendola (Bra'tac), Suanne Braun (Hathor), Colin Cunningham (Major Davis), Tom Butler (Trofsky), Samantha Ferris (Dr Raully), Kelly Dean Sereda (Lieutenant), Oliver Svensson-Tan (Marine), Alicia Thorgrimsson (Jaffa)

> Trapped on Hathor's planet, Jack is implanted with a symbiont. Hammond sends Makepeace and four Stargate units to rescue SG-1, and they succeed in freeing Sam and Daniel. Raully reveals that she is a Tok'ra spy and puts Jack in the cryogenic chamber, killing his Goa'uld. Meanwhile, on Chulak, Teal'c attempts to raise an army of rebellion to help his friends.

**ORIGINS OF THE SPECIES** Hathor's collection of guards is an eclectic mix, including Jaffa seemingly drawn from the service many other Goa'uld. She has clearly been gathering dissidents and defectors from across the galaxy. Hathor possesses the technology to generate a huge energy barrier, something that SG-1 have never before encountered.

Bra'tac is now 135 years old (see 'Bloodlines'). He still has some authority with the Jaffa formerly in service to Apophis, though many condemn his treason ('The Serpent's Lair') and some have tried to kill him. The people of Chulak fear that, with Apophis gone, Klorel will return to reclaim his inheritance. Bra'tac hid his ship about 100 years ago when he was First Prime of Apophis. Few people can fly this type of ship. Flying it through a Stargate is euphemistically called 'threading the needle' and requires great skill. 'They do not build as they once did' is an old Jaffa saying, apparently.

**SEX AND DRUGS AND ROCK 'N' ROLL** Daniel says he tries hard not to remember his night of hot steamy passion with Hathor (see 'Hathor'). Repressed, clearly.

**THE CONSPIRACY STARTS AT CLOSING TIME** Hammond discusses the creation of three new Stargate teams with Major Davis. Since SG-14 was mentioned in 'Show and Tell', this would make a total of at least 17 teams. SG-5, 6 and 11 accompany Makepeace and SG-3 on the rescue mission.

**POSSIBLE INFLUENCES** The title is a lyric from Duran Duran's 'View to a Kill' and a Bryan Adams song (see 'Hathor'). Also, *The Wizard of Oz, Casablanca* ('The start of a beautiful friendship'), *Monty Python's Flying Circus* ('She is no more... she's a former queen') and *Diamonds Are Forever, Goldeneye* and *Dracula, Prince of Darkness* (Hathor's death).

**LOGIC, LET ME INTRODUCE YOU TO THIS WINDOW** Time is found for Sam and Daniel to change clothes in the middle of a jailbreak. Reinforcements will be sent in six hours. During this time Hammond argues with Davis, goes to Chulak, finds Teal'c, despite never having been there before, waits for him to finish his rousing speech and searches for and finds Bra'tac's ship. Considering they seem to come from underground, how do the Jaffa get into the gun towers? Hathor calls Raully 'Jaffa'. She should have been able to tell the difference, surely (unless it's a general Goa'uld insult)? The Jaffa in the gun towers are *dreadful* shots. How did Hathor gather her forces? By breathing on them? Does that work on Jaffa?

**GOA'ULD LEXICON** 'Tal'bet' means 'surrender'. 'Kel nok shree Jaffa' translates as 'I am not a Jaffa.'

**QUOTE/UNQUOTE** Teal'c: 'I was witness to the final breath of Apophis. I saw him tremble in fear at what lay beyond.'

**NOTES** 'If the Tau'ri do not destroy you, know this, we will.' A high-octane beginning to the season with tons of over-the-top explosions and gunfights, and a bit of real drama thrown into the mix. Best bits: Hammond's 'Take one step forward' speech to his men. Jack killing Hathor.

**CAST AND CREW COMMENTS** Brad Wright describes the episode as 'a little too ambitious'.

**DID YOU KNOW?** The decision to blow up the 30-foot high gun tower was problematic for special-effects supervisor Wray Douglas. The structure was made from steel, wood, glass and plexi; '[these are] products we don't normally put into an explosion because they're hard-flying debris. So, we rigged it, sent everybody to a safe distance and then did the explosion. And it worked out quite spectacularly.'

# 46  SETH

US Transmission Date: 2 Jul 1999
UK Transmission Date: 29 Sep 1999
Writer: Jonathan Glassner
Director: William Corcoran
Cast: Robert Duncan (Seth), Carmen Argenziano (Jacob Carter), Mitchell Kosterman (Hamner), Stuart O'Connell (Tommy), Lucia Walters (Disciple), Greg Michaels (Joe Levinson), Rob Morton (Sheriff)

Jacob enlists SG-1 in a hunt for the Goa'uld Seth, whom he believes is hiding on Earth. SG-1 trace the alien to a heavily armed compound in Washington State, where Seth is posing as the leader of a fanatical religious cult. Jack, Sam and Daniel break into the compound but fall victim to a biological agent that Seth uses to brainwash his followers.

**ORIGINS OF THE SPECIES** The Tok'ra were impressed with SG-1 defeat of Hathor ('Into the Fire'). Jacob notes although there are thousands of Goa'uld, only dozen's of them are System Lords. The 'System Lords family tree' projection includes

13 Goa'uld, with the symbol of Ra at the top. Others on display include Apophis, Hathor and Heru'ur. Evidence from tombs in the Valley of the Kings suggest that many Goa'uld built their compounds with underground escape tunnels.

Setesh (also known as Set, Seti, Sutekh and Seth) was the Egyptian god of chaos. Said to be son of either Nut and Geb,[49] or Nut and Ra, Setesh's siblings include Osiris, Isis (see 'The Curse'), Horus and Nephthys.[50] All Tok'ra records of Setesh end when Earth's Stargate was buried and Setesh unsuccessfully tried to overthrow Ra. Jacob speculates that he's been hiding on Earth ever since, either using a sarcophagus or changing hosts approximately every 400 years. After Setesh was supposedly killed in Egypt, a similar god, Typhon, turned up in Greece. A cult of Setesh has existed in one form or another since around 1000BC. One instance was in the 1720s in England, near Stonehenge. Setesh, now calling himself Seth Fargough, is leading 'The Children of Seth'. Deprogrammed ex-cult members describe Seth as having magical powers and the ability to heal.

**"TWO JAFFA WALK INTO A BAR..."** Teal'c has met descendants of Setesh's Jaffa. Presumably, no Jaffa is currently loyal to Seth, since he has been hiding on Earth for thousands of years. The creature that represents Setesh was mythical.[55] Because of this, Setesh's Jaffa, who continue to wear this symbol, are the source of many jokes amongst the Jaffa. Teal'c gives an example: A Serpent guard, a Horus guard and a Setesh guard meet on a neutral planet. It is a tense moment. The Serpent guard's eyes glow. The Horus guard's beak glistens. The Setesh guard's nose drips. Teal'c finds this hilarious. It clearly loses much in translation.

**SEX AND DRUGS AND ROCK 'N' ROLL** Nish'ta, the Goa'uld biological compound used by Seth to control his followers, is similar to (but stronger than) the organism used by Hathor at the SGC ('Hathor'). Once inhaled it infects all body tissue, including the brain. It tends to make the mind pliable. Teal'c believes the substance is what Apophis used on Rya'c ('Family'). Once the effects are reversed with a strong electrical shock, however, the host becomes immune.

Historically, Seth used women as a harem attending to his every whim. The men within his compound are usually turned into eunuchs. (Jack is not, he says, looking forward to the prospect of waking up 'singing soprano'.)

**MILITARY INTELLIGENCE?** Jack asks Hamner if he can have one of those 'cool' ATF jackets (size double XL).

**POSSIBLE INFLUENCES** The *Doctor Who* story 'Pyramids of Mars' features a very different version of Sutekh. Also, *The X-Files* episode 'The Field Where I Died' and three real-life cult massacres, Jonestown,[52] Waco[53] and Heaven's Gate,[54] the

---

49 The children of Shu and Tefnut. Nut was the sky-goddess and Geb, the earth-god.

50 'The Mistress of the Enclosure', mother of the jackal-god Anubis (see 'Summit', 'Revelations').

51 At least most Egyptologists believe so. It looks rather like an aardvark to this author.

52 November 1978: 913 followers of Rev. Jim Jones's People's Temple committed mass suicide at Jonestown, Guyana by drinking cyanide-laced fruit-juice. Jones (who claimed to be a reincarnation of Christ), had recently ordered the murder of a US congressman investigating his cult.

53 February 1993: A controversial armed-conclusion to a 51-day stand-off between law enforcement officials and members of David Koresh's fundamentalist Branch Davidians cult, resulted in over 80 deaths.

54 March 1997: The mass suicide at Rancho Santa Fe, California, of 39 members of Higher Source, a cult

Three Stooges, *Song of the South* ('snippity-doo-dah'), *The Wizard of Oz* ('Hail Dorothy') and *Bill and Ted's Excellent Adventure*. Seth's physical appearance and costume owe much to the villain in the Hong Kong movie *The Black Sheep Affair*.

**'YOU MIGHT REMEMBER ME FROM...'** Mitchell Kosterman played Deputy Talbot in *Smallville*. Greg Michaels was in *Pumpkinhead*. Rob Morton appeared in *Who's Harry Crumb?* Lucia Walters was in *Mission to Mars*.

**LOGIC, LET ME INTRODUCE YOU TO THIS WINDOW** Daniel refers to a cult in the 'early 1800s', but the webpage he's reading from describes an 18th century cult leader (specifically, 1722 in Wiltshire). How did Seth know when Sam, Jack and Daniel were all within the circle of the rings? Seth comments on the lack of a scar on Sam's neck. But since he's aware of the Tok'ra, why would he be surprised by this? (It is possible, of course, that the Tok'ra took to entering their host body through the mouth in more recent centuries, whilst Seth has been stranded on Earth.) How do Jack and Daniel activate the rings the last time, and do they really leave the four cult members behind to be killed by the bomb? How did Hamner discover SG-1's names and ranks? How do SG-1 avoid hitting any of the cult twice with their zats? Sam says she hasn't seen her brother since either of his kids were born. In 'Cold Lazarus', she mentioned enjoying being an aunt. It must have been the wettest day in San Diego's history when Jacob and Sam went there. Sam says that Seth would be able to sense Teal'c's or Jacob's symbiotes within 50 feet. Given this, it seems ludicrous that no-one considered the possibility that Seth could sense Jolinar in Sam (something that both Apophis and Hathor previously had). Concerning Seth's name: Setesh is a Goa'uld name and not an Egyptian one. Seti was *not* an alternate name for Set, but rather a name that some Pharaoh's took to identify themselves as coming from his line. Before being associated with evil, Set was actually one of the good guys. He accompanied Ra in his barque and the pair joined forces to destroy Apophis. He is described as having red hair and being a northern barbarian warrior. The earliest representations of him date from 4,400BC. He is usually depicted as ambivalent - violent and cruel, but a good warrior to have on your metaphysical side. It's only from the Third Intermediate Period (circa 800BC) that he became viewed as an evil god, much associated with Ba'al (see 'Summit'). It's strange that after several millennia of building up false religions, Set is still only a cult leader to half a dozen loony rich kid. With his superior intelligence, knowledge and technology, wouldn't it have been more logical for him to have become the Pope or something?

**QUOTE/UNQUOTE** Jack: 'AK-47s, a couple of Uzis... Anyone think they observed the necessary fifteen day waiting period for those weapons?' And: 'Does the concept of overkill mean anything to anyone?'

**NOTES** 'Kinda gives "needle in a haystack" a whole new meaning.' A fantastic central idea (what's the *obvious* occupation for an undercover Goa'uld?) and, thanks to some real-world parallels and good acting (Robert Duncan is excellent as Seth: *love* his leather coat!), it scores on most levels. It's almost derailed, however, by the staggeringly pointless subplots about, first, Levinson and his son, and then Jacob

who believed that their souls were to rendezvous with a UFO hidden behind the Hale-Bopp comet.

119

SEASON 3

and *his* son. Rather obvious isn't it? Thankfully both get only a few minutes of screen time.

Jacob was assigned this mission by Garshaw ('The Tok'ra'). Selmac requested the assignment to allow Jacob an opportunity to reconcile with his son, Mark (see 'Cold Lazarus'). Jacob has been estranged from his son for years. Mark even refused to take Sam's calls or to visit Jacob when he was on his deathbed; something that hurt Jacob deeply.

**CAST AND CREW COMMENTS** 'Normally in the course of a show you start with a bible. As the show broadens, the stories lead to new paths,' noted Don Davis. 'Characters develop [and] the creative team want to explore new avenues. Art is not static. It moves. Every episode that's filmed opens up new possibilities. The writers have a need to express themselves and explore further.'

**DID YOU KNOW?** The scope and flashlight arrangement on the MP5s are police SWAT configuration, not military. The radios that SG-1 carry are commercially available civilian ones with a range of only a mile or so. They certainly couldn't work from underground caverns to the surface, or from ground to orbit.

# 47 FAIR GAME

US Transmission Date: 9 Jul 1999
UK Transmission Date: 6 Oct 1999
Writer: Robert C Cooper
Director: Martin Wood
Cast: Teryl Rothery (Dr Janet Fraiser), Jacqueline Samuda (Nirrti),[55] Ron Halder (Cronus), Vince Crestejo (Yu), Laara Sadiq (Technician), Michael David Simms (Secretary), TM Sandulak (Sgt Ziplinski), Dan Shea (Sgt Siler)[56]

> Thor tells Jack that the System Lords plan to attack Earth and offers his help in negotiating a peace treaty. Three System Lords attend. These are Yu, Nirrti and Cronus - the Goa'uld responsible for killing Teal'c's father. They agree to Asgard proposals on condition that Earth gives up its Stargate. But when Cronus is attacked, Teal'c is blamed and the two remaining Goa'uld vow total war.

**THE WIT AND WISDOM OF JACK O'NEILL** The presence of Yu provides Jack with the opportunity for a bunch of delicious puns. When Daniel tells SG-1 about some of Yu's more respectable achievements, Jack notes: 'Thank you'. And, on meeting the Goa'uld himself: 'Hello, Yu.'

**SAM'S TRAUMATIC LIFE** How ironic that Sam is the one to save Cronus's life, as she believes it was Cronus from whom Jolinar was fleeing and who sent the Ashrak to kill her.

· · · · · · · · · · · · · · · · · · · · · · · · · · · · · · · · · · · · · · · · · · · · ·

55 Jacqueline Samuda's official website spells the character name 'Nyerti'.
56 Uncredited.

**ORIGINS OF THE SPECIES** The Goa'uld are a relatively minor concern to the Asgard. According to Thor, the Asgard have an enemy in their home galaxy far worse than the Goa'uld (see 'Nemesis'). This seems to contradict Gairwyn's assertion that the Asgard are at war with the Goa'uld ('Thor's Chariot'). In keeping with the treaty, the Asgard allow the Goa'uld access to the Passage of Nilor, a strategically valuable sector of space.

The System Lords, Teal'c notes, reluctantly band together to defend Goa'uld territory against outside threats such as the Asgard and the Reetou ('Show and Tell'). However, they still battle amongst themselves for control of their own domains.

An influential System Lord, Cronus probably posed as a Greek god on Earth. The god of fate and time, Cronus was one of the 12 Titans who ascended to supremacy. He became father to Zeus, Hera, Poseidon and Hades.[57] This last relationship may indicate that Cronus has a blood relationship to Sokar, whom he and the other System Lords banished. Teal'c's father was once First Prime of Cronus, but was executed for failing him. For this reason, Teal'c vowed as a child to become one day First Prime of Apophis, Cronus's mortal enemy.

Nirrti is identified with an ancient Hindu goddess of darkness. She was responsible for the death of all but one of the inhabitants of P8X987 ('Singularity'). Like Hathor, Nirrti has also developed stealth technology, giving her the ability to become invisible.

Yu does not appear to have impersonated a god *per-se*, but may have been one of China's earliest emperors, founding the first dynasty. Legend says Yu sprang forth into the world from a dragon's body.[58]

**THE CONSPIRACY STARTS AT CLOSING TIME** Arthur Simms is the Secretary of Defense.

**IN THE INTERESTS OF NATIONAL SECURITY** Earth is now included in the Asgard-Goa'uld *Protected Planets Treaty*. Earth is still susceptible, however, to attack from other Goa'uld who rebel against the System Lords - such as Sokar. Thor says that if a rogue Goa'uld were to attack, the Asgard might not have sufficient resources to stop him.

**POSSIBLE INFLUENCES** *A Matter of Life and Death* (the Heavenly trial scenario). The 1940s song 'The Gang's All Here', *Between the Lines*, the *Friends* episode 'The One Where Everybody Knows' ('She doesn't know we know...') and the originator of psychoanalysis, Sigmund Freud (1856-1939).

**'YOU MIGHT REMEMBER ME FROM...'** Ron Halder was in *Tricks*. Jacqueline Samuda appeared in *One of Our Own*. Michael David Simms played Mitch Reed in *Underworld*

---

57 In Hesiod's *Theogony* Gaia (the earth), daughter of Chaos, bore Uranos (the sky) and then coupled with him to produce twelve Titans, the Cyclopes and the Hekatonchires. Uranos was, however, appalled by his children and locked them in the bowels of the Earth. Gaia persuaded Kronos, the youngest Titan, to castrate his father and seize power. An alternative myth, told by the Orphics, has Chronos ('time') and Adrasteia ('necessity') as the parents of Chaos.

58 The mythical Chinese emperor Shun appointed Yu to control the great flood. For thirteen years Yu laboured until his suffering was rewarded when Shun abdicated and Yu became the first emperor of the Xia dynasty c.2200BC. Yu was said to be half dragon. Another legend says that when working he would turn into a bear. There is a Chinese god named Yu Huang (better known as the Jade Emperor, supreme ruler of Heaven and Earth) but he's a completely separate entity to this Yu. However, see 'Summit'.

and was in *Alien Nation* and *The X-Files*.

**LOGIC, LET ME INTRODUCE YOU TO THIS WINDOW** The SGC computer appears to register the glyphs for an incoming wormhole. We've never seen this before, the implication always having been that they cannot tell where the wormhole comes from, or else they wouldn't have to await the GDO code. If Hammond intended Teal'c to act as Goa'uld liaison, what task was he going to assign to Daniel? It's doubtful that he would have been much use helping Major Castleman with security. The infirmary monitor appears to show brainwaves (see 'In the Line of Duty') but there are no EEG leads on Cronus. The three Goa'uld leave the conference room unescorted. Teal'c wasn't born on Chulak, implying that it's not the only Jaffa homeworld (the opposite to what we had previously been led to believe in, for instance, 'Children of the Gods'). How did the Goa'uld discover that the SGC had located a second Stargate on Earth? When the System Lords Gate to the SGC, the seventh chevron is Earth. It should be the point of origin. Though Earth is finally allowed to keep its Stargate, no mention is made of the treaty provision stipulating that Earth cannot advance technologically to a point where they may become a threat to the Goa'uld (with the definition of 'threat' resting solely with the Goa'uld). Is this now in effect and, if so, how's it going to be enforced? The 'Freudian' feelings that Jack suggests Sam may have for Cronus (hidden hatred) are not, actually, Freudian at all.

**GOA'ULD LEXICON** 'Gonach!' is an insult of some sort.

**QUOTE/UNQUOTE** Jack, on the Asgard: 'I've seen your work. It's great!'

Thor: 'I have been instructed by the Asgard High Council to leave Earth's orbit.' Jack: 'And that's, what, in line with your policy of limited benevolence?'

Daniel, as Nirrti is dragged off by her fellow System Lords: 'Boy, is she gonna get it!'

**NOTES** 'Did this get outta hand?' A thoroughly sharp piece of *realpolitik* as the SGC find out, to their cost, the wrath that messing with *The Big Boys* can bring down upon their house. A gritty revenge-saga with a cool subplot for Anderson. (Watching Jack's interaction with Thor is *always* worth the price of the DVD.) Robert Cooper, what a *star*.

Jack considers Daniel to be an extremely educated and articulate man. Daniel can, Jack continues, really grovel when he has to. Sam is promoted to the rank of major. Thor says that Asgard ships have never been detected in orbit around Earth. The Goa'uld healing device from 'Thor's Chariot' is used by Sam to heal Cronus.

**DID YOU KNOW?** Teryl Rothery believes that *SG-1*'s fans 'love the action as that's what the show is about. But you can't take away from the fact you have great characters and [the fans] care about these people. We're lucky to have this fanbase.'

# 48 LEGACY

US Transmission Date: 16 Jul 1999
UK Transmission Date: 13 Oct 1999

Writer: Tor Alexander Valenza
Director: Peter DeLuise
Cast: Kevin McNulty (Everett Rothwell), Teryl Rothery (Dr Janet Fraiser), Eric Schneider (Dr MacKenzie), Michael Shanks (Ma'chello)

SG-1 discover a room containing the corpses of a group of Goa'uld who challenged the System Lords. One holds a tablet which Daniel unwisely touches. He begins to suffer nightmarish hallucinations. Medical tests indicate schizophrenia. Daniel hears the voice of Ma'chello, declaring death to the Goa'uld, and realises that he has been infected by a deadly parasite that is also killing Teal'c. But will anyone believe him?

**ORIGINS OF THE SPECIES** The Tok'ra aren't the only Goa'uld who oppose the System Lords. The Linvris were a small group of nine Goa'uld who challenged their dominance. SG-1 find that the tablet in the Linvris chamber is similar to one found on Argos ('Brief Candle'). This is a data storage device, which requires a supplementary hand-unit (henceforth referred to as a PTD - Page Turning Device).

Ma'chello's creations do not kill the human host of a Goa'uld - only the parasite itself. The lives of Daniel, Jack and Janet were, therefore, threatened because without the presence of a Goa'uld the devices caused them insanity. Teal'c's life was at risk because the device attacked not him, but his symbiont, which serves as his immune system. The devices leave the body through the ear once the presence of a unique protein marker created by the death of the Goa'uld is detected. They can be deceived into leaving before the symbiont is dead, presumably, by injecting the victim with the blood proteins of someone who once carried a Goa'uld (as long as the Goa'uld died within the body and was absorbed). It doesn't leave a protein marker unless it has fully blended with the host body. Jack, for instance, was implanted with a symbiont that died before blending ('Into the Fire') and thus did not leave him with the marker that Jolinar left Sam ('In the Line of Duty').

The Goa'uld dialect used by the Linvris was akin to Latin.

**THE CONSPIRACY STARTS AT CLOSING TIME** The SGC has a medical containment unit, and a psychiatrist on staff who monitors the effects of Gate travel, Dr MacKenzie (previously seen in 'Fire and Water'). Fifty-three percent of SGC personnel have a history of headaches.

As Daniel notes, it's odd (not to mention, disturbing) that MacKenzie and Janet so quickly jump to the conclusion that he's a schizophrenic. Given the nature of SG-1's lifestyle - not to mention the numerous previous experiences of strange medical conditions induced by alien technology (see 'The Broca Divide', 'Brief Candle', 'Fire and Water', 'Hathor', 'Need', 'Bane', 'The Fifth Race', 'Holiday', 'Seth') one would expect them to be a bit more open to extreme possibilities. Quite apart from the fact that *something* weird medically always seems to happen to Daniel roughly once or twice a year...

**POSSIBLE INFLUENCES** *Altered States, The Lord of the Rings* ('the nine'), *The Quatermass Experiment, The Lion, The Witch and the Wardrobe, Poltergeist,* the *Buffy* episode 'I Only Have Eyes For You', *Jacob's Ladder, Repulsion, Scream and Scream Again* and *Tales That Witness Madness*. This sees the series' first reference to Jesus - as an exclamation of surprise by Daniel.

**LOGIC, LET ME INTRODUCE YOU TO THIS WINDOW** Ma'chello's planet, previously P3W924 in

SEASON 3

'Holiday', is designated P3C599 here. Is the psychiatric hospital exclusively for disturbed former-SGC members? There doesn't seem to be any security concern about nurses and attendants hearing tales of space-travel and aliens. Perhaps it's assumed that the staff will think Daniel is delusional? Did someone shave Daniel between the time that SG-1 visited and when Daniel convinces MacKenzie to call Jack? With SG-1's track record to date, one would think they would have better contamination facilities. Why is Jack inside the hazmat room with Sam and Janet instead of in the observation booth with Daniel? When SG-7 return, chevron seven lights up at the same time as chevron one. In the infirmary, Daniel's hand is on his forehead in close-up, but lying on his chest when Jack sits down. Sam doesn't balance the centrifuge when she places the yellow-topped tube into it. Intramuscular injections would not work as quickly as depicted here. All of that stuff about how to separate proteins from blood is scientifically implausible. Migraines are a first sign of schizophrenia, notes Janet. True, but they're also the first signs of, you know, *migraines*. Teal'c says that the Goa'uld are immune to bio-warfare. Something of a sweeping generalisation considering the subsequent events of 'Summit' and 'Last Stand'.

**QUOTE/UNQUOTE** Daniel: 'I'm just making sure you weren't figments of my imagination.'

Jack; 'I'd like to apologise in advance for anything I may say or do that could be construed as offensive as I slowly go *nuts*!'

**NOTES** 'You gotta admit, there's some holes in your theory.' Well-acted, if somewhat logically-flawed. (A constant problem for SF, generally, is the balancing act between stuff happening because it should and because it *can*!) Michael Shanks gets the acting awards this week (with an honourable mention for Teryl Rothery and her, ahem, interestingly *pornographic* reaction to alien infestation).

Neither Jack nor Daniel believes in ghosts. Of the two, Daniel is a better chess player. Jack's game is gin-rummy. Daniel has both shampoo and conditioner in his locker. It's been approximately six months since Ma'chello's death ('Holiday') during which time an SG team has returned to Ma'chello's planet and collected his technology, which is stored at Area 51.

**CAST AND CREW COMMENTS** This episode is a favourite of Teryl Rothery: 'We got to see a different side to Fraiser. The first time we see her vulnerable and out of control.'

**DID YOU KNOW?** Michael Shanks acknowledges Richard Dean Anderson's influence on his acting career. When Michael was attending business school at UBC, a friend told him about an acting audition. He wandered down to the beach where they were shooting an episode of *MacGyver*. 'It looked like a lot of fun,' Shanks noted.

'Daniel is a likeable character,' Shanks explained about his alter-ego. 'I admire his naiveté, passion, innocence and curiosity. The writers make Daniel the brunt of violence. He gets beat up a lot, which is because he's a pacifist.'

# 49 LEARNING CURVE

US Transmission Date: 23 Jul 1999

UK Transmission Date: **20 Oct 1999**
Writer: Heather E Ash
Director: Martin Wood
Cast: Teryl Rothery (Dr Janet Fraiser), Brittney Irvin (Merrin), Andrew Airlie (Kalan), Lachlan Murdoch (Tomin), Stephanie Shea (Solen), Diane Stapley (Mrs Struble), Rob Farrell, (SF Guard), Laara Sadiq (Technician), Sarah Goodwill (Student)

SG-1 take part in an exchange with the people of Orban. Jack accompanies a young Orbanian girl, Merrin, and her father, Kalan, to the SGC with a Naqahdah reactor. Merrin volunteers to teach Sam how to build such a device. As Sam and Jack spend more time with her, they become aware that she's not a typical eleven-year-old. Jack defies orders and shows Merrin the value of childhood. Well, he would, wouldn't he?

**THE WIT AND WISDOM OF JACK O'NEILL** Jack: 'Merrin, I understand you're a reactor expert... How old are you?' Merrin: 'I am eleven. How old are you?' Jack: 'So, Merrin, I understand you're a reactor expert...'

And, when looking at a child's portrait of himself: 'I look fat!'

**ORIGINS OF THE SPECIES** The Goa'uld have been on Orban within the past 100 years. The Orbanians may have come from Earth as recently as the eighth century (presumably in ships as both Stargates were buried) at the downfall of Teotihuacán, the 'city of the gods' in pre-Aztec Mexico (which suffered a 'great upheaval' c.750AD). Daniel also finds a symbol of the Aztec goddess of water, Chalchiuhtlicue, amongst Orbanian artefacts.

The Orbanians have accomplished in decades what it took humans over a century to achieve. They acquire this knowledge by selecting children (Urrone) and implanting them with nanites at birth, before their brains fully develop. These act as additional synapses, allowing the child to learn vast amounts of knowledge quickly. When an Urrone reaches approximately 12 years old, its nanites are harvested in the *Averium* ceremony, and one is given to every Orban citizen. The child's knowledge is, thereby, passed on, but the Urrone themselves are left in an infantile state. Merrin has studied Naqahdah technology for 10 years.

**SEX AND DRUGS AND ROCK 'N' ROLL** Half of the interesting things in Sam's life, she notes, didn't happen until she was 15. Though she seems reluctant to discuss them with Merrin.

**THE CONSPIRACY STARTS AT CLOSING TIME** The SGC now has a functioning Naqahdah reactor. The initial tests used up their supply of the mineral.

**POSSIBLE INFLUENCES** An oblique reference to *Doctor Who* ('reversing the polarity') with specific visual links to the stories 'Castrovalva' and 'Logopolis'. Also, the *Star Trek: Voyager* episode 'Innocence'.

**'YOU MIGHT REMEMBER ME FROM...'** Brittney Irvin played Amy in *Wasted*. Ron Farrell was in *She's the One*. Andrew Airlie appeared in *Breaker High* and *The Sausage Factory*. Lachlan Murdoch played Horney in *Cheaters*. Diane Stapley featured in her own TV comedy show in the 1970s.

**BEHIND THE CAMERA** Heather Ash wrote for *Glory Days.*

**LOGIC, LET ME INTRODUCE YOU TO THIS WINDOW** How does Jack manage to get Merrin off the base so quickly? (It happens during the time it takes to make one phone-call.) Teal'c says his larva will die if he doesn't find it a host when it matures. In '1969', he said it would take him over. Merrin asks first for '15 sheets of paper, 48 cm by 23 cm'. Later, she says '43 cm by 28 cm'. The edge of the leaf that Merrin painted before being stopped by Jack has disappeared from her final painting. Each of the millions of nanites in Merrin contains all the knowledge the Urrone gains, even though they are acting as the synapses in different parts of her brain? Most theories state that memory and knowledge are distributed across networks of neurons, not resident in single ones. If past Urrone children cannot accept new nanites, how do they learn to play? And how does Merrin remember what drawing was?

**QUOTE/UNQUOTE** Kalan: 'You claim to love knowledge, yet when you find something you do not like you demand we change to please you.'

**NOTES** 'When you say he gave you his knowledge, you meant literally.' An intriguing plot, with valid motives. But it fudges the central dilemma with a *nothing* ending. This suggests that an entire race has been taught the value of childhood. Okay, but to what end, exactly? Will that help them fight the Goa'uld? Message episodes can be fun if the message, itself, is worthwhile. But *this* seems to exist purely to demonstrate Jack's anti-square credentials.

Dogs are Jack's favourite people. (This is actually a quote from Anderson's biography in the *Stargate SG-1* press pack.) He speaks Italian. Sort-of. Whilst Sam and Janet were stuck in school learning to be doctors, Jack was out having fun. Apparently. Sam mentioned that she had *no* artistic talent whatsoever in 'Singularity', and she proves it again here. Cassandra is now in junior high school.

**CAST AND CREW COMMENTS** This episode is a particular favourite of Brad Wright. 'The third year was a diverse one,' he notes. 'I thought we started the season without some of the momentum we had at the end of the second year. However, we quickly got our stride. I especially liked 'Learning Curve'.'

**DID YOU KNOW?** 'I do a lot of reading - newspapers, *Discovery Magazine, New Scientist* and the like,' noted Heather Ash when asked where her ideas came from. 'What I really like about science fiction and what I do is when the gadgetry and the human merge. The idea of discovering new technological things in the future and how we would react is fascinating. In 'Learning Curve' it was the nanites in the brain. The plot came from an idea, which started when I read certain animals supposedly could learn by eating the brains of other animals.'

# 50 POINT OF VIEW

US Transmission Date: 30 Jul 1999
UK Transmission Date: 27 Oct 1999

Story: Jonathan Glassner, Brad Wright, Robert C Cooper, Tor Alexander Valenza
Teleplay: Jonathan Glassner, Brad Wright
Director: Peter DeLuise
Cast: Jay Acovone (Charles Kawalsky), Peter Williams (Apophis), Teryl Rothery (Dr Janet Fraiser), Tracy Westerholm (SF Guard), Ty Olsson (Jaffa #1), Shawn Reis (Jaffa #2)

Alternate reality versions of Sam Carter and Major Kawalsky are found in Area 51. To transport themselves to our Earth, they used the quantum mirror. The story of *their* reality is horrifying. Jack is dead and Teal'c is the enemy. Alternate-Sam begins to suffer from temporal distortion, a side-effect caused by the mirror. Sam believes that her other self will die unless she returns to her reality.

**THE WIT AND WISDOM OF JACK O'NEILL** 'The combined IQ of Earth might go up a few points having two Carters around.' And, on the Asgard: '*Love* those guys!'

**SAM'S TRAUMATIC ALTERNATE REALITY** Alternate-Sam uses the phrase, 'For crying out loud' during her interrogation. This, of course, is more commonly associated with Jack and indicates her relationship with O'Neill. In the two alternate realities seen, a romance between Sam and Jack is a key part of the differences. (In 'There But For the Grace of God' they were engaged; here, they had been married for a over a year.) Does this suggest that *our* Sam and Jack are hiding something (see 'Divide and Conquer', 'Window of Opportunity')?

**SUICIDE IS PAINLESS** Teal'c demonstrates the lengths he's willing to go for SG-1. Considering his alternate self to be 'the enemy' (and, presumably, incapable of making the same decision he did in rebelling against Apophis), Teal'c effectively kills himself. He justifies his actions, noting that 'ours is the only reality of consequence'.

**THE ALTERNATE REALITY STARTS AT CLOSING TIME** It was Sam, not Daniel, who made the Stargate work four years ago. The Goa'uld, led by Apophis, have started taking over every major city on Earth. The SGA (as they are called) knew of the impending attack six months in advance, but could do nothing to stop it. The SGC's reality was one of only a handful that Alternate-Sam saw which had not been overrun by the Goa'uld. She hypothesises that it's the differences between the parallel universes which contribute to the SGC's survival: Daniel and Teal'c joined the SGC and Sam joined the military. Alternate-Sam was prepared for the temporal entropic cascade failure, but believed it would take years, not days.

The SGA haven't had contact with the Asgard who, in that reality, have the power to resurrect humans (Hammond). The quantum mirror can, seemingly, be used to access a virtually infinite number of realities. The further one turns the dial, the further away the reality will be from our own. In one of the alternate realities that Daniel observes, Sam is still a captain. Hammond orders the mirror destroyed.

**POSSIBLE INFLUENCES** The alternate-reality Apophis and Teal'c have 'evil' facial hair, which may be a reference to Spock's beard in *Star Trek*'s 'Mirror, Mirror' and a famous episode of *Knight Rider*. For more 'evil twins', see 'There But For the Grace of God'. Plus, *Red Dwarf*'s 'Dimension Jump', *Doctor Who*'s 'Mawdryn

Undead' and *Buffy*'s 'The Wish'. Jack describes the Asgard as '*Roswell* grey' (see 'Thor's Chariot'). Not forgetting the *South Park* mirror universe.

**LOGIC, LET ME INTRODUCE YOU TO THIS WINDOW** Like a real mirror, the quantum mirror shows what is behind you in the other reality. So when transported through, you're on the same side of it that you left from. Yet when Daniel and Teal'c go through, they end up standing in the same arrangement (Teal'c on the left, Daniel on the right), but they are now touching it with the opposite hand. Daniel and Hammond are seen in the mirror waiting for Jack. When Jack goes through, however, Sam is where Daniel was. Where did all the girders littering the floor come from? The SGC is pretty much all concrete. How do the Jaffa know to evacuate so quickly when an Asgard ship appears? They start dialling before the ship appears on the monitor. Why is only Alternate-Sam affected by the entropic cascade failure? Why not both Sams? Sam says 'I had a hard time figuring out how to make this work the first time' regarding the Asgard power generator. Jack activated it in 'The Fifth Race'. Daniel recovers from the zat extremely quickly. As Daniel learns how to use the controller, several alternate realities are seen without Jaffa or any sign of damage in the hallway. If they're all fairly close to each other, that implies there was only a small set of circumstances that led to Earth's survival. If the alternate reality SG-1 never travelled to Apophis's ship would they be familiar with zat guns? One of the virtual-reality pods from 'The Gamekeeper' is stored at Nellis. Did SG-1 go back and retrieve it? In the photo that Alternate-Sam brings from alternate-Earth, she appears to have short spiky hair just like our Sam.

**QUOTE/UNQUOTE** Jack, to the Sams: 'For all we know you could be her evil twin. But then we'd be dealing with clichés and you know how I feel about those. No, actually, *you* know how I feel about those.' And: 'It's possible there's an alternate version of myself out there that actually understands what the hell you're talking about.'

**NOTES** 'Anywhere's better than the alternative.' The *It's a Wonderful Life* riff, mined for all it's worth by a production that's starting to have real fun with its expanding universe. 'Point of View' is a confident, articulate, funny vehicle with a plethora of 'nice hair' jokes. Excellent.

Kawalsky considers himself Jack's best friend.

**DID YOU KNOW?** 'We're given a lot of leeway,' cinematographer Peter Woestre notes on the job that he and colleague Jim Menard have. 'We can go almost anywhere we like in terms of the look of the show. We can experiment. The worlds are our oyster.'

## 51 DEADMAN'S SWITCH

US Transmission Date: 6 Aug 1999
UK Transmission Date: 3 Nov 1999
Writer: Robert C Cooper
Director: Martin Wood
Cast: Sam J Jones (Aris Boch), Mark Holden (Korra)

On PJ6877, SG-1 are captured by bounty hunter Aris Boch. He's hunting a Goa'uld who is wanted by Sokar. Boch promises SG-1's freedom in exchange for helping him. When the Goa'uld is captured, however, he reveals that he is a Tok'ra and, if given to Sokar, he may endanger many other operatives.

**ORIGINS OF THE SPECIES** Aris's blood reveals that his species aren't human. Their physical make-up rejects Goa'uld symbionts, making it impossible for them to be used as hosts. The Goa'uld wiped out most of their population because of this, and took the youngest as slaves. Those of Boch's race who were kept alive are addicted to a substance called Roshna, given to them in water by the Goa'uld. After many generations, they cannot live without it. According to Aris, the Goa'uld killed his wife and imprisoned his son in a Naqahdah mine. Korra, however, casts doubt on this. Boch possesses a device that tracks Naqahdah, enabling him to monitor anyone within range who carries Goa'uld weapons or other Naqahdah-based technology.

Goa'uld cargo ships travel at approximately twice the speed of light.

**I FOUGHT THE LAW (AND THE LAW WON)** Sizeable bounties exist on Teal'c and Sam and an only slightly smaller one on Jack. Daniel however, could be traded for only a day's rations, Aris speculates. He later tells Daniel that, actually, he is just as wanted as the others because he was the one who opened the Stargate. Strangely, this doesn't make Daniel feel any better.

**POSSIBLE INFLUENCES** *Adam Strange*, *The Punisher*, *Judge Dredd*, *Lobo* and other intergalactic bounty-hunter stories. *Beetlejuice* is mentioned. The cloaked ship suggests *The Arabian Knights*.

**'YOU MIGHT REMEMBER ME FROM...'** Sam Jones was Flash in *Flash Gordon* and appeared in *10*, *Baywatch*, *Psychotic* and *Hard Vice*.

**LOGIC, LET ME INTRODUCE YOU TO THIS WINDOW** If the SGC believed that the UAV was downed by the Goa'uld then why have SG-1 been sent to a potentially occupied world without another SG-team as backup? Where did Aris have the zat concealed? Why doesn't Jack use the zat to open the door? Teal'c says that the ship should have three crystals and that removing one will disarm it. Aris returns, replaces the crystal and says that it's now *armed*. Later, he says that the ship blew up after he removed a crystal. Daniel has a hard time unholstering his gun at Aris' request, then he trips over some gear as they prepare to enter the tel'tak. Aris pushes the bottom right button first when opening the door, but when he opens it later, he starts with the top left one. How did Boch, a member of a slave race, become a bounty hunter?

**GOA'ULD LEXICON** 'Mik'ta' is a Goa'uld slang word, equivalent to 'ass'. 'Tacs' are automatic remote heat-seeking weapons. The name is short for 'tacluchnatagamuntoron'.

**QUOTE/UNQUOTE** Aris: 'If you don't mind treating my wound.' Daniel: 'I'm an archaeologist.' Aris: 'I know, but you're also a doctor?' Daniel: '*Of archaeology*.'

Aris: 'My word is good on over 2,000 planets.' Jack; 'There are *billions*.'

**NOTES** 'Well, fancy that, we're famous.' An annoying sudden change of character motivation spoils what had been a pretty entertaining episode. It's interesting to see, for once, someone who is several paces ahead of SG-1 in all aspects. Fluid direction and a witty script all promise much, but that naff ending is a bitter disappointment.

**CAST AND CREW COMMENTS** Amanda Tapping suffered another on-location mishap during the filming of this episode, twisting her ankle. 'Good job these boots give lots of support,' she noted.

**DID YOU KNOW?** The part of Korra was played by Mark Holden, a British ex-policeman from Nailsea, Somerset who emigrated to Canada to become an actor. 'Often,' he noted, 'you arrive as a guest artiste and feel very much a spare-part, but not on this show. Everyone takes care to ensure you're included.'

## 52 DEMONS

US Transmission Date: 13 Aug 1999
UK Transmission Date: 10 Nov 1999
Writer: Carl Binder
Director: Peter DeLuise
Cast: David McNally (Simon), Alan C Peterson (Canon), Laura Mennell (Mary), Richard Morwick (Unas), John R Taylor (Elder), Christopher Judge (Voice of Unas)

> SG-1 arrive at a medieval village and free Mary, a young woman tied to a stake. Her guardian, Simon, explains that Mary is a sacrifice to the demon that plagues their village. SG-1 recognise the demon as an Unas and plot to destroy it, but the village Canon pronounces SG-1 evil and condemns them to be sacrificed.

**THE WIT AND WISDOM OF JACK O'NEILL** Jack: 'Do you read the Bible?' Teal'c: 'It is a significant part of your Western culture. Have you not read the Bible, O'Neill?' Jack: 'Yeah. Not all of it. Actually, I'm listening to it on tape. Don't tell me how it ends.'

And, to the Unas: 'You got the padre in your pocket, the hours are good. You probably get all the chicks, right?'

**ORIGINS OF THE SPECIES** Sokar still has Unas in his service ('Serpent's Song'). The Unas are a species, not just one creature (as Teal'c led Jack to believe in 'Thor's Hammer'). They served as Goa'uld hosts before humans were discovered on Earth by Ra.

**THE CRUCIFIXION STARTS AT THE LAST SUPPER** This mission represents the first sign of Christianity encountered in hundreds of missions. A plaque in the village is inscribed with a middle-English derivative of the Catholic Prayer for Suffering Souls. The villagers refer to the Stargate as the 'Circle of Darkness'.

**POSSIBLE INFLUENCES** *Austin Powers* (Jack's 'Dr Evil' impression), *Monty Python and the Holy Grail, Mark of the Devil, Matthew Hopkins - Witchfinder General, Blood on Satan's Claw, Hex, The Crucible, Captain Kronos: Vampire Hunter* (in fact, most of Hammer's late 60s output like *Twins of Evil* with Alan Peterson in the Peter Cushing/savant-monster role), *The Defiant Ones, Cool Hand Luke, Catch-22, The Mummy,* Geoffrey Chaucer (1340-1400) and loads of Biblical lore (David and Goliath, the resurrection, The Lord's Prayer).

**'YOU MIGHT REMEMBER ME FROM...'** Alan Peterson played the sheriff in *Shanghai Noon.* Laura Mennell was in *I've Been Waiting for You.* Rick Morwick was a stuntman on *Red Scorpion 2.*

**BEHIND THE CAMERA** Carl Binder wrote *Pocahontas* and for *Dr Quinn Medicine Woman.*

**LOGIC, LET ME INTRODUCE YOU TO THIS WINDOW** In 'Serpent's Song', Daniel discusses how Unas and human hosts coexisted on Earth. So why does Jack still believe that the Unas from 'Thor's Hammer' was the only one? After Teal'c apparently drowns, we see the Canon and the men retreat. So who dragged Teal'c's body out of the lake and brought it to the village? How often does the Unas come? He took Mary's parents last year. Based on the apparent size of the settlement, if he takes five adults every year, they'd have been wiped out long ago. Daniel supposes that Sokar took the people from medieval Europe through the Antarctic Gate. Impossible, as that has been buried even longer than the Giza Gate.[59] Why, anyway, would a Goa'uld take humans all the way to Antarctica when there are other populated planets to get slaves from? Haven't these people experienced chickenpox before (they seem very unfamiliar with it)? If not, from whom did Mary catch it (given that it's a contagion)?

**QUOTE/UNQUOTE** Daniel, on trepanning: 'They'd drill a hole in the person's head... Evil spirits are released, saving the person from eternal damnation.' Jack: 'Thus *saving* the person?' Daniel: 'They didn't call them the Dark Ages because it was dark.' Jack: 'You'd think these people never saw a guy rise from the dead.'

**NOTES** 'He isn't playing god, he's playing the devil.' Strange one, this. The script plays with potentially explosive subject matter, particularly the Teal'c subplot: the lad makes the greatest comeback since Lazarus. At once both virulently anti Christian piety and hypocrisy and yet, also, respectfully New Testament in its depiction of Simon's faith. 'Demons', at the very least, tackles the problem of Christian 'mythology' in the, essentially humanist, *Stargate*-universe without treading on too many toes. That's good. But, by trying to offend no-one, of course, they also end up truly satisfying no-one either. It's a good attempt, however, at something conceptually tricky and ethically dangerous.

• • • • • • • • • • • • • • • • • • • • • • • • • • • • • • • • • • • • • • • • • • •

59 Producer Joe Mallozzi has noted in an online interview: 'The Egyptian gate was buried when Egypt was a dominant civilisation on Earth; the Antarctic gate was presumably buried no later than the last time Antarctica didn't have an arctic climate, which puts it in the millions-of-years-ago club. Just how did the folks from 'Red Sky' or 'Demons' get taken from Earth? [These] are questions we'll be answering in due time.'

'All that is provided by "Demons" is the return of a rather uninspiring old enemy and a look at how unpleasant the Middle Ages were,' noted *Xposé*. 'It's not enough to gain this viewer's enthusiasm.'

**DID YOU KNOW?** Amanda Tapping has an unusual ambition. 'I want to be in *Coronation Street*,' the actress has claimed. 'I'm totally addicted to it and I want to come to England and appear as a long-lost Canadian cousin or something - anything - so long as I get to stand at the bar in the Rovers Return.'

# 53 RULES OF ENGAGEMENT

US Transmission Date: 20 Aug 1999
UK Transmission Date: 17 Nov 1999
Writer: Terry Curtis Fox
Director: William F Gereghty
Cast: Peter Williams (Apophis), Teryl Rothery (Dr Janet Fraiser), Aaron Craven (Captain Rogers), Dion Johnstone (Captain Nelson), Jesse Moss (Lieutenant Hibbard), Josh Byer (Sergeant)

SG-1 arrive off-world in the midst of a battle. But the mystery SG-team to whom they give assistance turn their weapons on SG-1. They find themselves in a training camp where the leader, Captain Rogers, recognises Teal'c as Jaffa. The soldiers' standing orders, Rogers explains, are to practice battle scenarios awaiting the return of Apophis, when they will be used in a stealth attack on Earth.

**THE WIT AND WISDOM OF JACK O'NEILL** Rogers: 'You're all casualties until 1400 hours.' Jack: 'Would that be daylight savings, or standard?' And: 'The whole "invasion of the Tau'ri" idea has been cancelled due to ... rain.'

**ORIGINS OF THE SPECIES** It's common practice amongst the Goa'uld to use humans as fodder during battles. The Rules of Engagement are the code of battle during a Jaffa's training. The Final Challenge is the day in a warrior's training when first blood is shed and the games become real. The Goa'uld wish only the strong to survive.

**THE CONSPIRACY STARTS AT CLOSING TIME** The SGC are experimenting with interfacing Goa'uld and Earth technology (see 'Tangent'). For unknown reasons (propaganda, maybe?) they videotaped Apophis's death ('Serpent's Song').

**IN THE INTERESTS OF NATIONAL SECURITY** The NID and Maybourne are mentioned. (Jack initially believes the training camp may be their work.)
    SG-11 were declared missing in action eight months ago on P89534. They were, actually, captured by Apophis, brought to the training planet, forced to reveal some minor details of indigenous crops in North America, and then murdered.

**POSSIBLE INFLUENCES** *The Battle Of The Bulge* (fifth columnists in fake uniforms), *Doctor Who*'s 'The War Games', *Psi-Warriors*, *The Eagle Has Landed*, *The Simpsons* ('Mmm ... Tuna!'). There's an allusion to John Lennon and Yoko Ono's 'Happy Xmas (War is Over)'.

**'YOU MIGHT REMEMBER ME FROM...'** Dion Johnstone was in *Josie and the Pussycats*. Jesse Moss played Jason in *Ginger Snaps*.

**LOGIC, LET ME INTRODUCE YOU TO THIS WINDOW** A general one not just applicable to this episode: how do SG-teams know the Stargate address to Earth from any given planet? Is it always the exact reverse of the address *to* the planet? The only alternative would be if it's the same first six symbols each time with a different seventh for the point of origin. That would make sense, but how does the dialler determine the unique seventh symbol for each world? Most of the glyphs that we see are constellations, not individual planets.

**GOA'ULD LEXICON** 'Shal'kek' means 'leave us'. 'Intar' are, basically, training stun-guns. A 'Vo'cume' is an orb-like holographic communication device.

**QUOTE/UNQUOTE** Teal'c: 'This is Colonel O'Neill. He is much-loved by Apophis.'

Teal'c: 'They are intar.' Jack: 'Short for?' Teal'c: 'Intar.'

Jack: 'Dr Fraiser says you haven't been eating.' Rogers: 'It's poison.' Jack: 'It's hospital food, *of course* it is.'

**NOTES** 'No rank is above strict adherence to the Rules of Engagement.' One of the series' finest pre-title sequences. Thereafter it gets a bit bogged down in semantics and rhetoric; but it's an interesting idea to have an, essentially, antiwar episode in a military-SF series.

Rogers's true name is Rophiapgisy. He and his fellow recruits have been on the planet for five 'cycles' (which Carter notes was approximately when SG-1 blew up Apophis's ship - see 'Within the Serpent's Grasp' - so, about a year and a half then).

**DID YOU KNOW?** 'I'm here at 6.30am meeting with the director,' Michael Greenburg noted, explaining a typical day in the life of an executive producer. 'We talk about the day's work, and then I'm managing the hundred departments it takes to do this type of show.'

# 54   FOREVER IN A DAY

US Transmission Date: 8 Oct 1999
UK Transmission Date: 24 Nov 1999
Writer: Jonathan Glassner
Director: Peter DeLuise
Cast: Vaitiare Bandera (Sha're), Teryl Rothery (Dr Janet Fraiser), Erick Avari (Kasuf), Jason Schombing (Robert Rothman)

During a rescue mission on P8X873, Daniel finds himself alone with Amaunet, who is intent on killing him. Teal'c prevents this, destroying the Goa'uld and its host. Daniel, distraught over his wife's death, resigns from the SGC. When Sha're appears to him in a dream, Daniel finds he must overcome his grief if he is to understand her message.

**THE WIT AND WISDOM OF JACK O'NEILL** How he and Kasuf entered Daniel's apartment: 'Got sick of waiting, so I let us in. You need a new lock by the way.'

**ORIGINS OF THE SPECIES** Amaunet returns to Abydos to locate her child. She told Apophis the child was stolen by Heru'ur ('Secrets'), but may have always known it was being kept by the Abydonians, many of whom she kidnapped to hide her true purpose. It's strictly forbidden for two Goa'uld hosts to bear a child (rather than producing Goa'uld larva offspring), indeed it's punishable by death. Each Goa'uld retains the genetic memory of its predecessors; but a Harsesis ('The one who holds the secrets') is a human with this knowledge. Such children are hunted and destroyed by the Goa'uld (see 'Maternal Instinct'). Heru'ur, the son of Ra and Hathor ('Thor's Chariot'), could be a Harsesis. But this probably refers to his symbiont and not his human host (as, for instance, Klorel is described as Apophis's son). The Harsesis of Amaunet has been taken by one of her closest aides to Kheb. In mythology this was where Isis hid Osiris from Set.

The ceremony that Daniel performs for Sha're is an accurate presentation of the ancient Egyptian funerary rite, presided over by the goddess Maat (balance), in which the dead declare their innocence of sin and their heart is weighed against a feather in judgment.

**THE CONSPIRACY STARTS AT CLOSING TIME** Because the Goa'uld ribbon-device is controlled in part by the emotion of the user, the host can have some influence over it. The device can, as this episode proves, be used to transmit detailed thoughts from the host to the victim. How these manifest themselves in the victim's mind may be subjective - interpreted as dreams or hallucinations. The device uses a modified version of the power source of a staff weapon, which it channels through amplification crystals.

**IN THE INTERESTS OF NATIONAL SECURITY** Daniel is in yet another new apartment (see 'Holiday'). He tells Hammond it was a free country last time he checked.

**POSSIBLE INFLUENCES** *Star Wars* ('Somewhere far away'), *Star Trek: The Next Generation*'s 'The Inner Light', *Quantum Leap*. Jack calls Rothman 'Bruce Jenner' (after the 1976 Olympic decathlon champion).

**'YOU MIGHT REMEMBER ME FROM...'** Jason Schombing appeared in *Whacked*, *The Whole Shebang*, *3 Ninjas Kick Back* and *Dirty Work*.

**LOGIC, LET ME INTRODUCE YOU TO THIS WINDOW** Why doesn't Teal'c just wound Amaunet? Daniel still has a swipe-card for the Gateroom after he's quit. He receives only a light forehead burn from the ribbon device. Daniel's birthday is July 8 (probably 1965). The events in '1969' took place in August, when Daniel said he was four and a half. Jack remembers Daniel saying: 'The SGC may be the single more important human endeavour for the future of mankind'. Actually, it was Sam who said this, in 'The Nox'. The box that Daniel carries to the elevator is obviously not the one he was packing earlier. When Sam blows up the Jaffa gun-post you can still see the stuntman standing after the first explosion and before the second.

**QUOTE/UNQUOTE** Daniel: 'I speak for Sha're who can no longer speak for herself. I had spoken no lies nor acted with deceit. I was once possessed by a demon who did these things against my will. The demon is gone and now, I am without sin.'

Daniel, to Rothman on Jack: 'He's just intimidated by you because you're *way* smarter than he is.'

**NOTES** 'Everytime I step through that Gate I was thinking about my wife. Now, everytime I go through it'd just be some *place* where that hope used to be.' Starting like the *SG-1* version of *The Longest Day* (the moment when, literally, *hundreds* of Jaffa come over the hill is breathtaking), 'Forever in a Day' mixes a quest saga with the lyrical theme of redemption. Surreal, in its depiction of Daniel's grief, and truly touching when the going gets tough. A great favourite of this author.

Daniel likes chocolate walnut cookies (hell, who doesn't?). When he was first on Abydos, Sha're saw him writing in his journal and thought that the ball-point pen he was using was magic. He says he's spent half his life studying the history of the written word. Daniel's SG-1 replacement (in his vision, at least) is Robert Rothman, who was Daniel's research assistant when he did his dissertation. He's a smart guy and a two-time college decathlon champion. Jack thinks he's a geek with two left-feet. Much like Daniel.

**CAST AND CREW COMMENTS** 'He's a type of moral conscience for the team,' Michael Shanks notes concerning his *alter ego*. 'He's a person who tries to see outside of the box. He's the naive one, the more innocent one.'

**DID YOU KNOW?** Goa'uld and Tok'ra voices are electronically enhanced in post-production by a method called 'flanging' in which a signal is processed via two conveyance routes, producing a 'shadow' signal slightly out of synch.[60]

# 55   PAST AN D PRESENT

US Transmission Date: 15 Oct 1999
UK Transmission Date: 1 Dec 1999
Writer: Tor Alexander Valenza
Director: William F Gereghty
Cast: Teryl Rothery (Dr Janet Fraiser), Megan Leitch (Ke'ra), Jason Gray-Stanford (Orner), Marya Delver (Mayris), Luisa Cianni (Woman)

> SG-1 discover an industrial society whose inhabitants are suffering from pandemic mass amnesia following an event they call the Vorlix. Their scientist, Ke'ra, returns to Earth with SG-1 hop-

60 The origin of this term is traditionally credited to John Lennon who, when an Abbey Road engineer in the 1960s attempted to explain the science behind the double-tracking process, said in very Jack O'Neill - eyes-glazing-over - moment, 'Fine, just use yer flanger on it...'

ing to find a cure. But as investigations proceed, SG-1 begin to suspect that the truth is more horrible than they could imagine.

**DANIEL'S TRAUMATIC LOVE-LIFE** Struggling with the recent loss of Sha're ('Forever in a Day'), Daniel hops straight into a relationship with Ke'ra, a woman with (literally) no past.

**ORIGINS OF THE SPECIES** Dargol, a chemical pesticide, affected Vyus's environment and caused infertility 20 years ago. Linea (see 'Prisoners') discovered that dargol could slow the ageing process. The Vorlix, which occurred a year ago, caused the entire population to become young and suffer from mass amnesia when the dargol settled between the synapses in the temporal lobes and hippocampus sections of the Vyusans brains. Linea, also a victim of the Vorlix, became Ke'ra, the Minister of Health, Science and Restructuring in the Vyus Transitional Government. Orner's true name is Nodaal. He's been married to Layale for 43 years.

**SEX AND DRUGS AND ROCK 'N' ROLL** Daniel compares the effects of dargol to those of DDT. Since the Vorlix, intimacy has been a taboo on Vyus. People fear they could, having regained their memories, find themselves waking up next to the wrong person.

**POSSIBLE INFLUENCES** Visually, *Star Trek*'s 'Return of the Archons'.

**'YOU MIGHT REMEMBER ME FROM...'** Megan Leitch was Samantha Mulder in *The X-Files* and appeared in *Daydrift* and *Revisited*. Marya Delver played Laurel in *Last Wedding*. Jason Gray-Standford was Ainsley in *A Beautiful Mind*.

**LOGIC, LET ME INTRODUCE YOU TO THIS WINDOW** How could the few drops of the antidote on the slide that Ke'ra stole be enough to cure her (especially after it had already worked on the tissue sample)? A specific point is made concerning the antidote needing to be injected into the carotid. So, even if this was enough, how did she inject it? The two compounds can combine and produce a lethal gas if mixed improperly yet Ke'ra and Janet are not working in a fume-hood under controlled conditions? And both vials and ampoules are kept in the same tray? The SGC let Ke'ra go back and assume that she will never take the antidote, despite their discovery of who she is? That's very trusting. She's only a homicidal maniac after all. Sam says the MALP didn't detect anything, but no MALP is visible in the warehouse. Exiting the Stargate, Daniel takes Ke'ra's arm twice (once at the top of the ramp and again further down). Isn't Sam just happening to find Linea's diary, a ridiculously obvious plot device?

**GOA'ULD LEXICON** 'Teal'c' means 'strength.'

**QUOTE/UNQUOTE** Daniel: 'Who would you trust with your life more than anyone else in the world? Don't worry, I won't be offended if you don't pick me!'
Jack, to Daniel: 'If she remembers who she is, you'll be the first to go.'

**NOTES** 'All you have to do is forget.' Poor Daniel,

he certainly knows how to pick them. 'Past and Present' features splendid characterisation but is castrated by a plodding pace and some painfully obvious twists. A startling lack of charisma in the guest cast doesn't help.

Sam says someone could stand at the DHD pushing glyphs randomly for months and never come across a valid address. The number of possible permutations from a fixed point is 3,010,936,385 ($38^6$+1 given that the origin glyph can only be the seventh).

A friend of Sam's suffered amnesia after a helicopter crash during the Gulf War.

**CAST AND CREW COMMENTS** On the subject of spoilers, Robert Cooper notes that: 'There's a poster in Paul [Mullie's] office, for the German DVD that has 'Forever in a Day' [on it]. In German, the episode's title is 'Sha're is Dead'. That's, kind-of, what's been going on with some of the *TV Guide* blurbs.'

**DID YOU KNOW?** 'We have a lot of weather problems in British Columbia,' notes John Smith. 'We *can* make a rainy day look sunny if we need to, but we often shoot as it is. If you don't back-light rain, you don't see it.'

# 56 JOLINAR'*S* MEMORIE*S*

US Transmission Date: 22 Oct 1999
UK Transmission Date: 8 Dec 1999
Writers: Sonny Wareham, Daniel Stashower
Director: Peter DeLuise
Cast: Peter Williams (Apophis), Carmen Argenziano (Jacob Carter), JR Bourne (Martouf), Daniel Bacon (Technician), Dion Johnstone (Na'onak), Bob Dawson (Bynarr), Peter H Kent (Kin'tac), David Palffy (Sokar), Eli Gabay (Jumar), Tanya Reid (Jolinar), Christine Kennedy (Young Carter), Dillon Moen (Charlie O'Neill),[61] William deVry (Aldwyn)[62]

> Martouf arrives with bad news: Jacob has been captured by Sokar and is imprisoned on Ne'tu - which Sokar has transformed into a, literal, hell. The Tok'ra believe that Sokar plans to attack the other System Lords. A rescue is planned but only one person has escaped from Ne'tu. Jolinar.

**THE WIT AND WISDOM OF JACK O'NEILL** He insists on calling Martouf 'Marty'.
Jacob: 'Are you crazy?' Jack: 'Apparently.'

**SAM'S TRAUMATIC LOVE-LIFE** Martouf uses Tok'ra technology to access Jolinar's memories. It would appear to be a modification of the device used by Hathor in 'Out of Mind'. (At least, it's the same prop, anyway.) However, what Sam recalls are painful remembrances from her own past and dark secrets that Jolinar never wished for Martouf to know while she was imprisoned on Ne'tu. Martouf now knows that she was tortured and escaped by having sex with Bynarr, using his ring transport to Sokar's homeworld, Delmak, and stealing a transport vessel.

Jolinar's recovery was long and painful.

----

61 Character previously played by Kyle Graham in 'Cold Lazarus'.
62 Although credited on screen as appearing in 'Jolinar's Memories' Aldwyn, in fact, doesn't.

137

**ORIGINS OF THE SPECIES** The Tok'ra have learned that Sokar is planning a major offensive against the System Lords. His fleet is ten times larger than the Tok'ra believed and he is poised to attack six enemies within 10 days. A victory would tip the balance of power since the feudal nature of the Goa'uld is the only thing that keeps them in check. Sokar would have a force great enough to rule the galaxy. The moon Ne'tu was once an industrialised colony of Delmak.

Apophis, under the assumed name Na'onak, is serving as first prime of Bynarr, warden of Ne'tu. Perhaps this was his punishment - to spend eternity in hell in service to Sokar. Since Jolinar once tried to overthrow a System Lord and was defeated when Apophis joined the battle ('In the Line of Duty'), it's possible Sokar was the intended victim (as she spent time in his prison). This could imply Apophis and Sokar were once allies.

**SYMPATHY FOR THE DEVIL** When Sokar conquered Delmak, he terraformed its moon to create a biblical representation of hell. He filled the atmosphere with barely-breathable toxins, then blasted holes in the surface to expose the molten core.

**THE CONSPIRACY STARTS AT CLOSING TIME** Transportation rings work like Stargates, transmitting a matter stream over shorter distances. Each ring mechanism has sensors that can locate other rings and detect the co-ordinates to make a connection.

**POSSIBLE INFLUENCES** Conceptually and visually the presentation of hell owes much to *Dante's Inferno*, *Doom*, *Paradise Lost*, the DC comics *The Sandman*, *The Demon* and *Hellblazer*, *Angel Heart* and *Left Hand Drive*. *The Wizard of Oz* ('Certainly not Emerald City', 'We're people of little consequence. Pay no attention to us'). Also, *Doctor Who*'s 'The Creature from the Pit' ('Throw them in ... the Pit').

**'YOU MIGHT REMEMBER ME FROM...'** Eli Gabay was Miguel in *Bordello of Blood*. Christine Kennedy played Melissa in *Air Bud*. Dillon Moen was Trevor in *Fear of Flying*. Tanya Reid appeared in *Hope and Redemption*. David Palffy's movies include *Replicant*, *Full Metal Jacket* and *The Net*. Peter Kent was Ashley in *Dark Angel*. He was also Arnold Schwarzeneggar's stunt double on *True Lies*, *Terminator 2: Judgment Day*, *Total Recall* and many others.

**LOGIC, LET ME INTRODUCE YOU TO THIS WINDOW** A moon's a pretty big place, so how did SG-1 know where to land the pods? Or was the settlement detectable from orbit, despite it being underground? Apparently 'doing covert', as Jack calls it, involves going into a situation with your SGC insignia visible. Sokar allows Bynarr to enter the room with his ribbon device on (whereas Kintac makes a point of noting that Sokar wouldn't allow Apophis to bring weapons in). The SGC don't close the iris until a wormhole is already established. Teal'c can fly the ship 'with great proficiency,' though in 'Within the Serpent's Grasp' he said he was qualified to fly only death gliders. Bynarr's symbiont couldn't heal his eye? Presumably they can heal only organs which are actually still there. (This may also explain the mysterious case of Rya'c's teeth - see 'Family'). How do the rings work between a planet and moon if both are rotating? Can you have such a thing as memories with a third-person narrative?

**GOA'ULD LEXICON** A 'tal'tak' is a transport vessel like the one seen in 'Deadman's Switch'.

**QUOTE/UNQUOTE** Daniel: 'You said hell, right?' Jack: 'Well, I'm gonna end up there sooner or later. Might as well check out the neighbourhood.'

**NOTES** 'To hell with us.' Very talky and slow to begin with, but this picks-up nicely and rattles along to a brilliantly-staged climax. The underworld setting is a visual treat.

Sam's mother died when she was a teenager. She occasionally gets Jolinar's memories in her dreams. The night before Jolinar was captured she and Martouf walked along the ridge of Noctana on a planet with at least two moons.

**DID YOU KNOW?** Christine McQuarrie's favourite costume on the show is the 'red guard' outfit worn by Eli Gabay in this and the next episode. 'Even though he was a background character we were able to go to town on him,' she notes.

# 57 THE DEVIL YOU KNOW

US Transmission Date: 29 Oct 1999
UK Transmission Date: 15 Dec 1999
Writer: Robert C Cooper
Director: Peter DeLuise
Cast: Peter Williams (Apophis), William deVry (Aldwyn), Carmen Argenziano (Jacob Carter), JR Bourne (Martouf), Daniel Bacon (Technician), Dion Johnstone (Na'onak), Bob Dawson (Bynarr)[63], Peter H Kent (Kin'tac), David Palffy (Sokar), Dillon Moen (Charlie O'Neill), Eli Gabay (Jumar), Tanya Reid (Jolinar), Christine Kennedy (Young Carter)

Attempting to rescue Jacob, SG-1 and Martouf are captured by Apophis, determined to use the information they have to overthrow Sokar. With the aid of the Tok'ra memory technology and a hallucinogenic drug, each prisoner is forced to relive painful memories. Meanwhile, an attack by Sokar's forces leaves Teal'c with no choice but to seek Tok'ra help. This involves a bomb that will destroy Ne'tu and his friends along with it.

**THE WIT AND WISDOM OF JACK O'NEILL** After Apophis's eye-rolling speech to the denizens of Ne'tu: 'This experience doesn't seem to have humbled him much.'

**ORIGINS OF THE SPECIES** The Tok'ra are currently located on the planet Vorash. However, Martouf lies that they're actually on Entac, a primitive world, recently conquered by Sokar. No weapons are capable of penetrating the shields of a Goa'uld mothership. Aldwyn's orders from the High Council are to launch a weapon at the core of Ne'tu, causing a chain reaction within 12 minutes, that will destroy the moon as well as Sokar's ship in orbit.

63 Appears only as a corpse.

**SEX AND DRUGS AND ROCK 'N' ROLL** The 'Blood of Sokar' is a powerful narcotic that induces very realistic hallucinations. 'They gave me something that reminded me of the 70s,' notes a very spaced-out Jack.

**THE REGRET STARTS AT CLOSING TIME** Sam's mother died in a car accident. Because Jacob was late and did not pick her up, she took a cab, which crashed. This is, seemingly, the event that tore Mark and Jacob apart (see 'Seth'). When forced to reflect on her past, Sam notes that if her father had not come to apologise to her on a particular day, she would've gone on hating the military and never joined up.

Jack never allowed Charlie to play with guns. Two weeks after a disagreement about a water pistol, Charlie accidentally shot himself (see 'Stargate', 'Cold Lazarus').

**POSSIBLE INFLUENCES** *Rosemary's Baby* ('This is not real'), *An American Werewolf in London* (It's that dream within a dream idea again.)

**'YOU MIGHT REMEMBER ME FROM...'** William de Vry played Joshua Doors in *Earth: Final Conflict*.

**LOGIC, LET ME INTRODUCE YOU TO THIS WINDOW** How does Kintac know that Daniel is concealing something? How did Apophis make Martouf see Sam as Rosha after he removed the memory device? Sokar intends to brand Apophis with his seal, but Bynarr wasn't, seemingly. The memory device doesn't leave a mark when removed. Daniel recovers from the Blood of Sokar more quickly than the others. Teal'c says he has 'entered hyperspeed' rather than hyperspace (see 'Enemies'). How did Sokar learn of Amaunet's death? It was he who told Apophis, seemingly. Apophis has also learned of the nonagression treaty between the System Lords and Earth ('Fair Game'), though that's probably universal common knowledge. How does Apophis insert himself into a memory so that he can guide it? Apophis (appearing to Daniel as Jack) says a Harsesis carries the knowledge of the Goa'uld who fathered him. This differs from Teal'c's observations in 'Forever and a Day'.

**QUOTE/UNQUOTE** Daniel: 'Your mate Amaunet is dead. Sorry to ruin your day. No, actually ... I'm not.'

**NOTES** 'You will be the means by which I reclaim my rightful power and position.' A suitably intense conclusion with lots of pyrotechnics and action. The final escape is, perhaps, a touch too easy, but the Apophis subplot is great.

Jack likes iced tea and air conditioning, he says. Sam has some leave due and Jacob suggests they go on a vacation to Alaska. Teenage Sam had a poster of Mars on her bedroom wall and owned several teddy bears. Martouf has endured torture before. When intercepting the matter stream from a ring transport, a ship must come to a complete stop. Otherwise, part of the stream may be missed, killing those *en route*.

**CAST AND CREW COMMENTS** 'The visual effects people and the directors, particularly Martin Wood and Peter DeLuise, are amazing in what they do on a week-to-week basis,' Robert Cooper proudly notes. 'You write it on the page and in your wildest dreams you couldn't imagine it coming off the way it does. It amazes me when

I see it all come together.'

**DID YOU KNOW?** Some of the walls of the Tok'ra base are actually hay bails painted silver.

## 58 FOOTHOLD

US Transmission Date: 5 Nov 1999
UK Transmission Date: 5 Jan 2000
Writer: Heather E Ash
Director: Andy Mikita
Cast: Teryl Rothery (Dr Janet Fraiser), Tom McBeath (Colonel Harry Maybourne), Colin Cunningham (Major Davis), Colin Lawrence (Sergeant Warren), Tracy Westerholm (Surveillance SF), Dan Shea (Sgt Siler), Biski Gugushe (SF Guard), Richard Leacock (Colonel Brogan), Alex Zahara (Alien Leader/Alien #1), Dion Johnstone (Alien #2)

> Returning from a mission, SG-1 learn that part of the SGC has been sealed due to a chemical leak. During routine medical examinations, Janet injects SG-1 with a sedative, rendering them unconscious. Teal'c and Sam eventually escape and realise that they cannot trust anyone in the SGC and must seek help from outside in order to save Earth from invasion.

**THE WIT AND WISDOM OF JACK O'NEILL** To Janet: 'How's a needle in my butt gonna get water out of my ears?' And, to the nurse: 'Listen, really *jam it in* this time, okay?'

**ORIGINS OF THE SPECIES** Based on the conversation that Teal'c overhears, the aliens are from another galaxy (Frasier says the Goa'uld are 'the dominant parasitical species of *this* galaxy') and are searching for a new home. Their infiltration of the SGC is to evaluate Earth's potential before invasion. They hid their activities by closing off Level 23 through causing a leak of tetrachloroethylene, a gas which causes hallucinations and paranoid delusions. It's likely that the aliens didn't replace every person at the SGC. Some of the soldiers that Teal'c subdues have human blood. In addition, the man who discovers the elevator operator unconscious checked for his cloaking device - presumably to determine whether he was a human or an alien. Replacing the base officers, it would be easy to maintain the deception without replacing everyone. The alien cloaking technology does not work when the wearer is dead.

**THE CONSPIRACY STARTS AT CLOSING TIME** All teams returning through the Stargate will be exposed to a high-frequency harmonic blast to compromise the cloaking technology. P3X18, where SG-6 were first replaced, has been locked out of the SGC dialling programme.

**MILITARY INTELLIGENCE?** Sam meets Maybourne at The Old Bailiff Café outside NID HQ in Washington, DC. Harry makes a colossal mistake in not following procedure when Sam informs him of a "foothold" situation and he, unwittingly, returns her to the aliens. But he redeems himself later and Jack makes the effort to thank him.

SEASON 3

**IN THE INTERESTS OF NATIONAL SECURITY** Sam notes that the SGC was designed to keep people out, not in. After the aliens took over the facility, the alien posing as Hammond asked Major Davis to come to Cheyenne Mountain. Presumably, the Pentagon was the aliens' next goal.

**POSSIBLE INFLUENCES** *Invasion of the Bodysnatchers*, *The Man Who Haunted Himself*, *Strange Invaders*, *Invasion*, *Doctor Who*'s 'The Faceless Ones' and 'The Android Invasion', *Die Hard*, *All the President's Men*, *The Manchurian Candidate* and *The Thing*. Also, *The X-Files* episode 'Jose Chung's *From Outer Space*' ('Yeh, that's an alien all right'). Jack refers to musical comedy star Ethel Merman (1908-84).

**BEHIND THE CAMERA** Andy Mitika was assistant director on *Portraits of a Killer*.

**LOGIC, LET ME INTRODUCE YOU TO THIS WINDOW** Tetrachloroethylene is a substance used in dry cleaning machines. It doesn't generally cause paranoid delusions. When Daniel and Jack are in the Gateroom, they're dressed as they were in the infirmary. So, how does the alien camouflage device manufacture civilian clothes for them when they're off base? When did Sam have time to get her leather jacket? Why didn't Sam have a doctor in DC check to see if she was suffering from tetrachloroethylene exposure? Why does Sam take the camouflage device off once she finds the right tone? Why do the aliens evacuate so quickly, even though they are still heavily armed? The same service shaft hatch seen in 'A Matter of Time' is used to enter the SCG, but now it has an interior ladder. (Cromwell's men had to lower by rope in the previous story.) What would Sam and Maybourne have done if the pilot had been an alien? Wouldn't it be easy for the aliens to change the frequency used by their cloaking technology, rendering Sam's tone ineffective? Maybourne informs the meeting that the alien impersonating Daniel has died. They must know this already since Daniel's *in* the meeting. (If the alien hadn't died, our Daniel would still be unconscious, surely?)

**QUOTE/UNQUOTE** Sam: 'Maybourne, you're an idiot every day of the week. Why couldn't you have just taken one day off?'

**NOTES** 'Where's the real Daniel? Is he still alive?' A great walloping slab of paranoid, *The X-Files*-like nonsense that's, again, logically flawed but *masses* of fun. Just don't think about it too much or it'll comes to pieces in your hands. Best bit: The sinister little sneers Teryl Rothery gives, firstly when sticking a needle in Carter's bum and then, later, announcing they're going to start "experimenting" on Teal'c.

**CAST AND CREW COMMENTS** '*Stargate* was my first foray into science fiction,' noted Andy Mitika. 'The biggest challenges early on were the technical ones related to special effects and the animatronic devices we use.' Plus after years as an assistant director and production manager, his first day in the directing chair was nerve-wracking. 'Imagine showing up on the set that first day and having 50 people look at you as if to say "What do we do?"'

**DID YOU KNOW?** 'Foothold' is one of James Tichenor's

favourite episodes: 'Not only was that very well-written, but I thought the effects came out looking very organic.'

# 59  PRETEN/E

US Transmission Date: 21 Jan 2000
UK Transmission Date: 19 Jan 2000
Writer: Katharyn Powers
Director: David Warry-Smith
Cast: Alexis Cruz (Skaara/Klorel), Garwin Sanford (Narim), Frida Betrani (Lya), Marie Stillin (Travell), Kevin Durand (Zipacna), Bill Nikolai (Technician)

> Narim invites SG-1 to participate in 'Triad', an ancient Tollan justice ceremony. Klorel's death glider has crashed on Tollana, allowing Skaara's personality to re-emerge and request asylum. This Triad will determine whether the body belongs to the host or the parasite.

**THE WIT AND WISDOM OF JACK O'NEILL** Narim: 'No harm will come to you. The Tollan will guarantee it.' Jack: 'Is that a "*money back if you're not completely alive*" guarantee?'

**SAM'S TRAUMATIC LOVE-LIFE** Because of her joining with Jolinar, Sam refuses to become involved with any potential romantic interests - in this case Narim.

**ORIGINS OF THE SPECIES** The Tollan relocated with help from the Nox (see 'Enigma') to their new homeworld, Tollana. Outside the Gate system, they've built their own Stargate. Chancellor Travell is head of the Curia, the Tollan government. Triad is an ancient Tollan ceremony in which two seekers select archons to represent them. A decision is reached by a third, neutral, party. The Tollan ability to pass through solid matter apparently extends to an animal (Schrödinger), seemingly *not* wearing one of their devices, and Narim, both of whom pass through the iris. The Tollan haven't been at war in many generations. Their law doesn't allow for the death penalty. The Tollan know how to contact the Tok'ra. (A friendship was mentioned by Martouf in 'Serpent's Song'.)

Zipacna was one of Apophis's most loyal underlords.[64] Klorel crashed on Tollana whilst fleeing two motherships dispatched by Heru'ur, knowing that they would be destroyed by the Tollan defence grid and ion cannons. The Tollan detachment device, worn around the chest, suppresses a Goa'uld's ability to silence his host. By Goa'uld law, people on a Goa'uld-ruled planet are the property of the Goa'uld. Skaara and the Abydonians were therefore considered Goa'uld slaves even after Ra's death. There seems to be a difference between a Jaffa and a Serpent guard. (Teal'c identifies those tampering with the ion cannons as 'two Jaffa and a Serpent guard'.) Jaffa may be a generic term for all who serve a Goa'uld, whilst the other term specifically refers to those who serve in the armies of Apophis and Klorel. Daniel points out that the Goa'uld have acquired virtually everything they own from other species - even the Stargate itself was developed by the Ancients ('The Fifth Race'). They are parasitic in nature culturally and techno-

64 In Mayan and Aztec mythology Zipacna was an arrogant giant (one of the four, the Popul Vuh, who ruled the Earth). He was turned to stone by the heavenly twins Hunahpu and Xbalanque.

logically, as well as biologically. The Tok'ra subsequently remove Klorel from Skaara.

The Nox remain pacifist. Well, sort of.

**THE WAR CRIMES TRIBUNAL STARTS AT CLOSING TIME** Skaara remembers with horror his attempts to kill his brother-in-law, Daniel, in 'Within the Serpents Grasp'. Enslaved within his own mind for two and a half years, Skaara has witnessed countless atrocities, many at his own hands.

**'YOU MIGHT REMEMBER ME FROM...'** Kevin Durand played Joshua in *Dark Angel* and appeared in *Austin Powers: The Spy Who Shagged Me*. Marie Stillin's movies include *Convergence* and *Can of Worms*.

**LOGIC, LET ME INTRODUCE YOU TO THIS WINDOW** Jack asks who Klorel's archon is whilst in Skaara's room but doesn't get an answer until they're back in the Triad hall. In 'The Tok'ra', they speak of trying to save the host when they remove Cordesh, as if there's some significant risk involved to both human and Goa'uld. Here, the Tollan suggest that the only risk is that Klorel may not survive. Zipacna says Abydos was under Goa'uld law until three years ago. It's closer to five. The Tollan had a banner displaying the symbol for each archon's world plus a split one for Skaara/Klorel. How did they make them so quickly? In order to mark every ion cannon on Tollana as a target, the Jaffa would have to travel vast distances in short amount of time. The blasts destroying Heru-ur's ships come from all over the planet's surface.

**QUOTE/UNQUOTE** Sam: 'They built their own Stargate?' Daniel: '*Way* smarter than us.' Jack: 'Ours is bigger.'

**NOTES** 'What I suffer each day is worse than death.' The stunning opening of a crashing death glider is followed by a talky, but fundamentally sound, essay on self-awareness, the problems of imposing a set of fixed moral values on other cultures and the impossibility of holding split personalities responsible for their actions. Beautifully directed. One of the best episodes of the season.

Heru'ur, Skaara says, is not dead.

**DID YOU KNOW?** Alexis Cruz made his acting debut in a Spanish-language commercial for boxed macaroni and cheese as a nine year old.

# 60 URGO

US Transmission Date: 28 Jan 2000
UK Transmission Date: 2 Feb 2000
Writer: Tor Alexander Valenza
Director: Peter DeLuise
Cast: Dom DeLuise (Urgo/Togar), Nickolas Baric (SF Guard), Bill Nikolai (Technician)

SG-1 have, they believe, been off-world for seconds. Hammond insists that they were gone for

15 hours. MALP data reveals a brief image of an alien lab. SG-1 experience intense cravings due to microscopic implants in their brains. And they, alone, can see an irritating man who identifies himself as Urgo.

**THE WIT AND WISDOM OF JACK O'NEILL** After SG-1's pie-fest: 'All desserts on the base are in grave danger.'

**FAKE ORIGINS OF THE SPECIES** P4X854 appears to be an untouched island paradise. This, however, is merely an illusion created by Togar.

**SEX AND DRUGS AND ROCK 'N' ROLL** The devices implanted in SG-1's brains by Togar were designed to observe, explore and experience alien cultures. They emit a barely measurable electromagnetic field, cause a sensitivity to the power of suggestion, and produce unexplained cravings and an increased acuity in the senses, especially taste and smell. An error in the visual communication interface allowed the subjects to see and hear Urgo.

**IN THE INTERESTS OF NATIONAL SECURITY** The SGC is looking for a planet on which to establish a research colony. Isolation quarters are located on Level 22 of the SGC.

**POSSIBLE INFLUENCES** The campfire song 'Row Row Row Your Boat', Jack bounces a baseball off the wall repeatedly whilst held in the cell in emulation of Steve McQueen in *The Great Escape*. Also, *Dirty Harry, Star Trek V, The Incredible Melting Man, The Hitch-Hikers Guide to the Galaxy* ('Don't panic'), Eddie Izzard ('Me ... or death?'), *The Simpsons* ('Mmm ... mineral survey'), *Quantum Leap* ('Oh boy!'), *Twin Peaks* (the coffee scene). Jack is thinking about actress Mary Steenburgen (*Time After Time, Back to the Future III, Nixon, The Butcher's Wife*). And, why not? Urgo looks like a famous tenor, according to Jack; a possible oblique reference to Luciano Pavarotti.

**'YOU MIGHT REMEMBER ME FROM...'** Legendary comic Dom DeLuise is best known as a long-running host of *Candid Camera*. He was Pizza the Hut in *Spaceballs*, Merlin Thorpe in *The Best Little Whorehouse in Texas* and appeared in *Cannonball Run, The Muppet Movie, Blazing Saddles* and *The Munsters*. Bill Nickolai was Richard Dean Anderson's stand-in on *MacGyver*.

**LOGIC, LET ME INTRODUCE YOU TO THIS WINDOW** How could Urgo remain in the briefing room after SG-1 had left? When Sam seals the room before sending out the EM pulse, why doesn't the guard outside get concerned? Four devices were removed from SG-1. Were all implanted in Togar? If SG-1 came back with no recollection of what happened yet again, wouldn't they make some attempt to find out, if only to ensure that Urgo survived (considering they had just decided that he may be sentient)? Daniel has a photo of Sha're on his desk. Where did he get it from? Watch the white-coated technician jump directly behind the MALP and back as SG-1 prepare to send the probe to the planet. In the locker room, each time there's a close shot of Urgo, he's shifted further to his left.

**QUOTE/UNQUOTE** Teal'c: 'Appearances may be deceiving.' Jack: 'One man's ceiling is another man's floor.' Daniel: 'A fool's paradise is a wise man's hell.'

SEASON 3

Jack: 'Never run with scissors?'

Hammond: 'Are we entirely sure that the members of SG-1 are, what's the word?' Janet: 'Sane?' Hammond: 'That's the one.'

**NOTES** 'What are you doing in our brains in the first place?' As funny as an afternoon at the genital torturers, 'Urgo' is narcissistic, cumbersome and proof that *SG-1* can't do 'straight' comedy. (It needs to be filtered through a layer of something else.) This entirely depends on whether you find Dom DeLuise amusing or annoying, because the episode is built completely around him. That, of course, means Anderson and co (who *do* all the comedy stuff normally) are pushed aside. Let's be charitable and put this one down to Peter doing his dad a favour. And a failed experiment in trying something different.

Jack doesn't like yoghurt. In addition to Italian (see 'Learning Curve') he knows how to say goodbye in German, French, Spanish and Japanese. As well as Mary Steenburgen, some of his thoughts involve the Hawaiian island, Maui. This is the first indication that he is knowledgeable about opera (see 'Shades of Grey'). Daniel has a 'dancing pharaohs' screensaver on his computer (also briefly seen in 'The Fifth Race'). Behind his photo of Sha're is one of himself in front of a pyramid. Sam has an uncle named Irving, of whom Urgo reminded her. (So, *very* annoying then?) Teal'c plays chess. Janet and Cassandra are going to the lake next weekend.

**DID YOU KNOW?** 'Urgo' is often said to include the series only reference to Jaffa cakes. It actually doesn't. (Urgo asks Teal'c to do some 'Jaffa *kicks*' on Togar.) For those outside the UK, Jaffa cakes are a British confectionery icon: chocolate-covered, orange-jelly-filled biscuits. At the first *Gatecon* convention in 2000, many British fans attended wearing Jaffa cakes on their foreheads and they have subsequently entered into *SG-1* lore.

# 61 A HUNDRED DAYS

US Transmission Date: 4 Feb 2000
UK Transmission Date: 26 Jan 2000
Story: Victoria James
Teleplay: Brad Wright
Director: David Warry-Smith
Cast: Teryl Rothery (Dr Janet Fraiser), Michele Greene (Laira), Shane Meier (Garan), Julie Patzwald (Naytha), Marcel Maillard (Paynan), Gary Jones (Technician)

SG-1 establish ties with a village on P5C768 and its leader Laira - with whom Jack shares a mutual attraction. Everyone gathers to watch the annual meteor shower, the Fire Rain. But an enormous shooting star prompts Sam and Daniel to conduct further research. Their results indicate that Edora periodically travels through an asteroid belt, and once every century the orbit hits a dense section of debris. A meteor hits the Stargate, burying it and trapping Jack on Edora.

**JACK'S TRAUMATIC LOVE-LIFE** After being on Edora for more than three months, Jack resigns himself to never returning to Earth. He would probably have married Laira had Sam not figured out a way to find him.

**SAM'S TRAUMATIC LOVE-LIFE**   Janet learns that Sam's feeling for Jack may be more than just a professional bond (which is the first hint of this, at least in *this* reality). Sam assures her, however, that this will not pose a problem (see 'Divide and Conquer').

**ORIGINS OF THE SPECIES**   Edora, a peaceful farming community, is the fourth planet in its solar system. Its orbit passes through an asteroid belt. The resulting meteor shower, known as Fire Rain, occurs on the same nights every year. Each 150 years the irregularity of the orbit causes an impact event. Edora has valuable and abundant Naqahdah resources.

**THE PREGNANCY STARTS AT CLOSING TIME**   As Jack leaves, the saddened Laira places her hands to her womb, which may indicate she's pregnant. Certainly it's implied that the two were intimate the previous night.

**YE CANNAE CHANGE THE LAWS OF PHYSICS**   Because the Stargate was buried with its wormhole active, molten Naqahdah hardened above the event horizon like an iris, allowing the Gate to be reactivated. Subatomic particles from the generator bombarding the Naqahdah produced heat enough to melt the barrier and create a pocket of super-heated gas. The unstable vortex of Gate activation expanded the pocket to form a cavern large enough for Teal'c to get through.

**SEX AND DRUGS AND ROCK 'N' ROLL**   Jack drinks tolka ('absolute gutrot') with Paynan and then dances with Laira at the hoe-down before nipping home for a bit of *how's-yer-father*. Needless to say, he pays for it in the morning. Yeh, been there, done that.

**POSSIBLE INFLUENCES**   A dead ringer for the *Star Trek* episode 'The Paradise Syndrome'. Daniel notes that something similar to the Fire Rain happened on Earth, almost destroying all life in the process. This probably refers to theories behind the extinction of the dinosaurs.

**'YOU MIGHT REMEMBER ME FROM...'**   Michele Green played Abbey Perkins in *LA Law* and appeared in *A Family Affair*, *Stranger in the House* and *Daddy's Girl*. Shane Meier had the title role in *The Matthew Shepard Story* and was the young MacGyver in *MacGyver*. Julie Patzwald was in *Disturbing Behavior*.

**BEHIND THE CAMERA**   Victoria James was script co-ordinator on *The Outer Limits*.

**LOGIC, LET ME INTRODUCE YOU TO THIS WINDOW**   Shouldn't there be some atmospheric effects from the dirt thrown up by the asteroid impacts? Even if the Gate hadn't been buried, would 24 hours be sufficient for the crater to cool? Why couldn't the SGC send more equipment (oxygen, for instance) with Teal'c? How long was Jack in the cave? Some dialogue suggests only one day but one of the villagers says: 'On the third day we could take no more.' What did SG-1 do during the three months? Every time we see Sam, she's working day and night on the particle beam generator, which suggests SG-1 was, effectively, stood down for the period. Although it's never actually stated, it is strongly implied that Laira is pregnant with Jack's child. (Subsequent comments by Richard Dean Anderson confirm this was intentional.) However, she's seemingly aware of this mere hours after she and Jack were intimate. It normally takes a couple of weeks at least for the first signs of pregnancy to show.

**GOA'ULD LEXICON** 'Tal pat ryn' is a term for a falling star.

**QUOTE/UNQUOTE** Laira: 'My mother taught me to be wary of men wishing to be closer friends.'

Jack: 'Just kind-of wondering what direction is home?' Laira: 'It's that way.'

**NOTES** 'I mourned my husband for a hundred days.' Unpopular with some fans, who regard it as a 'Mary Sue' story (an exercise in shipper wish fulfilment).[65] 'A Hundred Days' *is* cosy, bland and somewhat obvious (the ending in particular). But it's also warm, honest and with its heart in the right place, and Anderson is *fantastic* in it.

Jack's grandfather was from northern Minnesota. He's a fan of fireworks, and has trouble in explaining curling to the Edorans. Sokar, the Tollan and the Tok'ra are mentioned.

The episode was nominated for a Leo Award (which recognise excellence in British Columbian film and TV production) for 'Best Screenwriting in a Dramatic Series'.

**CAST AND CREW COMMENTS** 'Unfortunately we didn't have enough time to tell the story in the way it should have been,' Anderson has noted. 'Some of the emotional beats between my character and Michelle's are missing. Emotionally, it fell a little short. But that's the inherent problem with episodic TV. You only have 42 minutes and 30 seconds to tell your story.' On the possibility of a sequel, Rick adds: 'I asked Brad Wright if he'd consider doing a story in which O'Neill goes back to that planet and discovers he's got a child. If we did, I'd like it to be a daughter, only because he's already had a son.'

**DID YOU KNOW?** 'We did a lot of filming in a place called Bordertown,' revealed Lynn Smith. 'It's an outdoor Western set originally built for a TV series of the same name.' But when they got to the hamlet there were additional problems. 'According to the weatherman it was going to be fine. However, on the first morning we got locked in with fog so we had to switch filming around to the afternoon. Things like that put a little kink in your schedule.'

# 62 SHADES OF GREY

US Transmission Date: 11 Feb 2000

- - - - - - - - - - - - - - - - - - - - - - - - - - - - - - - - - - - - - - - - - - - - - -

65 Shipper is a fan-fiction term, in common use in TV circles, referring to relationship-based stories (often erotic) and also to the type of fans who enjoy this style of fiction in their favourite shows. See the chapter 'Stargate and the Internet' for further details.

UK Transmission Date: 9 Feb 2000
Writer: Jonathan Glassner
Director: Martin Wood
Cast: Teryl Rothery (Dr Janet Fraiser), Tom McBeath (Colonel Harry Maybourne), Marie Stillin (Travell), Steve Makaj (Colonel Makepeace), Christian Bocher (Major Newman), Linnea Sharples (Lt Clare Tobias)

> SG-1 travel to Tollana to negotiate a technology trade. Jack becomes annoyed when the Tollan refuse to co-operate, and steals a Tollan defence device. Relieved of his command, Jack resigns from the SGC. Then Harry Maybourne makes him an interesting offer.

**THE WIT AND WISDOM OF JACK O'NEILL** On the Tollan: 'We should never have saved their technologically superior butts.'

**ORIGINS OF THE SPECIES** PX3595 is an Asgard-protected planet. The indigenous population, known as Tiernods, are primitive and live in caves, using an Asgard stealth device. SG-9 have been unable to negotiate a trade for this. The Asgard themselves have the ability to traverse tremendous distances in an instant (previously alluded to in 'Thor's Chariot').

The people of Edora (with or without help from the SGC) appear to have moved their Stargate to a new location (as it looks nothing like the landscape seen in 'A Hundred Days').

**SEX AND DRUGS AND ROCK 'N' ROLL** Jack and Daniel share a Budweiser.

**THE CONSPIRACY STARTS AT CLOSING TIME** The Asgard and the Tollan approached the SGC with evidence of theft of technology. They, and the Nox, threatened to sever diplomatic ties. The Tollan suggested that the SGC apprehend their own rogue element, and the Asgard insisted that Jack be the only one involved. Maybourne led the rogue organisation, described as an offshoot of the NID, with command at *very* high civilian levels (see 'Secrets', 'Touchstone', 'Watergate'). Their standing orders are to use whatever means necessary to acquire alien technology (specifically weapons technology) that could help Earth in the battle against the Goa'uld, or other aggressors.

There has been a mole in the SGC since 'Secrets' (see also 'Touchstone'). It turns out to be Makepeace.

**MILITARY INTELLIGENCE?** The rogue group has multiple units, according to Maybourne, though we see only one. At least eight members were stationed at the off-world base, all of whom are arrested on their return to Earth (two more appear in 'The Sentinel'). They had access to all SG-1's mission reports (and, presumably, those of other SG-teams too), via Maybourne.

**IN THE INTERESTS OF NATIONAL SECURITY** After Jack's departure, Makepeace was the most senior field officer at the SGC (if not the most experienced; Ferretti is mentioned, for the first time since 'Within The Serpent's Grasp'). Clare Tobias, the engineer on the rogue Stargate team, was beaten for a position at the SGC by Sam.

**POSSIBLE INFLUENCES** *Seinfeld* ('Hello Newman'). Naples composer Ruggiero Leoncavallo's *I Pagiacci* (1892).

**'YOU MIGHT REMEMBER ME FROM...'** Christian Bocher was in *Total Exposure*. Linnea Sharples played Beth in *The Falling*.

**LOGIC, LET ME INTRODUCE YOU TO THIS WINDOW** It's a year since 'Touchstone', so how did the rogue team get people or equipment to their base from Earth during that time? Surely Makepeace couldn't have smuggled all those artefacts by himself. Some things (ammunition for their guns, for example), they could get *only* from Earth. How did Jack send the iris code before he went back to Earth? We see someone leaving the infirmary (Level 21) and walking around the corner to the Gateroom (Level 28). When Jack and Newman meet, Newman apologises for returning fire in the Utah hanger. But, in 'Touchstone', none of the four NID men fired a weapon. There appear to be seven symbols illuminated when Jack dials the gate but Jack presses only six panels before the centre, and a shot of the active DHD shows only six symbols lit. The Asgard locate the rogue base by looking at the DHD. This should have told them only the symbols used, not the order - leaving some 720 possible destinations.

When returning to Earth, Jack tells the rogue team that he will 'hold the door open' to prevent them from disconnecting the Stargate and dialling another planet. He does so, leaving his left arm submerged within the wormhole - which disengages as soon as he removes it. Though it's not been established what makes a wormhole stay open, this suggests that one cannot be terminated by traditional means as long as there is matter still in transit (see '48 Hours'). But, shouldn't the NID team still have been able to shut the Stargate down at their own end by interrupting the power supply?

The NID team are, seemingly, all military personnel and thus eligible for court martial. Which presumably means that they can be tried in military *diplock* courts (and, *in camera* as a bonus), which is useful given the Top Secret nature of the Stargate programme (but, see 'Chain Reaction' and 'The Sentinel' with regard to plausible deniability). Jack seems to have exactly the same framed poster of Mars in his house as the teenage Sam had in her bedroom in 'The Devil You Know'. Where is Daniel when Sam, Teal'c, Janet and Hammond see Jack off, ostensibly forever?

**QUOTE/UNQUOTE** Jack: 'Oh, here we go. Pop-pysch 101, right?' And, on the Asgard; 'They like me.'

Daniel, on why he went to see Jack: 'We drew straws. I lost.'

**NOTES** 'We do not steal from friendlies.' A truly *great* episode - not without its flaws (the ending seems perfunctory and rushed) but featuring another fabulous performance by Anderson.

Jack's (possibly fictitious) story is that a second SGC base was to be established off-world with him in command, but the Pentagon wouldn't grant the backing. He plays chess (see 'Legacy'), listens to opera and reads *Mad* magazine. Altogether he's had five counts of direct insubordination to a superior officer and a US senator (so, Kinsey grassed him up after 'Politics', well there's a surprise), two of refusing to obey orders and one concerning the kidnapping of an alien child (see 'Learning Curve'). In assuming his undercover role, Jack returns to the cold, hardened personality he showed before SG-1 was formed. To uncover Maybourne, the rogue team and the mole, Jack was forced to compromise his friendships. His relationship with Teal'c was strained, he told Sam she never really knew him and Daniel that their friendship had no real foundation. Hammond wears his watch on his right wrist, which may indicate that he's left-handed. There are references to Hammond recalling Jack from duty in 'Children of the Gods' (see 'Upgrades').

**DID YOU KNOW?** For the first three seasons of *SG-1*, except for effects shots, all episodes were filmed in 16mm. Starting with 'Nemesis', the final episode of season three, however, the decision was taken to move to 35mm stock.

# 63  NEW GROUND

US Transmission Date: 18 Feb 2000
UK Transmission Date: 16 Feb 2000
Writer: Heather E Ash
Director: Chris McMullin
Cast: Teryl Rothery (Dr Janet Fraiser), Richard Ian Cox (Nyan), Daryl Shuttleworth (Commander Rigar), Desiree Zuroski (Parey), Jennifer Copping (Mallin), Finn Michael (Soldier), Bill Nikolai (Technician)

> SG-1 find themselves in the middle of a religious war in which rival continents are engaged in a fundamentalist crusade. SG-1, by their arrival via the Stargate, threaten to shatter 2,000 years of faith amongst the Bedrosians. Though Teal'c escapes, Jack, Daniel and Sam are held prisoner and tortured.

**THE WIT AND WISDOM OF JACK O'NEILL** 'I have no friends. In the woods or otherwise.' And: 'You know that "We come in peace" business? Bite me.'

**ORIGINS OF THE SPECIES** Sam's cold-dialling programme searches for Stargates by periodically redialling cartouche Stargate addresses that hadn't connected the first time. P2X416 was the first connection made. Bedrosia and Optrica, rival continents, have been engulfed in an ideological war for decades. The Opticans believe (rightly) that humans were brought to the planet by aliens who travelled through a Gateway. During the Upheaval, a period of violent earthquakes and volcanic eruptions covering most of the continent 2000 year ago, the Gate was buried. The Bedrosians believe that the planet and its people were created by their god Nefertem. 'The Blue Lotus Blossum of Ra', Nefertem was son of Sekhmet, a minor System Lord and probably brought the people to the planet.

**THE CONSPIRACY STARTS AT CLOSING TIME** An SG team can bring the Naqahdah reactor (see 'Learning Curve') to a planet missing a DHD in order to power the Stargate.

**POSSIBLE INFLUENCES** *Apocalypse Now, A Clockwork Orange, I Love You I Kill You, Slaughterhouse Five, The Handmaid's Tale, Punishment Park, THX 1138,*

*Planet of the Apes*, *Starship Troopers*, *Butch Cassidy and the Sundance Kid* and *Fahrenheit 451*.

**'YOU MIGHT REMEMBER ME FROM...'** Daryl Shuttleworth was in *Replicant*, *Atomic Train* and *Killer Image*. Richard Cox played Manny Needlebaum in *Cold Squad*. Jennifer Copping featured in *Little Boy Blues* and *Protection*.

**LOGIC, LET ME INTRODUCE YOU TO THIS WINDOW** Nyan treats one of Teal'c's eyes, though it appears that both were injured. How did Rigar know how to operate the zat? Rigar destroys the MALP, but presumably the radios still work, so why did General Hammond shut down the wormhole? The Earth glyph is definitely present on the Bedrosian Gate. Daniel is dragged out to view the uncovered DHD, leaving Jack and Sam in the tent. Next shot, we see Jack and Sam being brought back into a tent that also has three cages, with Daniel already in one of them. Nyan becomes Daniel's research assistant ... and is never heard of again.

**QUOTE/UNQUOTE** Jack, after he gets no reaction from the Bedrosians: 'Wow, tough crowd.'

**NOTES** 'This is blasphemy.' A clever metaphor on the ideological war between religion and science; Nyan has no allegiances to abstract belief, but is prepared to change what he believes when presented with new evidence. The other Bedrosians are dedicated to their faith and are presented as arrogant and brutish. It's a clever idea (the Spanish Inquisition with 20th Century weapons and communication) but, just when you think that they're going to do something subtle with the dichotomy, the whole thing turns into a gun-battle-and-escape climax.

**CAST AND CREW COMMENTS** 'I love writing for Carter, not because she's a girl but because she's a science geek,' commented Heather Ash. 'I have a soft spot for Daniel for a similar reason. He's a little different - not a military man - and I've tried to give him back that sense of wonder; the little kid jumping up and down at each discovery.'

**DID YOU KNOW?** The location used for this episode was Red Rock quarry in Port Coquitlam, so-called because it was the site of *The X-Files* episode 'Anasazi' and the production crew of that show painted vast areas of the quarry red to simulate a valley in New Mexico. The site was also used for 'The First Commandment' and 'The Fifth Man'.

# 64 MATERNAL INSTINCT

US Transmission Date: 25 Feb 2000
UK Transmission Date: 1 Mar 2000
Writer: Robert C Cooper
Director: Peter Woeste
Cast: Teryl Rothery (Dr Janet Fraiser), Tony Amendola (Bra'tac), Steve Bacic (Major Coburn), Terry Chen (Monk), Carla Boudreau (Oma Desala), Aaron Douglas (Moac), D Harlan Cutshell (Jaffa Commander)

Chulak has been attacked by Apophis. Daniel believes he is searching for the Harsesis. Using the combined knowledge of Bra'tac and computer analysis, SG-1 decide on the most likely planet for Kheb. Bra'tac and SG-1 set out in search of Sha're's child. But will they get there first?

**THE WIT AND WISDOM OF JACK O'NEILL** 'I'm a huge fan of subtlety, but that's downright encrypted.' And: 'If we happen to make it out of this in one piece, remind me to harm Daniel severely.' And, after the lightning strikes: 'Well, *that* was cool!'

**ORIGINS OF THE SPECIES** Chulak was attacked by Apophis, searching for the Harsesis. Apophis has taken control of Sokar's forces. Moac, Bra'tac's newest apprentice, dies from injuries received in battle. He was, Bra'tac says, the bravest Jaffa he ever trained. Bra'tac is approaching the age when he can no longer carry a prim'ta. After his experience with the monk, Bra'tac finds he isn't ready to die, but takes comfort in the knowledge that the journey to the next world lies ahead of him. Bra'tac's father was also opposed to the Goa'uld. He once told Bra'tac the story of Kheb, wondering why gods would fear anything. Jaffa warriors' bodies are burned after death.

In mythology, Osiris once hid from Seth on Kheb (see 'Forever in a Day'). In Jaffa legend, Osiris hid on a planet of the Loc'na ko, a system whose resources were depleted by mining. Kheb, an untouched wilderness with mountains and a single temple in a valley distant from the Gate, is a world feared by the Goa'uld. It was discovered by a few Jaffa and kept secret. When a Jaffa could no longer carry a prim'ta, he journeyed to Kheb where his kah'lesh learned the path into the next life. When the Goa'uld themselves travelled to Kheb they did not return, so it was forbidden to speak of it. The temple on Kheb was built millennia ago, by an alien race who may have visited Earth. They discovered a means of ascending to a higher ethereal plane of existence and left the writings on the shrine for others to follow. 'Oma Desala' means 'Mother Nature'.

**THE CONSPIRACY STARTS AT CLOSING TIME** Bra'tac has a GDO to signal the SGC, designated Special Code 2. Special Code 1 probably belongs to the Tok'ra, who were given a GDO in 'Serpent's Song'.

**THE INTERESTS OF THE CHILD** Daniel struggles with his hatred for the Goa'uld which, the monk tells him, will lead to the child's death. Only when he gets what he wants (the Harsesis) does Daniel realise that he had never really been enlightened by the teachings. The Harsesis is taken to safety by Oma Desala, leaving Daniel without a purpose (see 'Absolute Power', 'Meridian').

**POSSIBLE INFLUENCES** Home and garden guru Martha Stewart, Snap's 'The Power', *Kung-Fu* ('Slow down there, Grasshopper'), *The Golden Child*, the Dalai Lama and, visually, *Superman II*, Tarkovsky's *Stalker* and *Lifeforce*.

**'YOU MIGHT REMEMBER ME FROM...'** Steve Bacic was in *21 Jump Street*, *Andromeda* and *Another Stakeout*. Carla Boudreau appeared in *Valentine* and *Saving Silverman*. Terry Chen was *Rolling Stone* editor Ben Fong-Torres in *Almost Famous*.

**BEHIND THE CAMERA** Peter Woeste worked on *Mortal Sins*, *Bingo*,

*In Cold Blood* and *Cousins.*

**LOGIC, LET ME INTRODUCE YOU TO THIS WINDOW** The Monk speaks in Zen koans, and Daniel suggests that the theology of Kheb may be an original basis for Buddhism on Earth. However, Zen philosophy post-dated the origins of Buddhism. In one shot you can clearly see Christopher Judge's pierced left ear. Daniel removes both boots and socks, but Bra'tac keeps his socks on. Janet is, seemingly, a surgeon as well as a physician. Kah'lesh is pronounced differently than it was in 'Need'. (The DVD-subtitles spell it 'Kalak' here.) The red address that Sam points to on the computer screen is actually a line that had just scrolled off the top of the screen and not the same one Bra'tac indicated. Daniel wears a short-sleeve shirt when he removes his backpack, but a long-sleeve one thereafter. Bra'tac hands his zat to Teal'c before entering the temple, but it looks like he has it when he exits later. Jack touches his earpiece to talk to SG-2, rather than the radio. Twice. It's almost impossible to believe that Daniel hadn't asked Teal'c if he knew anything about the legendary Kheb. Yet this episode seems to suggest that Teal'c knew of its location - in a roundabout way - all along. It appears that there can be more than one Stargate in the same solar system, contrary to what was established in 'Stargate'. Indeed, given that a glyph can represent a single planet and not an entire constellation (Earth) there's no reason why *every* planet in a system couldn't have one. Or two, also like Earth.

**QUOTE/UNQUOTE** Monk: 'Here, no bull can hide.' Jack: 'Oh, I don't know about that.'

Jack, on Apophis: '*Sonovabitch*! Somebody's gotta teach that guy how to *die*!'

**NOTES** 'I made a promise.' A fascinating dive into Buddhist texts, this beautifully restates the series' intellectual credentials and gives Daniel his first opportunity for growth since 'Forever in a Day'. His sad 'Bye' as the Jaffa are about to be destroyed by Oma Desala tells us much about the character.

The SGC database includes Stargate addresses from both the Abydos cartouche and the Ancients' map. SG-2, under Major Coburn, act as backup on the mission to Kheb.

**CAST AND CREW COMMENTS** This episode is a particular favourite of Robert Cooper. 'If it's not too corny to say, it has a little bit of soul. I like episodes with some nice character moments that focus more on the writing than the eye candy and all the explosions. I lean more towards the ones with a bit more heart, as I suspect the viewers do.'

**DID YOU KNOW?** In Robert Cooper's office there's a framed photo of SG-1 which Chris Judge has signed 'Thanks for all the great dialogue. Silently yours ...'

# 65 CRYSTAL SKULL

US Transmission Date: 3 Mar 2000
UK Transmission Date: 8 Mar 2000
Story: Michael Greenburg, Jarrad Paul
Teleplay: Brad Wright

Director: Martin Wood
Cast: Jan Rubes (Nick Ballard), Teryl Rothery (Dr Janet Fraiser), Russell Roberts (Psychiatrist), Jason Schombing (Robert Rothman), Jacquie Janzen (Nurse), Tracy Westerholm (Surveillance SF), Dan Shea (Sgt Siler), Daniel Bacon (Technician), Christopher Judge (Quetlzelcoatl voice)

A crystal skull is discovered on P7X377 that is identical to one that Daniel's grandfather, Nick Ballard, found in 1971. When SG-1 investigate, Daniel's body undergoes a phase shift and becomes invisible. Jack, Sam and Teal'c return through the Stargate without him. At least, that's what they think.

**THE WIT AND WISDOM OF JACK O'NEILL** Nick, on the invisible Daniel: 'He's standing right beside me.' Jack: 'He's lost a few pounds.'
Nick: 'Now we must wait for the giant aliens.' Jack: 'That just has a nice ring to it.'

**ORIGINS OF THE SPECIES** The pyramid on P7X377 is of Mayan design. Readings indicate lethal levels of muon radiation. The presence of leptons suggests that something is slowing down neutrinos. Such a material could change our understanding of physics.
The giant alien is called Quetlzelcoatl[66] and speaks in Mayan: 'Uy ah ualing ualing wetail' meaning 'The enemy of my enemy is my friend.'

**THE CONSPIRACY STARTS AT CLOSING TIME** Daniel's parents died when he was eight (see 'The Gamekeeper'). His grandfather chose not to adopt him. An archaeologist (it runs in the family, clearly), Ballard discovered the skull in 1971 in Belize in a temple which collapsed soon afterwards. Ballard was laughed out of the academic community because of his assertion that the skull is a teleportation device to giant aliens. He had a mental breakdown and is in a psychiatric institution in Oregon, where Daniel regularly visited him until four years ago. They fell out around the time that Daniel joined the SGC. The skull from Belize is now in the Smithsonian.

**POSSIBLE INFLUENCES** *Indiana Jones and the Last Crusade*, *Sole Survivor*, *Ghost* and *Star Trek: The Next Generation*'s 'The Next Phase'. Nintendo, *The Adventures of Rocky and Bullwinkle*, The Who's 'Naked Eye'. Jack says Janet is a Napoleonic powermonger.

**'YOU MIGHT REMEMBER ME FROM...'** Czech-born Jan Rubes was in Disney's *The Incredible Journey*, *Witness*, *Anthrax* and *Never Too Late* (which he also produced).

**LOGIC, LET ME INTRODUCE YOU TO THIS WINDOW** Daniel can walk through objects but still stands on the floor, leans against walls and sits on a desk (see 'Wormhole X-Treme!'). Don't SG-1 worry that Daniel may have been vaporised rather than transported somewhere? As Daniel lies unconscious on the dais, he is further from the edge in later shots then earlier ones. (He's reverted to his former position when Teal'c returns later.) The video appears to skip

*SEASON 3*

66 Meaning 'feathered serpent', Quetzalcoatl (note subtly different spelling) was a major god of the Aztec pantheon with origins in earlier Mesoamerican civilisations like the Mayans (c. 300-900AD). He appears in various guises throughout South American mythology. The Toltecs (c. 900-1180) perceived him as Venus, the morning star.

some frames as Nick replaces the skull on the pedestal. Why didn't Rothman know that the skull was an off-world artefact? Daniel's acrophobia (see 'Thor's Chariot') has disappeared. Sam is lying on her right cheek in close-ups after SG-1 return and collapse. In above shots she's in a different position. Nick says that Daniel hasn't published a paper in two years, but he's been at the SGC (and, before that, Abydos) for over four. Does this imply that he's published something since joining the programme (see 'The Curse')?

It's stated that Daniel claimed the Egyptian pyramids were landing sites for alien spacecraft, and that's why he was shunned by the scientific community. The claims he made in 'Stargate', though controversial, were a bit less radical than that (see 'Hathor'). Leptons are fundamental particles with no strong interactions. There are six types, and six anti-lepton types. Tau leptons and tau neutrinos tend to attract each other into rings or even massless mini-black holes.

**QUOTE/UNQUOTE** Sam: 'Normally neutrinos pass right through ordinary matter, no matter how dense. Something like 500 million billion just passed through you.' Jack: '"No matter how dense?"'

Daniel: 'You're not hallucinating.' Nick: 'Hallucinations always say that!'

**NOTES** 'Can you imagine what it feels like to go on the most incredible journey of your life, and have no-one believe you?' Two Daniel stories in a row. This one's terrific too, apart from an offensively stereotypical presentation of mental illness. Once that's out of the way, there's fun to be had with 'invisible' logistics (or lack of them). Best bits: Jack's rubbish attempts to get out of bed. Every scene featuring the excellent Rothman. Daniel's solo running commentary.

Hammond's granddaughters are mentioned again. (Kayla has a school play tomorrow.) Rothman (see 'Forever in a Day') couldn't figure out what an ashtray is for, Jack believes. The story of Nick's discovery of the crystal skull appears to be based on that of the most famous example in real life, the Mitchell-Hedges skull (which had a whole episode of *Arthur C Clarke's Mysterious World* to itself). Said to have been discovered at a Mayan settlement in British Honduras in 1924, in actual fact archaeologist F.A Mitchell-Hedges is alleged to have bought it at Sotheby's from a man named Burney in 1943.

**CAST AND CREW COMMENTS** An experimental episode, Brad Wright notes: 'We had a degree of success but, frankly, it wasn't as good as I [had] hoped in terms of the believability of the environment. Our actors were literally walking around in a green room. They had nothing real to work with. George Lucas can pull it off, but it's harder for us in terms of time and money.'

**DID YOU KNOW?** 'Crystal Skull' developed from a story that Michael Greenburg wrote involving O'Neill's past. When this didn't work, he amended it to Daniel. Michael Shanks, meanwhile, asked the writer to do a story concerning myths surrounding crystal skulls, which fascinated him. Greenburg was able to incorporate this.

# 66 NEMESIS

US Transmission Date: 10 Mar 2000

UK Transmission Date: 8 Mar 2000
Story: Robert C Cooper
Teleplay: Brad Wright
Director: Martin Wood
Cast: Gary Jones (Technician), Colin Cunningham (Major Davis), Guy Lee-Fraizer (Technician #2)

Jack is contacted by a dying Thor and learns that the *Biliskner* is being attacked by Replicators, spider-like metallic artificial organisms. The effects of the Replicators reaching Earth would be devastating. Jack plans to self-destruct the ship before that can happen. SG-1 disobey his orders and follow him.

**THE WIT AND WISDOM OF JACK O'NEILL** On Minnesota: 'Land of sky-blue waters. Loofas. "Ya sure y'betcha."' (A typical *How to speak Minnesotan* phrase; Sam repeats it in 'Small Victories'.)

**ORIGINS OF THE SPECIES** The Replicators, the enemy of the Asgard more dangerous than the Goa'uld (see 'Fair Game'), were discovered on an isolated planet. Their creators were apparently dead (see 'Menace'). They were brought aboard an Asgard ship for study, infested the ship, fed off the metals, replicating and becoming a plague on the galaxy. They have an extremely high ability for learning and are capable of functioning both independently and as a group. They're attracted to high bursts of energy (like the Asgard transporter) and are impervious to zat discharges. They reassemble after a shotgun blast, but a second shot appears to destroy them.

All Asgard ships are equipped with internal dampening fields. The *Biliskner* is powered by four neutrino ion generators. It's destroyed entering Earth's atmosphere. The ship crashes into the Pacific Ocean 400 miles off the Californian coast (see 'Small Victories').

**IN THE INTERESTS OF NATIONAL SECURITY** When the Asgard ship appears on Earth's radar screens, the Russians go to DefCon 2 (see 'Watergate').

**POSSIBLE INFLUENCES** *Bug*, *Lost in Space*, *The Terminator*, *Doctor Who*'s cybermats, *The Thing*, *Star Trek: First Contact* and *Aliens*. Also, the Apollo Moon landings ('One small step for Jaffa').

**LOGIC, LET ME INTRODUCE YOU TO THIS WINDOW** Has the DefCon indicator always been there? There's only one transporter still working with which to rescue Teal'c, but the SGC can pinpoint intraship transports? How does Sam know when they've waited long enough before blowing the ship? The monitor shows Jack and Teal'c in a corridor when they're in a room. How does Daniel convince Janet to let him out of the infirmary? Davis says that even disconnected there should be enough residual power in a Stargate for it to be used. Since when?

**QUOTE/UNQUOTE** Davis: 'I'll try to define "reasonable" to The Pentagon.'

Thor: 'The Replicators were brought aboard an Asgard ship before the danger could be fully comprehended.' Jack: '*We* do that all the time. Kinda expected more from *you* guys.'

SEASON 3

'This have anything to do with those bugs in the hall?' A shoot-'em-up finale which introduces a memorable new creation, the Replicators, and is visually impressive in spite of (or possibly *because* of) the amount of CGI involved. Excellent double-cliffhanger.

Jack likes bass-fishing in the Minnesota lakes and invites both Daniel and Sam to accompany him. Daniel's recently had his appendix removed. Teal'c is visiting his family (presumably in the Land of Light, see 'Family'). Sam has medical field training. SG-1 gate to P3X234 from the *Biliskner*. Davis says he spends all day reading of SG-1's exploits.

**DID YOU KNOW?** Daniel's surgery was written into 'Nemesis' to accommodate Michael Shanks, who suffered real appendicitis during 'Crystal Skull' and had an operation prior to this episode. That's his *real* scar we see in 'Small Victories'.

# STARGATE SG-1
# SEASON 4 (2000-2001)

'Sounds like a good idea for a TV show...

If you're into that sort of thing.'

# STARGATE SG-1™ SEASON 4 (2000-2001)

Double Secret Productions/Gekko Film Corp/
Metro-Goldwyn-Meyer

Developed for Television by Brad Wright, Jonathan Glassner

Executive Producer: Brad Wright

Co-Executive Producer: Michael Greenburg, Richard Dean Anderson

Executive Consultant: Jonathan Glassner

Creative Consultant: Peter DeLuise

Co-Producer: Joseph Mallozzi, Paul Mullie

Co-Executive Producer: Robert C Cooper, N John Smith

Post Production Consultant: Michael Eliot

SEASON 4

Regular Cast: Richard Dean Anderson (Jack O'Neill), Michael Shanks

(Daniel Jackson)[67], Amanda Tapping (Samantha Carter), Christopher Judge

(Teal'c), Don S Davis (General George Hammond)[68]

67 Does not appear in 'Prodigy'.
68 Does not appear in 'Exodus'.

161

# 67 SMALL VICTORIES

US Transmission Date: 30 Jun 2000
UK Transmission Date: 6 Sep 2000
Writer: Robert C Cooper
Director: Martin Wood
Cast: Gary Jones (Sgt Walter Davis)[69], Teryl Rothery (Dr Janet Fraiser), Dan Shea (Sgt Siler), Colin Cunningham (Major Davis), Yuris Kis (Yuri), Dmitry Chepovestsky (Boris)

SG-1's triumphant return to Earth is marred by news that one of the Replicators wasn't destroyed and has found its way into a Russian submarine. Jack and Teal'c lead a team to eliminate the threat. Sam, meanwhile, is taken to Thor's homeworld, which is on the verge of destruction by the Replicators. Thor believes that human knowledge could hold the key to the Asgard's survival.

**THE WIT AND WISDOM OF JACK O'NEILL** 'Would it be necessary for me to mention my insane aversion to bugs at this time?' And, memorably: 'Aw, *crap!*'

**ORIGINS OF THE SPECIES** Thor's planet (which may or may not be Othala, see 'The Fifth Race') is one of many Asgard worlds threatened by the Replicators. The Asgard have great respect for Jack, even naming their advanced warship prototype after him. The *O'Neill*'s hull is made of an alloy of Naqahdah, Trinium and Carbon. Asgard food comes in small coloured blocks.

The Replicators are a kiron-based technology. (Kirons are energy particles.) The Replicators on Earth are a different colour because they retain characteristics of the metals they consume. Each block making up a Replicator exerts an energy field on those surrounding it, allowing the Replicators to assume different forms.

**THE CONSPIRACY STARTS AT CLOSING TIME** It took more than a week to calibrate the beta Gate at the SGC. SG-1 remained on P4X234 until the connection was established.

**IN THE INTERESTS OF NATIONAL SECURITY** A tense political situation exists between the US and Russia, who spotted the *Biliskner* as it crashed. The Russians are also convinced that the Americans are involved with their missing submarine (see 'Watergate'). The destroyed Russian Foxtrot sub, codenamed Blackbird, is torpedoed by the *Dallas*, a Los Angeles class US submarine.

**POSSIBLE INFLUENCES** *The Simpsons* ('D'oh'), *Predator*, *Hunt for the Red October*, *Aliens*, *Jaws* (the music) and *The X-Files* episodes 'The Host', 'Apocrypha' and 'War of the Copraphages'.

**'YOU MIGHT REMEMBER ME FROM...'** Dmitry Chepovetsky was in *Dark Water* and *Saving Grace*.

• • • • • • • • • • • • • • • • • • • • • • • • • • • • • • • • • • • • • • • • • • • • •

69 First name given in dialogue as Walter in '2010'. Name-tag Sgt Davis seen in both 'The Other Side' and '2010' (but, see 'There But For the Grace of God').

**LOGIC, LET ME INTRODUCE YOU TO THIS WINDOW** The two Russian submariners actually speak in a Ukrainian dialect rather than Russian. The beta Gate has the regular point of origin rather than the one seen in 'Solitudes'. At the end of 'Nemesis', the planet that SG-1 escaped to was P3X234. Teal'c calls it P4X234 here. 'Entering hyperspeed'? They've just made that up! (See 'The Devil You Know', 'Enemies'.) When he boards the sub, it appears that Teal'c's gun-light flickers out unexpectedly. How did the Replicator get from the floating debris to the submarine? Jack, Daniel and Davis conclude that the new Replicators can't survive in the ocean because their metal will corrode. Eh? They're made out of bits of a submarine! When SG-1 return through the Gate at the start, we get a shot of the controlling SGC's PC booting up, and the monitor reveals it's a very primitive 286.

**QUOTE/UNQUOTE** Daniel: 'You're saying you need someone dumber than you are?' Jack: 'You may have come to the right place.' Sam: 'I could go, sir.' Jack: 'I don't know, Carter, you may not be dumb enough.'

Sam: 'We kicked their asses.' Jack: 'They *had* asses?'

**NOTES** 'That ship is everything they're looking for. It'll look like an all-you-can-eat buffet.' A thousand-miles-an-hour overture to the symphony that is *SG-1*'s most complete season. Pumped-up like a Schwarzenegger movie on steroids and as 'boys-with-toys' as *Stargate* ever gets, 'Nemesis' contains action movie visuals for a fraction of the price. *Fantastic.*

Jack is still going fishing (see 'Nemesis') and still wants Carter (and, later, Thor) to go with him. The submarine interiors were shot onboard the Whisky-class *Red Scorpion*, which is now anchored in Long Beach Harbor within a stone's throw of the location where the original *Stargate* movie was made.

**CAST AND CREW COMMENTS** Because he wished to get a shot from inside the torpedo tube, and the camera operator was claustrophobic, Martin Wood shot the 'replicators-eye-view' sequence himself. 'So, I'm twenty-five feet down a steel coffin and they close the door...'

The episode is also notable for the first appearance of the beard that Chris Judge returned with after the summer break and wanted to keep. It appears in several episodes until, as Wood notes, '[Chris] realised how silly it looked and shaved it off!'

**SEASON 4**

**DID YOU KNOW?** This episode, according to Joe Mallozzi, had some interesting outtakes. 'In one, Thor turns to the camera and orders a Mokochino. In another, Thor gooses Carter. If you translate what the two Russians at the beginning of the episode are saying, the conversation goes: "What's that noise?" "Maybe it's the bug from the last episode!"'

# 68  THE OTHER SIDE

US Transmission Date: 7 Jul 2000
UK Transmission Date: 13 Sep 2000
Writer: Brad Wright

Director: Peter DeLuise
Cast: Rene Auberjonois (Alar), Anne Marie Loder (Farrell), Stephen Park (Controller), Gary Jones (Sgt Walter Davis), Kyle Cassie (Eurondan Soldier), Mris Keeler (Zombie Pilot)

The SGC is contacted by Alar, from Euronda, whose people claim descent from Earth, and are at war. In exchange for heavy water needed to sustain their defensive fields, Alar offers SG-1 advanced technology. Jack agrees to the trade but Daniel is suspicious that the Eurondans have not been completely honest.

**GET A LIFE** Jack arrives at the SGC two hours early to find Sam not having left from the previous day. He ordered her to get a life but she, seemingly, hasn't had time.

**THE WIT AND WISDOM OF JACK O'NEILL** Jack: 'You've got that look.' Teal'c: 'To which look are you referring, O'Neill?' Daniel: 'The one that says, "I have misgivings about this mission, but deep-down I know we're doing the right thing"?' Jack: 'No, the other one!'

**ORIGINS OF THE SPECIES** The Eurondans discovered a Stargate when digging their bunker. They co-existed for centuries with their enemy, who now control most of the planet. They refer to the enemy as 'Breeders', who reproduce with no regard for genetic or ethnic purity. War began when the Eurondans built their underground facility and poisoned the planet's surface. Alar's father was among the leadership responsible for the war. The trade agreement provides for Eurondan technology, including nuclear-fusion reactors, defence-field generators, advanced aero-fighter weapons-systems and medicine, in-exchange for deuterium oxide fuel from heavy water. The aero-fighter system uses direct neural interface for targeting and vectoring.

**SEX AND DRUGS AND ROCK 'N' ROLL** Beta-cantin is a powerful Eurondan drug.

**POSSIBLE INFLUENCES** Footage from *Firefox* was used for the aerial shots. Also, *Star Wars*, *Doctor Who*'s 'Genesis of the Daleks' and *Blakes' 7* (fascist overtones). Product placement: the Sony amplifier.

**'YOU MIGHT REMEMBER ME FROM...'** Rene Auberjonois was Father Mulcahy in *M*A*S*H*, appeared in *The Big Bus*, *Benson*, *Inspector Gadget*, *The Man from Atlantis*, *The Patriot* and is best known as Odo in *Star Trek: Deep Space Nine*. Anne Marie Loder was Sophie in *Higher Ground*.

**LOGIC, LET ME INTRODUCE YOU TO THIS WINDOW** Jack isn't bothered about the details of the conflict, doing what he needs to get the technology. But as soon as he suspects that the Eurondans are genocidal racists, he acts against them without having had an opportunity to compare them to their enemies. What if the 'breeders' are even worse? If the shield-generator is so dependent on heavy water, why was the base built hundreds of miles from the ocean?

**QUOTE/UNQUOTE** Jack: 'So what's your impression of Alar?' Teal'c: 'That he is concealing something.' Jack: 'Like what?' Teal'c: 'I am unsure. He is concealing it.'

Daniel: 'We're about to turn the tide of a world war that we know nothing about against an enemy we know nothing about... Is it the right thing to do?'

**NOTES** 'Their whole world is in flames and we're offering gasoline. How's that "help"?' A brilliant analogy (what if aliens landed in 1945 Berlin, had a nice meal with Hitler and then provided the Nazis with advanced weapons?) with lots of subtle moments leading viewers into dark cul-de-sacs before they see the big picture. The central conflict between Jack's monochrome views and Daniel's more rationalist and ethical approach is an almost deliberate restating of the series' core dichotomy. Gets better with each viewing (particularly the war-as-a-video-game metaphor).

Daniel's grandfather is Dutch. (Probably Nick, see 'Crystal Skull', who certainly has a European accent.)

**CRITIQUE** '*Stargate SG-1* has matured,' noted Andy Lane in *DreamWatch*. 'In the early days almost every episode seemed to be a variation on the *Star Trek* "heroes arrive on a planet, find the inhabitants have a problem, solve it and leave" plot. Seasons three and four broadened the scope [to include] political machinations, terrorist activities, refugee problems and Earth-threatening disasters.'

**CAST AND CREW COMMENTS** 'It was like re-creating the Battle of Britain with the bunkers and [the] bombs going-off overhead,' Peter DeLuise remembers. 'It was a pleasure to work with Rene Auberjonois. He's such a powerful actor. My girlfriend (Anne Marie Loder) was in that. If you look carefully, you'll spot me as well.' (He plays the SGC soldier yelling 'move, move,' at the beginning.)

**DID YOU KNOW?** The extra climbing the ladder in the War Room as SG-1 enter is James Tichenor. The Eurondan generator was a reused prop from 'Into the Fire'.

## 69 UPGRADES

US Transmission Date: 14 Jul 2000
UK Transmission Date: 20 Sep 2000
Writer: David Rich
Director: Martin Wood
Cast: Teryl Rothery (Dr Janet Fraiser), Vanessa Angel (Anise/Freya), Dan Shea (Sgt Siler), Bill Nikolai (Technician #1), Laara Sadiq (Technician #2), Kristina Copeland (Waitress), Frank Topol (Big Guy), Daniel Mekes (SF #1), Tracy Westerholm (SF #2)

Tok'ra scientist Anise asks SG-1 to test armband devices which are believed to produce incredible strength and speed. Jack, Sam and Daniel volunteer, though Teal'c symbiont renders him immune. Anise suggests they attempt to destroy one of Apophis's warships. Fraiser's and Hammond's concerns grow as SG-1 begin to disobey orders.

**THE WIT AND WISDOM OF JACK O'NEILL** Anise: 'Your strength is five times that of a normal human.' Jack: 'So, no increase then?' And, to Hammond on their return: 'Just remember, I retired! *You* wanted me back!'

**ORIGINS OF THE SPECIES** The Atoniks' demise predates the Goa'uld. They probably became extinct because their armband technology stopped working, leaving them vulnerable. The wearer develops an antibody to combat the virus produced by the devices. The inscription on the armbands says, 'With great power comes great responsibility, and the ability to affect great consequences'.

The core of Apophis's ship is entirely encased in Trinium. Given the frequency with which this (supposedly rare) metal has been showing up recently (the Asgard use it in 'Small Victories', for instance), it's probable that PXY887 ('Spirits') isn't the only source. (This is confirmed in 'Between Two Fires'.) Goa'uld forceshields operate on a frequency oscillation principle.

Anise is a scientist and an archaeologist. She is driven and self-motivated. Her name means 'noble strength'. Her host, Freya, is more compassionate. She uses notebooks as she enjoys the tactile sensation of handwriting.

Weapons-grade Naqahdah is extremely dense.

**STEAK AND DRUGS AND A FIGHT** The virus released by the armbands causes increased hormones, producing a narcotic-like effect. It also increases metabolism to match the energy that the body requires, resulting in greater appetite and a fever which can cause organ failure. Under its influence, SG-1 go for a beer, a steak and a scuffle in O'Malley's Bar and Grill.

**THE CONSPIRACY STARTS AT CLOSING TIME** Hammond's intuition tells him that the Tok'ra are manipulating the SGC. Though early experiences with the Tok'ra proved invaluable for Earth ('Show and Tell', 'Into the Fire'), recently they've shown a lack of concern for the safety of Earth personnel and a desire to forward their own agenda (see 'Crossroads', 'Divide and Conquer'). Jack notes that the Tok'ra seem to show up only when they want something.

**POSSIBLE INFLUENCES** *Superman*, *The Flash*, *The Matrix* and *The Six Million Dollar Man*. Freya's name comes from the Norse goddess of fertility Freyja (see 'Red Sky').

**ACCIDENTS WILL HAPPEN** Siler suffers a broken arm after being accidentally knocked over a railing by Jack.

**'YOU MIGHT REMEMBER ME FROM...'** Vanessa Angel played Megan in *Baywatch* and Lisa in *Weird Science* and was in *G-Men from Hell* and *Kingpin*. Kristina Copeland appeared in *Catch Me if You Can*, *The Artist's Circle* and *Lured*. Frank Topol was in *Special Unit 2*.

**BEHIND THE CAMERA** David Rich wrote *Renegades* and episodes of *MacGyver*.

**HUSTLER!** Amanda Tapping found herself $100 richer

after Martin Wood wagered during rehearsals that she couldn't sink four strategically-placed pool-balls with one shot. She pulled it off. During filming, Wood unwisely repeated the bet. Amanda promptly repeated the feat.

**LOGIC, LET ME INTRODUCE YOU TO THIS WINDOW** How does Sam know with any accuracy how long it'll take for the cooling system to go critical? Daniel drinks beer, despite saying he didn't care for it in 'Shades of Grey' (see 'Children of the Gods'). When SG-1 go to O'Malley's, no-one notices that they're gone from Level 25, where someone is supposed to be observing them? Having done it once, they do it again to gear up for the mission (collecting hypodermics and sedatives). Teal'c gets into the Gateroom to watch SG-1 leave when no-one else is fast enough to beat the doors. When Jack picks up Hobbes' book, the light on his armband is white and Daniel's is off. As Jack is reading, his light appears to be off. It's on again when he says, 'I guess'. It's interesting that a Tok'ra, Freya, should have taken a Norse goddess's name. Is this a sign that they're being corrupted, perhaps?

**QUOTE/UNQUOTE** Jack: 'I'm Jack. It means ... what's in the box?'
Hammond: 'I thought the devices were supposed to enhance them physically, not make them stupid.'

**NOTES** 'If there's one thing I've learned in my time here it's that there's nothing wrong with a little prudence when dealing with alien devices.' The highlight of this episode is the pure joy that Sam, Daniel and Jack get from their new abilities. Daniel's delight that he can read 'really fast' is matched by Jack wanting to get out and hit things. 'Upgrades' balances a humorous story about the logistics of meta-human powers with a shading to the Tok'ra's agenda.

This is the first time we've seen Jack and Teal'c sparring since 'The Fifth Race'. Jack loves Jacob like a brother. Daniel notes that his name means 'God is my judge' in Hebrew. Under the armband's effect, Sam writes a thousand-page book on wormhole physics in under two hours. Sam prefers the taste of diet soda.

**CRITIQUE** SG-1 is, as John Mosby wrote in *DreamWatch*, 'even at its worst always watchable. The main cast have great chemistry and the dialogue (particularly from O'Neill) is dry comic timing at its best.'

**CAST AND CREW COMMENTS** According to Martin Wood, the speeded up sequences were shot at 96 frames-per-second so, during editing, SG-1 could acquire vapour trails. 'Upgrades' is one of producer Joe Mallozzi's favourite episodes. 'Robert Cooper did an amazing job on the rewrite. A lot of the time, the fans don't realise how many "good lines" are actually written by Brad or Robert. He's also one of the funniest writers I've ever seen. Before he got his hands on it, 'Upgrades' wasn't funny in the least.'

**DID YOU KNOW?** Four-foot pieces of Saran Wrap[70] stretched across the corridor were used for the Goa'uld forcefield. Watch closely and you'll see Anderson's nose impact with the material and squash. Eleven takes were required to per-

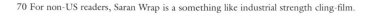

70 For non-US readers, Saran Wrap is a something like industrial strength cling-film.

*SEASON 4*

fect O'Neill casually tossing a ball of cellophane into a plastic cup, even though the ball landing in the cup wasn't the one leaving Rick's hand. The Norwegian ski-hat that O'Neill wears is the actor's own, a tribute to his Minnesotan roots.

# 70 CROSSROADS

US Transmission Date: 21 Jul 2000
UK Transmission Date: 27 Sep 2000
Writer: Katharyn Powers
Director: Peter DeLuise
Cast: Musetta Vander (Shan'auc), Vanessa Angel (Anise/Freya), Teryl Rothery (Dr Janet Fraiser), Peter Wingfield (Hebron/Tanith), Gary Jones (Sgt Walter Davis), Ron Halder (Cronus), Sean Millington (Ronac)

Shan'auc, an old flame of Teal'c, arrives from Chulak claiming to have communicated with her symbiont. She has convinced the Goa'uld to collaborate with the Tok'ra. They agree that Shan'auc's symbiont is of significant value and are willing to find it a host. But will they get one in time?

**TEAL'C'S (SUDDENLY) TRAUMATIC LOVE-LIFE** Shan'auc of the Red Hills had known Teal'c since before she became a priestess of the temple. Now believing the Goa'uld are false gods, she is sent to Earth by Bra'tac.

**ORIGINS OF THE SPECIES** A Jaffa's symbiont acts as an internal organ. There's an exchange of hormones and electrical impulses and, in the deepest state of kel-no'reem, communication can be achieved. There is much unrest on Chulak. Although the majority of Jaffa continue to worship Apophis, his attack on the planet ('Maternal Instinct') has resulted in some following Bra'tac. Amongst many Jaffa, Teal'c is as revered as the Goa'uld once were.

Queen Egeria, Roman goddess of fountains and childbirth and an advisor to Numa Pompilius, broke from the Goa'uld 2000 years ago and came to Earth to stop them taking humans as slaves. She founded the Tok'ra through her offspring before being killed by Ra. There are no Jaffa within the Tok'ra. Teal'c's father, Ronac, was killed by Cronus by having his symbiont crushed. Hebron of Paraval volunteered as a Tok'ra host for Tanith[71], knowing that he might end up being used as a counter-spy.

**SEX AND DRUGS AND ROCK 'N' ROLL** Teal'c emerges from Shan'auc's room with a massive grin on his face which suggests that something, ahem, *intimate* has occurred between them.

**THE CONSPIRACY STARTS AT CLOSING TIME** The Tok'ra suspected after Shau'nac's death that Tanith was deceiving them. They intend using him to pass on disinformation (see 'Exodus').

71 Phoenician goddess of fertility and the heavens. Tanith is also connected with the Egyptian Tanetu, goddess of light. She was the chief goddess of Carthage, and the Romans associated her with Juno.

**POSSIBLE INFLUENCES** Visually, *Silence of the Lambs*. The title is taken from a 1986 Walter Hill film based on Robert Johnson's 1928 song 'Cross Road Blues', about a bluesman bargaining with Satan.

**'YOU MIGHT REMEMBER ME FROM...'** Musetta Vander starred in the *Voyeur* computer game. She was Munita in *Wild Wild West* and appeared in *Buffy* and *The Cell*. Peter Wingfield will be familiar to British readers from *Soldier Soldier*. He was also Methos in *Highlander*. Sean Millington played Boswell in *Silencing Mary*. He's a star running back in the Canadian Football League with the BC Lions and was voted MVP in the 2000 Grey Cup.

**LOGIC, LET ME INTRODUCE YOU TO THIS WINDOW** Does Drey'auc know that Teal'c has a girlfriend? That may explain why she's living off-world. If the Tok'ra were able to find a host for the larva so quickly, why do they have so much trouble on other occasions? Tanith merges with Hebron awfully fast - he's able to speak almost immediately (see 'The Tok'ra'). The Vorash matte-painting shot from 'Jolinar's Memories' is reused. Of the five figures arriving, two are clearly Tok'ra and look nothing like Teal'c and Shan'auc. Is Tanith deceiving Hebron, his host, or impersonating him? This is never made clear. (However, see 'The Curse'.)

**GOA'ULD LEXICON** 'Tal'matte' is an expression of greeting. 'Kal'ma' means 'child'. 'Dal mek, creon te shree, tal'ma' means 'Our love does not end in death'. 'Kel'sha' is a greeting roughly equivalent to 'Good morning, I've just spent a night of passion with my girlfriend'.

**QUOTE/UNQUOTE** Anise: 'Your father asked that I shake your hand and give Colonel O'Neill a big kiss.' Sam: 'That might have been the other way around.'

**NOTES** 'This whole talking-to-two-people-in-one-body thing really sucks.' A hollow and far-fetched allegory about betrayal and guilt which, despite several fine performances (Judge, Musetta Vander and Peter Wingfield in particular), blows its big surprise ending.

Jack grows increasingly distrustful of the Tok'ra. He likes Freya, but isn't fond of Anise. He is amused that Bra'tac considers him Teal'c's apprentice. Or perhaps he's annoyed, and just covering it well? As a child, Teal'c was the strongest and bravest among his peers.

**CAST AND CREW COMMENTS** Peter DeLuise admits that the casting of Anise (a 'sexy alien chick') was influenced by the success of Seven of Nine on *Voyager* (see 'Wormhole X-Treme!').

**DID YOU KNOW?** A funeral scene for Shan'auc was filmed but cut from the episode as it was felt that the subtle confrontation of Teal'c and Tanith was a stronger ending.

## 71 DIVIDE AND CONQUER

US Transmission Date: 28 Jul 2000

UK Transmission Date: 4 Oct 2000
Writer: Tor Alexander Valenza
Director: Martin Wood
Cast: Teryl Rothery (Dr Janet Fraiser), JR Bourne (Martouf), Vanessa Angel (Anise/Freya), Bill Nikolai (Technician), Kirsten Robek (Lt Astor), Andrew Jackson (Per'sus), Phillip Mitchell (Major Graham), Roger Allford (The President)

During a meeting with the Tok'ra, Major Graham goes berserk before taking his own life. The SGC discover that Graham was a Zatarc, the victim of Goa'uld mind-control. There may be others within their ranks. Indeed, a subsequent Tok'ra test uncovers false memories in two more SGC personnel: Jack O'Neill and Sam Carter.

**SAM'S TRAUMATIC LOVE-LIFE** Faced with the possibility of being a Goa'uld assassin, Jack is forced to admit his feelings for Sam. He cares more for her than he should, considering his role as her commanding officer. Sam, herself, has a rotten day and ends it by having to kill Martouf, who's only just told Sam that he's fond of her.

**ORIGINS OF THE SPECIES** Supreme High Councillor Per'sus[72] comes to Earth to sign an official treaty with the president that outlines their alliance.
Zatarc programming, creates subconscious false memory. The victim is unaware of the programming which is triggered by visual or auditory signals. It can be detected only with Tok'ra technology: using a modified memory-recall device. Originally created to verify information retrieved from captured Goa'uld, the detector is unproven technology and can misread omissions as lies. Anise has documented three incidents in the past two months where Tok'ra operatives have suffered extreme behaviour ending in suicide. She presented her theory to the high council, but they didn't accept it.

**THE CONSPIRACY STARTS AT CLOSING TIME** During a mission to the Lasarians on P6Y325, SG-14 and SG-15 were attacked and six members were killed. SG-14 included Major Graham, Captain Blasdale, Lieutenant Astor and Sergeant Louis. The planet on which Apophis's new ship was destroyed ('Upgrades') was PX9757.

**IN THE INTERESTS OF NATIONAL SECURITY** Jack has done the 'drugged-out-strapped-to-the-bed thing,' possibly referring to his time in an Iraqi prison (see 'A Matter of Time').

**POSSIBLE INFLUENCES** *The Manchurian Candidate*, the *Star Trek: The Next Generation* episode 'The Mind's Eye', Ian Fleming's novel *The Man With The Golden Gun* and *Bladerunner*. The wheelchair-dolly shot of Fraiser and Hammond walking through the SGC may have been inspired by *The West Wing*.

**'YOU MIGHT REMEMBER ME FROM...'** Andrew Jackson was in *Specimen*. Kirsten Robek appeared in *Cats and Dogs* and *Cold Feet*.

**LOGIC, LET ME INTRODUCE YOU TO THIS WINDOW** One of the shot Tok'ra stays on his feet a few

72 Possibly named after Greek hero Perseus, son of Zeus, who slew Medusa the Gorgon and rescued Andromeda from the ocean god Nereus.

seconds, then falls. None of the scientists at the SGC question the reliability of the test - strange given that polygraphs (to which the Zatarc detector is compared) are inadmissible in courts. As Sam says: 'It's all based on assumptions, isn't it?' If it's so hard to detect a Zatarc, how can Anise be so sure that such operatives have been active only for two months? Why didn't anyone have a zat handy when they were trying to cure Astor? It takes a surprising amount of time for anyone at the SGC to realise that neither Freya nor Martouf has been tested. Much of Astor's flashback is stock footage from 'Into the Fire'.

**QUOTE/UNQUOTE** Daniel: 'I think these are the Jack O'Neill moments I'd probably miss the most.'

Freya: 'When we want to *lama-shen* ...' Jack: 'Excuse me?' Freya: 'I believe you call it ...' Jack: 'Something else!'

**NOTES** 'I didn't leave, because I'd have rather died myself than lose Carter. Because I care about her. A lot more than I'm supposed to.' The sin of omission is the central plank in this sequel to 'Upgrades' concerning Goa'uld suicide bombers. There was a hostile fan reaction to the death of the popular Martouf, but at least it provides the episode with some dramatic balance amid the, frankly disappointing, relationship-heavy script.

Freya has taken an interest in Jack, although her symbient favours Daniel for his intellect. She comes from a planet where people are free to share affection with each other and has heard that humans have many stigmas and inhibitions regarding intimacy.

**CAST AND CREW COMMENTS** Regarding reaction to Sam's and Jack's relationship Joe Mallozzi told *sci_fi.ign.com*: 'Military regulations strictly forbid fraternisation. The admission in 'Divide and Conquer' seems to have affected certain fans so deeply it's tainted their viewing of subsequent episodes. It will continue, subtle perhaps, but still there.'

On why Martouf was killed, Robert Cooper told a convention audience: 'Truth is we get flattered by the level of response when a character dies. It's drama. What attracted me to *Stargate* is that it's not a perfect world. It takes place as if it were happening now. These are people constantly faced with enemies with a higher level of advanced technology and they make mistakes. There are consequences. SG-1 makes mistakes and people are going to die. It doesn't always work out for the best.'

**DID YOU KNOW?** J R Bourne has worked three times with Martin Wood, and his characters have been killed on each occasion. (The others include the *Two* episode 'Armies of the Night'.)

# 72 WINDOW OF OPPORTUNITY

US Transmission Date: 4 Aug 2000
UK Transmission Date: 11 Oct 2000
Writers: Paul Mullie, Joseph Mallozzi
Director: Peter DeLuise
Cast: Robin Mossley (Malikai), Teryl Rothery (Dr Janet Fraiser), Dan Shea (Sgt Siler),

Daniel Bacon (Technician), Bill Nikolai (Technician[73]), Cam Cronin (Door Airman)

On P4X639, SG-1 meets Malikai, an explorer who shares Daniel's interest in what seems to be an alien computer. Malikai shoots Daniel and begins to programme the computer. As Jack and Teal'c attempt to stop him they find themselves back at the SGC earlier in the day, preparing to go on this mission. Then it happens again. And again. And again.

**THE WIT AND WISDOM OF JACK O'NEILL** 'What about Teal'c? Come on, is this the face of a crazy man? Bad example.' Jack endures the same 10 hours hundreds of times, unable to break the loop. He uses the time to learn pottery and an impressive amount of Latin, teach Teal'c how to juggle *and* resign his commission so that he can kiss Sam without official reprimand...

**SAM'S TRAUMATIC LOVE-LIFE** ... she doesn't seem too upset about it, either.

**ORIGINS OF THE SPECIES** The writings on the walls and the altar are a variation of the language of the Ancients, similar to Latin (see 'The Fifth Race'). They include a planetary history and description of the device, and reveal P4X639 thrived for thousands of years until it was struck by a cataclysm. The inhabitants built a time machine to change their own past but it didn't work, causing instead a continuous loop.

Malikai's wife died 12 years ago of a congenital heart weakness. He wants to go back in time to be with her.

**THE CONSPIRACY STARTS AT CLOSING TIME** SG-15 visited P4X639 two weeks ago and reported increasing solar activity. Coronal mass emissions, like giant solar flares, disrupt the planet's magnetic field and increase surface radiation. The device draws its energy from the ionisation in the atmosphere caused by geomagnetic storms which occur every 50 years. The beam from the device can access the Gate and create a time inversion. It establishes a simultaneous connection to 14 other worlds, including Earth and Alaris, creating a subspace bubble in which everything is cut off from the normal flow of time, resulting in a continuous loop repeating approximately each 10 hours.

According to Sam's theory, everyone on every planet within the bubble would be caught in the loop. Those planets with Stargates were able to access other Gates within the bubble (so, for example, Jack can dial Alaris for his golf game), but nothing outside of it. The Tok'ra have been trying to contact the SGC for three months, meaning that Jack and Teal'c lived through something like 200 loops - perhaps many more, as there's no of telling how long it was from the initial incident until the time that the Tok'ra first tried to establish contact.

**POSSIBLE INFLUENCES** Conceptually *Groundhog Day*, *The X-Files* episode 'Monday', *Star Trek: The Next Generation*'s 'Cause and Effect', *Buffy*'s 'Earshot' ('How hard can it be?'), *The Abominable Dr Phibes*, *Children of the Corn* (Malikai) and McDonald's ('Three fries short of a Happy Meal'). 'If at first you don't succeed,' is a quotation apocryphally attributed to Scottish king Robert the Bruce (1274-1329).

• • • • • • • • • • • • • • • • • • • • • • • • • • • • • • • • • • • • • • • • • • • • •

73 Character named 'Vern' in dialogue.

**'YOU MIGHT REMEMBER ME FROM...'** Cam Cronin played Clayton in *Cabin By the Lake* and Lyle in *No More Monkeys Jumpin' on the Bed*. Robin Mossley played Wilt in *MacGyver* and was in *The Man Who Used to be Me* and *Beyond Betrayal*.

**BEHIND THE CAMERA** Joe Malozzi also worked on *Mona the Vampire* and *Animal Crackers* and Paul Mullie's previous work includes *Largo Winch*.

**LOGIC, LET ME INTRODUCE YOU TO THIS WINDOW** The fruit loops are the same each time (they were actually glued to the spoon), but the people behind Jack in the mess aren't. How does Malikai have time to set-up the forcefield and still be able to work on the machine in each 10-hour loop? The Gate rotates during an incoming wormhole when the SGC are trying to set up the 'busy signal'. What did the gun do to Daniel? It looked similar to a zat, but Malikai later says that Daniel's 'living proof' the machine works, suggesting that he was killed. A figure is briefly reflected in Daniel's glasses. When Malakai activates the device, it establishes a wormhole, then immediately deactivates. But the electrical interference on Earth's Gate continues. What *was* the question Daniel that was constantly asking Jack at the start of each loop?

**THE ANCIENTS' LEXICON** 'Domavatus vestul motabilum' means 'master of the uncertain past'. 'Abicierum' is 'to give up'. 'Perennial adventus' means 'the approaching disaster'.

**QUOTE/UNQUOTE** Jack: 'What kind of archaeologist carries a weapon?' Daniel: 'I do!'

Jack: 'Every time we loop, Daniel asks me a question, and I wasn't paying attention the first time.'

Daniel, to Jack: 'I realise the Asgard returned you to normal, which is fortunate ... I suppose.'

**NOTES** 'Ask me tomorrow.' *Stargate*-goes-sitcom in a blisteringly funny (yet touching) tribute to *Groundhog Day*. Dozens of memorable little moments (including Jack's obsession with magnets and growing frustration with the banality of repetition and Teal'c getting hit in the face with the door). A *very* popular episode and rightly so; one that benefits from repeated viewing and a willingness on the part of the audience to suspend their prejudices for 45 minutes.

Jack, it's suggested, *never* reads briefing notes. Daniel seems to like waffles. He has a touch-screen PC. Continuity references to '1969', 'The Fifth Race' and 'Cold Lazarus'. The book Jack reads is called *Latin for the Novice* by Joseph Mallozzi Ph.D.

**CRITIQUE** 'Yes, it's *Groundhog Day* and the production team members *know* that *we know*, so they let O'Neill say so,' wrote *TV Zone*.

'A fan's dream,' noted Paul Spragg. 'Richard Dean Anderson's usually off the-cuff remarks translate wonderfully into a sequence of comic vignettes. Whether you want to see the normally stoic Teal'c release his frustrations by slamming an SG technician in the face with a door, listen to Hammond's horrified reaction to O'Neill's golf game through the Stargate or see the colonel finally making his feelings known in a passionate kiss with Carter, it's everything viewers could wish for.'

**CAST AND CREW COMMENTS** 'Our background's in comedy writing,' noted Paul Mullie, 'so this was an ideal story for us. It was fun to watch it being shot because everyone embraced it for the light-hearted adventure that it was.'

**DID YOU KNOW?** This episode originally under-ran by some three minutes, requiring several additional sequences to be filmed during 'Watergate'. These include much of the montage footage - Jack and Teal'c juggling, Jack learning pottery and Anderson finally fulfilling a long-held fantasy to drive a golf ball through the Stargate.

The image of Malakai's wife is that of production accountant Nicole Forest.

# 73  WATERGATE

US Transmission Date: 11 Aug 2000
UK Transmission Date: 18 Oct 2000
Writer: Robert C Cooper
Director: Martin Wood
Cast: Marina Sirtis (Svetlana Markov), Tom McBeath (Harry Maybourne), Gary Jones (Sgt Walter Davis), Daryl Scheelar (Co-Pilot)

The SGC learn that the Russians have a Stargate, recovered from Thor's ship. Furthermore, it's locked open, maintaining a perpetual wormhole. At the request of Svetlana Markov, SG-1 travel to Siberia. They find all the Russian personnel dead and the Stargate connected to a water-world. Daniel, Sam and Svetlana head through the wormhole in a submarine, attempting to shut the Gate. Jack and Teal'c find the frozen body of Harry Maybourne. Who promptly comes back to life.

**THE WIT AND WISDOM OF JACK O'NEILL** Jack: 'I suppose you expect my male bravado to kick in right about now.' Svetlana: 'I have read your file.' Jack: 'No mention of bravado, eh?'

**ORIGINS OF THE SPECIES** A water sample from the planet had unbelievable properties, spontaneously emitting energy in the form of heat. This was due to countless microscopic lifeforms in the water capable of entering and controlling a human body.

**THE CONSPIRACY STARTS AT CLOSING TIME** SG-1's mission before the discovery of the Russian Gate was the relocation of the Enkarans (see 'Scorched Earth'). Seven SG teams were trapped offworld by the Gate malfunction.

**YE CANNAE CHANGE THE LAWS OF PHYSICS** 'Watergate' destroys two long-held notions on Stargate physics. First, that a Gate filled with matter cannot open ('Children of the Gods', 'New Ground'). Here, the Gate is submerged underwater. It's also been established that the alpha Gate (recovered from Giza, used by the SGC and now in the possession of the Russians) supersedes the beta (discovered in Antarctica and now at the SGC). This means that if someone offworld gates to Earth, they will arrive at the alpha Gate. This can be changed only by overpowering the off-world Gate, thus causing the wormhole to jump to the second Gate instead (as in 'Solitudes', 'Touchstone').

Secondly, Svetlana says that a Stargate must be hooked up to a power source (a DHD or a computer) in order to receive an incoming wormhole. The Russians, thus, disconnect their Stargate when it's not in use, so that SGC teams and visitors like the Tok'ra go, instead, to the SGC. This violates evidence from 'Prisoners', where that Gate had no DHD and no power source - but received incoming wormholes daily. Additionally Stargates are said to retain some residual power even after disconnection - enough to dial once (see 'Nemesis'). This ought, therefore, to be enough to allow an incoming wormhole to connect to the Russian Gate even if it's disconnected from its DHD.

**IN THE INTERESTS OF NATIONAL SECURITY** The Russians recovered the Gate from the ocean two months ago after Thor's ship crashed. The DHD from Giza was confiscated from the Germans after World War II (see '48 Hours'). They are located in a decommissioned power plant in Siberian near the Kuybyshev Airbase. Doctor Svetlana Markov, chief science officer and second in command to Colonel Sokalov, helped to establish the Russian programme against the wishes of powerful people in her government, who wanted to expose the SGC. The project was in operation for 37 days and explored seven planets when a malfunction wouldn't allow the Gate to close (see 'The Tomb'). The Russians have access to extensive files on the SGC (provided by Maybourne). An 'Extreme Measures Protocol' releases Substance 35, a nerve gas, into the facility. Forty-seven people at the Russian base were killed.

**POSSIBLE INFLUENCES** *Voyage to the Bottom of the Sea*, *Goldeneye*, *The Abyss*, *The Thing* and *Dr Strangelove*. Also *Batman* ('Holy frozen bad guys'). The title is taken from the name of a hotel in Washington DC where, in 1972, a group of men employed by the re-election organisation of President Nixon were caught breaking into the Democratic Party HQ. The subsequent political scandal was exacerbated by attempts to conceal White House officials' approval of the burglary. The term now means any similar public scandal, especially one involving politicians and cover-ups.

**'YOU MIGHT REMEMBER ME FROM...'** Marina Sirtis was Deanna Troi in *Star Trek: The Next Generation* and numerous spin-offs. She also appeared in *Death Wish 3*, *The Wicked Lady* and *Minder*.

**LOGIC, LET ME INTRODUCE YOU TO THIS WINDOW** Jack says he's never been in a submarine before. He was in one four episodes ago! Maybourne's chest moves whilst he's still frozen (and well before Jack and Teal'c discover that he's alive). One of the dead scientists has his eyes open when we first see him, but closed in the next shot.

**QUOTE/UNQUOTE** Svetlana: 'I have read extensive files on all of you.' Jack: 'The question is how?' Svetlana: 'I learned to read English at the age of six. It is not difficult.'

Teal'c: 'This does not seem wise, O'Neill.' Jack: 'I said it was easy, not wise.'

Svetlana: 'The sub is Swiss.' Daniel: 'So they occasionally catch fire, but they keep perfect time. Sorry. I think I've been hanging around Jack O'Neill too much.'

**NOTES** 'The Russians have a Stargate?' What a disap-

*SEASON 4*

pointment that a series as sharp as *SG-1* is still stuck in the mindset of hawkish Cold War paranoia. For God's sake guys, the Berlin Wall's been down a decade (see also 'The Tomb'). Still, 'Watergate' features clever ideas. Svetlana and Sam make a good team (with Daniel throwing in pithy quips from the sidelines).

Jack has parachuted hundreds of times. Teal'c, seemingly, has not. There are continuity references to 'Solitudes', 'Touchstone', 'Nemesis' and 'A Matter of Time'.

**CAST AND CREW COMMENTS** 'I wrote the original outline during the first season,' revealed Robert Cooper. 'Everyone asked "Are you out of your mind?" Our visual effects supervisor said it would cost eight times the budget of the season to produce. Needless to say, we didn't do it.'

'We shot in an industrial kitchen at the old Expo site in Vancouver,' Lynn Smith remembered. 'The set decorators brought in everything from stacks of dishes to whole salamis to hang up. They even smudged the sink to make it look used. I often feel sorry for these guys because they don't get the credit they deserve.'

**DID YOU KNOW?** During the filming of this episode, Kurt Russell, who was shooting *3,000 Miles to Graceland* nearby, made a visit to the *SG-1* set. 'I told him that, with all due respect, I had to bring out a sense of humour in the guy,' said Richard Dean Anderson.

# 74 THE FIRST ONES

US Transmission Date: 18 Aug 2000
UK Transmission Date: 25 Oct 2000
Writer: Peter DeLuise
Director: Peter DeLuise
Cast: Gary Jones (Sgt Walter Davis), Jason Schombing (Robert Rothman), Steve Bacic (Major Coburn), Dion Johnstone (Chaka), Rob Lee (Pierce), Russell Ferrier (Captain Griff), Vincent Hammond (Unas), Barry Levy (Unas)

On P3X888, Daniel is captured by an Unas. SG-1 mount a rescue mission but discover that the planet's water supply is full of Goa'uld symbionts. Whilst Jack, Teal'c and Sam cope with the possibility that one of their colleagues has been inhabited by a Goa'uld, Daniel is trying to communicate with his captor.

**ORIGINS OF THE SPECIES** Daniel joins SG-11 for an archaeological survey of P3X888. He theorises that this was perhaps the planet from which the primordial Goa'uld originated and that they evolved for millions of years in the prehistoric oceans before taking Unas hosts. Those who did, subsequently learned to use the Stargate and left the planet. No traces of Naqahdah were found in Goa'uld fossils, suggesting that it became part of their make-up later in their evolution. The aboriginal Unas took refuge in the caves for protection against attack.

**THE CONSPIRACY STARTS AT CLOSING TIME** Members of the SG-11 archaeological team include Major Hawkins, Loder, Sanchez and Robert Rothman (see 'Forever in a Day'). Members of SG-2 joining SG-1 for search and rescue include Major Coburn and Captain Griff. Jackson and Rothman discovered multiple fossilised Goa'uld in three weeks on five sites. One was physically different, and they believed it could have been a queen. They named the fossils Cleo, Julius and Brutus.

**POSSIBLE INFLUENCES** 'My inspiration came from *Enemy Mine*, *Robinson Crusoe* and *Iceman*,' notes Peter DeLuise. Chaka was the ape-boy in *Land of the Lost*. Griff is a homage to director Sam Fuller, who had a character with this name in all of his movies. Allusions to *Julius Caesar*, *The Thing*, *Predator* (Hawkins), the rite-of-passage rituals of the Masai (young warriors killing a lion to prove their manhood) and the Australian Aborigines (walkabout), *Piranha*, *Casablanca* ('a beautiful friendship') and *Androcles and the Lion*. Rothman is named after Jonathan Glassner's lawyer. The Unas word 'nan' (eat) comes from the Hindi bread, excellent with a chicken biryani.

**'YOU MIGHT REMEMBER ME FROM...'** Russell Ferrier appeared in *Crying Freedom* and *Camouflage*.

**LOGIC, LET ME INTRODUCE YOU TO THIS WINDOW** Sam's hair is *very* long for a military officer. Daniel's wet clothes dry remarkably quickly. Why would the Ancients build a Stargate on this particular planet? And how did the Goa'uld learn to use it? Jack and Teal'c both address Major Coburn as "Sergeant". The arrow that Daniel scratches on the cave wall, indicating THIS WAY, is much more elaborate than he had time to achieve. Why are there still under-evolved Unas and Goa'uld? It seems logical that both species would continue to exist after some left the planet. But as the Unas learned to defend themselves (hiding in caves, wearing bone necklaces to guard their necks), the Goa'uld would be limited in their development. Daniel mentioned numerous outdated theories about alpha males - he's supposed to be an educated man, he should know better. In this episode the team switch from MP5s to FN P-90s as their weapon of choice. The P-90 is not, technically, either a submachine gun or assault rifle, FN market it as a Personal Defence Weapon. Though it would be a good choice for SG-1 to use against armoured Jaffa, they would have enormous problems with over-penetration against unarmoured opponents, or inside buildings with wood and plaster walls.

**QUOTE/UNQUOTE** Daniel: 'This is a radio. It's so my friends can find me. And shoot you.'

Teal'c: 'Trust in me, O'Neill.' Jack: 'What if I'm not O'Neill?' Teal'c: 'Then I was not talking to you.'

Daniel: 'Don't say "ka" till you've tried it.'

**NOTES** 'Anybody with a snake in their head, raise their hand.' Highly derivative, but another fundamental element in the *SG-1* mission statement, with Daniel proving his ability to talk his way out of being eaten. The game of *Toss the Symbiont Head* is fun.

Daniel gives chocolate to Chaka. 'I met my father-in-law like this,' he says referring to his initial meeting with Kasuf in the *Stargate* movie.

SEASON 4

DID YOU KNOW? 'Every week we get a script. It's amazing to see what these people are doing,' notes master sergeant Tom Giannazzo of the Air Force Entertainment Liaison Office who works closely with the production to ensure that military accuracy is maintained. 'The scripts come in via e-mail, we give [writers] notes for things that are problems, such as relationships and language.' Tom also keeps an eye on such minutiae as unmilitary hairstyles. The AFELO even managed to acquire a CF-130 coast-guard aeroplane for 'Watergate', from which SG-1 parachuted into Siberia. The co-operation works both ways. 'We've put the cast to good use,' notes Tom. 'They've all recorded announcements for the Air Force Recruiting Service.'

# 75 SCORCHED EARTH

US Transmission Date: 25 Aug 2000
UK Transmission Date: 1 Nov 2000
Writers: Paul Mullie, Joseph Mallozzi
Director: Martin Wood
Cast: Brian Markinson (Lotan), Marilyn Norry (Hedrazar), Alessandro Juliani (Eliam), Rob Court (Caleb), Nikki Smook (Mikka)

> Thanks to SG-1, the Enkarans are freed from Goa'uld slavery to a safer, more hospitable world. But one of their villages is attacked by a mysterious ship. When SG-1 investigate, they discover a terraforming exercise by a long-dormant species. Which means certain death for the Enkarans.

**THE WIT AND WISDOM OF JACK O'NEILL** 'We're talking about a bunch of freeze-dried aliens whose civilisation was lost a long time ago.'

**ORIGINS OF THE SPECIES** There's no Stargate on the Enkaran homeworld. The Goa'uld kidnapped their ancestors in ships and they were transported by the SGC to P5S381. They require a dense ozone layer to protect them against radiation, as even low levels cause blindness.

The Gad-Meer, whose physiology is sulphur-based, were an advanced and peaceful race who fell victim to a superior military power. They appear reptilian and have long tails. They placed all their knowledge and culture, from 10,000 years of civilisation, into the ship, looking for a world to colonise. The ship terraforms the planet by destroying all native organisms and replacing the atmosphere with sulphur-dioxide. Once the terraforming process has begun, it must be completed. The ship is two miles in diameter and the curtain of energy stretches for over 20 miles.

Lotan is a bio-mechanical representation of the Enkarans, assembled to facilitate communication.

**THE CONSPIRACY STARTS AT CLOSING TIME** If a feedback loop is created within a Naqahdah reactor, it creates a powerful bomb.

**POSSIBLE INFLUENCES** *E.T. The Extraterrestrial, Star Trek: The Next*

*Generation*'s 'The Measure of the Man' and 'Ensigns of Command'.

**'YOU MIGHT REMEMBER ME FROM...'** Brian Markinson appeared in *Bad Faith*, *Apollo 13*, *What Planet Are You from?* and *Star Trek: Voyager*. Marilyn Norry was in *Panic in the Skies* and *Mission to Mars*. Nikki Smook is Michael Greenburg's wife.

**LOGIC, LET ME INTRODUCE YOU TO THIS WINDOW** If the Enkarans require such specific planetary conditions to survive that, with the exception of their homeworld, there seems to be only one planet in the universe that can support them, then where have they been since the Goa'uld took their ancestors from the homeworld 'generations ago'? And, wherever it was, why haven't they all perished already?

**QUOTE/UNQUOTE** Jack: 'It's a no-win situation but we're not gonna sit around and watch these people gets slaughtered.'

**NOTES** 'Come back in a year and you will find this planet transformed.' A fantastic ethical debate on who has the greater right to life. The conflict between Daniel and Jack is well played, though O'Neill's solution (a big bomb) is simplistic and banal. Perhaps for that reason the episode wasn't popular with fandom in general and with Anderson himself.

Many of the visual effects were created at Windmill Studios in Ireland.

**DID YOU KNOW?** The interior of Lotan's ship uses redressed sets from the *Biliskner* in 'Nemesis' and Togar's lab in 'Urgo'. Location filming was briefly interrupted when a grizzly bear wandered onto set. 'Chris almost wet his pants!' noted Michael Shanks. Indeed, working on *SG-1* has been one (occasionally scatological) laugh after another. 'It's like working on a high school production', Shanks notes. 'We get our job done, but with the most adolescent behaviour possible. There's a lot of flatulence onset. We're into absurdist humour like *Monty Python* and *Austin Powers*. Anderson is the biggest kid you can imagine.'

# 76 BENEATH THE SURFACE

US Transmission Date: 1 Sep 2000
UK Transmission Date: 8 Nov 2000
Writer: Heather E Ash
Director: Peter DeLuise
Cast: Teryl Rothery (Dr Janet Fraiser), Gary Jones (Sgt Walter Davis), Russell Ferrier (Griff), Alison Matthews (Brenna), Laurie Murdoch (Calder), Kim Hawthorne (Kegan), Brian Drummond (Attendant), Jason Griffiths (Worker), Bruce Campbell (Worker)

> Jonah, Therra, Carlin and Tor are labourers working in the mines beneath an ice-covered planet who have no memories of their past lives as members of *SG-1*. Meanwhile, Hammond is faced with the possibility that SG-1 have perished on the planet's icy surface.

**SAM'S TRAUMATIC LOVE-LIFE** She lays her head on Jack's shoulder and looks fondly into his eyes. Sadly, they both believe that they're someone else. When memories of their true relationship resurfaces, the two obviously feel some regret.

**ORIGINS OF THE SPECIES** P3R118 is advanced in metallurgical and chemical technologies, despite a lingering ice age. Mine workers are given new personalities through a memory stamp, ensuring that they don't learn of true conditions in the idyllic domed city, which has no crime or unemployment. Nightsickness is the term given to failure of the memory stamp.

**THE CONSPIRACY STARTS AT CLOSING TIME** Major Griff and SG-2 are sent on a rescue mission to find SG-1.

**POSSIBLE INFLUENCES** Visually, *Metropolis, Max Max II: The Road Warrior, 1984, The Flintstones, Star Trek*'s 'For the World is Hollow and I Have Touched the Sky' and *Logan's Run*. Also, *The Simpsons* ('He's bald and wears a short-sleeved shirt and somehow he's very important to me. I think his name's Homer') and *Close Encounters of the Third Kind* (the dome). And, the two-part *Star Trek: Voyager* episode 'Workforce' (in which our heroes, believing themselves to be someone else, are working in an alien power plant; the main female having a romance and only the black guy resisting the mind-control). Except that the *Voyager* version was twice as long and half as good.

**'YOU MIGHT REMEMBER ME FROM...'** Alison Matthews played Emily Gordon in *Just Deal*. Kimberly Hawthorne appeared in *Voyage of the Unicorn*. Laurie Murdoch was in *Life, Or Somthing Like It*.

**LOGIC, LET ME INTRODUCE YOU TO THIS WINDOW** When Jack shoots out the skylight, why don't the glass shards fall on the miners below? Griff can only have been promoted in the last few weeks (as he was a captain in 'The First Ones'). Janet Fraiser also may have been promoted judging by the major's oak-leaves on her uniform. Where do they grow Kiwi fruit on an ice-planet (see 'Wormhole X-Treme!')?

**QUOTE/UNQUOTE** Sam: 'How do you stay so calm?' Jack: 'I think in another life I've handled dangerous explosives.'
    Jack: 'Where does Homer fit in?'

**NOTES** 'They passed judgment on us ... I'm simply doing the same.' A harsh allegory of forced allegiances, 'Beneath the Surface' is dramatically interesting in structure, and looks gorgeous, but it takes a while to get the audience's attention.
    Teal'c must perform kelno'reem daily (see 'Holiday'). Janet seems to be trained in covert operations, since she volunteers to join Griff's rescue team.

**DID YOU KNOW?** The broadcasts of the fourth season episodes (and, subsequently, the fifth) on Showtime's *Sci-Friday* at 10pm were prefaced by short monochrome trailers featuring the cast members announcing 'It's 10-sharp.'

## 77 POINT OF NO RETURN

US Transmission Date: 8 Sep 2000
UK Transmission Date: 15 Nov 2000
Writers: Paul Mullie, Joseph Mallozzi
Director: William Gereghty
Cast: Teryl Rothery (Dr Janet Fraiser), Willie Garson (Martin Lloyd), Robert Lewis (Tanner), Mars Andersons (Bob), Matthew Bennett (Ted), Francis Boyle (Sgt Peters)

The SGC is contacted by a conspiracy theorist, Martin Lloyd, who seems to have detailed knowledge of the Stargate programme. Jack meets Martin, who insists that he is really an alien. Jack initially believes that Martin is no more than a harmless crank, but a series of strange events suggest that there could be some truth in his story.

**THE WIT AND WISDOM OF JACK O'NEILL** Martin: 'A top-secret government programme involving instantaneous travel to other solar systems by means of a device known as a Stargate.' Jack: 'Sounds like a good idea for a TV show ... If you're into that sort of thing.' (See 'Wormhole X-Treme!')

**ORIGINS OF THE SPECIES** Martin's homeworld was under attack from the Goa'uld. He and his colleagues were sent to find allies. Realising that they were losing the war, they abandoned their ship in an escape pod and hid, as deserters, on Earth.

**SEX AND DRUGS AND ROCK 'N' ROLL** Tanner, Martin's psychiatrist, prescribes a number of medications including doxepin, haloperidol, perphenazine, lithium, and valium, mixed with indeterminate chemicals, to control Martin's memory and behaviour.

**THE CONSPIRACY STARTS AT CLOSING TIME** Martin calls the SGC from Butte, Montana and arranges a meeting with Jack at the New Clover Leaf restaurant in Billings. He alludes to numerous alleged government conspiracies, including Roswell, the Kennedy assassinations, CIA-sanctioned microwave harassment, crop circles, cow mutilations, the Apollo cover-up (the lunar landings *weren't* a hoax, he notes; that was a story created by the government to divert attention from the *real* cover-up), black helicopters and the 'lizard people' (a possible reference to David Icke's book *The Biggest Secret* and its alleged reptilian New World Order, the Illuminati). Martin learned the name Stargate in an online chatroom (most of the discussion of which, he says, was disinformation). Jack confirms that there *is* a Project Stargate, but it has nothing to do with aliens. (It's about, wait for it, *magnets*: see 'Window of Opportunity').

Martin's driver's licence number is 73890472398. His address is 10185 Mitchell Way, Billings, MT50619. He and his colleagues have clearly been on Earth for some time as the licence was issued in April 1996. Martin was once arrested for protesting outside a TV station claiming that subliminal advertising was controlling his thoughts.

**STRANGER THAN FICTION** The CIA really *did* operate something called Project Stargate during the 1970s. It was a study into using psychics for remote-viewing of Soviet military locations.[74]

**IN THE INTERESTS OF NATIONAL SECURITY** Not everyone at the vessel recovery site seems to have clearance and knowledge of the SGC. For instance, Teal'c hides his forehead seal from a soldier at one point.

**POSSIBLE INFLUENCES** *The X-Files* (especially 'Jose Chung's *From Outer Space*', 'Bad Blood', 'Unusual Suspects' and the characters of *The Lone Gunmen*), *Twin Peaks* (Jack ordering coffee and cherry pie) and *The Simpsons'* 'Grandpa Vs. Sexual Inadequacy'. Jack watches *The Day the Earth Stood Still* in the motel. Numerous lava lamps and UFO iconography decorate Martin's apartment. Big Sky Plumbing is a cover-organisation for the SGC, perhaps a reference to 'the Plumbers', the CIA dirty-tricks squad employed by the Nixon administration and heavily involved in Watergate. The title was the name of John Badham's 1993 US remake of *La Femme Nikita*. Also, Philip K Dick's letters and memoirs (microwave harassment).

**'YOU MIGHT REMEMBER ME FROM...'** In addition to appearing in *There's Something About Mary, Being John Malkovich, Mars Attacks!, Our Lips Are Sealed, Groundhog Day, Buffy, Spin City, It's a Shame About Ray* and *The Rock* and playing Henry Coffield in *NYPD Blue* and Stanford Blatch in *Sex in the City*, Willlie Garson has made something of a career of portraying Lee Oswald, in both *Ruby* and *Quantum Leap*. Mar Andersons was in *Seeking Winonas* and *First Shot*.

**LOGIC, LET ME INTRODUCE YOU TO THIS WINDOW** It seems irresponsible for Jack and Teal'c not to look around a bit more on Martin's planet before returning to Earth. There may have been survivors. One of the glyphs that Martin wrote doesn't match the address dialled. How does Martin acquire the specific information he has about the SGC (Jack's name, for instance, or its location)? A camera lens is reflected on the table in the opening shot. Why do the aliens refer to their escape pod as 'the experiment'? Why do they waste time clearing out Tanner's office? It is implied that this is to cast doubt on Martin's story but then, why leave a window with the man's name stencilled on it? Daniel does a very competent stunt-roll.

**QUOTE/UNQUOTE** Daniel: 'I've never been on a stakeout before. Shouldn't we have doughnuts or something?' And, to Tanner: 'You're not a *real* doctor, are you?'

Martin: 'Just because I'm from another planet, I have no rights? Doesn't the Geneva Convention cover extraterrestrials?'

**NOTES** 'Listen, Murray, I'm really sorry I tried to bite you.' Like *The X-Files* and *Buffy*, SG-1 discovers the ability to laugh at oneself isn't the turnoff

• • • • • • • • • • • • • • • • • • • • • • • • • • • • • • • • • • • • • • • • • • • • • • • • •

74 'Stargate' was one of a number of associated programmes conducted by the CIA to evaluate controlled remote-viewing as an intelligence tool. These were initiated in response to concerns about reported Soviets investigations of psychic phenomena. The resources devoted to Soviet psychotronics suggested that they had achieved some breakthroughs, though the matter was considered speculative and somewhat controversial. Remote-viewing research began in the US 1972 at the Stanford Research Institute. An operational unit employed remote-viewers to perform intelligence-gathering and psychic warfare.

that the more po-faced and snobbish end of SF fandom would have us believe. This is a fabulously silly exercise in one-liners with great performances from the regulars and Willie Garson. For once the woods around Vancouver play Earth instead of an alien planet.

Daniel is translating a cuneiform tablet that SG-1 found on P3O255. Sam can pick locks. She's currently calibrating the MALP sensors for long-term reconnaissance on P5X3D7. Teal'c rarely gets an opportunity to see much of Earth. But when he does, he finds something fascinating (on this occasion, a vibrating bed in a cheap motel). The waitress who brings Jack and Martin their bill was, apparently, the winner of an internet competition to appear in an episode. The headline of the *Whistle Blower* magazine Teal'c reads is the brilliant HEADLESS ALIEN FOUND IN TOPLESS BAR - AS DANCER SWUNG AROUND POLE SHE NOTICES DECAPITATED ALIEN WASN'T GROOVIN'.

**CRITIQUE** 'A nice comedic episode with a twist,' noted *space.com*'s Michael Bender. 'We have a crank alien enthusiast who really turns out to be an alien as well as some great scenes with Teal'c as "Murray", wearing all sorts of amusing hats. I also like the bits of seriousness they throw in such as our heroes' rather ominous ability to disregard civil rights in the name of national security.'

**CAST AND CREW COMMENTS** A chance remark by a fan gave the writers a spark of inspiration for this episode. 'Some people apparently believe that the Stargate is real, that the TV show is a cover by the military,' Paul Mullie notes. 'I thought, there's a story there about the world of conspiracy theories.'

**DID YOU KNOW?** 'You can only fool people with smoke and mirrors and special effects for so long before it becomes *blah!*' Anderson said with refreshing honesty. 'We ebb and flow, we're not hitting home runs every week but we're consistently getting better at telling good stories in our arena. I'd no expectations at the beginning, but I'm working with great people on a good project.'

# 78 TANGENT

US Transmission Date: 15 Sep 2000
UK Transmission Date: 22 Nov 2000
Writer: Michael Cassut
Director: Peter DeLuise
Cast: Peter Williams (Apophis), Carmen Argenziano (Jacob Carter), Colin Cunningham (Major Davis), Steven Williams (General Virdrine)

A test of X301, an experimental aircraft adapted from Goa'uld technology, sends Jack and Teal'c hurtling out of Earth's orbit An attempt to alter the craft's course fails, so Daniel seeks off-world help. He learns that the Tok'ra have a ship capable of reaching the stricken X301, but it's on a covert mission in Goa'uld territory.

**THE WIT AND WISDOM OF JACK O'NEILL** Jack: 'We didn't spring a leak. Though I may have just taken one.' And, to Jacob: 'D'you know your ship's bigger than ours?'

**ORIGINS OF THE SPECIES** P2C257 is a Goa'uld-occupied world within a scout-ship's range of Earth. SG-14 spent several days observing a mining operation and Jacob is on a mission to blow it up. After Teal'c's betrayal ('Children of the Gods'), Apophis placed a homing device in all his death gliders.

The Tollan didn't have a ship close enough to Earth to reach Teal'c and Jack within a year. The Tok'ra high council refuse to contact Jacob and jeopardise him but, thanks to clues from Anise, Sam locates him.

**THE TECHNOLOGY STARTS AT CLOSING TIME** The X301 is a hybrid made from the Goa'uld death gliders recovered in 'The Serpent's Lair'. The power source doesn't exert force against gravity but takes inertia out of the equation, making pilots immune to G-force. It's equipped with stealth technology and two AIM-120A air-to-air missiles that could destroy a Goa'uld mothership if armed with Naqahdah-enhanced warheads (see 'Redemption Part 1').

**POSSIBLE INFLUENCES** An overt homage to *Apollo 13* and *Marooned*. Also, *Spies Like Us*, *Top Gun*, *The Right Stuff*, *Empire of the Sun*, *Star Trek* ('"Beam them out"? What am I, Scotty?') and *The Wizard of Oz*.

**'YOU MIGHT REMEMBER ME FROM...'** Steven Williams is best known as Mr X in *The X-Files*. He also appeared in *Route 666*, *21 Jump Street*, *Corrina Corrina*, *The Dukes of Hazzard* and *Better Off Dead*.

**LOGIC, LET ME INTRODUCE YOU TO THIS WINDOW** It seems odd that Apophis's homing device didn't activate until now. Teal'c has piloted the X301 *at least* twice prior to the test flight (for General Vidrine at the beginning and in 'The Serpent's Lair'). Transport rings don't need a specific receiving end to work. A ship's rings can transport aboard something floating in space, but it must be within five metres. Some of rear-screen work on Jupiter is badly superimposed. One of Jack's radio messages is different at the SGC from when he recorded it. There are a few time anomalies, particularly surrounding the missile burn. Sam tells Jack and Teal'c to perform the burn at 16:22. They do, and the SGC receives preliminary data indicating that it didn't work, which Sam immediately radios back to them. At 18:13 (nearly two hours later). Why doesn't the warhead explode when it hits the X301? Teal'c and Jack are in the vacuum of space with no protection suits. Only for five seconds, maybe, but still they should freeze to death (as the temperature of space is near absolute zero) even if they didn't asphyxiate (as the sudden decompression should collapse their lungs). On the DVD commentary of this episode, Peter DeLuise makes a good fist of suggesting that it *is* possible to survive for a very brief time in space, but this author wonders if Peter has ever tried it for himself just a make sure? Thought not.

**QUOTE/UNQUOTE** Jack; 'Is that what I think it is?' Teal'c: 'If you think it is Earth, yes.' Jack: 'It's *shrinking*.' Teal'c: 'Its size remains constant. Rather, it is we who are moving away at extreme velocity.'

**NOTES** 'You can't just stick a US Air Force sticker on the side of a death glider and call it yours.' One of the best episodes, 'Tangent' triumphantly wears its source material ('Cheyenne, we have a problem!') in a postmodern, almost abstract way. The drama comes from the emotions of those involved - the quiet anguish of Don Davis and Colin Cunningham is a fine example. When other series do this kind of thing it feel forced and hackneyed. When *SG-1* does so, it can usually manage to make it feel *right*.

Location for the opening sequences was Pitt Meadows Airfield near Vancouver.

**CAST AND CREW COMMENTS** Peter DeLuise notes: 'This is a credit to Brad Wright's ingenuity in how to make two guys floating in space into an hour of television.'

**DID YOU KNOW?** Within hours of this episode's broadcast, internet newsgroups were filled with fans talking about 'a simple, elegant visual-effects shot,' as Brad Wright described it. Yet hundreds of posters were compelled to ask: if the ship was leaving the solar system, how could it possibly have crossed the sun's path at 90°? This amused Wright, though not as much as one fan who subsequently posted a series of animated diagrams elaborately describing the exact orbital path that the ship *could* have taken to cross in front of the sun.

# 79 THE CURSE

US Transmission Date: 22 Sep 2000
UK Transmission Date: 6 Dec 2000
Writers: Paul Mullie, Joseph Mallozzi
Director: Andy Mikita
Cast: Teryl Rothery (Dr Janet Fraiser), Anna-Louise Plowman (Sarah Gardner/Osiris), Ben Bass (Steven Rayner), David Abbott (Dr Jordan), Lorena Gale (Curator), Dan Shea (Sgt Siler)

> Daniel's archaeology professor dies in an explosion, and Daniel goes to his funeral. But as he reacquaints himself with his former colleagues, he begins to suspect that Jordan's death may not have been an accident. One of the items that the professor was studying contains a perfectly preserved Goa'uld symbiont.

**ORIGINS OF THE SPECIES** Isis was the Egyptian mother-goddess and consort of Osiris, the first Pharaoh. According to legend, he was placed in a box and dumped in the Nile by his brother Setesh (see 'Seth'). Normally, a Goa'uld symbiont is capable of withstanding a sedative (see 'Crossroads'). Osiris learns that the SGC was responsible for the deaths of Ra, Seth, Hathor and Sokar (see 'Stargate', 'Seth', 'Out of Mind', 'The Devil You Know').

The convincing performance by Osiris-as-Sarah supports evidence that Goa'uld can impersonate their human hosts, suppressing the change in voice and glowing eyes. Osiris even has some access to his host's memories, recognising Daniel and their past relationship. This is consistent with, for instance, Tanith's suppression of Hebron in 'Crossroads'.

**THE CONSPIRACY STARTS AT CLOSING TIME** David Jordan was Daniel's archaeology professor along with associates Steven Rayner and Sarah Gardner. The latter had a relationship with Daniel before he disappeared five years ago. Daniel originally distanced himself from Jordan to spare him the embarrassment of being associated with Daniel's unorthodox theories.

The artefacts were discovered by the Stewart Expedition near Cairo in 1931. Each member of the expedition died within a year, their fate attributed to the 'Curse of Osiris', whilst the ship carrying the artefacts sank off the coast of New Jersey six months later. The wreck was recently recovered and the collection is on-loan to the Museum in Chicago. It includes two ceramic canopic jars with an inner chamber holding a sedative liquid and using a Naqahdah power source to keep a Goa'uld symbiont in stasis. An inscription reads, 'Woe to all who disturb this, my final resting place.' The gold amulet represents Osiris carrying an ankh, symbol of immortality. It is carbon-dated as 10,000 years old.

**POSSIBLE INFLUENCES** *The Curse of the Mummy's Tomb*, *Doctor Who*'s 'Pyramids of Mars', *Raiders of the Lost Ark*, the discovery of Tutankhamun's tomb (and the alleged curse upon it),[75] Percy Bysshe Shelley's *Ozymandias*.[76] Several character surnames are taken from *The Green Lantern* (Jordan, Gardner, Rayner, Stewart). Allusions to *The Man from Atlantis*, the parable of the Prodigal Son (Luke 15) and Exodus 7 ('The rivers... shall run red with blood').

**'YOU MIGHT REMEMBER ME FROM...'** Lorna Gale was in *Freddy Got Fingered*, *Screwed*, *Wild Thing* and *Echo*. Bass Bass played Javier Vachon in *Forever Knight*. Anna-Louise Plowman was Gabriella in *The Adulterer*.

**LOGIC, LET ME INTRODUCE YOU TO THIS WINDOW** When Daniel reads Jordan's notebook, he holds the book much higher up in some shots than in others. It's odd that Hammond would send only Daniel, Sam and Janet to Egypt. A powerful Goa'uld ought to warrant a much larger operation. Hathor managed to locate the Stargate easily enough (see 'Hathor'), yet Osiris, seemingly, can't. Who erased the computer records, Sarah or Steven? Daniel travels from Chicago to Colorado and back in a few hours, and all wearing the same shirt. How does Daniel smuggle the Isis jar out of the Museum to the SGC without anybody noticing? Although not revealed in the episode itself, Sarah's surname was given as 'Kane' on the official *Stargate* website. However, in 'The Fifth Man', we find that it's actually Gardner.

**GOA'ULD LEXICON** The inscription on the Isis jar is 'Hakoor kra terak shree' ('banished to oblivion').

**QUOTE/UNQUOTE** Teal'c: 'We have caught nothing. We are fishing.' Steven: 'The last time I saw you, you were giving a lecture to an empty room.' Daniel:

• • • • • • • • • • • • • • • • • • • • • • • • • • • • • • • • • • • • • • • • • • • • • • • •

75 Tutenkhamun (c.1345-1327BC) was the Boy-Pharaoh of the 18th Dynasty, and son-in-law of, and successor to, Akhenaten (Amenhotep IV). His unspoiled tomb was discovered in 1922 by Egyptologists Howard Carter (1873-1939) and the Earl of Carnarvon (1866-1923). It contained the most spectacular collection of discoveries of modern times. Recent x-ray evidence on the mummy suggests that Tutenkhamun may have been murdered.

76 An epic poem inspired by the blue granite statue of Rameses II (c.1304-1237BC) taken from the Funerary Temple at Thebes and exhibited in the British Museum, this tells of Ozymandias, the King of Kings and includes Shelley's most quoted line: 'Look upon my works, ye Mighty, and despair!'

'It was full when I started.'

'What the world knows about Ancient Egypt barely scratches the surface.' A terrific moment to re-establish *SG-1*'s Egyptology credentials. A cool modern-day murder mystery set against an insular academic backdrop, with some fine performances. And it's nice to see Janet out in the field for once.

Jack goes fishing at his cabin in Minnesota. Sam is restoring an Indian motorcycle. Teal'c has developed a taste for tabloid journalism (see 'Point of No Return') but not, seemingly, fishing.

*Glimmer* magazine headlines include AARF AARF!! PET DOG WINS 162 MILLION IN STATE LOTTO, CURSE OF OSIRIS RETURNS: NOTED ARCHAEOLOGIST DIES IN LAB EXPLOSION and an advert for GOOD OL' AMERICAN HAMBURGERS (CALL 1-800-555-2348).[77] Steven's drives a BMW though he's getting a Porsche soon as his book's on the best-sellers list. His e-mail address is srayner@snunl.edu. The labtech who performed the carbon dating test of the amulet has the address tech17@thelab.pm.edu.

The episode was shot in late July 2000, with location filming at the Vancouver Maritime Museum and Richmond Sand Dunes. The scene of Daniel and Jack in the briefing room was shot during the filming of '2010'.

According to Andy Mitika 'The desert scenes were filmed with the second unit at the Richmond sandpits, where we shot 'Cold Lazarus'. It was a rather difficult day because the fuel pump on the jeep that Mike, Amanda and Teryl were driving gave out just as we were ready to shoot.'

# 80  THE JERPENT'J VENOM

US Transmission Date: 29 Sep 2000
UK Transmission Date: 29 Nov 2000
Writer: Peter DeLuise
Director: Martin Wood
Cast: Peter Williams (Apophis), Douglas H Arthurs (Heru'ur), Carmen Argenziano (Jacob Carter), Obi Ndefo (Rak'nor), Paul Koslo (Terok), Art Kitching (Ma'kar), Wren Roberts (Red Guard), Daniel Bacon (Technician), Nicholas Harrison (Red Guard), Kyle Hogg (Jaffa Boy), Chris Duggan (Heru'ur's Jaffa), Dan Shea (Sgt Siler)[78]

> While on Chulak to gather support for a rebellion, Teal'c is captured. SG-1, unaware of his fate, are dispatched to thwart a potential alliance between Apophis and Heru'ur. But they soon dis-

77 Ever wondered why 555 is used as a telephone prefix in many US TV series? When exchange names were part of phone numbers, digits also corresponded to letters, the first three signifying the exchange that the caller was dialling. Unfortunately '5' was J K and L and there aren't many English place-names using a combination of those. Due to the low number of 555 codes, Hollywood was encouraged to quote them in their productions to prevent real subscribers being harassed by people trying out numbers that they'd heard in the movies. Now the 555 code is used by various service providers. Only 555-0100 to 555-0199 are set aside by Bellcore for the entertainment industry. This episode doesn't use one of those so, presumably, the producers visited the website www.home.earthlink.net/~mthyen/, which lists numbers available to movies and TV shows.
78 Uncredited.

SEASON 4

cover that Heru'ur has brought a gift for his former enemy: Teal'c. Can SG-1 rescue their friend? Or, as Jacob argues, does the success of their mission outweigh one life?

**ORIGINS OF THE SPECIES** Heru'ur is allied with the System Lords against Apophis. The pair control the two largest armies of the Goa'uld. An alliance between them could topple all other System Lords and shift the balance of power. They've agreed to meet within the minefield of the Tobin System to discuss a possible alliance. Their transmission was intercepted by the Tok'ra through Tanith.

The Tobin originated from Earth thousands of years ago and have been extinct for several centuries. They left behind a large orbiting minefield designed to protect the planet. Symbols on the mines are similar to Phoenician letters and translate as 'Three to the blue, four to the orange, three to the blue.'

On Chulak, Teal'c plans to meet Kol'na of the High Cliffs and Hak'nor of the Cordai Plains at the Chamka Groves (where R'yac was rescued in 'Family'). Ma'kar of the Gomai Foothills is an old friend of Teal'c. Rak'nor is the son of Delnor, who was spared by Teal'c when he was First Prime. Delnor followed Bra'tac's rebellion, but when his family was killed by Apophis, Rak'nor became loyal to Heru'ur. Teal'c is told that Bra'tac died under torture. (This proves to be a lie.) Jaffa religious belief appears to include the concepts of sin, a soul and an afterlife (see 'The Warrior').

**IN THE INTERESTS OF NATIONAL SECURITY** Jacob's been on Earth (probably since 'Tangent'). His ship is held, cloaked, at a classified military airstrip.

**POSSIBLE INFLUENCES** *Edward II* and *Matthew Hopkins - Witchfinder General.* Tobin was the name of one of Dax's previous hosts in *Star Trek: Deep Space Nine*.

**'YOU MIGHT REMEMBER ME FROM...'** Obi Ndefo played Bodie in *Dawson's Creek* and was in *Angel, 3rd Rock from the Sun* and *Star Trek: Voyager*. Paul Koslo appeared in *Coyote Moon, Chained Heat II, Heaven's Gate, Cleopatra Jones, The Omega Man, Django* and *CHiPs*.

**LOGIC, LET ME INTRODUCE YOU TO THIS WINDOW** Jacob removed the bulkhead and escape pods from his ship, anticipating the need for extra room when bringing the mine on board. When? He's only just learned of the Apophis/Heru'ur meeting. Sam's not a linguist, so why is she reading one of Daniel's Phoenician books? One of the Red Guards mispronounces 'Heru'ur'. Twice.

**QUOTE/UNQUOTE** Hammond: 'Sounds very risky.' Jack: '"Insane" might be another word.'

Daniel: 'I just couldn't find *Beck's Ancient Phoenician Symbology* on CD at *archaeology.com*, so...'

Sam: 'It's all Phoenician to me.' And: 'Trust me, it's a math-thing.'

**NOTES** 'Heru'ur attacks!' A massively ambitious story, its success or failure probably depends on how strong a stomach you've got for graphic torture (with Teal'c getting the full 'red-hot-poker-up-the-symbiont' routine). There are Christ-like allusions, which work within the context. It's also interesting to see the SGC taking part in what is, in effect, a piece of terrorist sabotage.

Sam's laptop is an Apple Mac.

**CAST AND CREW COMMENTS** When Paul Koslo did his audition for the role of Goa'uld torturer Terok, he was so convincingly evil that he actually frightened Martin Wood and Robert Cooper. He got the part.

**DID YOU KNOW?** The location of Teal'c's rendezvous, 'the third moon of Tichenor', is of course in honour of James Tichenor. The Tobin system is named after the art department's Nolleen Tobin.

# 81 CHAIN REACTION

US Transmission Date: 5 Jan 2001
UK Transmission Date: 13 Dec 2000
Writers: Paul Mullie, Joseph Mallozzi
Director: Martin Wood
Cast: Ronnie Cox (Senator Kinsey), Tom McBeath (Harry Mayborne), Gary Jones (Sgt Walter Davis), Dan Shea (Sgt Siler), Lawrence Dane (General Bauer), Patti Allan (Kinsey's Wife), Gina Stockdale (Maid), Mark Pawson (Reporter), Norma Jean Wick (Reporter), Jacquie Janzen (Aide)

> When Hammond announces that he's leaving the SGC, claiming that he no longer has the stomach to send friends out to die, Jack suspects another motive. He discovers that the NID was behind the change of command. When Hammond's replacement breaks up SG-1 and assigns Sam the task of building a planet-killing Naqahdah bomb, Jack takes matters into his own hands with an unlikely ally.

**THE WIT AND WISDOM OF JACK O'NEILL** 'I realise the format of my reports is of vital importance and if you'd like, someday we can get together and talk about fonts and margins...' And: 'If it wasn't for SG-1, you'd be sitting there with a snake in your head, instead of your head up your ass.' And: 'I see you're on that famous beer and mustard diet. How's that working out for you?'

**ORIGINS OF THE SPECIES** On Chulak, when a great warrior retires from the field of battle, it's customary for his fellow Jaffa to sing a song of lament.

**SEX AND DRUGS AND ROCK 'N' ROLL** Maybourne has a fridge full of beer. When he phones Jack from some tropical paradise, he says he's going to have a few Margaritas.

**THE CONSPIRACY STARTS AT CLOSING TIME** Two weeks prior to the events of this episode, representatives of the NID suggested that Hammond take a more aggressive approach to gaining access to off-world technology and threatened dire consequences if he refused to comply. The next day, two men in plain clothes and an unmarked car picked up his granddaughters from school before bringing them home. Hammond promptly resigned.

SEASON 4

The NID is 'as powerful as the CIA,' and above the law, according to Hammond. Maybourne also confirms that they were behind the off-world operation he oversaw ('Touchstone', 'Shades of Grey'). Their goal remains the acquisition of advanced technology by any means necessary, no matter how illegal or unscrupulous. But they've been deprived of their means of obtaining it. (It is confirmed that Maybourne was in Russia at the NID's behest.) Jack holds damaging information over Senator Kinsey - a high-profile player in NID-activity - which prevents them from blackmailing SGC personnel again.

After Jack's forced removal, Teal'c is temporarily reassigned to SG-3. On a mission to P3S452 to acquire Naqahdah, Major Waite is killed.

**MILITARY INTELLIGENCE?** The NID is made up of cells who communicate via internet bulletin boards like *findorama.net*. The systems are firewall-protected with usernames and passwords. One of Maybourne's is *Menard*.[79] Kinsey's online activities link him to NID actions over the last year and a half - including Maybourne's operations and the blackmailing of Hammond. The NID has funnelled money into Kinsey's election fund. They'll now, presumably, be backing his presidential campaign (see '2010').

Maybourne was arrested after the events of 'Watergate' and convicted of treason. He was awaiting execution in a federal penitentiary. After Maybourne helps Jack (and acquires evidence against former NID associates), he blackmails Kinsey into transferring him to a nicer facility - and promptly escapes (see 'Desperate Measures'). Maybourne has many aliases, one of which is Charles Bliss. He and Kinsey go 'way back.'

**IN THE INTERESTS OF NATIONAL SECURITY** After the events of 'Watergate', the Pentagon forced the Russians to cancel their programme in exchange for the continued sharing of information and technology.

**POSSIBLE INFLUENCES** *The Parallax View, Mission: Impossible, Silence of the Lambs, Starsky and Hutch, JFK* ('He's just a patsy'), Matthew 7:1 ('Judge not, lest ye be judged') and *Not Waving But Drowning* by Stevie Smith (1902-71). The title was also used for Andrew Davis's 1996 nuclear thriller.

**'YOU MIGHT REMEMBER ME FROM...'** Patti Allan played Queen Victoria in *The Secret Adventures of Jules Verne*. Norma Jean Wick appeared in *Not Our Son* and *Circle of Deceit*. Lawrence Dane played Jack Kinney in the US *Queer as Folk* and was in *Scanners, The Clown Minders, Airwolf, The Virginian* and *Bonanza*.

**LOGIC, LET ME INTRODUCE YOU TO THIS WINDOW** Jack seems to have considerable influence over the President, probably due to the frequency with which he and SG-1 have saved the world (see '2001'). He's granted permission to get a convicted traitor out of jail, which presumably takes some doing. So, let's get this straight. Harry Maybourne was charged with treason, tried (presumably in some form of Diplock military court to prevent any knowledge of the Stargate from becoming public), convicted and he's now on death-row awaiting his execution. Why? What's the hold-up? There can surely be no appeals procedure. (If there is, then to whom?) So, why didn't the military just take him

79 Almost certainly a reference to director of photography Jim Menard, although there is also a famous hardware chainstore in the Midwest called Menard's.

out the back the second that the sentence was passed and shoot him? (See, also, 'The Sentinel'.) Why do SG-1 just stand around on the ramp after coming through the Gate when they could easily have been hit by the hostiles blasting after them?

### QUOTE/UNQUOTE

Kinsey: 'Have you completely taken leave of your senses?' Jack: 'I'm hanging around Maybourne. What does that say?' Kinsey: 'How dare you come into my house waving a gun.' Jack: 'Not waving. Pointing. Sit down.'

Jack: 'One day, I may ask you to buy back my soul.'

### NOTES

'Given the chance, half of all American citizens won't even vote. And the half that do are too stupid to know what they're doing.' Wey-hey, another comedy epic from Mallozzi and Mullie (who really seem to have got the right idea of the series' fundamental dichotomy in their scripts). The Jack/Maybourne double-act is *inspired*.

Jack seems to be a close friend of the entire Hammond family (as George's granddaughters address him by his first name). Kinsey has three children and seven grandchildren.

### CAST AND CREW COMMENTS

'He's a good man, conservative, well educated. As a young man he was a hands-on officer,' Don Davis has noted regarding Hammond. 'In the Pilot we're told he's on the verge of retirement, writing his memoirs. He cares deeply for O'Neill and his team because he experienced that reality of being on the front-line. He knows what it is to be afraid in the dark. This is the basis for his concern for them. Each time he sends them through the Gate, he looks after them and knows that feeling of fear. Also, he's a little bit of a poet, loves those grandkids of his and loves his dead wife - obviously since she's been gone for several years and he still wears the ring.'

### DID YOU KNOW?

'Besides the private mansion used for Kinsey's house, we also filmed on the beach in English Bay,' Lynn Smith remembers. 'We hired a hot dog vendor to be in one scene. We fell a bit behind and by late afternoon he got bored and started selling his hot dogs!'

Kinsey's dog, Oscar, is played by Richard Dean Anderson's dog, Zoe. The two extras buying hot dogs behind Jack and Maybourne were German journalists on the set to interview the crew.

## 82 2010

US Transmission Date: 12 Jan 2001
UK Transmission Date: 3 Jan 2001
Writer: Brad Wright
Director: Andy Mikita
Cast: Teryl Rothery (Janet Fraiser), Ronnie Cox (The President), Gary Jones (Walter Davis), Christopher Cousins (Ambassador Joe Faxon), Dion Luther (Mollem), David Neale (Dialer), Linnea Johnson (Guide), Bryce Hodgson (Kid), Liza Huget (Waitress)

It's 2010. The Goa'uld have been defeated and disease wiped-out by Earth's new friends, the Aschen. Despite vast medical advancements, Sam and her husband, Joe, are unable to conceive. Aschen doctors insist that Sam is fine, but Janet reveal something very different: an insidious plot to wipe out humanity through sterilisation.

**THE WIT AND WISDOM OF JACK O'NEILL** On the contents of the note they're sending back in time: 'Can we at least mention who won the Super Bowl in 2004?'

**SAM'S BIZARRE LOVE TRIANGLE** Sam's finally found a caring man to share her life with. One who doesn't have a snake in his stomach or who's obsessed with fishing. Sadly, even in this future-fantasy, she's still not happy. Consequently, there's a definite *Bring Your Own Subtext* to the scenes between Jack, Sam and Joe.

**ORIGINS OF THE SPECIES** When SG-1 first met the Aschen, the aliens were friendly and willing to share advanced technology. But, as Jack noted in his mission report, they were too good to be true.

**THE CONSPIRACY STARTS AT CLOSING TIME** *The Washington Examiner* is dated 27 July 2010 (ASCHEN PROMISE ANTI-AGING VACCINE WORLDWIDE). It's the tenth anniversary of SG-1's visit to P4C970. Earth is now a member of the Aschen Confederation.

**FUTURE IMPERFECT** Thanks to the Earth/Aschen alliance, the Goa'uld were defeated and the Tok'ra scattered. Kinsey is President. Hammond died six years ago of a heart attack, under suspicious circumstances. Jack retired and moved to Minnesota, bitter that his warnings about the Aschen were ignored. (Last time he was in the Oval Office, he got kicked out.) Sam married Joe Faxon, an ambassador, over three years ago. There's no longer a military. Jack and Sam were both colonels when they retired. With the Goa'uld overthrown, Teal'c returned to Chulak and doesn't see his friends very often. Janet has a private practice in Washington though, with Aschen medical advances (including anti-ageing and anti-cancer vaccines), she feels obsolete. The world's birthrate has dropped by 91% in two years. Joe (and presumably others within the government including Kinsey) agreed with the Aschen to sterilise around a third of the population to limit growth.

The Stargate is housed at the JR Reed Space Terminal in Washington, where it's used routinely for space travel. The SGC is a tourist attraction and Walter Davis works there as Operations Tech Advisor. (The annoyingly cheerful guide refers to the Gateroom as 'the Embarkation Room', see 'Children of the Gods'.) The Jupiter Ignition Project is designed to convert the planet into a star. Aschen computers are capable of predicting solar flares.

**POSSIBLE INFLUENCES** Arthur C Clarke's *2010: The Year We Make Contact* (Jupiter Ignition Project), *Star Trek: The Next Generation*'s 'Future Imperfect', *Earth: Final Conflict*. Future-Jack's death owns much to the climax of *The Roaring Twenties* (specifically the lingering death of James Cagney's character). A tourist does a Vulcan hand greeting whilst being photographed.

**'YOU MIGHT REMEMBER ME FROM...'** Christopher Cousins was in *As the World Turns*. Dion Luther appeared in *The Stalker* and *Follow the Bitch*.

**LOGIC, LET ME INTRODUCE YOU TO THIS WINDOW** How could humanity in general *not* know about the rapid decline in births? Something *that* significant should have been spotted by somebody, somewhere, even if only in whispers, regardless of Aschen control of the world's media. There's some poor dubbing in the scene at Jack's cabin. Sam's mouth movements don't match what she's saying. Interestingly, the public revelation of the existence of alien life doesn't seem to have changed fundamental Judeo-Christian beliefs. (Kinsey mentions God twice during his speech.)

**QUOTE/UNQUOTE** Jack: 'Personally, I like things the way they are. No more saving the world, just a nice pond with no pesky fish in it. The single most pressing issue in my life is whether or not to get a dog.'

Guide: 'These people comprise the famous SG-1. Arguably the most important, although not my personal favourite, team!'

**NOTES** 'Not working out, is it? Gosh, wish I'd seen that coming. Oh wait, I *did*.' A Byzantine plot is sweetened by an eloquent and astute script which tackles the truism 'Be careful what you wish for, it might come true'. In this period, when it seemed that *SG-1* could do virtually no wrong, '2010' restates many of the series' core values through numerous smart criteria. A potentially pessimistic (even nihilistic) *denouement*, in which all the heroes die, turns into a rainbow of hope. Many wonderful moments: the dinner between old friends, the hologram of Jupiter and its moons, Jack's leap of faith to, in death, secure a future for humanity. Excellent.

**CAST AND CREW COMMENTS** Teryl Rothery would like to see more of the background of Dr Fraiser - her home life and what makes her tick. And she hankers for romance. 'I'd love Janet to go to some planet and fall in love and have to say goodbye like a summer fling.'

**DID YOU KNOW?** Walter's name is a tribute to Radar O'Reilly, as played by Gary Burghoff, in *M\*A\*S\*H* due to Gary Jones's resemblance to Burghoff. The location for the Space Terminal is the Plaza of Nations from the 1986 Vancouver Expo. The scenes at Jack's cabin were shot (before the script was even completed) during location filming of 'The Curse'. Other sequences, notably the opening meeting of Sam and Joe, were filmed during the shooting of 'Chain Reaction'.

**SEASON 4**

# 83  ABSOLUTE POWER

US Transmission Date: 19 Jan 2001
UK Transmission Date: 10 Jan 2001
Writer: Robert Cooper
Director: Peter DeLuise
Cast: Peter Williams (Apophis), Gary Jones (Sgt Walter Davis), Teryl Rothery (Dr Janet Fraiser), Erick Avari (Kasuf), Colin Cunningham (Major Davis), William deVry (Aldwyn), Steven Williams (General Virdrine), Lane Gates (Shifu), Michelle Harrison (Assistant), Yee Jee Tso (Left Tech), Jenn Forgie (Right Tech), Barbara Fixx (Rear Tech), Coleen Christie (Reporter), June B Wilde (Maid)

On Abydos, SG-1 investigate a sandstorm that whispers Daniel's name. They find Shifu, the Harsesis, and bring him back to Earth. The boy is wise beyond his years, possessing the genetic memory of the Goa'uld. He could prove a powerful weapon. But Shifu has come to teach Daniel a valuable lesson.

**THE WIT AND WISDOM OF JACK O'NEILL** 'If I may, Sir, I think what he means is the wick is the centre of the candle and, ostensibly, a great leader like yourself is essential to the whole ball of wax. Basically, what it means is that it's always better to have a ... big long wick.'

**ORIGINS OF THE SPECIES** 'Shifu' means 'light'. Nanite technology caused his age acceleration, but they're currently inactive. Oma Desala taught him to forget the Goa'uld knowledge he was born with. He came to Abydos to learn about his mother, Sha're.

Teal'c says that all Goa'uld are born evil because of their genetic knowledge. The SGC's treaty with the Tok'ra includes the full exchange of all potential sources of information.

**SEX AND DRUGS AND ROCK 'N' ROLL** Daniel and Jack celebrate the AG3 launch with a $2,000 bottle of champagne.

**DREAMING (AS BLONDIE ONCE SAID) IS FREE** 'Dreams teach,' Shifu tells Daniel. Just as a vision given by Sha're taught Daniel to forgive Teal'c ('Forever in a Day'), so he learns here that Goa'uld genetic memory cannot be used, even by people with good intentions. Dreams are depicted as the battleground of the conscious and subconscious. In Daniel's, he believes that the ribbon device requires Naqahdah in the user's blood to activate it. The AG3 are designed as a defence system to be deployed orbiting Earth. They're capable of detecting approaching Goa'uld ships thousands of light years away.

**IN THE INTERESTS OF NATIONAL SECURITY** The Russian Stargate remains closed. Daniel describes blowing up Moscow as 'Like cutting out your enemy's heart with a scalpel'.

**POSSIBLE INFLUENCES** *Watchmen*, *You Only Live Twice*, *Moonraker*, *Twister*, *The Manchurian Candidate*, *Dr Strangelove*, *The West Wing*'s 'A Proportional Response' and *Buffy*'s 'Who Are You?'. *The Wizard of Oz* ('Try to keep it in Kansas'), Exodus 3 ('a burning bush'), Nazi dictator Adolf Hitler (1889-1945). The title's a quotation by Baron Acton (1834-1902): 'Power corrupts, absolute power corrupts absolutely.' It was also the title of Clint Eastwood's 1997 political intrigue caper movie. The broadcast journalist Amy Jensen, seen reporting on the launch, works for Fox News, seemingly. Product placement: second time this season for Fruit Loops.

**'YOU MIGHT REMEMBER ME FROM...'** Barbara Fixx played Alicia in *Traces of Us*. Lane Gates was Jason in *Major Crime*. Michelle Harrison played Sarah Laughlin in *Pressure*. Yee Jee Tso was Chang Lee in *Doctor Who*.

**LOGIC, LET ME INTRODUCE YOU TO THIS WINDOW** Sam says that she's never heard of liquid Naqahdah. That's what powers Goa'uld staff weapons, and was discussed by Sam and her alternate-reality twin in 'Point of View.'

**QUOTE/UNQUOTE** Shifu: 'If the instrument is broken, the music will be sour.' Daniel: 'The music does not play the musician.' Shifu: 'Normally there is truth in that.' Daniel: 'Really? Good. Because I really didn't have any idea what I was talking about.'

Jack: 'I didn't wanna miss watching you save the world.' Daniel: 'Sam thinks I'm trying to take it over.' Jack, 'Oh, how *arch*!'

**NOTES** 'Ultimately a man travels his chosen path alone.' Still they come. 'Absolute Power' sees Daniel given the *gift* of vision, learning that evil knowledge can never be used for good because it automatically corrupts. He watches himself slip into megalomania until he's able to find his true path. A simple Buddhist allegory ('suffering ceases when desire is eradicated' is one of the 'four noble truths' central to *Hsi Yu Chi*), given a powerful twist in a Byronic-fable of lost innocence surrounding Daniel's descent. Fabulous.

Numerous continuity references to 'Forever in a Day' and 'Maternal Instinct'.

**CAST AND CREW COMMENTS** 'The cornerstone of science-fiction is the ability to use supernatural circumstances to put your character in interesting situations,' notes Robert Cooper.

**DID YOU KNOW?** For the destruction of Moscow, stock footage of the Kremlin was mixed with foreground shots of members of the visual effects department (including Shannon Gurney and Michelle Comens).

# 84 THE LIGHT

US Transmission Date: 26 Jan 2001
UK Transmission Date: 17 Jan 2001
Writer: James Phillips
Director: Peter Woeste
Cast: Teryl Rothery (Dr Janet Fraiser), Gary Jones (Sgt Walter Davis), Kristian Ayre (Loran), Link Baker (Sgt Barber)

SG-5's Sgt Barber commits suicide after visiting a temple on P4X347. Other men with him, including Daniel, become gravely ill. SG-1 discover a room with a mesmerising light display. But they aren't alone.

**THE WIT AND WISDOM OF JACK O'NEILL** 'Great. All those years of just sayin' no!' And: 'Nice digs. Reminds me of my first apartment, How are the people upstairs?'

**ORIGINS OF THE SPECIES** Loran's parents were explorers who became addicted to the light. When Loran turned off the device, they went into withdrawal and drowned in the ocean.

**SEX AND DRUGS AND ROCK 'N' ROLL** The temple was once a Goa'uld pleasure palace (and it's compared to an opium den). A light-matrix hologram is projected, the colour and light interact with the optic nerve and trigger chemical responses.

Accelerated neural activity causes dopamine-like effects. When exposure ends, neural activity decreases, resulting in cold turkey-type withdrawal. Perception of time, Daniel notes, is one of the first things to go when you're high.

**THE CONSPIRACY STARTS AT CLOSING TIME** There's an acknowledgement of the problems inherent in controlling the information (or lack of it) which can be given to the families of SGC members killed in the line of duty.

**POSSIBLE INFLUENCES** *Saving Private Ryan* (Hammond's letter to Barber's family). Dialogue allusions to *The Usual Suspects* (itself a reference to *Casablanca*). Teal'c uses an NEC computer in Daniel's office.

**'YOU MIGHT REMEMBER ME FROM...'** Kristian Ayre was in *Running Home*. Link Baker played Kul in *Living With Monsters*.

**BEHIND THE CAMERA** James Phillips wrote *The Lost Idol* and, as an actor, appeared in *Prison Planet*.

**LOGIC, LET ME INTRODUCE YOU TO THIS WINDOW** Barber is credited as a sergeant, though Hammond refers to him twice as a lieutenant. Daniel's got yet another new apartment. The man goes through more houses than Salman Rushdie. Why did the Goa'uld need a pleasure palace? Don't they get enough kicks from enslaving worlds?

**QUOTE/UNQUOTE** Sam: 'Daniel bet on curling?' Jack: 'Oh yes. His team won the big bonspiel.'

**NOTES** 'It is hard to believe something so beautiful could be dangerous.' An episode about vulnerability, 'The Light' is hampered by an unbelievable story and a namby-pamby stab at social comment which really doesn't work. Some good scenes (including the startling moment that Jack finds Daniel about to throw himself to his death), but it's very lethargic.

Daniel and Jack bet on whether or not Sam will work through yet another period of leave. Teal'c will be 102 years old in 47 days. Jaffa don't celebrate birthdays.

**DID YOU KNOW?** This episode was originally to have been entitled 'Suicide Mission'. The visual effects on 'The Light' won Richard Hudolin and his team a 'Best Production Design' prize at the 2001 LEO awards.

# 85 PRODIGY

US Transmission Date: 2 Feb 2001
UK Transmission Date: 24 Jan 2001
Writers: Brad Wright, Joseph Mallozzi, Paul Mullie
Director: Peter DeLuise
Cast: Russell Ferrier (Major Griff), Elisabeth Rosen (Jennifer Hailey), Michael Kopsa

(General Kerrigan), Hrothgar Mathews (Dr Hamilton), Bill Dow (Dr Lee), General Michael Ryan (Himself), Keith Martin Gordon (Professor Monroe), Roger Haskett (Dr Thompson), Ivon R Bartok (Cadet)

Visiting the Air Force Academy, Sam meets Jennifer Hailey, a promising cadet with a rebellious streak who could be an asset to the SGC. They travel to M4C862, where Jack and Teal'c are babysitting a group of stubborn scientists. But the seemingly routine mission takes a deadly turn when they're attacked by a microscopic lifeform.

**ORIGINS OF THE SPECIES** The energy-based lifeforms can pass through matter. Electrical fields repel them. Sam theorises that their behaviour is retaliatory. Hailey suggests that the moon's eccentric orbit is the cause. We never find out which of them, if either, is correct.

A zat blast temporarily alters the electrical field of whatever it hits, even inanimate objects. When Teal'c shoots the ground next to the DHD, the lifeforms are repelled.

**THE CONSPIRACY STARTS AT CLOSING TIME** Hailey has great potential but seems determined to sabotage her future. She's fiercely independent and resentful of Sam, with whom she's constantly compared.

**IN THE INTERESTS OF NATIONAL SECURITY** M4C862 is a moon orbiting a gas giant, 42,000 light years from Earth. A team of scientists have been there for six weeks. Before the lifeform is encountered Hammond was proposing a permanent off-world research station.

**POSSIBLE INFLUENCES** *The Swarm*, *The X-Files*' 'Darkness Falls', *Good Will Hunting*, *An Officer and a Gentleman*, *The Birds*, Muriel Sparks' *The Prime of Miss Jean Brodie*, Glenn Chandler's *The Sanctuary* and *Star Trek* ('those phaser things'). There's a reference on the whiteboard to the string theory of 26 dimensions.

**'YOU MIGHT REMEMBER ME FROM...'** Bill Dow was in *Big Bully*, *Scorn* and played Chuck Burks in *The X-Files*. Elisabeth Rosen appeared in *Bless the Child* and *Sanctuary*. Hrothgar Mathews's movies include *Legs Apart*, *Nuremburg* and *Mother, May I Sleep With Danger*.

**LOGIC, LET ME INTRODUCE YOU TO THIS WINDOW** When everyone runs into the base, Dr Lee almost collides with the cameraman. Sam's on the right and Hailey the left as they step into the Gate. When they emerge on M4C862, they've switched. How convenient that the diagram of the moon's orbital-path is on the blackboard so that Hailey can describe her theory. That's a photo of Paul Mullie on Kerrigan's desk playing, in the writer's own words, 'his half-wit nephew'.

**QUOTE/UNQUOTE** Teal'c: 'Are you ready, O'Neill?' Jack: 'No. Give me a warning.' Teal'c: 'I am going to shoot you.'

**NOTES** 'Wormholes and hyperspace may seem like science-fiction but, take my word for it, the future is a lot closer than you might think.' A poorly designed essay on science-versus-the-military, which is deprived of Daniel's influence and is much poorer for it. On the plus side, Hailey is a rather cool little Carterclone - smart, sassy and *really* full of herself. Just like Sam was back in season one.

Jack complains of a bad back and dodgy knees (see 'Threshold'). This author, who suffers from both, totally sympathises. Sam avoids telling Monroe that parallel realities can overlap. Just (see 'Point of View'). Monroe calls Sam a 'leader in the field of astrophysics'. Hailey's thesis is entitled *Toward a New Cosmology of Multiple Realities.* She was graded D, as rewriting the laws of physics was not her assignment. Michael Shanks doesn't appear in this episode as he was preparing for his directional debut. Daniel is said to be off-world with SG-11.

**CAST AND CREW COMMENTS** 'Richard likes to ad-lib,' Paul Muzzie noted. 'Often we'll agonise for hours over a quip but know he's just going to make it up on the spot.'

'Unlike other sci-fi shows, SG-1 has a fairly rigid structure,' added Joe Mallozzi. 'In "Prodigy", we focus on a cadet. We wanted her to go AWOL and get punished. The Air Force said, "You can't do that. She'd be kicked out." We had to find another way to tell the story.'

**DID YOU KNOW?** Invited to visit the set by Hank Cohen, Air Force Chief-of-Staff Michael Ryan was press-ganged into a cameo appearance. 'Do you have colonels like me?' Richard Dean Anderson asked during rehearsals. 'Yes,' noted the General. 'And worse.'

# 86 ENTITY

US Transmission Date: 9 Feb 2001
UK Transmission Date: 7 Feb 2001
Writer: Peter DeLuise
Director: Alan Lee
Cast: Teryl Rothery (Dr Janet Fraiser), Gary Jones (Sgt Walter Davis), Dan Shea (Sgt Siler)

> The SGC is infected by an alien probe that downloads itself into the computers. Sam and Daniel feel that they should attempt to communicate. Sam tries, only for the entity to take over her body.

**ORIGINS OF THE SPECIES** Co-ordinates for P9C372 come from the Ancients' repository ('The Fifth Race'). MALP transmissions reveal an entirely alien landscape. The entity piggybacked on the radio signal to travel to Earth through an outgoing wormhole.

**THE CONSPIRACY STARTS AT CLOSING TIME** There's an 'emergency disconnect' system in the Gateroom, which cuts all power to the Gate. The SGC's computer data is archived at the Pentagon. The MALP storage room is on sublevel 24.

**IN THE INTERESTS OF NATIONAL SECURITY** Hammond implies that he is aware of Jack's feelings for Sam, reminding him that hard decisions may have to be made.

**POSSIBLE INFLUENCES** *2001, Highlander, Aliens, The Matrix* and *The X-Files*' 'Kill Switch'. The title comes from a notoriously lurid Sidney Furie movie about supernatural rape.

**BEHIND THE CAMERA** Alan Lee was previously editor on *Rollercoaster* and *Home Movie*.

**LOGIC, LET ME INTRODUCE YOU TO THIS WINDOW** Jack's first name was Jonathan in *Stargate*. It's John now. Lee Van Cleef's date-of-birth is given using the European dating system (17/6/46) rather than the American one (6/17/64). How much of the SGC's data was lost in the system reformat? And as for Sam's consciousness being "stored" in a computer...

**WHERE WE WENT ON OUR HOLIDAYS** Selective use of freeze-frame when the entity is viewing mission logs can be very rewarding.

Å Mission 614-2615B: 'The team and I went to a planet called P3X917 which had tons of cool stuff like arcade games.'

Å Mission 617-4316B: 'I really like cheese. On planet P5X391 they have lots of cheese and it's very delicious. The gouda is especially tasty.'

Å Mission 618-9249A: 'There's this planet called Tichenor. It's very nice and has a good climate.'

Å Mission 910-1726B: 'There are lots of ways to skin an Unas. Even though they are large and intimidating the Unas are easy to deal with...'

Å Mission 734-2597A: '... on the barbecue they are especially nice as we found out when visiting planet P4X512 running out of food.'

Å Mission 292-8391A: 'This planet was filled with bugs. Really big ones.'

Å Mission 715-4261A: 'June was a pretty month. There were many flowers which we loved.'

Å Mission 766-9172A: 'Having no anthropologist we felt there wasn't much chance of the military strike coming off, but...'

Å Mission 872-4159A: 'Enjoyed our visit to Tichenor, a holiday planet with plenty of coast.'

**QUOTE/UNQUOTE** Jack, to Hammond: 'For the record, I want to blow it to hell. These folks wanna chat with it.'

Daniel: 'We won't send any more probes.' Jack: 'Yes, we will. We'll send dozens of them, one after another.'

**NOTES** 'Whatever's got into our computers has, apparently, built a nest.' Logically *insane* and with a gallery of non-sequiturs and a literal *deus ex machina* climax, 'Entity' nevertheless features fine performances from Tapping and Anderson. (Love his little non-verbal double-act with the entity-influenced camera.) Visually impressive, too. It's just when you start to analyse the ridiculousness of the plot that it falls apart.

Jack's service number is 69-4-141. Sam's is 36-6-349. She has a living will, requesting no extraordinary measures to sustain her life in case of accident.

**DID YOU KNOW?** Peter DeLuise makes his usual cameo in the SGC's computer records as Lee Van Cleef ('Master' of SG-1, apparently). Other SGC members would appear to include Kent Matheson (Captain SG-3), Maureen O'Boyle (Major SG-9), Richie Jarvis (Captain SG-7) and Kim Matheson (Captain SG-3). Kent Matheson is the production's matte-painter whilst Maureen O'Boyle is the host of the syndicated news shows *Extra* and *A Current Affair*.

This was the first *SG-1* episode shot on HighDef 24 video. The original title was 'Child's Play'.

SEASON 4

# 87  DOUBLE JEOPARDY

US Transmission Date: 16 Feb 2001
UK Transmission Date: 31 Jan 2001
Writer: Robert Cooper
Director: Michael Shanks
Cast: Jay Brazeau (Harlan), Daniel Bacon (Technician), Ron Halder (Cronus), Matthew Harrison (Darien), Belinda Waymouth (Ja'din), Bill Croft (Sinder), Tracy Hway (Hira), Michael Jonsson (Juna Warrior), John DeSantis (Jaffa), Paul Stafford (Jaffa)

> SG-1 travel to P3X729 and are recognised by villagers whom they once helped free from Heru'ur. Now, facing a vengeful Cronus, SG-1 find themselves unwelcome and captured. But when Daniel is executed, a shocking discovery is made.

**THE WIT AND WISDOM OF THE TWO JACK O'NEILLS** Jack: 'What the hell do you think you're doing?' Duplicate-Jack: 'Same thing you do. Only better.' Jack: 'What does that mean?' Duplicate-Jack: 'It means *bet-ter!*'

**ORIGINS OF THE SPECIES** SG-1 led a rebellion on P3X729 against Heru'ur. The Juna were told to bury their Gate, but Cronus's army arrived in ships and claimed the planet. A Goa'uld mothership can carry as many as 1,000 Jaffa.

Contrary to what he promised in 'Tin Man', Duplicate-Jack never intended to bury the Altair Stargate. Duplicate-SG-1 have been going on short-term missions for three years. Duplicate-Sam created a portable powerpack which lasts 48 hours before needing recharging.

**THE CONSPIRACY STARTS AT CLOSING TIME** The Asgard treaty doesn't protect humans when they're on other worlds, as Cronus warned ('Fair Game').

**POSSIBLE INFLUENCES** *Blakes' 7* (Ja'din's Servelan-style Lesbian-Dominatrix overtones), *Doctor Who*'s 'The Three Doctors' (the squabbling Jacks), *Westworld* and *Star Trek* ('Affirmative'). The episode shares its title with Bruce Beresford's 1999 revenge saga.

**'YOU MIGHT REMEMBER ME FROM...'** Matthew Harrison was Mick Jagger in *The Linda McCartney Story*. Tracy Hway appeared in *Dogmatic* and *Forever Knight*. Belinda Waymouth was in *Murder One*, *Melting Pot* and *User Friendly*.

**LOGIC, LET ME INTRODUCE YOU TO THIS WINDOW** Sam knows about the internal operations of a Goa'uld mothership. (She knows how to lock the doors, for instance.) Where did she learn this? How does Harlan transmit 'comtrya' to the SGC?

**QUOTE/UNQUOTE** Hammond, to Jack: 'It would seem your robot counterpart is equally as good at following orders as you.'

Sam: 'This kind of thing happens to us all the time.'

**NOTES** 'Is this the first time you've lied to yourself?' Taking one of the series' worst episodes and making a sequel was brave. And, thanks to brilliant pairing of Richard Dean Anderson and... Richard Dean Anderson, it works very well. Shanks's direction is fluid, all the regulars get good death scenes and the concluding firefight is a season highlight.

Cronus tries to kill Teal'c by crushing his symbiont, just as he did with Teal'c's father (see 'Crossroads'). Sam acknowledges that Harlan *was* annoying (see 'Tin Man'). Yes, we know.

**CAST AND CREW COMMENTS** 'He's done his homework and he's making a go of it,' Anderson noted concerning first-time director Michael Shanks. 'I've thought about it, but there's no way in hell I'd want to direct a show of this size. It's a nightmare!'

Shanks himself commented: 'We had a lot of twinning ... That involved split-screens and photo-doubling. We also did two days on location in a forest.'

**DID YOU KNOW?** The interior of the pyramid was a redressed set from 'Absolute Power'.

# 88 EXODUJ

US Transmission Date: 23 Feb 2001
UK Transmission Date: 14 Feb 2001
Writers: Paul Mullie, Joseph Mallozzi
Director: David Warry-Smith
Cast: Peter Williams (Apophis), Carmen Argenziano (Jacob Carter), Peter Wingfield (Tanith), Mark McCall (First Guard), Renton Reid (Red Jaffa), Paul Norman (Apophis' Red Guard), Kirsten Williamson (Tok'ra #1), Anastasia Bandey (Tok'ra #2)

> SG-1 loan the Tok'ra Cronus's ship to help them move to a new planet. Tanith is finally exposed as a spy but he escapes, and soon Apophis's fleet is heading for Vorash. Sam and Jacob devise a daring scheme to turn the Vorash sun nova and destroy Apophis's army. Everything goes according to plan until a Goa'uld ship decloaks and fires.

**THE WIT AND WISDOM OF JACK O'NEILL** 'It was kind-of a trade deal. Cronus gave us his ship. And he got what was coming to him.' And: 'That guy is a living cliché.' And: 'This is *so* the last time I help someone move.'

**ORIGINS OF THE SPECIES** 'Al'Kesh' is a Goa'uld midrange bomber with cloaking capabilities.

The Tok'ra don't possess a ship large enough to transport all their people, plus a Stargate. They are moving to a world outside the network of Gates known to the Goa'uld, to create a permanent base. They have been moving periodically since the movement's foundation 2,000 years ago. This confirms that a Gate can be moved to a new world and still used (see 'Within the Serpent's Grasp', 'Nemesis').

In four years, SG-1 have played a part in the deaths of Hathor, Seth, Sokar, Heru'ur and Cronus. Jacob, however, makes a valid point: the resulting power vacuum has been filled by Apophis, who is now poised to rule the galaxy. The Tok'ra plan is less proactive than SG-1's 'if it moves, shoot it' policy, and more long-term: to undermine the Goa'uld and keep them fighting amongst themselves.

SEASON 4

**THE CONSPIRACY STARTS AT CLOSING TIME** Tanith has been used by the Tok'ra to relay disinformation to Apophis (see 'Crossroads'). His sentence, declared by the High Council, is to be extracted from his host, Hebron, and left behind on Vorash when the Tok'ra evacuate.

The plan to destroy Apophis's fleet is to dial P3W451 (see 'A Matter of Time'). The Stargate will be drawn into a black hole, allowing the removal of stellar matter to disrupt the balance between the forces of fusion and gravity in Vorash's sun.

**POSSIBLE INFLUENCES** The title comes, either, from the second book of the Bible or a Bob Marley and the Wailers LP. The cliff-hanger recalls the opening of *Star Trek: Voyager*'s pilot (and the episode 'Scorpion').

**'YOU MIGHT REMEMBER ME FROM...'** Kirsten Williamson appeared in *Road Movie*.

**LOGIC, LET ME INTRODUCE YOU TO THIS WINDOW** How did Tanith overpower his well-armed guards and escape? Where did he acquire a Goa'uld communications device? Why doesn't the ship get sucked into the Gate when the black hole-planet is dialled? The Gate rotates anti-clockwise when leaving the ship but in the opposite direction as it enters the sun.

**QUOTE/UNQUOTE** Sam: 'I've never blown up a star before.' Jack: 'They say the first one's always the hardest.'

Daniel: 'I figured that flashing wasn't good news. And the fact that in Goa'uld it says, "Warning, Warning..."'

**NOTES** 'A Jaffa revenge thing.' A fine end to a thoroughly enjoyable season. Peter Wingfield is at his nostril-flaring best, Anderson displays some tasty sarcasm, the effects are outstanding (they blow'd up the sun real good) and it's got a stupendous cliff-hanger. What more can you ask from a season finale?

High Councillor Per'sus (see 'Divide and Conquer') is mentioned. This episode was nominated for a visual effects Emmy (see 'Wormhole X-Treme!'). 'We lost, of course,' notes James Tichenor wryly.

**CAST AND CREW COMMENTS** During the Wolf SG-2 convention, Peter Williams noted that Apophis wants to get the Tok'ra out of the way so that he can take on the Asgard next. Whilst in Sydney for a convention, Williams was on Oxford Street, the main drag of the Sydney Gay and Lesbian Mardi Gras and home to a stretch of drag-queen boutiques. 'I stopped to ask directions from a guy and a girl. While I'm talking to the girl, the guy is hanging back, with a cigarette in his mouth, looking at me very strangely.' Obviously wondering if Apophis is coming out?

**DID YOU KNOW?** 'This is really a collaborative effort,' said James Tichenor. 'The producers will say "We need a spaceship that can do this". They'll also give me a specific idea they have on how they'd like the effect to look. Next, I'll look at the drawings done by Richard Hudolin to make sure the basic effect matches the style Richard and his people have come up with. Finally, I'll go off and do my own research and work up a series of designs to present to Brad Wright and Robert Cooper.'

# STARGATE SG-1
# SEASON 5 (2001-2002)

'Dammit, colonel, just because they're aliens
and their skulls are transparent doesn't mean
they don't have rights!'

# STARGATE SG-1™ SEASON 5 (2001-2002)

Double Secret Productions/Gekko Film Corp/
Metro-Goldwyn-Meyer

Developed for Television by Brad Wright, Jonathan Glassner

Executive Producer: Robert C Cooper, Brad Wright

Co-Executive Producer: Michael Greenburg, Richard Dean Anderson

Executive Consultant: Jonathan Glassner

Creative Consultant: Peter DeLuise

Supervising Producer: Joseph Mallozzi, Paul Mullie

Co-Executive Producer: N John Smith

Story Editor: Ron Wilkerson

Post Production Consultant: Michael Eliot

SEASON 5

Regular Cast: Richard Dean Anderson (Jack O'Neill), Michael Shanks (Daniel Jackson)[80], Amanda Tapping (Samantha Carter), Christopher Judge (Teal'c), Don S Davis (General George Hammond)[81]

80 Does not appear in 'Revelations'.
81 Does not appear in 'Last Stand'.

# 89 ENEMIES

US Transmission Date: 29 Jun 2001
UK Transmission Date: 12 Sep 2001
Story: Brad Wright, Robert C Cooper, Joseph Mallozzi, Paul Mullie
Teleplay: Robert C Cooper
Director: Martin Wood
Cast: Peter Williams (Apophis), Carmen Argenziano (Jacob Carter), Gary Jones (Sgt Walter Davis), Jennifer Calvert (Ren'Au), Thomas Milburn Jr (Jaffa), Dean Moen (Jaffa), Dan Shea (Sgt Siler)[82]

The supernova sends both ships to an uncharted region of the universe 125 years distant from Earth. The shields of SG-1's ship are damaged and the hyperdrive controls destroyed. But they have other things beside this, and Apophis, to worry about. Replicators.

**THE WIT AND WISDOM OF JACK O'NEILL** On the mystery ship that attacks Apophis: 'I'm enjoying their style. Shoot first, send flowers later.'

**ORIGINS OF THE SPECIES** Since SG-1's last encounter with them, the Replicators have begun to take on more varied forms. Several larger Replicators have wings. Once Replicators reach a critical number, they look for new sources of technology. By destroying the control crystals of the ships' sublight engines, SG-1 prevent deceleration after exiting hyperdrive, resulting in an uncontrolled re-entry, crashing the ship into Delmak (see 'The Devil You Know').

SG-1's actions will throw the Goa'uld into chaos, and the resultant power void could see the remaining System Lords fighting each other for years (see 'Summit'). The Tok'ra had two ships in the vicinity of Vorash, which confirm the detonation of the star and the destruction of Apophis's massive fleet. Jacob is in control of his body for most of the time, Selmak only assuming control when communicating with Apophis's ship.

A Ha'tak-class mothership can travel through hyperspace at a maximum speed of 32,000 times the speed of light.

**POSSIBLE INFLUENCES** Bug, The Terminator, Star Trek: The Next Generation's 'The Best of Both Worlds', Star Trek: Voyager 'The Caretaker' and the novels of C J Cherryh (uncontrolled near-light speed crash into planet used as a weapon).

**'YOU MIGHT REMEMBER ME FROM...'** British actress Jennifer Calvert was Cheryl Boyanowsky in Brookside and appeared in The Fast Show, Red Dwarf and Randall and Hopkirk (Deceased).

**LOGIC, LET ME INTRODUCE YOU TO THIS WINDOW** The Replicators altered the mothership's engines to travel at more than 800 times its previous maximum speed. But even at this rate, with four million light-years to cover, it would take nearly two months to reach

82 Uncredited.

home. Since the ship reached Delmak in just hours, its speed must have increased to in excess of 100,000 times maximum. 'The course has been plotted for Delmak,' notes a Red Guard. How? It can't be possible to plot an exact course over such a distance. Why do the Goa'uld have a box containing four P-90s in storage? 'Hyperspeed' is mentioned again (see 'Nemesis'). With the cargo-bay doors open, how was Jacob planning to get Sam, Jack and Daniel aboard without using the transportation rings? During the climactic gun battle the explosive charges to simulate gunfire are clearly visible on the walls.

### GOA'ULD LEXICON

'Rak'lo najaquna, shel're hara kek,' means something like 'It is time for you to die'. 'Harek rel kree lo'mak. Onak rak shel'na.' translates as 'I know everything. There's nothing you can do to help. I will destroy you.' 'Kla mel harek,' means 'Too late.'

### QUOTE/UNQUOTE

Jacob: 'I am Selmak of the Tok'ra, commander of this ship.' Jack: 'Commander?' Jacob: 'You want to bicker about rank now?' Jack: '*That* is a big bug!'

### NOTES

'You'll forgive me for holding out hope a little longer. SG-1 has a surprisingly good habit of beating the odds.' A nice character exercise (Daniel trying to get Jack to talk about Teal'c's loss is particularly well-done), but ultimately, like 'Nemesis', this is largely a collection of fantastic gun battles amid a cacophony of explosions. The expositions are a bit perfunctory and the logic is almost non-existent. Great to look at though.

Jack can, as we know, be a real pain in the arse sometimes. Mind you, so can Jacob. He likes to be right all the time, even to the point of extreme pessimism. ('Welcome to my life,' Sam tells Jack after one such instance.) Daniel demonstrates that he's had training in the use of military weapons and combat tactics. (He handles a P-90 like a veteran.)

### CAST AND CREW COMMENTS

'A terrific season opener,' commented Brad Wright. 'What I wanted to do was take our two big nemeses of the last two years and put them together, with a whole load of twists that will leave our audiences gasping.'

'I remember calling Joel Goldsmith and discussing the music for this episode,' Robert Cooper noted. 'Usually, there are natural spots in a scene where the music begins and ends. For 'Enemies', I said to Joel, "After the opening credits, jump on in, and then right before the end credits, jump out." That's pretty much how things went.'

### DID YOU KNOW?

How much notice do the producers take of internet postings, and do they have any influence on decisions? 'Yes, we do read the net,' Peter DeLuise has admitted. 'Though understandably we don't have much time for it.' 'Ascension', however, *was* inspired directly by comments on the net from fans wishing to see some of Carter's home life.

## 90 THRE/HOLD

US Transmission Date: 6 Jul 2001

UK Transmission Date: 19 Sep 2001
Writer: Brad Wright
Director: Peter DeLuise
Cast: Peter Williams (Apophis), Teryl Rothery (Dr Janet Fraiser), Tony Amendola (Bra'tac), Brook Parker (Drey'auc), Eric Schneider (Dr MacKenzie), Karen van Blankenstein (Nurse), David Lovgren (Va'lar)

Teal'c has not recovered from the brainwashing he suffered at the hands of Apophis, and still believes that SG-1 are his enemy. In desperation, they call on Bra'tac's help. He proposes a kill-or-cure treatment.

**THE WIT AND WISDOM OF JACK O'NEILL** 'I am 100% sure ... 99% sure Apophis is dead.'
To Teal'c: 'That would make you the most ineffective double agent in the history of double agenting.'

**ORIGINS OF THE SPECIES** The Rite of M'al Sharran could save Teal'c by taking him to the threshold of death. Bra'tac has tried it twice before, but both occasions resulted in death. Va'lar and Teal'c were friends. Both were Jaffa in-training under Bra'tac when he was First Prime, and served together in Apophis's personal guard. Va'lar was ordered killed for failure in battle against Ra, but was freed by Teal'c, banished, then later killed when Teal'c burned his village under orders from Apophis. Bra'tac is now 137 (see 'Into the Fire'). His symbiont will mature in two years and will be his last, as a new symbiont would reject a host of his age.

Several things contributed to Teal's rebellion against Apophis, including Apophis's punishment of Teal'c for defending his father's honour; Bra'tac's influence; Apophis ordering Teal'c to kill his friend Va'lar; the subsequent discovery that Apophis was not all-knowing, and, eventually, meeting O'Neill (see 'Children of the Gods').

**IN THE INTERESTS OF MAXIMUM SECURITY** If the Rite of M'al Sharran had failed, and Teal'c survived, he would've been incarcerated in a high-security prison facility. Hammond believes that Teal'c's symbiont will mature in four or five years.

**POSSIBLE INFLUENCES** *Star Trek: The Next Generation*'s 'Sins of the Father', 'Redemption' and other Klingon-based episodes. *Jacob's Ladder*, *Silence of the Lambs*, *Gladiator*, *Kung Fu*, *The Empire Strikes Back*, *Apocalypse Now*, *ER* and *The Exorcist*. Allusions to *Field of Dreams* ('He will come'), *Trainspotting* ('I choose freedom'), Matthew 6:24 ('The servant of two masters') and the My Lai massacre (Teal'c's memory of burning a village).[83]

**'YOU MIGHT REMEMBER ME FROM...'** David Lovgren played David in *Sea* and Neill in *Madison*.

**LOGIC, LET ME INTRODUCE YOU TO THIS WINDOW** Teal'c's father was called Ronac in

83 March 1968: The slaughter of 347 inhabitants - including women and children - in the South Vietnamese village of My Lai, by US troops. The incident was exposed to the world by a *Life* photographer and, ultimately, led to the court-martial of the officer responsible, Lt William Calley, in 1971.

'Crossroads'. Here, it sounds like Ranoc. Teal'c's symbiont looks very different to the last time we saw it. (It's a different colour for a start.) It's obviously grown. Teal'c's Jaffa skullcap in the newly-shot sequences doesn't match the one he wore in footage taken from 'Children of the Gods'.

**QUOTE/UNQUOTE** Daniel: 'Did he just call me a woman?'

Bra'tac: 'Men such as you and I have only the comfort of those times we make a difference. *Make* a difference.' And: 'I saw you play the game with those who would play god.'

**NOTES** 'His god? You mean that scum-sucking, overdressed boombox-voiced snake-in-the-head? Latest on our long list of dead bad guys?' Teal'c's development into a quasi-Messianic figure (see 'The Serpent's Venom') continues with what amounts to an science-fiction version of *The Last Temptation of Christ*. This is a good, solid episode, full of nice dramatic moments and thoughtful philosophy. But it's not, perhaps, the epic it should have been.

Jack considers himself Teal'c's best friend (at least, on Earth). Teal'c asks Sam if she believes in a god. She pointedly avoids making any reply. Bra'tac was present on Chulak during the events of 'Children of the Gods'. This is the first occasion in the series in which we've seen any of Ra's Jaffa.

**CAST AND CREW COMMENTS** Chris Judge was worried during the making of the pilot episode and even asked Michael Shanks and Jay Acavone if they thought that the audience would understand what his character was all about. An actor fears stillness and silence, yet that was Teal'c's *raison d'être*. Shanks reassured him: 'Sure they will.' 'Now I think he's almost talking too much,' Judge said. 'Everyone is used to [Teal'c] not saying much that when he *does* it automatically becomes important.'

**DID YOU KNOW?** Location filming for this episode took place at the magnificent Mount Seymour. 'We were supposed to have nice weather,' noted Lynn Smith, 'but instead it was rainy, snowy and foggy. However the scenes with Teal'c and Bra'tac came out beautifully.' The fog was a particular problem. 'We could probably have done it easier on a soundstage,' noted Peter DeLuise.

In the scene where Hammond and Jack are in the observation room, the reflection of a group of candles - forming the letters PD (Peter DeLuise) - can be seen for several seconds.

# 91 ASCENSION

US Transmission Date: 13 Jul 2001
UK Transmission Date: 26 Sep 2001
Writer: Robert C Cooper
Director: Martin Wood
Cast: Sean Patrick Flanery (Orlin), Teryl Rothery (Dr Janet Fraiser), Eric Breker (Reynolds), John de Lancie (Frank Simmons), Ben Wilkinson (O'Brien), Rob Fournier (Special Forces Commander)

SG-1 find a world devastated by war, with no apparent survivors. But Sam is touched by a powerful energy blast while studying an alien device. Once home, she finds herself being stalked by a handsome young man who knows a lot about her.

**THE WIT AND WISDOM OF JACK O'NEILL** Sam: 'Tense? Me? When did you first notice?' Jack: 'As we *met!*'

**SAM'S BIZARRE LOVE TRIANGLE** When she is forced to take time-off work, we see, clearly, just how little life outside the SGC Sam has. This was implied in previous episodes ('Nemesis', 'The Other Side', 'The Curse'). Suspicious of Orlin, Sam eventually confides in him, though she doesn't believe a relationship would be possible despite his claim to love her. Jack is understandably a bit surprised when he discovers that Sam has a date, and seems somewhat jealous.

**ORIGINS OF THE SPECIES** The civilisation of Velona may be 3000 years old, but the weapon dates to 400 years ago when the Goa'uld attacked. Orlin gave the Velonans the knowledge to build the weapon, and they defeated the Goa'uld. But, when they began to use the weapon for conquest, the Others destroyed them. The Others, the race to whom Orlin and Oma Desala (see 'Maternal Instinct') belong, have a sacred rule not to accelerate other races' natural development (see 'Abyss'). For breaking this, both Orlin and Oma were banished. The Others were once human (or, human-*like*, at least), but learned to ascend to a higher plane of existence in which they became non-corporeal. They can retake human form, but cannot ascend again. The Others continue to monitor Velona. (Orlin says that they would know if the weapon is activated, and they do indeed return to the planet when it is.) The Others are capable of manipulating the weather (including the ability to make lightning strike in specific places). Orlin reads some of Sam's books and watches overnight television to learn how to talk to her.

**THE CONSPIRACY STARTS AT CLOSING TIME** Reynolds (see 'Touchstone'), now a colonel, has been transferred from Area 51 and leads SG-16 during the long-term analysis of P4X636 and the testing of the weapon. The power core had been removed, but a Naqahdah reactor is used to replace it.

Concerning Sam's medical history, Janet mentions the events of 'In the Line of Duty', 'Beneath the Surface' and 'Entity', 'just for starters'.

**IN THE INTERESTS OF NATIONAL SECURITY** Hammond objects to the government bugging Sam's house, but is helpless to do anything.

**POSSIBLE INFLUENCES** *Star Wars.* (Jack's never seen it, Teal'c has. Nine times.) The Sam and Daniel phone-call is *very* Mulder and Scully. Sam has a Denver Broncos plaque in her basement.

**'YOU MIGHT REMEMBER ME FROM...'** Sean Patrick Flannery played the title role in *The Young Indiana Jones Chronicles* and appeared in *Kiss the Bride*, *Powder*, *Simply Irresistible* and *Suicide Kiss*. John de Lancie was Q in *Star Trek: The Next Generation* and several spin-offs and Al Kiefer in *The West Wing*. He was also in *Good Advice*, *Legend*,

*Andromeda, The Onion Field, Multiplicity* and *The Fisher King*.

**BEHIND THE CAMERA** Rob Fournier is the series' armourer.

**LOGIC, LET ME INTRODUCE YOU TO THIS WINDOW** It is, seemingly, possible to build a Stargate using materials available online, including 100 pounds of pure raw titanium, 200 feet of fibre-optic cable, seven 100,000-watt industrial-strength capacitors. And a toaster. Who has the authority to approve the bugging of Sam? Jack's never seen *Star Wars*, yet he knew who Luke Skywalker was in '1969'. To be fair, you don't have to have seen a movie to know the name of one of the characters in it. Note that when Orlin is rigging the junction box in Sam's basement, he pulls *out* the wire taking power into the box. What could those strange coloured liquids seen in the conical flasks in the infirmary possibly be?

**QUOTE/UNQUOTE** Janet: 'Make sure you come back if you start speaking an alien language.'

Teal'c: 'Do you believe Major Carter has become mentally unstable?' Jack: 'No more than the rest of us.'

Simmons: 'Need I remind you of the dangers we're trying to defend Earth against?' Daniel, at his most sarcastic: 'Could you? I mean, go slow.'

**NOTES** 'You wouldn't believe the things you can make from the common simple items lying around your planet. Which reminds me, you're going to need a new microwave.' Being a Rob Cooper story, this has plenty of good moments. (The Jack/Sam scenes are great, particularly his defence of her against Simmons' insinuations.) And Teal'c in a silly hat is always worthwhile. But the episode never quite engages the viewer, possibly because of the lack of sparkle in the relationship between Sam and Orlin.

Sam's birthday is in May, with a birthstone of emerald. She and Orlin share glasses of red wine and a pizza.

**TRIVIA** Many of the photos in Sam's house were from Amanda Tapping's own family collection. Similarly, some of the household items (quilts and ornaments, for instance) were gifts sent to Amanda by fans. The little girl, (supposedly a teenage Sam), seen in the photo with Carmen Argenziano, is actually Carmen's stepdaughter Mia. According to Martin Wood, one of the videotapes on a shelf seen briefly behind Richard Dean Anderson in Sam's house contained a label with a *very naughty word* on it. This author has tried to find out what it was. And failed miserably. The first five episodes recorded in season five all include references to toiletry functions (especially for all of those people who bemoan the fact that no one ever seems to pee on television).

**CAST AND CREW COMMENTS** 'This is a huge episode for Carter,' noted Amanda Tapping. 'We get to see where she lives, I wear normal clothes, I drive an amazing car. You know what? I think Carter is cool. She has a 1940 Indian motorcycle, a 1961 vintage Volvo and a Harley in her garage. How great is that? It's not like she's a complete loser!'

**DID YOU KNOW?** 'He's a consummate professional and a very intelligent man,' Don Davis noted concerning John de Lancie. 'He's such a joy to listen

SEASON 5

to. John is articulate without being rigid. When he's playing a villain, John can look at you and, without having to snarl and behave like Charles Bronson or Clint Eastwood, let you know if you get in his way he *will* destroy you.'

## 92 THE FIFTH MAN

US Transmission Date: 20 Jul 2001
UK Transmission Date: 3 Oct 2001
Writers: Joseph Mallozzi, Paul Mullie
Director: Peter DeLuise
Cast: Dion Johnstone (Tyler), John de Lancie (Frank Simmons), Teryl Rothery (Dr Janet Fraiser), Gary Jones (Sgt Walter Davis), Karen van Blankenstein (Nurse), Brad Kelly (Jaffa), Shawn Stewart (Jaffa), Dario DeIaco (Jaffa)

> Daniel, Sam and Teal'c hurriedly return to the SGC and tell Hammond that he must send immediate help to P7S441, where Jack and Lieutenant Tyler are trapped by enemy fire. Unfortunately, no-one at the SGC has any idea who Tyler is, despite SG-1's protestations that he's a valued member of their team.

**THE WIT AND WISDOM OF JACK O'NEILL** 'I wasn't going to let you die, Lieutenant. That's, like, a ton of paperwork... It's a joke. My way of deflecting attention from my own obvious heroism. You'll get used to it.'
Jack: 'Do you know what the Goa'uld really want from us? Minnesota, that's what. For the fishing, mostly. I'll take you some time.' Tyler: 'Fishing?' Jack: 'Oh, yeah. Ask Teal'c. He can't get enough.'

**ORIGINS OF THE SPECIES** The Reole are a race who shun technology and conflict. Their natural defence is a chemical in their bodies which resembles cortical acetylcholine, a neurotransmitter affecting the temporal lobe and associated with memory and recognition. This induces the mind to produce a sense of familiarity. Kaiael was captured by the Goa'uld for study, escaped and crashed on P7S441. He uses the chemical on SG-1, and the 'Made in Tyler, Texas' label on an MRE makes them believe that he is Lieutenant Tyler, newly assigned to SG-1. The Reole are the victims of what amounts to a systematic Goa'uld genocide programme. A group have established a hidden colony in an isolated part of the galaxy.

**THE CONSPIRACY STARTS AT CLOSING TIME** Simmons's chain of command is still unclear. He can access secure SGC files (including mission logs and briefings) as 'User 4574' (see 'Desperate Measures').

**IN THE INTERESTS OF NATIONAL SECURITY** Hammond's inability to speak to the President to overrule Simmons's investigations are reminiscent of the situation in 'Touchstone' (though, as Simmons points out, he may well try to play that card once too often).

**POSSIBLE INFLUENCES** *The Usual Suspects*, *The Man Who Never Was*

and *So Long at the Fair*. The title's an allusion to *The Third Man*. There's a dialogue reference to *That Thing You Do*. The alien creature itself is similar to Species 8472 in *Voyager*.

**LOGIC, LET ME INTRODUCE YOU TO THIS WINDOW** The death-glider canon that Teal'c uses has a pathetically small kickback for such a massively powerful weapon. Sam says that Daniel's name doesn't appear in any of her reports. What, *none* of them? Not even those like 'Crystal Skull', 'Maternal Instinct' or 'The Curse', that he should have featured rather prominently in? How do Sam, Daniel and Teal'c return to P7S441 and rescue Jack and Tyler? The Stargate is *very* well guarded at the far end by Jaffa. Why does Tyler revert to human form once he's captured by the Jaffa whilst in his natural state?

**QUOTE/UNQUOTE** Daniel: 'We obviously have Lieutenant Tyler issues. I say he exists. You say he doesn't.' Simmons: 'This is not just about Lieutenant Tyler.' Daniel: 'Someone else doesn't exist?'

Daniel: 'I would've asked him, but I was too busy being unconscious.'

**NOTES** 'That may be the way they are, but we're the way we are, so ... there you are!' Another so-so episode. Nothing fundamentally wrong with it except that it has the feeling of being lots of good bits from previous episodes randomly assembled. It kind-of works, but there's a sense of tiredness about the production.

Jack confirms that he was born in Chicago but raised in Minnesota (see 'Children of the Gods', 'Nemesis', 'The Curse'). Sam has considerable hacking ability. Simmons mentions Sam harbouring Orlin ('Ascension'). Daniel refers to the events of 'There But For the Grace of God'.

**CAST AND CREW COMMENTS** 'In this episode we get the largest number of corpses ever on the show. O'Neill's really trying to outdo *The Terminator*. We kill everybody. Twice,' noted Peter DeLuise.

**DID YOU KNOW?** As she's bought a house in Vancouver, does this mean that Amanda Tapping is planning to stay there for good? 'I thought I should invest the money I was going to earn with *Stargate*,' she confirmed. 'Since I knew I was going to be away for a long time, I decided to settle down there instead of living like a nomad.'

Richard Dean Anderson, meanwhile, spent part of his summer break in Tibet filming a documentary on the great rivers of the world. Fatherhood also provides a pleasant distraction for Rick. His daughter, Wylie, lives in California with her mother. 'I'm a great dad,' noted Richard. However, he believes he'll be able to control any rebellious teenage problems. 'Her mum's already said that she's going to tell our daughter with pride about her father's reputation because, essentially, I'm a survivor.'

## 93  RED *J*KY

US Transmission Date: 27 Jul 2001
UK Transmission Date: 10 Oct 2001
Writer: Ron Wilkerson

Director: Martin Wood
Cast: Fred Applegate (Elrad), John Prosky (Malchus), Norman Armour (Dr MacLaren), Brian Jensen (Freyr)

K'Tau is a peaceful, agrarian world populated by a spiritual people who worship the Asgard. SG-1's arrival is heralded as the coming of friendly emissaries from the gods but, when the planet's skies turn red, suspicions about the new arrivals mount.

**THE WIT AND WISDOM OF JACK O'NEILL** 'I have great confidence in you, Carter. Go on back to the SGC and confuse Hammond.'

**ORIGINS OF THE SPECIES** K'Tau is part of the Protected Planets Treaty. However, according to Subsection 42, people on such planets (including Earth) can't be artificially advanced through a technological means. Thus interference from the Asgard nullifies the treaty and leaves all protected planets open to Goa'uld attack. The K'Tau civilisation has its roots in Norse culture, using runic symbols and praying to the Norse god Freyr, Lord of the Aesir.[84] 'Annulus' is the K'Tau term for the Stargate. Odin is mentioned.[85]

**YE CANNAE CHANGE THE LAWS OF PHYSICS** The margin for error in calculating planetary shift causes an occasional rough ride during Gate travel. An unstable superheavy element, probably plutonium, may have piggy-backed onto the wormhole from another system and been introduced to K'Tau's sun as the wormhole passed directly through it, causing a shift in the light spectrum toward infrared. Sam's solution is to introduce a more stable superheavy element with an atomic weight above 200 into the sun's core, either by rocket or by prematurely disengaging the wormhole. HU2340 is the element artificially created by Dr MacLaren. Hammond will recommend its proposed name, 'Maclarium'.

The Asgard believe that K'Tau's religious belief system is essential to the population's development. But Jack suggests that a 'benevolent' advanced race posing as gods is no different to the Goa'uld doing the same. The Asgard's refusal to compromise the terms of the treaty carries implications that the Goa'uld are monitoring protected planets to ensure this provision is not violated (though there's a hint at the end that the Asgard used the SGC's presence as a screen and did provide the ultimate solution). The war with the Replicators still rages. Thor has apparently received a new ship since the destructions of the *Biliskner* and the *O'Neill*.

**POSSIBLE INFLUENCES** Ron Wilkerson's vision for the planet's inhabitants was 'a cross between Bergman's *The Seventh Seal* and an Amish-type community as in *Witness*.' Also, *The Wicker Man* and *The Day the Earth Caught Fire*. The title was an episode of the BBC's 1970s eco-drama *Doomwatch*.

**'YOU MIGHT REMEMBER ME FROM...'** Fred Applegate was in *Newhart*, *Remington Steele*, *Spaced Invaders* and *Stuart Saves His Family*. John Prosky appeared in *24*,

84 Freyr, not to be confused with his sister, Freyja (see 'Upgrades'), is the Viking god of sky, land and water, ally of Thor and ruler of the elves. Although not an Aesir (Sky god) himself, but rather a Vanir (Earth god), Freyr dwelt in Asgard. The cult of Freyr began with the Yngling kings in Sweden and subsequently spread to Iceland and Norway.

85 In Viking mythology Odin, the All-Father, was ruler of Asgard who lived in his Hall of the Slain, Valhalla.

*Artificial Intelligence: A.I.* and *Bowfinger.*

**LOGIC, LET ME INTRODUCE YOU TO THIS WINDOW** Sam notes that the SGC had to override some of the normal dialling protocols to get a lock on the K'Tau Stargate. This is the first we've heard of any such protocols (see '48 Hours'). Cimmeria may not be in the Protected Planets Treaty, Daniel speculates. But in 'Thor's Hammer', Thor's hologram clearly tells Jack and Teal'c that it *is*. A controlled shutdown forces the Stargate to disengage prematurely, causing the energy in transit to dissipate between gates. However, 'Shades of Grey' established that a Gate can be held open if there's matter in transit. What, exactly, is the *point* of that scene between Carter and MacLaren, a character who appears for no other reason than to be name-checked. It doesn't advance the plot an inch. A sizeable rocket is sent through the Stargate bit by bit and reassembled on K'Tau (including the building of a Houston-style staging tower) in three weeks. It's *possible*, but the task must have employed literally hundreds of labourers and technicians working on it, which raises questions about who they were, whether they had all signed a non-disclosure agreement and where they stayed whilst on the planet. (Or, did they all come back through the Stargate at the end of their shift each day?)

**QUOTE/UNQUOTE** Jack, on Sam: 'It's your call, General. I only understand about 1% of what she says half the time.'

Jack, describing Freyr's spaceship: 'Big machine like the one we were building. Only his is way-better. And not blown-up.'

**NOTES** 'We've saved your little grey butts. And now we want your help.' Conceptually this is brilliant - the Daniel/Jack conflict as to whether or not to influence the K'Tauans religious beliefs is a very interesting spin on an age-old *SG-1* dilemma (and one that Daniel has found himself on the opposite side of on more than one occasion). The imagery, a beguiling little essay on religious fanaticism and Jack's hilarious meeting with the Asgard are also feathers in its cap. But 'Red Sky' is fundamentally an opportunity missed. There was real potential to ask some hard questions about the ham-fisted way in which the SGC is wandering around the galaxy messing things up and expecting the Asgard to put it right. Pity we didn't get them.

**CAST AND CREW COMMENTS** 'I'd written an episode of the VH-1 series *Strange Frequencies.* That was the script that got me noticed by *Stargate*,' explained Ron Wilkerson. 'I was invited to pitch storylines over the phone to Robert Cooper and Peter DeLuise. Unfortunately, they were similar to things already in development, so they didn't go with any of them.' In September 2000, Wilkerson pitched several more, one of which was 'Red Sky', the idea for which came from 'flipping through an encyclopaedia. I looked at the visual spectrum of light that comes from the sun. I thought, what if sunlight somehow shifted to either extreme? It would kill a planet.'

**DID YOU KNOW?** 'We had to create an environment with a sky that progressed from blue to red. You can't do that with filters,' Michael Greenburg commented. 'We ended up building an exterior set on a soundstage so we would have complete control of the lighting. We also shot some live-action footage on location using filters, blue screen and trick photography. That material then went through a bleached bypass, which is a neat visual effect. Visually, 'Red Sky' is a beautiful show to watch.' The filming location was the town of Cloverdale.

# 94  RITE OF PASSAGE

US Transmission Date: 3 Aug 2001
UK Transmission Date: 10 Oct 2001
Writer: Heather E Ash
Director: Peter DeLuise
Cast: Teryl Rothery (Dr Janet Fraiser), Colleen Rennison (Cassandra)[85], Jacqueline Samuda (Nirrti), Karen van Blankenstein (Nurse), Richard de Klerk (Dominic)

> It's Cassandra's birthday but, whilst she enjoys a passionate first kiss with her boyfriend, Dominic, sparks fly. And not in a good way, either. SG-1 return to P8X987, the dead world they left four years ago, to search for a cure. But they bring back more than they expected.

**ORIGINS OF THE SPECIES**  Nirrti's experiments were designed to create a new advanced human host for herself. She infected the Hankan children (see 'Singularity') with a retrovirus causing symptoms of telekinesis, then cured them so that the altered DNA would be passed on to the next generation. The virus can exist in the body for years before symptoms appear. (The symptoms include a high fever, seizures, increased brain activity and cells generating an electromagnetic field.) During puberty the retrovirus rewrites the individual's DNA in order to replicate. When SG-7 were on P8X987 ('Singularity') they witnessed two instances of the virus, which the Hankans called '*mind-fire*'. Affected teenagers went alone into the forest and returned cured.

**POSSIBLE INFLUENCES**  *The Exorcist* ('until your head spins round'), *Carrie*, *Firestarter*, *The Tomorrow People*, *X-Men* and *The X-Files* episodes 'D.P.O' and 'Eve'. Visual influences include *Wolfen* and *The Matrix*.

**LOGIC, LET ME INTRODUCE YOU TO THIS WINDOW**  *All* cells generate an electromagnetic field, albeit so small as to be virtually unnoticeable - life itself is, in effect, one massive electro-chemical reaction. Why all the panic about Cassandra? She *can't* die here as it has already been established that she will live to old age (see '1969'). When did Cassandra turn into a sulky little madam (puberty, probably ...)? Her cake has 14 candles but she was 12 in 'Holiday' and '1969', so she should be 15 at least. TER scans failed to detect Nirrti when she followed SG-1 through the Stargate (see 'Show and Tell'). Nirrti doesn't appear to have modified her technology so that TERs *can't* detect her, as one of the SF guards later makes her partially visible with one. How can Teal'c tell that a fire burned in the forest on Hanka when it's been uninhabited for four years - the ground should surely have lost all traces of the fire by now. Come to that, the forest doesn't look as overgrown as you'd expect for an uninhabited planet. Sam described herself as a lousy cook in 'Emancipation', but she's man-

---

86 Character previous played by Katie Stuart in 'Singularity'.

aged to both bake and decorate a very professional looking birthday cake. Cassandra says Nirrti 'ran away' when she screamed. Is she a Goa'uld or a mouse?

**GOA'ULD LEXICON** 'Hok'tar' is a colloquialism from 'Hok' meaning 'advanced' and 'Tar' a slang term for the Tau'ri (humans).

**QUOTE/UNQUOTE** Cassandra on Jack: 'He always pretends he's not as smart as he really is.'

**NOTES** 'What do you see when you look at me now?' A somewhat strained attempt to take *SG-1* into *Buffy/Roswell* territory by focusing on the only teenager the series has access to. Colleen Rennison (see 'Bane') puts in a fab performance in a story which has energy and excitement, if not focus. But there are many nice moments (for instance, a gorgeous little scene between Daniel and Janet, that's rather unexpected but *very* in character for both). The climax is disappointing, however. Best bit: Janet holding Cassandra's hairbrush threateningly.

Every other Saturday when she's on Earth, Sam plays chess with Cassandra.

**CRITIQUE** 'Teenage angst is something we haven't seen much of in *Stargate*,' wrote Jan Vincent-Rudzki in *TV Zone*. 'It's interesting to see the reaction of both Fraiser and Carter as their sweet young girl wants to become her own person.'

*scifi.ign.com*'s Daniel Solis noted: 'Considering the recent trend of episodes centering on a specific character (Teal'c and Carter have both gotten the spotlight this season), I was wondering when the writers would devote a story to Frasier. We don't learn all that much about her, but at least we get to see her focused [as] *One baaaad momma*. Finally, Nirrti. Samuda was *born* to play Catwoman.'

**CAST AND CREW COMMENTS** 'Katie Stuart, who originally played Cassandra, is quite busy these days and wasn't able to reprise the role,' Teryl Rothery explained. 'They hired a lovely girl named Colleen Rennison. When I heard her name it sounded familiar but I couldn't place it. It was only after we met I realised she played one of my daughters in a film I did with David Bowie called *Mr. Rice's Secret*.'

**DID YOU KNOW?** For the series' first look at Janet Fraiser's home, the crew filmed at an old farmhouse in the small town of Ladner.

# 95 BEAST OF BURDEN

US Transmission Date: 10 Aug 2001
UK Transmission Date: 17 Oct 2001
Writer: Peter DeLuise
Director: Martin Wood
Cast: Dion Johnstone (Chaka), Larry Drake (Burrock), Alex Zahara (Shy One), Vince Hammond (Big Unas), Noel Callaghan (Boy), Dean Paul Gibson (Man from Store), Herbert Duncanson (Guard), Finn Michael (Guard), Wycliffe Hartwig (Unas), Trevor Jones (Unas)

SG-1 discover a community who oppress the Unas as slave labour. When they find that Daniel's friend Chaka is amongst the latest captives, they have to decide if they are morally obligated to liberate the Unas from bondage and become involved in the genesis of a war.

**ORIGINS OF THE SPECIES** Generations ago, the Unas served the Goa'uld and enslaved the population of the planet. When the Goa'uld left, the humans learned to use their weapons and led an uprising against the Unas. The Beast Wars lasted many years until the slaves became the masters. The villagers refer to staff weapons as 'firesticks'.

**THE CONSPIRACY STARTS AT CLOSING TIME** Daniel returns regularly with SG-11 to P3X888 to reset a surveillance camera and leave chocolate bars for Chaka (see 'The First Ones'). He uses the footage to study the Unas culture and has identified up to 70 words of their language.

**SEX AND DRUGS AND ROCK 'N' ROLL** When told it is the custom of the village to offer visitors a drink, Jack notes: 'It's our custom *to* drink.'

**POSSIBLE INFLUENCES** *Roots, Doctor Who*: 'Warriors' Gate' (aliens now the sympathetic and mistreated enslaved of their former human slaves). The title is that of a song by The Rolling Stones.

**'YOU MIGHT REMEMBER ME FROM...'** Larry Drake played Natalie's Dad in *American Pie 2* and Benny in *LA Law* and appeared in *Bean* and *Darkman*.

**LOGIC, LET ME INTRODUCE YOU TO THIS WINDOW** Burrock explains how he acquired the symbols to get to P3X888, but not how he managed to get *back*. How come nobody notices Sam sneaking around the village's main square planting explosives in broad daylight? Daniel's hair is very different during the first scene in the barn (indicating that those scenes were filmed after the rest of the episode had been completed). Daniel's pacifism has been suspect since his Chow Yun Fat impression in 'Within The Serpent's Grasp'. Here, the writers may be making a deliberate point concerning the real-life irony that many self-proclaimed pacifists are often to be found throwing petrol bombs over the barricades. Nobody gets so violent in a protest as a riled pacifist.

**QUOTE/UNQUOTE** Jack: 'I'm chained up in a madman's barn with a bunch of Unas. Who's to blame is not at the top of my list of concerns. Yet.' And: 'Dogs sniff each other's butts and they're friends for life. We still keep them as pets.'

**NOTES** 'We've meddled in other planets' cultures before.' True, though it's usually Daniel doing the complaining and Jack the meddling. Some strange messages come from this episode, not least the final scene in which Daniel Jackson, one of the last *great* liberal TV characters, becomes a gun runner. 'We didn't come here to arm them,' Jack notes as Daniel gives Chaka his zat and, in effect, signs his approval to what's likely to be a bloody conflict. Odd behaviour for an alleged pacifist. The slavery metaphor works up to a point, but that was an issue raised and won in real-life by the changing of consciences through dialogue, not with guns.

The filming location for this episode was Bordertown (see 'A Hundred Days').

**CAST AND CREW COMMENTS** 'One of the things we're doing more now is dealing with darker aspects of storytelling,' commented Robert Cooper. Both 'Red Sky' and 'Beast of Burden' 'embody the *Stargate* philosophy, which is *we're not perfect*. We're humans who make mistakes and get into situations that can't be solved by reversing the polarity of a device on your spaceship. We certainly don't have a *Prime Directive*. Our heroes poke their noses into things. They do their best to help but they're not always successful.'

**DID YOU KNOW?** 'I remember when I first read the script,' said Martin Wood. 'I thought "this is going to be big."' And, the director was happy to report that, in the end, it was. 'Because each of our characters was a different take on the slavery issue. "Beast of Burden" sets up an interesting dynamic between O'Neill and Daniel.'

# 96 THE TOMB

US Transmission Date: 17 Aug 2001
UK Transmission Date: 24 Oct 2001
Writers: Joseph Mallozzi, Paul Mullie
Director: Peter DeLuise
Cast: Garry Chalk (Russian Colonel), Earl Pastko (Colonel Zuckov), Alexsander Kalugin (Major Valarin), Jennifer Halley (Tolinev), Vitaliy Kravchenko (Lt Marchenko)

SG-1 reluctantly accompany a Russian unit on a mission to P2X338, where they investigate the disappearance of a Russian Stargate team 10 months ago. They find a desert, bodies and a tomb containing some dark secrets.

**THE WIT AND WISDOM OF JACK O'NEILL** 'I'm a big fan of the Russians and international relations are a bit of a hobby of mine, however, I do believe that SG-1 should handle this one alone.' And, on how Marduk died: 'Okay, that's *officially* the worst way to go.'

**ORIGINS OF THE SPECIES** P2X338 is an arid, deserted planet. The average temperature is 135 degrees in the shade. The ziggurat[87] is over 4000 years old. Its inscriptions were written in Babylonian cuneiform (which Daniel understands - see 'Fire and Water').

The Babylonian tablet refers to the Eye of Tiamat, a large jewel which supposedly endowed the Babylonian god Marduk (see 'Thor's Hammer', 'Fire and Water') with magical abilities. The entrance code is a retelling of the Babylonian creation myth in which Marduk slew the winged serpent Tiamat, cut her in two and used half to create the sky and half to create the Earth. Marduk was such an evil tyrant that his own priests rebelled against him, and sealed him in the sarcophagus with a very nasty creature that has no translated name. The sarcophagus continually tried to keep Marduk alive, so the creature eating him would have clearly taken some time.

- - - - - - - - - - - - - - - - - - - - - - - - - - - - - - - - - - - - - - - - - - - - - -

87 A distinctive type of Mesopotamian temple, described as a ladder to Heaven. Jacob's Ladder in Genesis may have been a ziggurat.

**THE CONSPIRACY STARTS AT CLOSING TIME** Major Valentine Kirensky was serving under Colonel Sakolov in Siberia and taking secret orders from certain hard-line elements in Russian Army Intelligence (see 'Watergate'). He disappeared six days before the SGC was called in to deactivate the Russian Gate, along with two other officers and Alexander Britski, an archaeologist and expert on ancient Mesopotamia. Two years ago Britski began an excavation near Rafha in southern Iraq. He found several stone tablets engraved with Babylonian cuneiform, and one with a set of Gate symbols - the co-ordinates for P2X338. The results of the dig became classified when the Russians connected the symbols to the Giza DHD discovered by the Germans in 1906 and taken by the Red Army at the end of World War II (see 'Watergate'). The co-ordinates were added to the list of addresses supplied to them by Maybourne.

**IN THE INTERESTS OF NATIONAL SECURITY** The Russians have been pushing for more direct involvement in the SGC as part of their agreement to share information.

**POSSIBLE INFLUENCES** *Alien, Indiana Jones and the Last Crusade, The Mummy, The Fly, Predator* and *The Beast Must Die*. Dialogue references to *The Russians Are Coming The Russians Are Coming*.

**'YOU MIGHT REMEMBER ME FROM...'** Earl Pastko played Satan in *Highway 61* and appeared in *Century Hotel, Dog Park, Sodbusters* and *Lexx*.

**LOGIC, LET ME INTRODUCE YOU TO THIS WINDOW** How long was Marduk sealed in the sarcophagus? Although it's never stated specifically, the implication is for many centuries. Yet, in 'Thor's Hammer', Kendra says that she was taken from her planet by Marduk and freed a mere ten years ago. (It's possible that Kendra was a Goa'uld for a long time, though other dialogue exchanges in 'Thor's Hammer' imply otherwise.) P2X338 looks very well-vegetated considering its arid climate. A grenade explodes in Valarin's hand, yet Zuckov and Jack, mere feet away, aren't killed. Daniel mispronounces Iraq.

**QUOTE/UNQUOTE** Sam: 'We've got a problem.' Jack: 'We've got a lot of problems, Carter. Can you be a little more specific?'

Daniel, to Valarin: 'Yes, you go down the dark hallway alone, and I'll wait here in the dark room alone ...'

**NOTES** 'We take risks, but we don't hand out cyanide pills and we don't leave our people behind.' Jack O'Neill can be a fairly petty individual at times. His constant baiting of Daniel is a good example. So is his reduction of every story involving Russians to a game of *wind-up Johnny Foreigner*. 'Whose side are you on?' he asks Sam at one point. Because Jack, seemingly, is on the side of Ronnie Reagan and mom's apple pie, right? It's really annoying that a series as sharp and sussed elsewhere as *SG-1* is still living deep in the past when it comes to international politics. Do the writers believe that it comforts the audiences to think of Russia as a nuclear bogey-state like some John Milius, *Red Dawn*-style throwback to the early-80s rather than, as in reality, a country that can't even feed its own people? Full of posturing, shallow stereotypes and clichés, 'The Tomb' should be ruddy awful. That it, actually, *isn't* is largely down to style over content.

Svetlana ('Watergate') is mentioned. She speaks highly of SG-1. Jack seems to be an expert on Russian commandos. (Given his time in Special Ops that's unsurprising.)

**CAST AND CREW COMMENTS** 'I want to direct,' stated Amanda Tapping. 'I asked at the beginning of season three, at the same time as Michael. For whatever reason, I wasn't allowed to, and that's a source of frustration to me. I'm sure my lack of a penis had nothing to do with it.'

**DID YOU KNOW?** A version of 'The Tomb' was pitched during season four but rejected as too expensive. Jennifer Hally had auditioned for the part of the similarly-named Jennifer Hailey in 'Prodigy'. The photos of the original Russian team are actually images of Peter DeLuise, Peter Woeste (see 'Maternal Instinct'), Wray Douglas (see 'Into the Fire') and Doug McLean (see 'Singularity'): 'The four shiftiest people we could find,' noted Paul Mullie.

## 97 BETWEEN TWO FIREƧ

US Transmission Date: 24 Aug 2001
UK Transmission Date: 31 Oct 2001
Writer: Ron Wilkerson
Director: William Gereghty
Cast: Gary Jones (Sgt Walter Davis), Garwin Sanford (Narim), Marie Stillin (Travell), Peter Wingfield (Tanith), Ryan Silverman (Tollan Gurad)

> The Tollan High Council announce that they are willing to share weapons technology with the SGC, contrary to their previous stance. Jack is delighted, but others (including Narim) are suspicious, wondering what sinister motive could be behind the change of heart.

**THE WIT AND WISDOM OF JACK O'NEILL** Jack: 'If you're going to recommend I continue to be suspicious and sceptical ...' Hammond: 'I wouldn't waste my time.' Jack: 'Good thinking, Sir.' And, to Travell: 'Do you people practice being vague?'

**SAM'S TRAUMATIC LOVE-LIFE** She's having a bad run of luck lately. Narim (whom Teal'c notes has strong feelings for Sam) is left to almost-certain death at the end. His computer featured Sam's voice.

**ORIGINS OF THE SPECIES** The final transmission from Tollana reports defences failing, the Stargate destroyed and ships attempting to leave the planet being shot down.

**THE CONSPIRACY STARTS AT CLOSING TIME** The line fed to SG-1 is that because of the Goa'uld threat, the Curia has been forced to change its isolationist views. Omac continued to favour the old ways. His death was probably murder, the aim being to shift the Curia vote and allow the trade of technology with Earth. Every Tollan has a small implant that monitors health. These are linked to a central system allowing the immediate dispatch of health officers in an emergency. Crime is very rare on Tollana. Tollan law considers lying by the government to be even more heinous than murder.

The SGC has access to an off-world Trinium mine (see 'Spirits', 'Upgrades'). A trade agreement is reached for a supply of Trinium to the Tollan in exchange for 38 ion cannons to provide an effective network to protect Earth from attack. Trinium is required in order to house any device that generates Tollan phase-shifting technology.

Tanith left Apophis's ship in an escape pod before the fleet's destruction by the Vorash supernova (see 'Enemies'). He now serves a powerful Goa'uld whose identity he refuses to reveal (see 'Summit'). His mothership has shields making it impervious to the ion cannons. The Curia was forced to agree to build weapons of mass destruction to prevent Tollana's annihilation. The weapons will penetrate solid matter prior to detonation.

**SEX AND DRUGS AND ROCK 'N' ROLL** Is Jack entirely comfortable with his sexuality? He seems *very* hung-up about having to hold hands with Teal'c.

**IN THE INTERESTS OF NATIONAL SECURITY** America's relationship with the Russians is described as 'tenuous at best'. So, what else is new (see 'The Tomb')?

**POSSIBLE INFLUENCES** *Star Wars* (the hologram), *JFK* (the cover-up), *Enemy of the State*.

**LOGIC, LET ME INTRODUCE YOU TO THIS WINDOW** There seem to be a lot of rainy days on Tollana. Both times that SG-1 visit during this episode, it's chucking it down. One could almost believe it was Vancouver. Where's Schrödinger? Narim finds what he's looking for in Travell's records remarkably quickly. In a distance shot of the site where the Tollan bombs are stored, several technicians can be seen in the background. But, when Jack and Teal'c go to disarm the bombs, they're seemingly alone.

**QUOTE/UNQUOTE** Daniel: 'So, push on blindly, then?' Jack: 'Blindly, yes, but we still have our slightly heightened sense of smell.'

**NOTES** 'There seems to be an evil conspiracy among the Tollan Curia, whose apparent goal is to give us everything we ever wanted.' A sinister tale of government duplicity and secret agendas. It's interesting to see Jack and Daniel for once on exactly the same wavelength when it comes to things not adding up. The finale is a let-down, however, with the bombs destroyed very easily (and, if they were so destructive, with very little damage) and a huge reported off-screen space battle. Best Bit: Jack's and Daniel's fumbling embarrassment at asking Travell for, not one ion cannon, but 38.

**CAST AND CREW COMMENTS** 'The idea changed a lot from the initial concept,' noted Ron Wilkerson. 'At first, I thought it would be interesting if the Tollan made a deal with an old enemy of SG-1's to build a weapon for them. One of the Tollan engineers leaks this and SG-1 is sent on a mission to stop them. The story became a more complex psychological study and, in many ways, a detective story.'

**DID YOU KNOW?** The filming location for the Tollana city

complex in this episode (and 'Pretense') is the Simon Fraser University in Vancouver.

## 98  2001

US Transmission Date: 31 Aug 2001
UK Transmission Date: 7 Nov 2001
Writer: Brad Wright
Director: Peter DeLuise
Cast: Gary Jones (Sgt Walter Davis), Ronnie Cox (Senator Kinsey), Rob Lee (Pierce), Christopher Cousins (Joe Faxon), Dion Luther (Mollem), Robert Moloney (Borren), Howard Siegel (Keel)

SG-1 encounter a powerful potential ally, the Aschen, but discover that the aliens' homeworld is one about which they once received a cryptic warning from the future. Can SG-1 find proof of their suspicions before the politicians repeat the mistakes of 2010 all over again?

**THE WIT AND WISDOM OF JACK O'NEILL** On the Aschen: 'They don't get excited in general, General. It's like an entire planet of accountants.'

**SAM'S TRAUMATIC LOVE-LIFE** She blinds Joe Faxon with science and, in return, he accompanies her to the SGC mess. Unfortunately, he subsequently joins Martouf and Narim in the *Sam's Dead Boyfriend* club so there's no chance of the marriage seen in '2010' actually happening.

**ORIGINS OF THE SPECIES** Aschen technology includes medical advances (see '2010'), transporters, harvesters, the ability to create a secondary star by igniting a gas giant, and bio-weapons containing radioactive genetic material designed to destroy only a specific enemy. They seek new planets to colonise, but their ships travel only within their Confederation, and their Stargate was found buried, with no DHD and no Gate addresses.

The search for an Aschen homeworld close to the Volian system reveals four planets, including P4C970 which SG-1 received a warning about from the future seven months ago (see '2010'). Two hundred years ago, the Volians were a thriving urban civilisation approximating 1910 North America in technological development. Newspapers reveal a language similar to Celtic Welsh. A pandemic killed millions, then the Aschen arrived in ships, offered a vaccine and were seen as heroes. The Volians joined the Confederation but it was eventually discovered that the Aschen vaccine caused sterility in the Volians. There were street riots, the urban society abruptly ended and all evidence of it was buried. In 200 years, P3A194 has gone from an industrialised civilisation of millions to an agrarian population of thousands.

**THE CONSPIRACY STARTS AT CLOSING TIME** The President is under enormous pressure to present some concrete benefits of the Stargate programme before the next election. He puts Kinsey in charge of the Aschen negotiations. (Given that Kinsey has already announced his intention to run for President himself - see 'Chain Reaction' - is the President hoping Kinsey will make a mess of this?)

**IN THE INTERESTS OF NATIONAL SECURITY** Jack has an open invitation to the White House from the last time he saved the planet (probably after 'Small Victories').

**POSSIBLE INFLUENCES** *Planet of the Apes, They Live* and *Logan's Run*. The title comes from Stanley Kubrick's *2001: A Space Odyssey* (based on a novel by Arthur C Clarke, who is also name-checked), *The Wizard of Oz* ('Just when you think you're not in Kansas anymore') and *Starsky and Hutch*. Again. Visually, *The Rocketeer*. Daniel mentions the 1918-19 influenza pandemic which killed over 20 million people and the Luddite movement of the early 18th Century in which European textile workers organised the destruction of automated machinery, believing that the existence of such machines would lead to their own unemployment.

**LOGIC, LET ME INTRODUCE YOU TO THIS WINDOW** Sam's laptop boots up remarkably quickly. How convenient that she had a length of rope in her backpack with which to lower herself into the Stargate. The Volians have very Earth-like barbed wire on their farms. At the end as Carter lies injured in the SGC, Jack, Daniel and Teal'c do not seem concerned enough about her to check on her condition.

**QUOTE/UNQUOTE** Sam, on Jack's note: 'You were probably trying to limit the causality violation by keeping it simple.' Jack: 'I wonder whose idea that was?'

**NOTES** 'You'll find we are a very patient people.' A fantastic prequel to '2010', in which the audience is, for once, five steps ahead of the characters. This reinforces our faith in SG-1 - they all suspect that something's amiss with an offer too good to be true. Aided by beautifully colourful locations and a cunningly layered plot, this is another real gem.

Daniel has been to Wales. The DHD is designed to compensate automatically for stellar drift. Sam believes the outer limit for a lock between two Stargates without a DHD is 300 light years (see 'Children of the Gods').

The lost Volian city used redressed building sets from 'Red Sky'. Herbert Duncanson (see 'Wormhole X-Treme!') plays one of three SG Leaders whom Hammond intends to send to specific Stargate addresses which might be the Aschen homeworld.

**CAST AND CREW COMMENTS** 'We write smart stuff for him but he likes to play it dumb,' Robert Cooper notes regarding Rick Anderson. 'We know Jack is really smart but he likes to tease Carter with the fact he doesn't get her technobabble.'

**DID YOU KNOW?** 'I'm very surprised [the series] took off the way it did,' Michael Shanks noted. 'I didn't think it would last more than a year or two and here we are at five years.'

# 99 DESPERATE MEASURES

US Transmission Date: 7 Sep 2001
UK Transmission Date: 14 Nov 2001

Writers: Joseph Mallozzi, Paul Mullie
Director: William Gereghty
Cast: Teryl Rothery (Dr Janet Fraiser), Tom McBeath (Harry Mayborne), John de Lancie (Frank Simmons), Bill Marchant (Adrian Conrad), Andrew Johnston (Doctor), Ted Cole (Doctor), Carrie Genzel (Diana Mendez), Robert Manitopyes (Guard), Jay Kramer (Guard), Frank C Turner (Homeless Man), Tammy Pentecost (Assistant), Sasha Piltsin (Driver), Raoul Ganeev (Roadblock Soldier), Igor Morozov (Roadblock Soldier)

When Sam is abducted by a gang of *ninjas*, Hammond gives Jack authorisation to find her using any means necessary. Meanwhile, Sam wakes up in a hospital where doctors are performing experiments on her.

**THE WIT AND WISDOM OF JACK O'NEILL** Daniel: 'You think Maybourne's a fan of Godzilla movies?' Jack: 'Strikes me more as a Mothra guy.'
Maybourne: 'Jesus, Jack, you're stealing my routine.' Jack: 'Consider it an *homage*.'

**THE CONSPIRACY STARTS AT CLOSING TIME** On the second mission when the Russian Stargate was active (see 'Watergate'), a Jaffa was captured and held by a renegade faction of Russian military intelligence. Maybourne arranged for the theft of the symbiont and was paid $3 million into his off-shore bank account by a company in the Cayman Islands, a subsidiary of a multinational, Zetatron Industries, run by Adrian Conrad. Immunologist Neil Brooke took delivery of the symbiont.

**MILITARY INTELLIGENCE?** Conrad is in the late stages of the incurable Burchardt's Syndrome, which affects the immune system. Sam is taken to St Christina's, a deserted hospital in the suburbs of Seattle, to determine a safe means for implanting, and then removing, a symbiont.

Simmons is confirmed as User 4574 (see 'The Fifth Man'). Shooting Jack at the climax, he now has his own Goa'uld to play with (see '48 Hours'). He loathes his predecessor, Maybourne. The feeling appears to be mutual.

**IN THE INTERESTS OF NATIONAL SECURITY** The NID is a legitimate organisation financed by the government, with a mandate to provide civilian oversight of top-secret military operations (see 'Touchstone'). Agents use websites such as *movieorbit.com* ('Everything for the B-Movie fanatic') to post coded messages to each other (see 'Chain Reaction'). The FBI and Interpol are searching for the missing Goa'uld, and for Maybourne, believing that *he* was responsible for shooting Jack.

**POSSIBLE INFLUENCES** Dialogue allusions to *National Geographic*, *Godzilla* and *Starsky and Hutch*. Jack refers to G Gordon Liddy (the notorious Watergate burglar and, latterly, celebrity author). Also, *The X-Files* ('I wonder if glowing aliens have anything to do with it?' and, specifically, Scully's abduction in 'Ascension'), *Trading Places* ('I was in 'Nam'), *The Godfather Part II* (Maybourne turning the ornamental cannon towards Diana) and a misquote of Roman satirist Decimus Juvenal (c.55-140) 'Who watches over you?' It's a very *New Avengers*-type pre-title sequence (including the music). The title comes from Barbara Schroeder's 1998 thriller,

**'YOU MIGHT REMEMBER ME FROM...'** Bill Marchant featured in *Mysterious Ways* and *Millennium*. Ted Cole appeared in *Scary Movie*. Tammy Pentecost was in *Valentine*. Carrie Genzel played Ali McIntyre in *Days of Our Lives* and appeared in *Married... with Children*. Andrew Johnston was in *Best in Show* and *The X-Files*. Frank Turner appeared in *The Duke*, *Sliders*, *Insomnia* and *Needful Things*.

**LOGIC, LET ME INTRODUCE YOU TO THIS WINDOW** How isn't Sam's scalpel spotted by the cameras? Why doesn't Sam suggest contacting the Tok'ra for Conrad? He'd make an ideal host.

**QUOTE/UNQUOTE** Homeless Guy: 'I was in 'Nam.' Jack: 'What company?' Homeless Guy: 'Vacation. It was a long time ago.'

Maybourne on *hide-and-seek*: 'I could always find anyone, anywhere, but they could never find me.' Jack: 'Because they didn't want to?'

Daniel: 'I think I just electrocuted myself. Do you have any idea what that feels like?' (Shoots zat.) 'Something like that!'

**NOTES** 'That overwhelming desire to shoot you has come back.' A very impressive piece of recontextualisation which explores the dark corners of *SG-1*'s espionage world. Anderson and Tom McBeath form one of the best comedy double-acts on TV.

Jack drives a Ford F250. Sam attends a fitness club 12 blocks from her home and is still driving her vintage Volvo (see 'Ascension'). Vancouver's Rainview Psychiatric Hospital was a filming location. (Often used for episodes of *The X-Files*, the fourth floor is alleged to be haunted.) Aerial stock footage of the Pentagon also features.

**DID YOU KNOW?** 'I owe my whole career to Richard Dean Anderson and Michael Greenburg,' Don Davis revealed. 'I was a college professor who was semi burned-out teaching, and starting out in the film business. They gave me my first break, my first guest-star role, they took care of me. Those two guys have more integrity than anybody I've ever met in this business.'

# 100 WORMHOLE X-TREME![88]

US Transmission Date: 14 Sep 2001
UK Transmission Date: 21 Nov 2001
Story: Brad Wright, Joseph Mallozzi, Paul Mullie
Teleplay: Joseph Mallozzi, Paul Mullie
Director: Peter DeLuise
Cast: Teryl Rothery (Dr Janet Fraiser), Willie Garson (Martin Lloyd), Robert Lewis (Tanner), Mar Andersons (Bob), Michael DeLuise (Nick Marlowe/Colonel Danning), Peter DeLuise (Director), Jill Teed (Yolanda Reese/Stacy Monroe), Benjamin Ratner (Studio Executive), Don Thompson (Props Guy), Christian Bocher (Ray Gunne/Dr Levant), Peter Flemming (NID Agent Barrett), Herbert Duncanson (Doug

[88] Though the episode is entitled 'Wormhole X-Treme!' the fictitious series does not include an exclamation mark.

Anderson/Grell), David Sinclair (Bill A.D.), Kiara Hunter (Alien Princess), Laura Drummond (Security Guard), Keath Thome (Head SF), Hank Cohen[89] (Studio Executive), Brad Wright[90] (Exec-Producer), Michael Greenburg[91] (Exec-Producer), Robert Cooper[92] (Writer), Joseph Mallozzi[93] (Man Looking for Doughnuts), N John Smith[94] (Man in Pink Shirt), Martin Wood[95] (Armed NID Man), Ron Wilkerson[96] (Man on Cellphone), Jan Newman[97] (Makeup Lady), Andy Mikita[98] (Actor whom Marlowe head-butts), Wray Douglas[99] (Special Effects Supervisor), Nikki Smook[100] (Very Tall Alien Female)

A campy SF TV series, *Wormhole X-Treme*, has worrying implications for the SGC. The Creative Consultant is someone with obvious knowledge of the Stargate. At the same time, a mysterious alien ship arrives in Earth's orbit. Are these events connected? *Of course* they are.

**WHO ARE THESE GUYS ANYWAY?** *Wormhole X-Treme* stars Nick Marlowe as the wry Colonel Danning ('As a matter of fact it *does* say "colonel" on my uniform'), Yolanda Reese as the brilliant Major Stacy Monroe, Raymond Gunne as Dr Levant and Douglas Anders as Grell. *A robot.*

**ORIGINS OF THE SPECIES** Tanner's surprising decision to blow up his escape pod ('Point of No Return') is finally explained. A spacecraft was waiting nearby, which would eventually return for him and his colleagues. Fully aware that the NID is after them, Tanner is astute in turning to the SG-1 for help. Or, maybe they have had a run-in with the NID before and know that Jack is the lesser of two evils.

**THE CONSPIRACY STARTS AT CLOSING TIME** The NID has had Martin under surveillance since his experience with the SGC ('Point of No Return'). They're motivated by the desire to locate Tanner and the others. It seems odd, therefore, that they haven't confiscated the recall device that Martin took from Tanner. Barrett tells Sam and Daniel that the NID has been given full authority over the investigation. By whom? The SGC's remit doesn't extend far beyond Cheyenne Mountain ('Cold Lazarus, 'Desperate Measures') but it *was* the Air Force who had Jack appointed as an advisor to *Wormhole X-Treme*.

**IN THE INTERESTS OF NATIONAL SECURITY** The Air Force got Martin a job in real estate, but he hated it and began taking vitamins laced with memory suppressing chemicals (see 'Point of No Return'). Martin tells Jack that he isn't sure how the studio first heard of his short story, *Going to Other Planets*, on which the TV series is ultimately based. Was it sent by the Air Force? Jack implies that they have knowledge of, and control over, television programme development, so this seems likely. The Air Force could have shut down *Wormhole X-Treme* whilst it was in pre-production as a violation of national security. Instead they have allowed the series to continue specifically to maintain plausible deniability about the existence of the Stargate. Should anyone threaten to expose it (see 'Secrets', 'Point of No Return'), the Air Force can simply say, 'That's the television series *Wormhole X-Treme* you're describing', thus making the accuser look ridiculous.

**POSSIBLE INFLUENCES** *The X-Files* and *Mutant X* ('Research says

89-100 Uncredited.

SEASON 5

shows with *X* in the name get higher ratings'), *Men in Black* ('Please, Mr Man-In-Black, don't pretend you don't know about the Aliens'), *The Six Million Dollar Man* (one of Tanner's men is called Steve Austin), *Battlestar Galactica* (time measured in 'bleems'), *The Matrix* (Agent Smith), *Star Trek* ('positronic feedback compositors are off-line'; Colonel Danning grabbing all the women by their shoulders before kissing them, like Jim Kirk used to do; the effect used when beaming-up Tanner and his men to their ship), *Mars Attacks!*, *Doctor Who* ('Try reversing the polarity'), *UFO* (a movie studio as a cover for nefarious alien skulduggery), *Galaxy Quest*... and just about every other science-fiction film and TV series ever made. Visually, *Traffic* (the NID's arrival). The Kepler probe is named after German astronomer Johannes Kepler (1571-1630), who wrote the laws of planetary motion.

**'YOU MIGHT REMEMBER ME FROM...'** Michael DeLuise was Tony Piccolo in *SeaQuest DSV* and Andy Sipowicz in *NYPD Blue* and appeared in *Wayne's World*. Jill Teed was in *Bad Company*, *Mission to Mars*, *Roommates* and *The Final Cut*. Kiara Hunter played Tamara in *Bordello of Blood* and Suzanne in *Blackmail*. Benjamin Ratner was in *Crash*, *Dirty*, *The Last Wedding* and *Leaving Normal*.

**BEFORE THE CAMERA (FOR ONCE)** Amongst the *SG-1* crew making cameos are property master David Sinclair, Chris Judge's stand-in Herbert Duncanson and chief lighting technician Rick Dean (who plays the crewman avoiding the smell of Teal'c's food).

**LOGIC, LET ME INTRODUCE YOU TO THIS WINDOW** *Logic?!*

**WE SUFFERED FOR OUR ART, NOW IT'S YOUR TURN** Martin: 'You think aliens eat apples?' (see 'Beneath the Surface'). Props Guy: 'Why not? They speak English.' (See 'Emancipation'.)

Studio Executive: 'Know what this show needs? *Sexy female alien.*' (See 'Upgrades'.)

Yolanda asks why, if Major Monroe is 'out of phase', she doesn't fall through the floor. (See 'Crystal Skull'.)

**QUOTE/UNQUOTE** Levant: '*Dammit*, colonel, just because they're aliens and their skulls are transparent doesn't mean they don't have rights!'

Hammond: 'In the event of a future breach of security we'll be able to point to this television programme. That's if it stays on the air.'

Producer: 'Where are all the doughnuts?' Teal'c: 'They were consumed by the drivers before they retired to sleep.'

Daniel: 'Why would somebody with two PhDs become a teamster?' Sam: 'Money, I guess?'

**NOTES** 'That's the stupidest Act-4 opening *ever*. You should stick with the Air Force.' Okay, so this is extremely self-indulgent, but milestones occasionally deserve celebrating. An episode that revels in dozens of great self-aware one-liners ('The real money's in syndication', 'Don't worry, it's on cable') and TV-industry jokes ('We're gonna win an Emmy for this. *Visual Effects* category'). There's even a great Mary-Sue joke at the expense of fan-fiction writers (specifically, Martin's original concept featuring himself as the 'handsome fifth crewmember'). As with 'Point of No Return', the discovery that you *can* clown around without looking stupid can be a liberating one. Best bit: Daniel biting his lip and looking distressed as he watches his

*Wormhole X-Treme* equivalent deliver a very Danielesque 'alien have rights too' speech. And, by contrast, Carter's little grin at *her* SF-cliché counterpart.

*Poochinsky* was a TV series about a crime-solving talking dog. It ran for a hundred episodes and won a *Cable Ace* award. Jack was a big fan ('*Great show!*'). Daniel's getting rather good at all the James Bond cloak-and-dagger stuff, isn't he? *Dust Off That Old Screenplay And Sell It!* is a national bestseller by one Robert Cooper.

**CRITIQUE** 'For the hundredth episode, the *SG-1* team settled on this tongue-in-cheek offering, taking one of last season's dafter premises and making it even sillier with the addition of a *Stargate* take-off,' noted *Xposé*. 'As a chance to make knowing jokes, it works nicely, the only letdown being the plotting doesn't make a lot of sense under close inspection.'

**CAST AND CREW COMMENTS** 'I thought *Twin Peaks* was going to be one of the high points of my life,' Don Davis noted. 'It's a show people still remember - even though we only did 30 episodes. This one, we've done 100! I think that says something.' Asked about the underlying theme of *SG-1*, Don notes: 'It's a humanist viewpoint. You have two choices in life: make a difference or make a profit.'

Brad Wright added: 'Rather than do a heavy, expensive episode like we normally would do, we did a show that was a parody of ourselves, kind-of a *Galaxy Quest* version of *Stargate SG-1*.'

'Even when we were working on the outline, people were coming by and saying, "You should do this,"' Paul Mullie told *cinescape.com* website. 'Everybody pitched ideas, it was a big collaboration. It was easy to do all of the spoof elements. Having an actual *Stargate* story underneath the parody was the hard part. It had to be there, otherwise the episode wouldn't mean anything.'

**DID YOU KNOW?** 'I think the fact we did the self-parody episode means we can concentrate on other ideas this year,' Amanda Tapping commented. 'Wormhole X-Treme!' got lots of mileage from SF's treatment of women as either window-dressing, or men with tits. Fortunately, that's never been much of a problem for *SG-1* unlike, for instance, *Voyager*. *Poltergeist: The Legacy*'s Helen Shaver has called Sam Carter one of the strongest women on television. 'I ran into her in the gym in Toronto,' Tapping notes. 'I told her she's a huge inspiration to me, not only because she continues to act but that she has this entirely different directing career.'

*SEASON 5*

# 101 PROVING GROUND

US Transmission Date: 8 Mar 2002
UK Transmission Date: 28 Nov 2001
Writer: Ron Wilkerson
Director: Andy Mikita
Cast: Elisabeth Rosen (Jennifer Hailey), Michael Kopsa (General Kerrigan), Courtney J Stevens (Elliott), David Kopp (Grogan), Grace Park (Satterfield)

While training cadets at a secret facility, Jack learns of a possible alien incursion at the SGC.

Knowing that other teams may be compromised, he has no choice but to take his young troops into a battle situation. Or so it seems.

**THE WIT AND WISDOM OF JACK O'NEILL** 'These, and other clichés, will be available to you all for one more day of training.' And: 'I like people with attitude. In fact, I much prefer them to people who suck up.'

**THE CONSPIRACY STARTS AT CLOSING TIME** The SGC trains new recruits consisting of top graduates from the Air Force Academy (and probably other military academies). General Kerrigan now has knowledge of the programme (he didn't in 'Prodigy'). Each SG-team participates in training exercises on rotation. The scenarios occupy several floors of Stargate Command every few months and are observed and reviewed by the SGC and the Pentagon. The intars recovered from Apophis's camp ('Rules of Engagement') have been adapted for use in this training. No recruit can be assigned to an SG-team without the recommendation of an existing SG commander. In next year's budget, Hammond is proposing an off-world training facility (see 'Shades of Grey', 'Prodigy').

**MILITARY INTELLIGENCE?** When the trainees arrive at the SGC, they discover that the Stargate is active. Though the SGC may have co-ordinated an off-world team to dial-in at an appropriate time, it's probably an outgoing wormhole.

**IN THE INTERESTS OF NATIONAL SECURITY** SGC training scenarios include rescuing captured team members, recovering alien technology and neutralising a 'foothold' situation (see 'Foothold'). Trainees gain access to classified information about SGC technology and previous missions. Elliott, for example, knows about Argos ('Brief Candle'). Since not all trainees are successful they, presumably, have to sign non-disclosure agreements.

The access shafts from Cheyenne Mountain are locked with electronic mechanisms. If an incorrect code is entered (if Jack's telling the truth), tear gas is released. The dialling computer is isolated from the base mainframe, making it impossible to hack from outside the control room.

**POSSIBLE INFLUENCES** *Star Trek II: The Wrath of Khan* and the *Next Generation* episode 'Lower Decks', *Under Siege* and *Die Hard*.

**'YOU MIGHT REMEMBER ME FROM...'** Grace Park played Shannon Ng in *Edgemont*. David Kopp was in *Josie and the Pussycats*.

**LOGIC, LET ME INTRODUCE YOU TO THIS WINDOW** Hailey is a 2nd lieutenant. In 'Prodigal' she was an underclassman, which means not yet in her final year at the academy. So she should still be referred to as a cadet. When did Elliott take Sam's access card? Those shot SFs are bloody good actors - managing to bleed on cue and not to breathe when closely observed by Elliott. How do Sam, Hammond and Jack get from the observation room on Level 16 to the gateroom 12 floors below in less than a minute to applaud Elliott's rescue of Hailey?

**QUOTE/UNQUOTE** Jack: 'I was *never* their age.'
Sam: 'Sir, if you don't mind, your wound is bleeding all over my lab.'

**NOTES** 'They're the future of the Air Force, the programme, the entire planet. God help us.' This plot (an outsiders look at the regular cast) has become something of a standard for most long-running series. Not very ambitious perhaps, but as far as it goes, it's a worthy attempt at something different, with Elliott as a cunning Jack-*wannabe*. Though he's hardly in it, Daniel gets most of the best bits: love his sharp-shooting and his decadent pleasure at how comfortable Hammond's chair is.

Sam's lab is on Level 19. Daniel's office is on Level 18. Elliott was at the top of his class at the academy. He is assigned to SG-17, commanded by Major Mansfield (see 'Summit'). SG-3 is still a Marine unit (see 'The Broca Divide').

**DID YOU KNOW?** Among the charities that Richard Dean Anderson is happy to associate with are the Water Keeper Alliance, who prosecute corporate polluters; the Challengers, an inner-city recreation club for boys and girls in Los Angeles; and the Sea Shepherd Foundation, a conservation organisation who protect marine life.

# 102  48 HOUR∫

US Transmission Date: 15 Mar 2002
UK Transmission Date: 5 Dec 2001
Writer: Robert C Cooper
Director: Pete F Woeste
Cast: Tom McBeath (Harry Mayborne), John de Lancie (Frank Simmons), Garry Chalk (Colonel Chekov), Colin Cunningham (Major Davis), Bill Marchant (Adrian Conrad), David Hewlett (Rodney McKay), Gary Jones (Sgt Walter Davis), Tracy Westerholm (SF), Dan Shea (Sgt Siler), Peter Wingfield (Tanith)[101], Jeff Seymour (Mr Black), Martin Blaiz (NID Guard), Ken Phelan (Food Server)

> As SG-1 return to Earth, Teal'c is lost in transit. Sam tries to fashion a way to bring him back, whilst Daniel negotiates with the Russians and Jack seek the help of Harry Mayborne.

**ORIGINS OF THE SPECIES** Thanks to Tok'ra intelligence, knowledge of Tanith scouting P3X116 for a new base reaches SG-1. The Goa'uld cannon that Teal'c recovered in 'The Fifth Man' is used to avenge Shau'nac (see 'Crossroads').

**THE CONSPIRACY STARTS AT CLOSING TIME** An event horizon dematerialises an object, turning it into matter and transmitting it through a subspace wormhole. The receiving Gate translates the energy signature and reconverts it back to its original form (see 'Children of the Gods'). The Stargate has massive amounts of memory, like a computer buffer which temporarily stores energy signatures before reconverting them to make sure that the information is complete before reintegration. One of the Gate's safety protocols erases the energy imprints from the control crystals each time a new wormhole is established, like a system reset. The Stargate is capable of emitting up to 400 feedback signals and safety protocols during a dialling sequence. Using a computer rather than the DHD ignores as many as 220 of these.

101 Uncredited.

SEASON 5

**LOST IN SPACE** Destruction of the sending Gate severs the wormhole prematurely; however, a local DHD would compensate for the loss of power and allow the receiving Gate to finish the reintegration process. Removing the control crystal from a DHD before connecting will create an event horizon without connecting to a wormhole. Daniel and Major Davis negotiate a loan of the DHD from the Russians to facilitate this.

**MILITARY INTELLIGENCE?** Maybourne recruited Frank Simmons to the NID. Harry confirms that it was Simmons who shot Jack in 'Desperate Measures'. And offers to kill Simmons for Jack if he'd like.

**IN THE INTERESTS OF NATIONAL SECURITY** McKay's been studying the Stargate at Area 51 for over a year and is considered by the Pentagon to be the world's foremost expert. If not by the SGC, who prefer Sam Carter. The NID has several bases for its special operations. The Goa'uld in Adrian Conrad (see 'Desperate Measures') is being held in Minot, North Dakota.

**POSSIBLE INFLUENCES** The title is from a 1982 Walter Hill comedy starring Eddie Murphy. Maybourne is staying at the Accent Inn under the name Cassidy. 'David[102]' or Shaun[103]?' asks Jack. 'Butch[104]' is the reply. Also, *Die Hard* ('Teal'c is *toast*') and *Apollo 13* ('That never happened in any of the simulations').

**'YOU MIGHT REMEMBER ME FROM...'** Jeff Seymour appeared in *Liberty Stands Still*. Gary Chalk was in *Cold Squad* and *M.A.N.T.I.S.* David Hewlett appeared in *Century Hotel*, *Chasing Cain*, *Company Man*, *Amateur Night*, *The First Circle*, *Autoerotica*, *Cube* and *ER*.

**LOGIC, LET ME INTRODUCE YOU TO THIS WINDOW** Lots of timing issues. Much travelling is done by both Daniel and Jack in a *very* short space of time. What happened to the Goa'uld? Did Jack hand him over to Maybourne? Or leave him with the NID? (They were bound-up, of course, which leaves the possibility of escape. That's the last thing, surely, the SGC would want?) Attempt to reconcile the "transporter" and "wormhole" versions of Gate-travel gives us some of the worst scientific technobabble in the series, particularly the description of what an event horizon actually is. In reality, it's the point at which matter is irrevocably crushed into a singularity: a mathematical concept with infinite mass and no dimensions.

**QUOTE/UNQUOTE** Sam: 'Is there any chance you can get the Russians to give us their DHD?' Daniel: 'Not without giving back Alaska.'

**NOTES** 'We can't just ignore the laws of thermodynamics. Entropy dictates that the crystals won't retain the energy patterns permanently.' A turbo-charged plot racing along at dizzying speed. Wish it all made more sense, but the acting is good. (It's primarily Tapping's and Shanks's episode.) There are some inter-

---

102 One of the biggest TV stars and pop idols of the 1970s via *The Partridge Family* and hits like 'Daydreamer'.
103 Never as huge in Britain as his half-brother David, Shaun was also a best-selling 70s teenage popstar and played Joe in *The Hardy Boys Mysteries*. He later became a noted TV writer/producer, co-creating the series *American Gothic*.
104 Pseudonym for Robert Leroy Parker (1866-1909), a notorious train robber who died in a hail of bullets in Bolivia. His story was somewhat romanticised by Paul Newman in *Butch Cassidy and the Sundance Kid* (1969).

esting issues highlighted. McKay may be a pain in the neck, but he is correct when he says that Sam's experimentation with Gate protocols is dangerous and mostly guesswork. Similarly, despite more Cold War rhetoric (see 'The Tomb'), Chekov is justified not to play the SGC's game, regardless of Davis's and Daniel's assurances that whatever agreements have been broken in the past, tomorrow is another day.

McKay is allergic to citrus. ('Go suck a lemon', says Sam, after he's insulted her.) Much to his *chagrin*, he's sent to Russia to supervise the construction of their Naqahdah generator programme (see 'Redemption'). SG-2 are about to go to P4C796.

**DID YOU KNOW?** The original working title was *Teal'c Interrupted*.

## 103 SUMMIT

US Transmission Date: 22 Mar 2002
UK Transmission Date: 19 Dec 2001
Writers: Joseph Mallozzi, Paul Mullie
Director: Martin Wood
Cast: Gary Jones (Sgt Walter Davis), Carmen Argenziano (Jacob Carter), William deVry (Aldwyn), Vince Crestejo (Yu the Great), Kevin Durand (Zipacna), Anna-Louise Plowman (Osiris), Jennifer Calvert (Ren'Au), Courtney J Stevens (Elliott), Cliff Simon (Ba'al), Anthony Ulc (Mansfield), Kwesi Ameyaw (Olokun), Suleka Mathew (Kali), Paul Anthony (Slave), Andrew Kavados (Zipacna's Jaffa), Simon Hayama (Jarren), Natasha Khadr (Bastet), Bonnie Kilroe (Morrigan)

> The Tok'ra learn that the System Lords are negotiating an alliance and request Daniel's help to infiltrate the summit. As SG-1 aid the Tok'ra in their evacuation of their current base, Sam makes a surprising discovery.

**THE WIT AND WISDOM OF JACK O'NEILL** 'It's always suicide-mission this, and save-the-planet that. No-one ever just stops by to say "Hi" any more.' And: 'We really should come up with a new strategy. One that doesn't include us *dying*.'

**SAM'S BIZARRE LOVE TRIANGLE** Sam is angry about Martouf's death (see 'Divide and Conquer') and the subsequent choice by the Tok'ra to save the symbiont at the expense of the host.

**ORIGINS OF THE SPECIES** The deaths of Cronus and Apophis created a power vacuum among the System Lords (see 'Double Jeopardy', 'Enemies'). Anubis has attacked several and exacted heavy losses, sowing discord among the other Goa'uld. Zipacna and Osiris act as his emissaries. (Tanith also seemed to be serving him in 'Between Two Fires', so he's got a tasty bunch of lieutenants.) He is said to have methods of extracting information from even the most determined spy (see 'Revelations'). Seven System Lords arrange a summit in the Hatara system (considered neutral territory) to discuss the new order. Those attending are: Ba'al[105], Bastet[106], Kali the Destroyer[107], Morrigan[108], Olokun[109], Svarog[110], and 'The Jade Emperor Yu Huang Shang-ti' (see 'Fair

*SEASON 5*

Game'). Ba'al wiped out the inhabitants of two star-systems (60 million lives) rather than lose them to Sokar (see 'The Devil You Know') in a territorial dispute. Bastet and Kali made a treaty with Sobek[111], then moved against him during a celebratory feast. It is rumoured that his head still decorates Bastet's palace in Bubastis. Zipacna suggests that Osiris once served Isis (see 'The Curse'). Nirrti is still *persona-non-grata* among the System Lords. For the first time in thousands of years, the Goa'uld are showing zero population growth. (The number SG-1 and their allies have killed in the last five years might be a factor. See 'Last Stand'.) A dying symbiont usually releases a deadly toxin which will kill its host. A Lo'tar is the highest rank among human slaves of the System Lords, a kind-of personal attendant, considered to be a position of great honour. One of Yu's former servants revealed sensitive information to Morrigan's lo'tar and was killed in a surprise attack that followed.

The Tok'ra's new planet is called Revanna (see 'Enemies'). Aldwyn has prepared a lecture for new SGC recruits on the development of Tok'ra insurgency techniques since the collapse of the second world dynasty. Elliott is blended with the dying Tok'ra Lantash who, apparently, survived the death of former host Martouf (in 'Divide and Conquer').

**SEX AND DRUGS AND ROCK 'N' ROLL** The Tok'ra use a modified version of the chemical that SG-1 obtained from Tyler (see 'The Fifth Man') to pass Daniel off as Yu's lo'tar.

**POSSIBLE INFLUENCES** *Star Wars* ('Welcome to the Dark Side'), *The Godfather* (the meeting of the warlords), *The Simpsons* ('Let the good times roll').

**'YOU MIGHT REMEMBER ME FROM...'** Cliff Simon was in *Egoli: Place of Gold*.

**LOGIC, LET ME INTRODUCE YOU TO THIS WINDOW** If the plan was for Daniel to release the dead-

105 Ugaritic (Canaanite) storm-god (also known as Hadad) who defeated Yam (the sea) and Mot (death). Also associated with a Phoenician sun-god, several Semitic fertility deities (*bá'al* means 'lord' in Hebrew), *Baalberith* (lord of the covenant) of the Shechemites and *Báalzebúb* (lord of flies) of the Philistines. Shrines to Ba'al were objects of Yahweh's wrath in Leviticus. The Israelites were commanded to destroy such idols when entering Canaan (Deuteronomy 33:29), but Ba'al's cult was still active during the reign of King Hezekiah in 7th Century BC.

106 The Egyptian cat-goddess of sex and fertility. The daughter of Ra, she was worshipped primarily in the city of Bubastis. During the New Kingdom (1539-1075BC), Bastet became equated with Sekhmet, the lioness deity of war. Images portray Bastet playing a *sistrum* (an Egyptian percussion instrument) with figurines of kittens surrounding her feet.

107 'The Dark One'. Hindi mother-goddess and consort of Shiva, Kali is frequently depicted as a laughing, naked hag with blood-stained teeth. Kali's worshipers purportedly appeased her with human sacrifices (see the shenanigans of *Help!* for a comic western-take on this). As *Bhavani*, she was invoked by the secret brotherhood of 18th Century assassins and scoundrels called *Thugs*. Calcutta gets its name from *Kalighata*, a temple dedicated to Kali.

108 The Morríghan: Irish Celtic war-goddess known as *The Phantom Queen*. One of the Tuatha Dé Danann ('Tribe of Danu'), she helped defeat the Firbolg at the First Battle of Mag Tuireadh. Frequently depicted as either a hooded crow or as part of a triumvirate with Badb and Nemain.

109 Yoruban (West African) ocean-god. Olokun lived in a huge underwater palace with both humans and fish as servants.

110 Senior Slavic elemental-god. Had two sons, Svarozhich (fire) and Dazhbog (the sun).

111 Egyptian crocodile-god, son of Neith, worshipped at Kom-Ombo where there was an extensive cemetery of mummified crocodiles. Sobek was the principal god among the Greek and Roman settlers in Faiyum during the 12th and 13th dynasties.

ly poison and then return to Jacob's ship, surely this would be dangerous for Jacob if Daniel carried any of the poison with him on his skin or clothing? Yu wasn't 'The Jade Emperor', that was a different Chinese god called Yu (see 'Fair Game').

### QUOTE/UNQUOTE

Elliott's looking forward to meeting the Tok'ra. Jack: 'You'll get over it.'

Jacob: 'Yu will be among the System Lords attending.' Sam: 'I thought you said he was going in as a slave.' Jacob: 'The System Lord Yu.' Sam: 'Little joke there.' Jack: '*Funny.*'

Jacob: 'Just don't jab yourself with it.' Daniel: 'Why?' Jacob: 'Actually, I don't know, exactly. That, in itself, should scare you.'

### NOTES

'Oh swell, it's kind-of like Goa'uld Mardi Gras here.' A brilliant set-up as Daniel goes undercover to infiltrate the System Lords. The Goa'uld internal politics stuff is fascinating and really well played, but the rest of SG-1 get stuck in a painfully obvious 'base under siege' story that isn't resolved by a cliffhanger that's signposted *miles away.*

### CRITIQUE

'Pulling together so many threads from past episodes that it's impossible to remember where half of them were last left dangling, the story throws SG-1 headlong into cosmos-wide war,' noted John Binns. 'Barely letting up for breath, it builds slowly to an almighty climax after a series of surprise revelations and astonishing special effects.'

### CAST AND CREW COMMENTS

'There are still quite a few of the Egyptian gods we haven't used,' Peter DeLuise commented. 'Anubis was killed in the movie, but he was just Ra's First Prime. He seemed to like the jackal's mask so he adopted the name, but he wasn't the god himself.'

'Each Lord [has] some historical base,' Christina McQuarrie noted. 'There's a Celtic god called Morrigan. In myth she appeared as a raven. We took an S&M twist with it, black leather, feathers and studs. Another is based on an Egyptian cat god. [We used] iridescent fabric, metallic chainmail for the head-dress and ornate jewellery.'

### DID YOU KNOW?

J R Bourne was invited to resurrect Martouf in 'Summit' and 'Last Stand', but was prevented from doing so by prior commitments. It's unknown whether the episode would have brought the character back from the dead, or if the actor was to appear in a flashback or a dream. 'We really wanted to bring Martouf back, but no matter how hard we tried to move the schedule around to accommodate him, [J R Bourne] was shooting a movie [*Cover Story*], and was booked for months,' noted Brad Wright.

## 104 LAST STAND

US Transmission Date: 29 Mar 2002
UK Transmission Date: 9 Jan 2002[112]

112 Shown as part of a two-hour movie version of 'Summit' and 'Last Stand'.

Writer: Robert C Cooper
Director: Martin Wood
Cast: Carmen Argenziano (Jacob Carter), Vince Crestejo (Yu the Great), Kevin Durand (Zipacna), Anna-Louise Plowman (Osiris), Courtney J Stevens (Elliott), Cliff Simon (Ba'al), Kwesi Ameyaw (Olokun), Suleka Mathew (Kali), Paul Anthony (Slave), Andrew Kavados (Zipacna's Jaffa), Natasha Khadr (Bastet), Bonnie Kilroe (Morrigan)

> With time running out to complete his task, Daniel is confronted by Osiris before he's able to release the biological weapon. At the same time, Zipacna's forces attack Revanna.

**ORIGINS OF THE SPECIES** Over a thousand years ago, Anubis was banished by the System Lords (only Yu remains from the ruling council in those days) because his crimes were unspeakable, even to the Goa'uld. The System Lords tried to murder him and believed him dead. He now plans to destroy Earth before rejoining the ranks of the System Lords, thus working outside the restrictions of the Protected Planets Treaty.

Sacred ritual cannibalism of symbionts is rampant among the System Lords. (Daniel notes this may explain why Goa'uld numbers are dwindling.)

**SAM'S BIZARRE LOVE TRIANGLE** Lantash, through Elliott, tells Sam that he loves her as much as he once loved Jolinar. Then he dies. She's not having *any* luck at all, is she?

**POSSIBLE INFLUENCES** *Star Trek* ('I'm diverting power to the shields').

**LOGIC, LET ME INTRODUCE YOU TO THIS WINDOW** The blood on Sam's face changes position several times. Anna-Louise Plowman mispronounces 'Tau'ri' as 'Tory'. How convenient that Jacob's ship crashes within easy walking distance of SG-1 when it had the whole planet to choose from. There's a huge logic flaw in Elliott's plan at the end. He speculates, if he allows himself to be captured, he'll be taken to the Jaffa base close to the Stargate, where he intends to release the poison. That still doesn't explain how Jacob and Teal'c are going to get through the Gate without being exposed to it. They couldn't have been planning to use the time to fix Jacob's ship (since it's still on Revanna in 'Fail Safe').

**QUOTE/UNQUOTE** Daniel: 'You'd think a race advanced enough to fly around in spaceships would be smart enough to have seat belts.'

**NOTES** 'You know what's at stake. No single person's life is worth more. Complete your mission.' A disappointing melange of thud and blunder with lots of loud gun battles but little common sense. The fact that Daniel fails in his mission renders the complete two-parter a colossal waste of time.

**DID YOU KNOW?** 'We're introducing a new villain at the end of season five who'll become our primary antagonist throughout season six building towards a climax in the *Stargate SG-1* feature film,' Brad Wright told *cinescape.com* (see 'Future Imperfect'). 'We've been taking some of the mythologies and the storylines we have set up, and bringing those to a head. Season five has been about wrapping-up loose ends,' Robert Cooper added.

# 105 FAIL SAFE

US Transmission Date: 5 Apr 2002
UK Transmission Date: 12 Dec 2001
Writers: Joseph Mallozzi, Paul Mullie
Director: Andy Mikita
Cast: Teryl Rothery (Dr Janet Fraiser), Gary Jones (Sgt Walter Davis) Colin Cunningham (Major Davis), David Bloom (Speilman), Gren Anderson (Webber), Michael Teigan (Telescope Guy), Kirsten Williamson (Jalen)

Earth finds itself threatened by something even more destructive than the Gou'ald: an asteroid on a collision course with the planet. SG-1 put together a plan to avert an armageddon.

**THE WIT AND WISDOM OF JACK O'NEILL** Sam: 'This close to Earth, it would probably be enough to set the atmosphere on fire and boil the oceans.' Jack: 'Okay, *this* was not in the movie.'

To Sam: 'I'd like to take this opportunity to say this is a *very* poorly designed bomb and we should say something to somebody when we get back.' And: 'Carter, I can see my house!'

**ORIGINS OF THE SPECIES** The Tok'ra have been on the run since the events of 'Last Stand'. Revanna is approximately 8 days flight from Earth in a Tok'ra ship.

**IN THE INTERESTS OF WORLD SURVIVAL** The asteroid, 137 kilometres in length, was first located in Cassiopeia on a collision course to wipe out all life on Earth. With a core composed almost entirely of Naqahdah (which doesn't occur naturally in the solar system), the asteroid was probably a Goa'uld creation to circumvent the Protected Planets Treaty (see 'Fair Game') by making the destruction of Earth look like a natural disaster. The only way to stop it is with a nuclear weapon which, enhanced by the Naqahdah, would have the force of a small nova.

SG-1 expanded the Tok'ra ship's hyperspace field beyond its usual envelope to encompass the asteroid, taking it out of normal space long enough to avoid collision with Earth.

**POSSIBLE INFLUENCES** *Quatermass II*, *Doctor Who*'s 'Spearhead from Space', *The Simpsons*' 'Bart's Comet', *Armageddon*, *Deep Impact* and *Asteroid* ('I've seen this movie. It hits Paris'), the Beatles ('a little help from our friends') and *Julius Caesar*. The episode shares its title with Sidney Lumet's 1964 nuclear paranoia classic.

**'YOU MIGHT REMEMBER ME FROM...'** Michael Teigan played Lou in *A Guy Thing*.

**LOGIC, LET ME INTRODUCE YOU TO THIS WINDOW** How can Sam predict so precisely where the asteroid will impact on Earth. (That's not an exact science; there are all sorts of considerations like atmospheric conditions to take into account.) The Tok'ra are on the run. What Tok'ra? 'Summit' and 'Last Stand' suggested that pretty much all, bar Jacob, had been wiped out. The hull breaches cause depressurisation of the ship astonishingly quickly. Jack and Teal'c can walk (and run) in zero-g without too much difficulty. Sam,

**SEASON 5**

among her many other achievements, is seemingly an expert on bomb disposal.

Jack: '… And, after that, I kind-of lost my temper.' Daniel: 'Let's just say Jack made a reference to Freyr's mother.'

Sam: 'We can detonate it right here. What's our position?' Daniel: 'Personally, I'm against it. But if you want to know where the ship is, we're about five metres above the surface.'

**NOTES** 'We came, we saw, we planted the bomb, we had a little fun with a meteor shower, we went home. It's a great story.' Yeh, it is, actually. Once again, the plot wears its reference texts on its sleeve (*Armageddon*, especially) but it's great to see SG-1 in an utterly hopeless situation with only their wit and skill to get them out, the rather *faux* arrival of the Tok'ra notwithstanding.

Continuity references to 'Red Sky' (the K'Tau's hall of wisdom), 'Between Two Fires' (the Goa'uld influencing the Tollan to send a bomb through the SGC's iris) and 'Tangent' (the X301 and the recall device). SG-1 use Jacob's cargo ship which crashed on Revanna (see 'Last Stand'). Davis, Janet and Walter are amongst the last group leaving for the alpha site. Hammond refuses to go with them, however, as resources will be limited. If SG-1 are unsuccessful, Jack's orders are to proceed to the alpha site and take command. The most powerful warhead ever developed carries 1200 Naqahdah-enhanced megatons, equivalent to one billion tons of TNT. Filming began in August 2001 when the production team returned from their summer hiatus.

**DID YOU KNOW?** This episode was shown out of order (before 'Summit' and 'Last Stand') by Sky in the UK, which completely ruined the surprise attack on the Tok'ra in 'Summit'.

# 106 THE WARRIOR

US Transmission Date: 12 Apr 2002
UK Transmission Date: 16 Jan 2002
Story: Christopher Judge
Teleplay: Peter DeLuise
Director: Peter DeLuise
Cast: Rick Worthy (Kytano), Kirby Morrow (Tara'c), Tony Amendola (Bra'tac), Vince Crestejo (Yu the Great), Obi Ndefo (Rak'nor)

A charismatic Jaffa leader tries to rally his people against the Goa'uld and seeks an alliance with Earth. SG-1 agree to supply weapons, but encounter resistance both from the Jaffa and within their own ranks.

**ORIGINS OF THE SPECIES** Imhotep, the first pyramid-builder during the Third Dynasty, was deified by the ancient Egyptians[113]. Daniel believes that he was

113 A high court official during the reign of Djoser (c.2660BC), Imhotep was the architect of the Step Pyramid at Saqqara. In death, he was credited as author of *The Book of Wisdom*, deified, and became a patron-god of Scribes. The Greeks associated him with their medicine-god, Asklepios.

an insignificant Goa'uld from a backwater planet. Kheb (see 'Maternal Instinct') is regarded as a Jaffa version of *nirvana* - a place of eternal freedom. Mast'aba is a form of martial art practised by Imhotep's Jaffa.

**THE CONSPIRACY STARTS AT CLOSING TIME** Kytano, Imhotep's former First Prime, says he led a rebellion against his god and killed him. He now leads a raggle-taggle but growing army of disaffected Jaffa from various System Lords. He has recently attacked the forces of both Zipacna (see 'Pretense') and Nirrti (see 'Fair Game') and sends Teal'c on a mission against Yu, who survived being stabbed by Osiris ('Last Stand') with the aid of a sarcophagus. However, Kytano has deceived his followers and is really Imhotep using the cover of a Jaffa revolution to grab a slice of power for himself.

**POSSIBLE INFLUENCES** *Deliverance* ('Any idea what happened to the guys in that movie?'), *The Matrix* (Teal'c's and Kytano's fight), every movie by Jackie Chan and John Woo, *Apocalypse Now* and Matthew 14 ('Kytano believes he could walk on water').

**LOGIC, LET ME INTRODUCE YOU TO THIS WINDOW** One of the 'wooden' staff weapons can be seen wobbling when shaken.

**GUN LORE** Jack confirms that the P-90 carries a 50-round top-loading magazine of Teflon-coated ordinance with a cyclical firing rate of 900 rounds per minute, accurate within a range up to 350 yards (see 'The Tomb'). The subsequent weapons demonstration goes a long way towards explaining why the Jaffa seem to be such lousy shots in many episodes. The blast area of a staff weapon is so big they don't have the pinpoint accuracy that Sam demonstrates with a P-90. Basically, the staff weapon seems to be largely a weapon for crowd control, intended to make a big noise and a flash, to intimidate and shepherd groups of people.

**GOA'ULD LEXICON** 'Tek ma'tek' means 'friends well met'. 'Tek ma'-tae' is a greeting of respect. 'Jolma'sheku' means a challenge of leadership. 'Kalach shal'tek' is 'victory or death'. 'Ya'duru arek kek'onac' is translated as 'I honour he who would kill his god.'

**QUOTE/UNQUOTE** Bra'tac: 'I would stake my life on it.' Jack: 'Ours too, apparently.'

Kytano: 'I see you are one who speaks your mind, O'Neill.' Jack: 'Which is why I don't say much.'

**NOTES** 'We have our freedom.' Slow and ordinary until it turns into a kung-fu movie and gets interesting in the last ten minutes. Teal'c being swept along with intoxication at Kytano's charisma is a real surprise. A thoughtful story, with a cynical edge, but it could have used a more effective exposition than a reported off-screen conversation.

The Tok'ra are 'severely weakened' and the Tollan 'may be gone forever' after the events of 'Last Stand' and 'Between Two Fires' respectively.

**CAST AND CREW COMMENTS** The concept for this story came from

Christopher Judge. 'The plot plays into Egyptian mythology and, in particular, an historical figure called Imhotep who designed the pyramids,' he noted. 'He claimed the design was given to him by the gods, which ties in perfectly with our show's mythology.'

**DID YOU KNOW?** New *SG-1* episodes were usually broadcast in America from July to September, then return in early January. So why not this year? Allegedly, the terrorist attacks of 11 Sept 2001 prompted Showtime to delay their new post-apocalyptic show *Jeremiah*. So, what has *that* got to do with *SG-1*? New episodes of *Stargate*, say Showtime, were essential to *Jeremiah* to attract viewers. Well, *I'm* convinced ...

# 107 MENACE

US Transmission Date: 26 Apr 2002
UK Transmission Date: 16 Jan 2002
Story: James Tichenor
Teleplay: Peter DeLuise
Director: Martin Wood
Cast: Danielle Nicolet (Reese), Teryl Rothery (Dr Janet Fraiser), Gary Jones (Sgt Walter Davis), Dan Shea (Sgt Siler), Biski Gugushe (SF Guard), Colin Lawrence (SG-3 Leader), Kyle Riefsnyder (SF), Tracy Westerholm (SF)

> SG-1 visit a world seemingly destroyed by the Replicators and find one survivor, a young girl who may hold the secret to the survival of the Asgard. But, returning to the SGC, they make a horrifying discovery.

**THE WIT AND WISDOM OF JACK O'NEILL** 'Hasn't it occurred to anyone this thing may've been lying around that planet for some time. Maybe it's *broken*?'

**ORIGINS OF THE SPECIES** Daniel notes that the Greeks, Romans, Chinese and Babylonians all envisioned synthetic beings long before the words 'robot' and 'android' were invented.[114]

Once an advanced civilisation, the people of Reese's planet were destroyed by her toys (the Replicators), who protected their creator when she was threatened. The nanobots that Reese uses for self-repair are able to reorder matter on a microscopic level.

**POSSIBLE INFLUENCES** *Sleeping Beauty* ('Why don't you kiss her?'), *Frankenstein, The Terminator, Aliens, The Shrine, Firestarter, The Bad Seed* and *The Midwich Cuckoos.*

**'YOU MIGHT REMEMBER ME FROM...'** Danielle Nicolet played Cheryl in *Shadow of Doubt* and Caryn in *3rd Rock from the Sun* and appeared in *The Prince.*

**LOGIC, LET ME INTRODUCE YOU TO THIS WINDOW** What is an Air Force recruitment poster

114 'Robot' comes from the Czech word robota (work) and was first used in Karel Capek's satirical play *R.U.R.* 'Android' is a twentieth century bastardisation of the Greek word androeidēs (manlike).

doing on the wall of an SGC bunker? Who's going to see it? Who placed the cloth covering Reese's face? Everyone else on the planet was dead. Sam says that Reese is more advanced than any android SG-1 have encountered. To be fair, they've only met *four* (and they were all pretty advanced). Love the CD-player in Reese's neck. Jack fires once at Reese, yet it appears that she's been hit by several bullets.

### QUOTE/UNQUOTE

Daniel: 'She did seem pretty upset.' Jack: '... For a *machine*.'

Daniel: 'I don't think she meant to hurt me. I just don't think she liked what I was saying.' Jack: '*I* don't like most of what you say. I try to resist the urge to shove you through a wall.'

### NOTES

'I'm saying we should avoid slapping her in the face with the reality of her existence moments after telling her that her planet was destroyed.' The usual tone of the series, which had always previously been fairly light with a witty quip to accompany each saving of the world, from the beginning of season five is largely absent ('Wormhole X-Treme!' being an obvious exception). Possibly this reflected wider tensions within the camp, episodes taking on a far more serious note and the camaraderie between SG-1 being frequently diminished. This episode is the *nadir* of this trend. It's also a *huge* disappointment. For the creator of its deadliest foes, *Doctor Who* had Davros, *The Avengers* had Dr Armstrong. *SG-1*, by contrast, has a petulant child. That says something significant.

Daniel says that he doesn't have as much fun as he'd like to. There's an easy remedy, man. SG-2 was unable to contact the Asgard using the K'Tau Hall of Wisdom (see 'Red Sky', 'Revelations'). There are continuity references to 'Tin Man'.

### DID YOU KNOW?

The announcement of the imminent departure of Michael Shanks from *SG-1* by Brad Wright during a convention Q&A session, brought a tidal wave of emotion from the actor's many fans. Dismay quickly turned to anger in some quarters when comments made by Shanks, in various interviews, suggested his leaving was not, entirely, voluntary. The, self-styled, 'Danielites' organised their own pan-continental cyber-campaign, vehemently drowning MGM in protest calls - more than 1,000 within the first day. They raised thousands of dollars to buy ads, including a full-page in the trade journal *The Hollywood Reporter*, and aggressively questioned the producers at any given opportunity (Joe Mallozzi suffered a couple of particularly harsh online attacks.) The reaction surprised Shanks who commented: 'I think it's great [if] a bit overwhelming.' He also admitted, 'I've read one site - *www.savedanielajckson.com*. For the most part I agreed with it. I couldn't sit there and go "Well, you shouldn't really say that..." [because] they've got a point!'

# 108 THE SENTINEL

US Transmission Date: 3 May 2002
UK Transmission Date: 23 Jan 2002
Writer: Ron Wilkerson
Director: Peter DeLuise

Cast: Henry Gibson (Marul), Frank Cassini (Sean Grieves), Christina Cox (Kershaw), Gary Jones (Sgt Walter Davis), David Kopp (Grogan), Colin Lawrence (Major Lawrence), Shaw Reis (Jaffa Commander), Carrie Ann Fleming (Secretary), Chris Newton (Caretaker)

After SG-9 run into trouble on P2A018, Jack turns to a pair of convicted criminals for help. They must repair an alien device, that the couple once deactivated, in order to protect a world from Goa'uld annihilation.

### ORIGINS OF THE SPECIES

Lotona has enjoyed 300 years of peace thanks to the Sentinel, a powerful defensive weapon. The Lotonans are egalitarians, non-materialistic and don't use currency. The civilisation has technologically regressed since the building of the Sentinel and no-one now knows how to operate it. SG-9, under Major Benton, were sent to re-establish diplomatic relations with the Lotanas whose world was one of a number visited by the rogue NID team (see 'Shades of Grey').

The Caretaker, whom Grieves killed, had a symbiotic relationship with the Sentinel and, when he died, the machine stopped providing protection to Lotona. P2A463 has a language similar to that which Daniel reads on the Sentinel. The Sentinel is protected by a force-field that must first be deactivated. The code to shut off the force-field constantly changes, using a mathematical progression of the harmonics between the tones being emitted in each of over a hundred randomly changing patterns, relative to its spectral equivalent. The Caretaker wears a wristband that is, in effect, a dead man's switch, keeping the flame in Marul's chamber burning as long as he lives. The symbols on the Sentinel mean 'Life Force' or 'Life Energy' and 'Two as One', indicating that the symbiosis of man and machine is necessary to activate the Sentinel. The Goa'uld who attacks Lotona is Svarog (see 'Summit').

### IN THE INTERESTS OF NATIONAL SECURITY

Grieves and Kershaw were members of the NID's rogue unit arrested in 'Shades of Grey'. Maybourne is mentioned (when Jack asks if he's visited Grieves lately). Whilst stealing a powerful beam-weapon from P3Y294, Grieves turned the weapon on his pursuers, killing three of them. The government of P3Y294 would have nothing further to do with the SGC even after the device was returned to them.

### POSSIBLE INFLUENCES

*The Dirty Dozen*, *The Rock* and other examples of the 'prisoner recruitment' genre.

### 'YOU MIGHT REMEMBER ME FROM...'

Henry Gibson played Thuston Howell in *Magnolia* and was in *The Blues Brothers*, *Bewitched*, *Rowan & Martin's Laugh-In* and *Sunset Beach*. Claire Fleming appeared in *The Swishy-Washy*, *Get Carter* and *One Hot Summer Night*.

### LOGIC, LET ME INTRODUCE YOU TO THIS WINDOW

Again, if Grieves and Kershaw were convicted of high treason, what are they doing on death row (see 'Chain Reaction')? There can be no appeal from a military tribunal, so they should have been executed straight after sentencing. Which also brings up the question of what their families have been told (if they have any, of course). Do they think they're dead? If not, then somebody, somewhere is surely going to start asking questions about *what crimes* these people have been convicted of. Treason's a good cover, but you'd think some enterprising investigative journalist from CNN would have got hold of this story by now. It's a *huge* cheat to place shots of Frank Cassini and Christina Cox into the 'previously on' footage from 'Shades of Grey', making it appear that they're playing returning characters. How does Grieves know how to become the Caretaker? Jack says that he's read the report on the Sentinel. Wait a minute. O'Neill's *read* a file? That's got to be a first.

**GUN LORE** Daniel's pistol is a Beretta M92F, a standard-issue handgun to US Forces and many police officers. The USAF don't deploy the Heckler & Koch MP-5 (used by SG-1 prior to 'The First Ones') or the Belgian FN P-90 to their regular troops (who mainly use M16 Assault Rifles). But then SG-teams are *special*. The guards at the SGC carry a mix of MP5s and AR15 variants. We also sometimes see SAWs (Squad Automatic Weapon) and USAS 12s (an auto shotgun made by Daewoo).

**QUOTE/UNQUOTE** Kershaw: 'I feel better knowing there's an archaeologist watching our backs.'

**NOTES** 'People are starting to die here.' Illogical, burdened by pointless changes of character motivation (especially of Grieves), and not helped by a ludicrously signposted *denouement*. The regulars seem oddly distant too (as in Jack's fumbling opening scene with Hammond, for instance).

Major Lawrence commands SG-3 (having, presumably, replaced Makepeace; see 'Shades of Grey', 'Menace'). UAVs have a new targeting system enabling the SGC to send guided missiles through the Stargate and destroy strategic positions in advance of SG-teams.

**CRITIQUE** Michael Shanks's impending departure saw a fierce debate rage in the letters pages of numerous UK genre magazines, not least *Starburst*, in which editor Gary Gillatt's comment that most of the people complaining seemed to be female fans who (perhaps) fancied Shanks brought a predictably vociferous response.[115]

By contrast, whilst *SFX* went down a conspiracy theory route (see 'Meridian'), *Starlog*'s coverage (a lengthy Shanks interview/vox-pop piece by Thomasina Gibson), took a more personal but, perhaps, less balanced approach in quoting many angry and emotional reactions from fans. This author does not wish to belittle, in any way, the sadness often associated with the departure from a popular TV show of a favourite character (particularly as I was, and remain, as sad *anyone* to see Daniel go). Gibson is a *fine* writer, who has produced many impressive and worthwhile articles on the series (not to mention two official books). But whether her heart-rending description of a letter received from the mother of a young fan who had 'cried well into the night' after watching 'Meridian' actually added anything worthwhile to the debate, is somewhat questionable. That anonymous death threats were allegedly made to members of the production team around this time by 'fans' outraged at Shanks's departure suggests that, maybe, some people were taking it all a shade too seriously.[116] At the end of the day, let's

*A* SEASON 5

---

115 Joe Mallozzi noted online during this period: 'Our writing isn't geared toward a specific demographic. While, for instance, *Star Trek*'s core audience is males 14-35, our core audience appears to be women 30-45.'
116 Brad Wright's decision not to do conventions in 2002 appears to be directly related to this. As he told a *sci-fi.com* online chat, 'If the hate mail dies down, maybe then.'

remember, *SG-1* is still *just* a television programme.

# 109 MERIDIAN

US Transmission Date: 10 May 2002
UK Transmission Date: 30 Jan 2002
Writer: Robert C Cooper
Director: William Waring
Cast: Corin Nemec (Jonas Quinn), Teryl Rothery (Dr Janet Fraiser), Carmen Argenziano (Jacob Carter), Gary Jones (Sgt Walter Davis)[117], Mel Harris (Oma Desala)[118], David Hurtubise (Tomis), Kevin McCrae (Scientist)

An alien civilisation is threatened with extinction when they attempt to build a weapon of mass destruction and, during a test, expose Daniel to a massive dose of radiation. But Daniel is walking another road, and one from which there may be no return.

**THE WIT AND WISDOM OF JACK O'NEILL** On Jonas: 'He's a nerd, sir. He and Daniel got on great.'

**SAM'S TRAUMATIC LOVE-LIFE** In a (completely unsignposted) moment, Sam weeps over the dying Daniel's body and tells him she regrets never telling him her true feelings. Huh? Where'd *that* come from?

**ORIGINS OF THE SPECIES** Kelowna is one of three major political and military power blocs on P3X4C3. They are at a similar stage of development to America in the 1940s, and have a tasty Cold War brewing (see 'Shadow Play'). They discovered their Stargate approximately 15 years ago, but their knowledge of its uses is limited. Jonas Quinn is an advisor to the High Minister. A highly educated man with an interest in ancient civilisations, Jonas quickly forms a bond with Daniel. One of Jonas's responsibilities is overseeing weapons research from an ethical perspective. He ultimately leaves his world as a traitor, having stolen a quantity of the super-powerful element Naqahdriah, which his government intend to use in creating weapons of potential mass destruction. Jack assures him that the element will be used on Earth to create defensive shields (see 'Redemption'). Jonas asks that, should these prove successful, the SGC will share them with his own people.

Ten thousand years ago a Goa'uld tried the same Naqahdriah experiments as the Kelownans and nearly blew the whole planet to bits. Daniel prevents a disaster and, in doing so, exposes himself to massive doses of radiation (the equivalent, notes Sam, of eight or nine grades of neutron radiation). He is very knowledgeable about the horrific symptoms he will subsequently suffer.

**DEAD MAN WALKING** Daniel once gave Teal'c a miniature Egyptian sarcophagus and told him of the ancient Egyptian belief was that the spirit for whom the

• • • • • • • • • • • • • • • • • • • • • • • • • • • • • • • • • • • • • • • • • • • • • • • • • • •

117 Just to confuse an already confused situation (see '2010') Walter's name-tag reads 'Norman Davis' in 'Meridian'.
118 Character previous played by Carla Boudreau.

sarcophagus was originally made would one day serve its present owner in the afterlife.

**A POOR PLAYER THAT STRUTS HIS HOUR UPON THE STAGE** Daniel believes that his entire life has been a failure. Oma (see 'Maternal Instinct'), with the abstract help of Jack, Sam and (especially) Teal'c, shows him that this simply isn't true and that once he can unburden himself from the worthless baggage of his insecurities, he can choose a new path.

**POSSIBLE INFLUENCES** Conceptually, *Fat Man and Little Boy* (aka *Shadowmakers*), *Insignificance*, *Watchmen* and *Captain Atom*, *Flatliners* and numerous 'near-death' episodes of *The X-Files*, *Star Trek: The Next Generation* and *Quantum Leap*.

**'YOU MIGHT REMEMBER ME FROM...'** Corin Nemec was the star of the early 90s cult high school comedy *Parker Lewis Can't Lose*. His movies include *Free*, *Mojave Moon*, *Drop Zone* and *I Know My First Name is Steven*.

**BEHIND THE CAMERA** William Waring was a camera operator on *Screwed*, *Hoods*, *Daughters* and *Underworld*.

**LOGIC, LET ME INTRODUCE YOU TO THIS WINDOW** A big one. How doesn't Jonas suffer from radiation poisoning when Daniel dives through the safety glass? That must, surely, have flooded the viewing room with deadly radiation?

**QUOTE/UNQUOTE** Teal'c: 'If you are to die, Daniel Jackson, I wish you to know that I believe the fight against the Goa'uld will have lost one of its greatest warriors. And I will have lost one of my greatest friends.'

Jack: 'You cannot capitulate to these people. They are lying bastards.'

Daniel, to Oma: 'Maybe I did something good every now and again, but nothing I've ever done seems to have changed anything.'

**NOTES** 'Just let him go.' Well, *that* was emotional. So, is this mawkish and sentimental rubbish, or not? It's *really* difficult to say, to be honest, because, despite an ending that's straight out of *E.T.*, 'Meridian' shares with Spielberg's movie a (possibly naive, but fundamentally valid) faith in the basic decency of humanity. And *that*'s the episode's salvation. It's still hard to be objective about the manipulative nature of much of the drama. But the dialogue is beautifully poetic (this is Robert Cooper, what did you expect?). Daniel's quest for absolution before he can embark on his new path is perfectly in-keeping with the character and it's fabulously acted. (I love Janet admitting to Sam that she's considering euthanasia, or Teal'c's moment of honest regret.) Something of a curate's egg, then. You'll cry and then feel hollow after watching this but, for a few moments, the episode gets right to the heart of what makes *SG-1* great.

Jack, touchingly, says that it's possible he may admire Daniel. A bit. Despite the fact that Daniel can be a pain in the ass. Jacob has been on a mission to rescue the last undercover Tok'ra. There are continuity references to 'Maternal Instinct', 'Absolute Power', 'Ascension', 'Stargate' and 'Children of the Gods'. Daniel feels guilt and responsibility for the fates of Sha're ('Forever in a Day') and Sarah ('The Curse'). SG-3 found a heavily guarded sarcophagus three months ago. Hammond is reluctant to order a mission to retrieve it as he knows it will cost many lives.

**CONTROVERSY!** 'A number of agendas had to be resolved,' Michael Shanks told *TV Zone* in one of a lengthy series of 'final interviews' the actor gave in early 2002. 'I thought there was a bit of chickening out with how it happened. The big problem, I think, was they were so intent on saying to the audience, "Daniel's not dead!" This was mainly for the benefit of the same viewers who got upset when Martouf was killed. The powers that be wanted to quell any backlash.'

Shanks also, seemingly, had problems with the introduction of a replacement in the same episode: 'I think that was poor form. Really tasteless,' he told *SFX*. 'The character's not even cold yet and [they're] bringing in someone to carry on.' In *Xposé*, Shanks praised Robert Cooper's work in general and on this particular episode, but felt 'me leaving is a kind of indicator of how satisfied I was [with season five].'

'People don't realise, I think, how close you get to being when you're on a series as regulars together,' Don Davis told *Xposé*. 'You spend more time with each other than you do with your own family. So when one makes a decision - for whatever reason - to leave, it's like a member of your family saying, "I can't be here any more." It tears you apart.'

Robert Cooper, however, is more forthright on the subject, telling *Cult Times*: 'For some reason, [Michael] said "I want to leave"; because nobody begged him to stay, he assumed we all wanted to push him out, which was not true. Personally, if I have someone over to dinner and they stand up in the middle and say, "You're a lousy cook, I don't like you, I'm outta here," I don't go, "Please stay, dessert will be much better!"'

In April 2002, *SFX* made a series of allegations concerning Michael Shanks's departure. They stated that they had 'solid rumours from a reputable source' (unnamed, of course), which suggested another cast member had made his displeasure known concerning Shanks's popularity. This led to Shanks becoming increasingly sidelined. Shanks complained to the producers about his 'shoddy treatment,' *SFX* continued, saying he may as well leave. He received, they allege, a curt 'goodbye'. The same issue of the magazine carried an interview with Shanks himself, who noted 'It wasn't like they did everything they could to keep me ... The success of the character was [his] downfall.'

**CAST AND CREW COMMENTS** It's hard not to feel sorry for Corin Nemec, walking blindly into a withering hail of gunfire from disgruntled Daniel fans who, before his character had even been seen, were filling the internet with their wrath. 'I know an amount of correspondence has been coming in,' he noted in one of his first major interviews. 'People are upset because there's been this change with the character they're used to. For me, change is a beautiful thing. If you're unwilling to change you're going to fight a losing battle.'

**DID YOU KNOW?** The first broadcast of a scene from this episode in North America came in January 2002 when Chris Judge appeared on the Canadian talkshow *Vicki Gabereau*.

# 110 REVELATIONS

US Transmission Date: 17 May 2002

UK Transmission Date: 6 Feb 2002
Writers: Joseph Mallozzi, Paul Mullie
Director: Martin Wood
Cast: Teryl Rothery (Heimdall), Anna-Louise Plowman (Osiris), David Palffy (Anubis), PJ Johal (Jaffa), Shaker Paleja (Jaffa), Martin Sims (Jaffa), Dan Shea (Sgt Siler)[119]

The SGC is contacted by the Asgard, who state that Thor has been killed by the Goa'uld, and that SG-1's help is needed to rescue a stranded scientist. When SG-1 arrive on the planet, they discover that Thor is very much alive, but has been captured by Osiris.

**ORIGINS OF THE SPECIES** The planet has an atmosphere with 80 per cent carbon dioxide and a surface temperature of 420 degrees Fahrenheit. The Asgard war with the Replicators has reached a critical stage, with the Asgard finally gaining an upper-hand. They have, seemingly, been given Reese (see 'Menace') and are studying her construction.

Osiris's ship has defensive shields that can withstand Asgard weapons. Anubis has a device which is implanted into Thor's brain and forms a neural link between his mind and the ship's computer (see 'Summit'). Thor's knowledge can, therefore, be simply 'downloaded'. Sam notes that, after his rescue, Thor lapsed into a coma and the Asgard are unsure if they will be able to save him. Yu is maintaining a powerful offensive against Anubis's forces (and seems to be doing quite well).

**SEND IN THE CLONES** Heimdall[120] is conducting research into the genetic history of the Asgard. They can reproduce only through a process of cloning. For nearly 1,000 years they have been incapable of sexual reproduction. They have achieved a degree of immortality through this - as each Asgard's body fails its consciousness is transferred into a younger version of itself. Unfortunately the lack of genetic diversity has started to become a problem. They have created a process of controlled mutation which has helped them to avoid complete genetic breakdown. But, Heimdall confesses that the Asgard race are in danger of dying out.

Thirty thousand years ago an Asgard ship was launched with its crew in stasis. Due to a malfunction it drifted for millennia. The Asgard found the ship six months ago. They are hoping that the one remaining specimen of an Asgard from their past will give them clues to help stave off their potential genetic degradation.

**IN THE INTERESTS OF NATIONAL SECURITY** When Hammond served in Vietnam, he saw his best friend's plane shot down. Although he was certain that the man survived (seeing a parachute open) Hammond's friend was never found and the Vietnamese authorities refused to acknowledge that he'd been taken prisoner. He was declared M.I.A. Hammond says that he learned to live with the situation.

**POSSIBLE INFLUENCES** *Star Wars* (Anubis/Darth Sidious), *The Way of the Warrior*, *Star Trek* ('Why don't you just beam him out?'). The title is a misquotation of the final book of the Bible.

- - - - - - - - - - - - - - - - - - - - - - - - - - - - - - - - - - - - - - - - - - - -

119 Uncredited.

120 In Norse mythology Heimdall, 'the White god', was the watcher over Asgard, the father of mankind and the sworn enemy of Loki.

**LOGIC, LET ME INTRODUCE YOU TO THIS WINDOW** Hammond and Sam are in Daniel's office on Level 16. A call comes through asking them to go to the Gateroom. Hammond says 'Let's get up there,' but it's *down*. Heimdall says that the Asgard have been cloning for a thousand years. However, some of her dialogue with Sam concerning her ancestor from 30,000 years ago indicates that the race were experimenting with the process even then. Heimdall is described as 'he' by both Jack and Thor, despite being voiced by a female actor. One could argue, perhaps, that the Asgard are hermaphrodite, but the suggestion that, before they turned to cloning, their method of procreation was sexual indicates otherwise.

**QUOTE/UNQUOTE** Heimdall, when admitting that the Asgard have not practised sexual reproduction for a thousand years: 'It is not something we usually discuss with other races.' Jack: '*This*, I understand.'

Teal'c: 'Our chances of escape are negligible.' Jack: 'Oh, I don't know. All we've gotta do is bust out of here, take out every Jaffa between here and the peltak, commandeer the ship and fly on home.' Teal'c: 'I stand corrected.'

**NOTES** 'This is the job, we lose people all the time.' Jack asks, 'That's *it*?' at one point, and it's hard to disagree, especially with another (literal) *deus ex machina* in Jack's and Teal'c's escape from the holding cell. A *very* low-key episode to end the season, though it does have some redeeming features. Best bits: Sam tearfully wandering around Daniel's office, and her little heart-to-heart with Hammond. And the final scene: a quiet, dignified end to a generally disappointing year; a proposal for dinner amongst good friends and a tiny suggestion that Daniel is still around in some form and, perhaps, always will be.

**CRITIQUE** 'This show continues to get better each season', noted Dean Kaufman in *Intergalactic Enquirer*.

Reviewing MGM's impressive DVD series in *Shivers*, Stephen Foster notes: '[The] presentation is impeccable; the commentary tracks are as interesting as the episodes and the bonus videos are genuinely revealing.'

**CAST AND CREW COMMENTS** 'I understand why Michael wanted to move on,' said Amanda Tapping. 'On a personal level, as a friend of Michael's and someone who spent five years hanging out with him, I don't know how it's going to affect the show. I'm excited about next season in some ways because it is going to be different. I just find it incredibly sad that we couldn't have finished what we started [with Michael].' The final two episodes of season five had been particularly hard for the cast, she continued: 'Christopher Judge and I couldn't even look at each other without bursting into tears. On Michael's last day of shooting the three of us couldn't get through a scene without crying. It was heartbreaking.'

**DID YOU KNOW?** During January 2002 a telephone poll on Channel 4's teletext service asked viewers to chose their favourite SF TV programme. After over 20,000 votes were registered, *SG-1* beat off formidable opposition (*The X-Files*, *Doctor Who*, *Star Trek* and *Blakes' 7*) to win comfortably.

# STARGATE SG-1
# SEASON 6 (2002-2003)
# ...AND BEYOND

'I leave, and look at the mess

you get yourself into.'

# STARGATE SG-1™ SEASON 6 (2002-2003)

Double Secret Productions/Gekko Film Corp/

Metro-Goldwyn-Meyer

Developed for Television by Brad Wright, Jonathan Glassner

Executive Producer: Brad Wright, Michael Greenburg,

Richard Dean Anderson, Robert C Cooper

Executive Consultant: Jonathan Glassner

Creative Consultant: Martin Wood

Co-Producer: Peter DeLuise

Producer: Andy Mikita, Damien Kindler (114-121)

Supervising Producer: Joseph Mallozzi, Paul Mullie

Co-Executive Producer: N John Smith

Post Production Consultant: Michael Eliot

Regular Cast: Richard Dean Anderson (Jack O'Neill)[121], Amanda Tapping

(Samantha Carter), Christopher Judge (Teal'c), Corin Nemec (Jonas Quinn),

Don S Davis (General George Hammond)

Note: Season six is being transmitted in the UK at the time of going to press.

121 Does not appear in 'Nightwalkers'.

# 111 REDEMPTION (PART I)

US Transmission Date: 7 Jun 2002 (Sci-Fi Channel)
UK Transmission Date: 25 Sep 2002
Writer: Robert Cooper
Director: Martin Wood
Cast: Gary Jones (Sgt Walter Davis), Tony Amendola (Bra'tac), Neil Denis (Rya'c), Dan Shea (Sgt Siler), Tobias Mehler (Lt Graham Simmons), Garry Chalk (Colonel Chekov), David Hewlett (Robert McKay), David Palffry (Anubis), Christopher Kennedy (Dr Larry Murphy), Aleks Paunovic (Shaq'rel), Ivan Cermak (Hagman), Craig McNair (Technician), Carrie Richie (Technician), Michael Soltis (Medic)

> Tragedy reunites Teal'c with his son, Rya'c, who demands proof that the Goa'uld can be defeated. Jack and Sam launch a dangerous mission when the SGC comes under sonic attack from Anubis. Jonas tries hard to fit into his new home.

**THE WIT AND WISDOM OF JACK O'NEILL** Carter: 'It looks like a 605/3 error.' Hammond: 'Forgive me?' Jack: 'It's the one after 605/2, sir.'

**SAM'S TRAUMATIC LIFE GENERALLY** Robert McKay (see '48 Hours') returns from his exile building Naqahdah reactors in Russia, at the Pentagon's request to help Sam. She, needless to say, is *delighted* by this.

**ORIGINS OF THE SPECIES** P2X374 is described by Sam as unfriendly and fairly primitive.

Dray'auc refused to accept a new symbiont. The Goa'uld are said no longer to trust Jaffa priests with their young as they once did. Abydos remains the closest planet with a Gate to Earth (see 'Children of the Gods').

Although Anubis has grown powerful, he still rules on only a small number of worlds. He has, however, got access to a weapon that bombards energy through one Stargate to another, creating a wormhole that cannot be shut down and will, ultimately, destroy the receiving Gate and, probably, the entire planet as well. His first target is Earth, obviously. Anubis appears at the SGC using Asgard holographic technology stolen from the mind of Thor ('Revelations').

**THE CONSPIRACY STARTS AT CLOSING TIME** Colonel Chekov wants a Russian officer to be assigned to SG-1. Both Jack and Hammond are less than keen.

The XL302 (a development from the X301, see 'Tangent') is a human-built spacecraft containing retro-engineered Goa'uld systems and a hyperspace window generator made possible by Naqahdriah. It is, in short, the first human vehicle capable of interstellar travel. The only problem is, it doesn't work (the Naqahdriah's instability making the establishment of a stable wormhole impossible).

**MILITARY INTELLIGENCE?** Daniel, notes Hammond, provided SG-1 with not only linguistic skills and invaluable knowledge but also a 'beneficial viewpoint', which Hammond wishes to see replaced. Since Daniel 'ascended' (see 'Meridian'), SG-1 have tried out nine replacements, the latest being Captain Hagman. This number includes Captain Mathieson, who lasted just two hours.

**POSSIBLE INFLUENCES** *Titanic, Star Trek: The Next Generation*'s 'Sins of the Father', *Star Trek* ('Phasers?').

**'YOU MIGHT REMEMBER ME FROM...'** Michael Soltis played Lt Pierce in *Taken*.

**LOGIC, LET ME INTRODUCE YOU TO THIS WINDOW** Both Jonas and Hammond refer to the XL302 as the X302 (as does Sam in the next episode).

**QUOTE/UNQUOTE** Jack, to Sam: 'How come you're not downstairs with the rest of the eggheads? Not that you're an egghead. Well, you are. But in a good way.' And: 'You do have a penchant for pulling brilliant ideas out of your butt.'

Jack, after Anubis's 'Prepare to meet your doom,' rant: 'Oh, *please*!'

**NOTES** 'Hammond is insisting SG-1 needs a sociological nerd to offset our overwhelming coolness.' A very confident start to the new era. Something of a continuity overload, but with a decent basic storyline. It's also a nicely laid-back introduction to Jonas, with Nemec getting a couple of smashing little scenes under his belt. Sam seems unusually testy throughout, even before the wonderfully abusive Robert McKay arrives.

It's three months since the events of 'Meridian'. Jack likes cake. Again, one has to ask *who doesn't*? It is suggested, by Jonas, that Jack holds Jonas responsible for Daniel's fate. Jack subsequently, and with some dignity, denies this in 'Redemption Part 2'. Teal'c seems to enjoy a hearty snack after sparring sessions. As Teal'c mourns the death of his wife, he is able to become reconciled with Rya'c. Since being brainwashed by Apophis ('Family'), the boy has believed that he will never measure up to his father. Teal'c tells Rya'c of his own brainwashing ('Enemies') and says that he has never lost his trust in his son.

Jonas hasn't left the SGC since defecting to them - his first trip off-base is to Area 51 to see the XL302, which the Naqahdriah he supplied has helped to develop. (Wasn't he told in 'Meridian' that the SGC would use the element only for defensive shields?) He has spent most of his time studying nearly all of Daniel's library, becoming versed in everything from ancient Earth cultures (Babylonian, for instance) to the Goa'uld. He seems to be fascinated by The Weather Channel. He boxes with Teal'c (and gets chinned with the same regularity and force that Jack does - see 'The Fifth Race') and says that he is as fit as anyone on the base. He also notes that Dr Fraiser believes he has an ability to learn much faster than most humans.

The episode contains numerous continuity references to 'Bloodlines', 'Family', 'Fair Game', 'Serpent's Song', 'The Warrior' and 'Threshold' amongst others.

**CRITIQUE** 'Redemption' brought *SG-1* it's biggest publicity in years within the non-genre media. The *Chicago Tribune* ran a feature story on the show's move to Sci-Fi whilst the *L.A. Times* reviewed the season premiere, noting: 'Anderson and co-stars Amanda Tapping, Christopher Judge and newly-added Corin Nemec have a smooth rapport, and their sly quippery combined with all the interplanetary carrying-on make for a rollicking good time.' Brian Ford Sullivan also gave a good review at *The Futon Critic*. 'The show has never looked or played better. ['Redemption'] balanced multiple storylines, exciting battles and a surprisingly easily accessible [plot] with the same flair and wit the show has provided throughout its run.' On the other hand the *Boston Herald*'s critic wrote: 'If *Stargate*'s premiere is an example, the series has run out of stories to tell. The episode is titled 'Redemption,' but the producers could have called it 'Tangerine' or 'Dandruff' for all the relevance to the plot.'

**CAST AND CREW COMMENTS** 'As for Anubis,' Joe Mallozzi told an online chat, 'we'll be peeling the layers on that onion. For those who haven't seen 'Revelations', he's not your typical Goa'uld.'

'Redemption' is, according to Corin Nemec 'a really wonderful show. It introduces the audience to Jonas, to his abilities, and it gives you a glimpse of what he had to offer ... It shows his enthusiasm.'

**DID YOU KNOW?** The new season featured not only a new title sequence (albeit a temporary one, see 'Frozen'), but also a series of linking trailers featuring the slogan: 'You're watching *Stargate SG-1* on SciFi Friday.'

# 112 REDEMPTION (PART II)

US Transmission Date: 14 Jun 2002
UK Transmission Date: 25 Sep 2002
Writer: Robert Cooper
Director: Martin Wood
Cast: Gary Jones (Sgt Walter Davis), Tony Amendola (Bra'tac), Neil Denis (Rya'c), Garry Chalk (Colonel Chekov), David Hewlett (Robert McKay), Christopher Kennedy (Dr Larry Murphy), Aleks Paunovic (Shaq'rel)

> Sam and Jack must find a way to save Earth from destruction at the hands of Anubis, who has turned the Stargate into a bomb. Teal'c and Bra'tac, meanwhile, are stranded off-world, with only Rya'c to come to their rescue.

**THE WIT AND WISDOM OF JACK O'NEILL** Sam, as Jack embarks on his insanely dangerous mission: 'I wish I could go with you, sir.' Jack: 'Yes, I'm sure you do. And I find that quite *bizarre*.'

**SAM'S BIZARRE LOVE-LIFE** When McKay was a child his ambition was to be a concert pianist. (How typical of Sam, to have an admirer who suffers from pianist envy.) McKay had a 'not so comfortable' childhood and sought solace in music. Having been told that, whilst he was a fine clinical musician, he had no feel for the art he instead turned to science. But, he admits that science is just as much of an artform as music and he considers Sam as a brilliant artist. He also fancies her something rotten (as alluded to, between insults, in '48 Hours'). Hospital gowns, he notes, turn him on. Sam eventually grows to tolerate and, perhaps, even quite like McKay, and gives him a kiss as he leaves to return to Russia. But, she tells him, this is bad news for him in some ways as she was more attracted to him when she hated him. Ah well, another one bites the dust.

### ORIGINS OF THE SPECIES
Teal'c describes Anubis's weapon as having been built by the Ancients (see 'The Fifth Race'), and says he has seen such designs before.

### THE CONSPIRACY STARTS AT CLOSING TIME
Jonas comes up with an ingenious plan to get the Stargate off Earth. Sam provides the means (the XL302), leaving Jack the simple task of flying the craft. Of course, you didn't think it was going to be easy, did you?

Until news of Rya'c's destruction of Anubis's weapon reaches Hammond it seems that, with the transportation of the beta Stargate from Earth, and its destruction, the Stargate programme is, effectively, over. The SGC could not take the risk of activating the alpha Gate in case Anubis tried the same attack, and were in process of shutting down the operation. Once it is clear that this will not happen, the Russians offer to 'rent' the alpha Gate to the SGC in exchange for a great deal of money, access to the development of the XL302 (and the subsequent XL303) and a Russian presence in the SGC.

### POSSIBLE INFLUENCES
*Watchmen*, *Apollo 13*, *Star Wars* ('a galaxy far, far away'), *The Hitch Hikers Guide to the Galaxy* ('... and still falling').

### LOGIC, LET ME INTRODUCE YOU TO THIS WINDOW
Teal'c tells Rya'c that it is difficult to hit a moving target, and this was why Rya'c got shot when they landed on the planet. But neither Teal'c nor Bra'tac was moving a great deal more than Rya'c and neither of them were hit. Maybe Anubis's Jaffa are just lousy shots? The original US broadcast of this episode seems to have mistakenly included the end credits of 'Descent', listing, as they do, John Shaw and Peter DeLuise as appearing in 'Redemption Part 2'.

### QUOTE/UNQUOTE
McKay, after Sam receives a massive electric shock: 'She's not gonna be happy when she wakes up, is she?'

Sam, as the XL302 plummets towards Earth: 'We're going to write a new subroutine. It'll be ready to upload in a few minutes.' Jack: 'Right, well, in the meantime I'll just keep falling.'

### NOTES
'I knew you'd think of something.' A cracking conclusion, with the four separate plots all dovetailing nicely at the end. I love Sam and McKay's brilliantly spiky dialogue, and it's a real shame that he's not going to hang around at the end as they're very amusing to watch. The episode is a bit oddly structured, however, with Jack missing entirely for about the first twenty minutes.

The Stargate weighs 64,000 pounds. Teal'c says that Rya'c is going to help Bra'tac spread news of the Jaffa rebellion.

### CAST AND CREW COMMENTS
'I'd heard of [*SG-1*] but I hadn't seen any of it,' recalled Corin Nemec. 'When I had my first meeting with Hank Cohen, he got me copies of the show so I could check it out. I was really blown away by the quality, the production values and the writing and performances. The whole mythology of it was very exciting.'

In an online interview in June 2002, Joe Mallozi revealed: 'Amanda wanted to be funnier this year. She got the chance to be a bit of a smart-ass in the two-parter. [Sam and McKay] were my favorite parts of "Redemption".' He also revealed that the production team understand that the more vocal disgruntled internet fans are a minority. '[We know] about the majority of fans who love and support the show. The premier's ratings proved my point that you haven't gone anywhere.'

**DID YOU KNOW?** The jacket worn by the SG-teams is (the now outdated) G8 WEPS jacket, which is actually a Navy/Marine Corps piece of kit from the Vietnam war era and not Air Force issue at all. The SGC tac vest is an Omega Medic/Utility vest intended for wear by medics and backup personnel.

# 113 DESCENT

US Transmission Date: 21 Jun 2002
UK Transmission Date: 2 Oct 2002
Writers: Jospeh Mallozi, Paul Mullie
Director: Peter DeLuise
Cast: Carmen Argenziano (Jacob Carter), Colin Cunningham (Major Davis), Gary Jones (Sgt Walter Davis), John Shaw (Dr Friesen), Peter DeLuise (Lieutenant), Dan Shea (Sgt Siler)[122]

> A salvage operation on Anubis's abandoned mothership goes drastically wrong, leaving SG-1 and various colleagues trapped at the bottom of the Pacific.

**ORIGINS OF THE SPECIES** Despite Sam's initial belief that Thor may have planted an intelligent virus in Anubis's computer during his capture in 'Revelations', it is subsequently revealed that Thor actually, in effect, downloaded his consciousness into the mothership, explaining why he had been in a coma ever since.

**THE CONSPIRACY STARTS AT CLOSING TIME** This is not only the first time that Jonas has been in space but also, probably, a first for Major Davis too. Jacob warns Jack about slapping an Air Force sticker on the side of the mothership, exactly the same observation he made to Sam and Daniel about the X-301 in 'Tangent'.

**POSSIBLE INFLUENCES** *Voyage to the Bottom of the Sea, Das Boot, The Poseidon Adventure* (Jonas's underwater escapades). Jack twice quotes Mr Burns from *The Simpsons* ('Ahoy-ahoy' and 'Excellent!'). The Trojan Horse is mentioned (see 'Singularity').

**LOGIC, LET ME INTRODUCE YOU TO THIS WINDOW** Sam punches the buttons to operate the door control in a different order on the first two occasions she does it. Later, Jonas demonstrates a third different sequence. Maybe it's not the order that you hit them that operates it at all? It is established that the ship automatically closes off flooded areas allowing no-one in or out, except when Thor overrides this to let Sam and Jack escape. So, once Thor's influence is deactivated, how does Jonas gain entry to the flooded control centre?

122 Uncredited.

Jack: 'Next time we crash our brand new mothership, what do you say we do it in the Tropics?'

Sam gets the crystals containing Thor's mind: 'Here he is.' Jack: 'Sure you've got all of him in there? He's a smart guy, you know.'

**NOTES** 'Well, I guess we're going in.' A terrific
episode which, whilst low on clever dialogue, more than makes up for it with a series of blood-pumping set-pieces. It's nice to see Major Davis getting a share of the action for once and Teal'c and Jonas have a couple of interesting scenes together. Best bit: Teal'c taking out Anubis's three kung-fu *ninja* Jaffa.

Teal'c still isn't entirely conversant with human euphemisms - 'holding our breath' in this particular case. Or, is this simply an example of his bone-dry humour that Jonas has been warned about. (Warned by whom, we wonder?) Jonas eats a banana. (It was grapes in 'Redemption'; is this some kind of subliminal advertising by the American Fruit Growers Association?) Colonel Chekov is mentioned.

**CAST AND CREW COMMENTS** Colin Cunningham writes a regular diary of his
experiences on the *SG-1* set for his website, *ColinCunningham.com*. He noted that this episode originally included a scientist character named Nolan. But, having been alerted to this by his agent, Colin suggested to Peter DeLuise that it would be an ideal role for Major Davis. 'First actor I know that has ever suggested himself ... and turned out to be right,' Brad Wright apparently noted. 'Make Up can truly do some amazing things,' Colin adds. 'You'd never know it, but Christopher Judge is actually 90 pounds and white!'

**DID YOU KNOW?** As usual, Peter DeLuise gets a cameo. He's the
third man who enters the ship with Jonas and Teal'c. Michael Shanks's voice can be briefly heard when one of Thor's lines from 'Revelations' is repeated.

# 114  FROZEN

US Transmission Date: 28 Jun 2002
UK Transmission Date: 9 Oct 2002
Writer: Robert C Cooper
Director: Martin Wood
Cast: Teryl Rothery (Dr Janet Fraiser), Bruce Harwood (Dr Osbourne), Venus Terzo (Dr Francine Michaels), Gary Jones (Sgt Walter Davis), Paul Perri (Dr Woods), Dorian Harewood (Torin), Ona Grauer (Ayana)

> The SGC's study of the Antarctic Gate site reveals a woman frozen and buried in the ice and, with her, evidence that humans may have evolved on another planet before coming to Earth. But, unfortunately, that's not all she brings with her from the past.

**ORIGINS OF THE SPECIES** The DHD found in Antarctica (see
'Solitudes') was taken to Area 51, but after being used a few times it stopped working. This was the first indication that the power sources of the Stargates may have a limited

life span. Having compared this DHD with others that they have access to, the SGC is now believes that the Antarctic Stargate was one of the oldest within the entire Gate system.

Anaya, the woman found in the ice, certainly seems to be human, although her brain chemistry is said to be different and she has the amazing power to heal with a touch (ala the Nox). It is speculated that she could be an Ancient, one of the original Stargate builders (see 'The Fifth Race'). And that, perhaps, human evolution was not an accident but a deliberate part of the Ancients plans for the universe. The virus that she carries, and which comes close to killing Jack, is similar to cerebral spinal meningitis.

The Tok'ra offer Jack a symbiont, Kanan, whose former host recently died before he could reveal vital information that he learned on an undercover mission.

**THE CONSPIRACY STARTS AT CLOSING TIME** An SGC base, called White Rock, was established in the Antarctic after the events of 'Solitudes' approximately four years ago. Regular excavations into the ice, however, have been disappointing, with only the bodies of two Jaffa found during the first year and nothing since. Until now.

**POSSIBLE INFLUENCES** *The X-Files* movie (and various episodes of the series like 'Ice' and 'Gethsemene'), the *Star Trek: The Next Generation* episode 'The Chase' and the *Doctor Who* story 'City of Death' (the extraterrestrial origins of mankind) and *The Thing*. Also, *Airplane!* ('Doctor', 'Major', 'Doctor', 'Major'), *Roswell* (Ayana's healing powers) and Charles Darwin (1809-82), the English naturalist who formulated the theory of evolution by natural selection. Jack is horrified that he forgot to set a videotape for *The Simpsons*. (He tells Teal'c, sulkily, that it's important to him. See 'Beneath the Surface'.)

**'YOU MIGHT REMEMBER ME FROM...'** Venus Terzo's movies include *Born to Run*, *Echo*, *It* and *I Know What You Did*. She also provides the voice of Jean Grey on *X-Men: Evolution*. Bruce Harwood was terrific as John Byers in numerous episodes of *The X-Files* and as one of the stars of its spin-off series *The Lone Gunmen*. He also played Willis in *MacGuyer* and appeared in *The Outer Limits*, *Bingo* and *The Fly II*. Paul Perri was in *Dead Men Can't Dance*, *Live Nude Girls*, *Demolition Man*, *A Bronx Tale*, *Manhunter*, *Dark Angel*, *Melrose Place* and *Sirens*. Dorian Harewood was Morgan Hamilton in *7th Heaven* and appeared in *Glitter*, *Hendrix*, *Pacific Heights*, *Full Metal Jacket*, *Roots: The Next Generation*, *Panic in Echo Park* and *Kojak*. Ona Grauer was in *Sliders*, *First Wave* and *My Five Wives*.

**BEHIND THE CAMERA** Assistant director Alex Pappas previously worked on *Dead Man's Gun*, *Rare Birds* and *Brokers*.

**LOGIC, LET ME INTRODUCE YOU TO THIS WINDOW** Jonas says that Daniel postulated that when the Giza Stargate was buried two thousand years ago, attempts were made off-world to activate the Antarctica Gate (which, presumably, resulted in the trapping in ice of the Jaffa found by Jack and Sam in 'Solitudes', and two further Jaffa mentioned as having been discovered here). However, Daniel theorised that the Giza Gate was buried *ten* thousand years ago in *Stargate*. In talking about the Stargate found in Antarctica, Sam says that it could be as much as fifty million years old. Later, however, she contradicts this by noting that Ayana is at least three million years old, the same as the Antarctic

Gate. The Tok'ra offer a symbiont to Jack to save his life. They say that this could be a temporary arrangement and that, once another host is found, it can be removed. (Sam subsequently uses this as a major factor in getting Jack to agree to the process, see 'Abyss'.) This completely contradicts what Jacob was told by Selmac in 'The Tok'ra' - that a symbiont is for life, not just for Christmas.

The same Air Force recruitment poster that seems to appear in every holding cell in the SGC (see, for instance, 'Menace') is also present on the wall of the SGC's Antarctic base. Is it the only one the production team have? Why does Jonas keep speaking English to Ayana rather than at least trying other languages? There are lots of unanswered questions, like: did Ayana come to Earth in order to put herself into a frozen state away from her people until a cure for her disease was discovered? Or, is this disease part of the reason why the Ancient Ones are no longer around?

**QUOTE/UNQUOTE** Jack, on the prospect of becoming a Tok'ra: 'Over my dead body.'

**NOTES** 'We could be looking at evidence that human beings evolved long before we thought they did.' Some fantastic Big Concept ideas marble this episode, which is a major building block in the series mythology. It's nicely played too and, although Ayana's death is a little melodramatic, the unresolved ending is very well done. The only real problems are a couple of continuity errors which seem so out of character for a writer like Robert Cooper.

There are references to Nirrti's experiments on Cassandra in 'Rite of Passage', the Ancients' downloading of information into O'Neill's mind in 'The Fifth Race' and Daniel's ultimate fate in 'Meridian'.

**CAST AND CREW COMMENTS** 'Richard Dean hates playing the hero,' notes Brad Wright. 'It's always a writer's instinct to make the hero [act like] the hero. That's what I love about the way Rick plays O'Neill. And I think I'm finally getting it.'

**DID YOU KNOW?** Outrageous, isn't it? You wait five years for a new title sequence to come along and then you get two in the space of four episodes. The latest model is a combination of the 'Stargate exterior' sequence used on the previous this season, with various clips from episodes like 'The Fifth Race' and '48 Hours'. At the same time, Richard Dean Anderson fronted an amusing trailer called 'Stargate 101' in which O'Neill describes to viewers (in very basic terms) what the Gate and the event horizon are and then introduces his team who have, he says, saved the world six times. 'Seven' corrects Teal'c.

# 115  NIGHTWALKER**J**

US Transmission Date: 12 Jul 2002
UK Transmission Date:
Writers: Joseph Mallozzi, Paul Mullie
Director: Peter DeLuise
Cast: Blu Mankuma (Sheriff Knox), Vincent Gale (Agent Cross), Michael Eklund (Dark

Haired Man), Peter Anderson (Fleming), Adrian Holmes (Special Ops. Sergeant), Scott McNeil (Townsperson), Carin Moffat (Snake Townsperson), Sean Tyson (Barkeep/Agent Singer), Dave "Squatch" Ward (Antagonistic Bar Guy), Christie Wilkes (Delivery Woman)

Carter, Teal'c and Jonas investigate the death of a research scientist with connections to Adrian Conrad's company, and discover a small town whose inhabitants are part of a sinister Goa'uld operation.

**THE CONSPIRACY STARTS AT CLOSING TIME** Sam is awakened by a call from Dr Fleming. He tells her that 'The project was never finished' and mentions Adrian Conrad (see 'Desperate Measures', '48 Hours'). Fleming asks for protection, just as his car crashes. Sam, Teal'c and Jonas are sent to investigate the small town where the biotech firm that Fleming worked for is located. The local sheriff suspects foul play, especially as Fleming's lab mysteriously burned down prior to SG-1's arrival.

Most of the townspeople have been implanted with immature Goa'uld, cloned from Conrad's symbiont by Fleming and his partner, Peter Stofer. As in the case of Kawalski (see 'The Enemy Within'), the symbionts are weak and can't control their hosts except at night when they are sleeping. The Goa'uld have been building a spaceship to escape from Earth, but now their plan has changed to one of conquest.

**IN THE INTERESTS OF NATIONAL SECURITY** Sam uses the excuse that Fleming may have access to information pertaining to national security to get the sheriff's co-operation.

The NID, in the form of Agents Cross and Singer, have been monitoring the situation in town for the last three months and are waiting for the completion of the ship, which they plan to acquire and use as the first line of Earth's planetary defence. The half-built ship is, subsequently, transferred to Area 51.

**POSSIBLE INFLUENCES** Another *very The X-Files/Invasion of the Bodysnatchers* influenced episode. (SG-1 look incredibly cool in their Men in Black-style undercover clothes.)

**SEX AND DRUGS AND ROCK 'N' ROLL** Amphetamines were found in Fleming's car. Sam believes that he might have been suffering from drug-induced paranoia. (In fact he was using them to stay awake and avoid his symbiont taking over his mind.) Sam sends Janet a sample of the liquid in the syringe. Dr Fraiser believes that it may be a sulpher-based antibiotic. The symbionts had been engineered with an in-built kill-switch, a susceptibility to the antibiotic. Hence, Sam injecting herself with it kills the implanted symbiont within moments. The SGC use the cover of an inoculation against a meningitis outbreak when they organise a mass injection of townspeople with the antibiotic.

**'YOU MIGHT REMEMBER ME FROM...'** Blu Mankuma appeared in *Stakeout*, *Blacktop*, *Convergence*, *Bliss*, *Cadence*, *Bone Daddy* and *Forever Knight*. Vincent Gale was in *Last Wedding*, *Trixie*, *True Heart* and *Dirty*. Michael Eklund's CV includes *The Lone Gunmen* and *Stark Raving Mad*. Peter Anderson was in *Leaving Normal* and *The X-Files*. Adrian Holmes appeared in *Valentine* and *Highlander*. Scott McNeil is best known as the voice of Wolverine on *X-Men: Evolution*. Carin Moffat was in *Avenging Angelo* and *Sex, Lies and Obsession*. Dave "Squatch" Ward appeared in *So Weird*, *Spooky House* and *Mask of Death*. Christie Wilkes played Kristen in *Kanadiana*.

**LOGIC, LET ME INTRODUCE YOU TO THIS WINDOW** Sam Carter sleeps in a vest, seemingly. Amanda Tapping mispronounces 'Zetatron'. Twice. Sam notes that 'we' (presumably meaning the SGC) took Adrian Conrad into custody 10 months ago after the events of 'Desperate Measures'. But, of course, the SGC didn't, Simmons and the NID did. Sam says that the symbionts in the townspeople will just 'break down' after the injection of the antibiotic. Is she sure? Mightn't lots of people, including herself, be walking around with a dead Goa'uld symbiont inside them?

**QUOTE/UNQUOTE** Teal'c: 'The people of this town *are* behaving strangely. Even for humans.'

**NOTES** 'They only come out at night.' A cracking episode that, despite the lack of Anderson's presence, includes loads of funny moments and a genuinely sinister atmosphere. Given, for once, the chance to lead the team, Amanda Tapping has lots of fun doing all of the cool detection stuff. There's also a sub-plot about the ethics of stem-cell cloning research, which seems to be a red herring to the main plot, but is actually a key part of the *denouement*. Best bits: Teal'c and Jonas in the bar, and their conversation about human customs and fitting in. Plus, Jonas, realising that everybody thinks he's strange because he knows everything about everything, claiming not to know who Adrian Conrad is. Sam assures him that no-one thinks he's strange. But, when he asks about Jack, she changes the subject.

Jack is still with the Tok'ra after the events of 'Frozen' (see 'Abyss'). Richard Fleming was a biologist, formerly a Professor of Advanced Genetics at Stanford, famous for developing hybrid strains of disease-resistant quorn. Jonas read an article about him in the *American Journal of Evolutionary Science*. (The SGC library has a subscription.) Two years ago, Fleming joined Immunotech Research, a wholly-owned subsidiary of Zetatron Industries. The company's headquarters used to be in Phoenix until the events of 'Desperate Measures'. Within a week they had moved to the small shipbuilding town of Stevestown, Oregon. Jonas is starting to enjoy traditional American food. He has very keen observational skills. Both he and Teal'c drink ginger ale in the bar. (Jonas seems less than impressed.) In addition to her other numerous and impressive abilities, Sam also seems to be a crack codebreaker.

**DID YOU KNOW?** This episode allowed Richard Dean Anderson the opportunity for a well-deserved holiday. Peter DeLuise makes his regular cameo appearance as one of the men coming out of the cafe when the townspeople go on their nightly zombie-march.

# 116 ABYSS

US Transmission Date: 19 Jul 2002
UK Transmission Date:

Writer: Brad Wright
Director: Martin Wood
Cast: Michael Shanks (Daniel Jackson), Teryl Rothery (Dr Janet Fraiser), Cliff Simon (Ba'al), Gary Jones (Sgt Walter Davis), Dorian Harewood (Torin), Ulla Fris (Woman), Patrick Gallagher (Jaffa Commander)

Jack is captured and tortured by Ba'al and must rely on an old friend to survive until help comes. Daniel Jackson.

**THE WIT AND WISDOM OF JACK O'NEILL** Ba'al: 'Do you know the pain you will suffer for this impudence?' Jack: 'I don't know the meaning of the word. Seriously, "impudence". What's that mean?'

**ORIGINS OF THE SPECIES** Having agreed to receive the Tok'ra symbiont, Kanan (see 'Frozen'), Jack is now fully healed. However Jack/Kanan has gone missing from the Tok'ra base. Torin says that the Tok'ra are baffled as to why he would leave. The Tok'ra blame Jack for the disappearance, whilst Hammond and SG-1 believe that Kanan must be responsible. Jack has, in fact, travelled to a secret test facility where, several months ago, Kanan worked undercover in Ba'al's court (see 'Summit'). Kanan's agenda is to rescue Ba'al's Lotar, Shaylin, whom Kanan loved and was forced to leave behind.

Taken prisoner, Kanan leaves Jack's body, and the symbiont, presumably, dies. Ba'al wants the information that Kanan possessed and, believing Jack may have retained his Tok'ra memories, tortures Jack, repeatedly killing him and then reviving him in a sarcophagus.

**THE CONSPIRACY STARTS AT CLOSING TIME** Daniel confirms that he has now ascended to a higher level of existence and is, basically, energy. ('How's that workin' out for you?' asks Jack. 'Good,' Daniel replies.) He is, however, unable to break Jack out of jail (any more than Oma was able to cure Daniel's radiation sickness; see 'Ascension', 'Meridian'). Daniel suggests that he can help Jack to release his burden and to ascend as he, himself, did. However, there is a time limit involved as, once the sarcophagus has changed Jack fundamentally, he will be unable to ascend even if he wants to. Daniel says that the hardest part of being what he is now, is having the power to change things and not being able to. Because, ultimately, he has no more right to play God than the Goa'uld do.

Jonas and Sam suggest that it was the exposure to Jack's code of ethics ('We don't leave our people behind') that made Kanan risk everything to rescue the woman he loved.

**POSSIBLE INFLUENCES** *Quantum Leap*, the *Next Generation* story 'Chain of Command', John Wyndham's *Random Quest*, *Return of the Jedi*. The title is also that of a James Cameron movie. *Groundhog Day* is mentioned (see 'Window of Opportunity').

**'YOU MIGHT REMEMBER ME FROM...'** Ulla Fris appeared in *The Void*. Patrick Gallagher played Jake Goss in the *Apocalypse* movies, and appeared in *Felony*, *Mom's Got a Date with a Vampire*, *Bad to the Bone* and *Dark Angel*.

**LOGIC, LET ME INTRODUCE YOU TO THIS WINDOW** Where did Daniel get the chunky jumper from? And, the suede shoes? It seems that those on a different plane of existence get a poor fashion sense as an optional extra. Isn't the off-screen cry of 'Lord Yu attacks!' the most ridiculously cheap and nasty *deus ex machina* imaginable?

Jack: 'They did the implantation - a word I intend *never* to use again - and I woke up here. That's *my* week so far!'

Daniel, to Jack: 'You think the Asgard named a ship after you because they thought it was a cool name? Now's not the time to play dumb, you're a lot smarter than that. They saw our potential in you. Because of who you are and what you've done.'

**NOTES** 'I leave, and look at the mess you get yourself into.' A fantastically designed, beautifully acted and intelligently assembled curate's egg. The Jack/Daniel sequences are blissful, and very funny - some of the best moments of *SG-1* ever. But the rest of the episode feels somewhat forced, with a long-winded plot and several perfunctory, clearly filler, scenes. Best bits: 15 minutes of pure Richard Dean Anderson and Michael Shanks at their very best. Worst bit: Jack's escape, which is moronically simple.

The attack on the Tok'ra base on Revanna (see 'Summit') is mentioned. Both Janet and Sam confirm that whilst a mature symbiont can take control of a host body, it doesn't work both ways. Karan's last mission was as an operative on a mothership in Zipacana's fleet. He escaped during a battle with Yu's forces. Article nine of the Tok'ra/Earth treaty covers mutual provision of mission reports. Jack says that Jonas is at least as smart as Daniel. Jacob Carter's attempts to heal Daniel ('Meridian') are mentioned. The Tok'ra are a very passionate race, Sam notes. And she should know. The SGC leak the location of Ba'al secret base to Yu so that his attack can act as a diversion to aid Jack's escape. Torin is outraged by this and threatens to break off diplomatic relations. However, as Hammond notes, the Tok'ra need the SGC far more than the SGC needs the Tok'ra at this time. Jack will probably have some withdrawal symptoms from the sarcophagus (see 'Need'), but he should be fine, at least physically. Shaylin intends to stay with the Tok'ra to carry on Kanan's fight in his honour.

**CAST AND CREW COMMENTS** Michael Shanks made his much-anticipated return to *SG-1* here. Brad Wright noted that, in addition, he was working on another Daniel story for later in the season. 'I've received some pretty nasty letters, and so has Joe Mallozzi,' Wright added, sadly. 'We know how disappointed everyone was that Michael left, but I promised I'd have him back and he'll *be* back. Michael and I had a long talk at the end of last season. I wanted him to stay. We're still friends and he's welcome back on *Stargate*.'

# 117 SHADOW PLAY

US Transmission Date: 26 Jul 2002
UK Transmission Date:
Writers: Joseph Mallozzi, Paul Mullie
Director: Peter DeLuise
Cast: Dean Stockwell (Dr Keiran), Teryl Rothery (Dr Janet Fraiser), Gillian Bartber (Ambassador Dralok), Joel Swetow (First Minister Valez), Doug Abrahams (Commander Hale), Gary Jones (Sgt Walter Davis), Rob Daly (Resistance Leader), Paul

Schiele (Kelownan Soldier), Susie Wickstead (Kelownan Aide)

Jonas returns to his homeworld to face the consequences of his treason in 'Meridian'. His nation, on the brink of all-out war, is prepared to use any means to avert defeat.

**ORIGINS OF THE SPECIES** Terania, and the Andari Federation, Kelowna's main enemies on P2X 4CE, have signed a non aggression pact ending 200 years of mutual mistrust. The last major conflict between any of the sides was 20 years ago and nothing was solved. Jonas explains that Kelowna has always felt safe because the Teranians and the Andari hate each other as much, if not more, than they hate the Kelownans. He adds that their new pact is merely a marriage of convenience. He notes that the planets' conflicts are the result of a thousand different grievances that go back centuries. Unknown to the other powers, the Kelownans have finished building a Naqahdriah bomb (see 'Meridian', 'Redemption' Part 1) and have successfully tested it. The politicians have decided that a pre-emptive strike may be necessary. This will, of course, mean war, so they want to make a deal with Earth for advanced weapons - particularly aircraft. A Kelownan official tells Sam that his people wish to open trade negotiations with SG-1. ('I hope you diplomatically told him where to shove it,' snarls Jack.) In return for offensive weapons, Kelowna's diplomats offer SG-1 consignments of Naqahdriah. By the end of the episode, the Kelownans have broken contact with the SGC and may, in fact, be at war.

**THE CONSPIRACY STARTS AT CLOSING TIME** Dr Keiran, Jonas's mentor, approaches Jonas and asks for help. Keiran, and the other scientists, have realised that using the bomb violates their ethics, he says. They believe that the Kelownans are on the brink of destroying their planet. Keiran wants Jonas to get the SGC to support an underground resistance network that is planning a coup. They have, Keiran continues, successfully infiltrated many levels of the civil service and the government. It subsequently becomes clear that the resistance is, in fact, a figment of Kieran's delusional state.

**POSSIBLE INFLUENCES** The title comes from a song by Joy Division. The plot includes elements reminiscent of *Shadowmakers*, *Insignificance*, *Oppenheimer*, *1984*, *A Beautiful Mind* and *I, Claudius*. Valez paraphrases John Kennedy's 'Ask not what you can do for your country …' inaugural address.

**'YOU MIGHT REMEMBER ME FROM...'** The son of a Broadway legend (his father, Harry, sang the voice of the Prince in Disney's *Snow White and the Seven Dwarfs*), Dean Stockwell was a Hollywood child star in the 40s, appearing in *Anchors Aweigh*, *The Boy With Green Hair* and *The Secret Garden*. He left acting at 16 and travelled extensively, returning a decade later with an acclaimed performance in the New York production of *Compulsion*, a role he reprised in the film adaptation. He solidified his reputation with mature, sensitive performances in *Sons and Lovers* and *Long Day's Journey into Night*. Later, he again left the profession, taking only occasional roles in films like *The Last Movie* and *Tracks*, both with his close friend Dennis Hopper. In the 80s, Stockwell made a second, spectacular, comeback with memorable performances in *Dune*, *Blue Velvet*, *Tucker: The Man and His Dream* and *Paris, Texas*. This culminated in an Oscar nomination for *Married to the Mob* and possibly his most famous role, the holographic Al Calavicci in the much-loved series *Quantum Leap*.

His massive CV also includes *Limit Up*, *The Player*, *Psych-Out*, *The Dunwich Horror*, *Human Highway* (which he also wrote and directed), *To Live and Die in L.A*, *They Nest*, *Buffalo Soldier*, *Naked Souls*, *Enterprise*, *The A-Team*, *Cannon*, *Mission: Impossible*, *Bonanza*, *Wagon Train* and *Dr Kildare* (as Rudy Devereux).

Gillian Barber was in *Hollywood Off-Ramp*, *The X-Files*, *Shadow Realms*, *Cats & Dogs*, *Double Jeopardy* and *Bliss*. Joel Swetow appeared in *Days of Our Lives*, *See No Evil Hear No Evil* and *L.A. Law*. Doug Abrahams has guest-starred in *The X-Files* no less than five times, playing different characters on each occasion. His movies include *Road Rage*, *3000 Miles to Graceland*, *Run* and *Big Bully*.

**LOGIC, LET ME INTRODUCE YOU TO THIS WINDOW** The shot of the Kelownan city shows a very modern-looking helicopter flying in the distance. Odd, for a planet with a technology at the level of 1940s Earth. Schizophrenia isn't caused by exposure to radiation or anything even remotely like it. In 'Meridan', the planet's designation was P3X4CE, now it's P2X4CE.

**QUOTE/UNQUOTE** Jonas, on the negotiations: 'After four hours the only thing we could agree on was to adjourn for the day.'

**NOTES** 'What are they fighting for anyway?' An episode about trust in all its forms, 'Shadow Play' works well within the context of a characterisation exercise, features yet another magical Teal'c/Jonas scene discussing loyalty and betrayal, and also a great performance by Dean Stockwell. Yet, somehow, despite having a load of things going for it, the viewers are never, quite, as engaged as they should be. Best bit: Jack giving Hammond several excellent reasons why Earth shouldn't give the Kelownans any weapons, and Hammond noting, with a smile, 'You sound like Doctor Jackson!'

Jonas was recruited to the Naqahdriah project by his mentor, Keiran, six years ago. Keiran notes that Jones was always a dreamer. In Daniel's old office at the SGC, Jonas has installed a tropical fish tank (with fish), and has a poster of the Moon on the wall. There are specific continuity references to the mistakes that the SGC almost made in 'The Other Side'. The three original members of the Naqahdriah project were Keiran, Tomas Leage and Dr Silas. All three eventually developed advance schizophrenia from long-term exposure to the Naqahdriah. The symptoms of this include paranoia, delusions and hallucinations. Keiran's condition isn't life-threatening but he remains delusional and the SGC intend to put him in a facility for the terminally bewildered.

**CRITIQUE** '*Stargate SG-1* may lack the visceral flash and labyrinthine imagination of *Farscape*,' noted *TV Guide*. 'But it's a smart, well-scripted series in its own right, driven by a charismatic cast and consistently intriguing plot twists.'

**CAST AND CREW COMMENTS** Concerning the Kelownans, 'What they're saying [to Jonas] is, "We're willing to let you come home, because it serves our own best interests,"' noted Robert Cooper.

# 118 THE OTHER GUYS

US Transmission Date: 2 Aug 2002
UK Transmission Date:
Writer: Damian Kindler
Director: Martin Wood
Cast: John Billingsley (Simon Coombs), Patrick McKenna (Jay Felger), Adam Harrington (Hu'rak), Michael Adamthwaite (Kon'su), Gary Jones (Sgt Walter Davis), Martin Sims (Dol'ok), Randy Schooley (Meyers), Michael Daingerfield (Big Jaffa)

To gain favour with Anubis, a minor Goa'uld plots to capture SG-1, who are currently on a mission looking after a group of physicists. After an attack, two of the scientists, one of whom idolises SG-1, attempt a daring rescue. Much to Jack's annoyance.

**THE WIT AND WISDOM OF JACK O'NEILL** To Felger: 'Just what part of "Gate home" did you not understand?'

**ORIGINS OF THE GEEKS** Jay Felger is a lecturer in residence at M.I.T. He has four post-graduate degrees. He based his doctoral thesis on Sam Carter's wormhole stability theories. He's studied every mission that SG-1 have ever been on, and Jack O'Neill is his hero. Simon Coombs teaches applied math at Yale. He has a Vespa scooter and two cats and is an extremely anal *Star Trek* fan. The pair receive the Air Force Civilian Award for valour after rescuing SG-1. Or not, as the case may be.

**THE CONSPIRACY STARTS AT CLOSING TIME** Kon'su of Amon Shuk is, apparently, a minor Goa'uld in the service of Anubis. In reality he is a Tok'ra who has collected vital information on where Anubis is acquiring his technology from. His identity is uncovered by Hu'rak, however, and he's killed.

**POSSIBLE INFLUENCES** Loads of *Star Trek* references (red shirts, Vulcans, Klingons etc.).

**'YOU MIGHT REMEMBER ME FROM...'** Most famous for his role as Doctor Phlox in *Enterprise*, John Billingsley has also appeared in *High Crimes*, *The Glass House*, *Crocodile Dundee in Los Angeles*, *The Others*, *Kate's Addiction*, *Eden*, *I Love You to Death*, *Roswell*, *The West Wing*, *Gilmore Girls*, *Felicity* and *NYPD Blue*. Patrick McKenna's CV includes *Duct Tape Forever*, *Xxxposed*, *Elvis Meets Nixon*, *Traders*, *Who's Harry Crumb?* and *Eerie, Indiana: The Other Dimension*. Comedian and singer Michael Daingerfield voiced Ace Ventura in the animated series *Ace Ventura: Pet Detective*, played Bill Haley in *Mr Rock 'n' Roll: The Alan Freed Story*, and appeared in *Earth: Final Conflict* and *Special Unit 2*. Michael Adamthwaite was in *Spasms*. Martin Sims appeared in *The Lost World*, *Suspicious Minds* and *Red Dwarf*. Randy Schooley's CV includes *Bones*, *Skullduggery* and *The Christmas List*.

**LOGIC, LET ME INTRODUCE YOU TO THIS WINDOW** Leaving the control room, Felger gets to the armoury, takes several zat guns and then makes it to the door of the room in which SG-1 are being held, all in the space of approximately 30 seconds. During the gun battle between SG-1 and the Jaffa, one of the shot Jaffa clearly throws himself into the lake and, as he's doing so, he throws his staff weapon in another direction so that it doesn't get wet. Teal'c seems remarkably dry just a minute or so after having been fully submerged in the lake.

**QUOTE/UNQUOTE** Felger: 'Jaffa don't kill each other for fun.' Coombs: 'They *don't*?'

Hu'rak: 'No matter what you have endured, you have never experienced the likes of what Anubis is capable of.' Jack: 'You ended that sentence with a preposition. Bastard!'

**NOTES** 'We're here to rescue you.' A dreadfully uneven episode. Includes some of the worst dialogue in the history of popular television. ('I don't know how you can call yourself a scientist and not worship at the alter of Roddenbury,' for example.) Yet, for all that, and despite some very laboured comedy, bits of 'The Other Guys' are actually quite funny. Nevertheless, it is a disappointment, and the final scene, suggesting that the entire episode may be nothing more than Felger's hackneyed daydream, is clichéd beyond belief.

Jack mentions the ice hockey Lord Stanley Cup and asks who Teal'c fancies to win it. He doesn't seem very impressed by Teal'c's suggestion of Vancouver.

**CAST AND CREW COMMENTS** 'Everything is coming together nicely,' Joe Mallozzi noted. 'Season six will be the best yet. Some are looking at it as the end of *Stargate* when, in reality, it's actually a new beginning. Season six introduces a whole new dynamic and will essentially be the launch point for the movie and the spin-off.'

# 119 ALLEGIANCE

US Transmission Date: 9 Aug 2002
UK Transmission Date:
Writer: Peter DeLuise
Director: Peter DeLuise
Cast: Teryl Rothery (Dr Janet Fraiser), Peter Stebbings (Malik), Tony Amendola (Bra'tac), Carmen Argenziano (Jacob Carter), Obi Ndefo (Rak'nor), Link Baker (Artok), Rob Lee (Pierce), Kimani Ray Smith (Ocker), Herbert Duncanson (SG Gurad), Dan Payne (Ashrak)

> The SGC's alpha site is crowded with Tok'ra and Jaffa refugees, and tensions mount between them when both Tok'ra and Jaffa are mysteriously killed in sabotage attacks. Jacob Carter and Bra'tac try to keep their respective sides restrained as SG-1 investigate the deaths. They eventually realise that an Ashrak, a Gou'ald assassin, is at work.

**ORIGINS OF THE SPECIES** This episode attempts to answer two questions that many fans have been asking: what has happened to the Tok'ra after the events of 'Last Stand' and to the Jaffa since 'The Warrior'?

Jacob explains the mistrust between the two races. Most Tok'ra hosts come from worlds that were conquered by the Goa'uld and were born into a feudal system where the only choices open to them were forced labour or death. For 2,000 years, he continues, every time that a Tok'ra died, shot by a staff weapon, it was a Jaffa who was responsible for the killing.

**THE CONSPIRACY STARTS AT CLOSING TIME** Jacob tells Jack that the blending of two separate personalities in a Tok'ra does sometimes have its drawbacks, hence the reason that many humans and Jaffa find the Tok'ra somewhat arrogant. He goes on to note that Kanan, the symbiont implanted into Jack (see 'Abyss'), had committed one of the worst crimes known to the Tok'ra when he used Jack's body without Jack's consent. Even if Kanan's motives were honourable.

**POSSIBLE INFLUENCES** *Star Trek: The Next Generation*'s Klingon stories, particularly 'Sins of the Father' and 'Redemption', *Henry V* and *Predator*.

**'YOU MIGHT REMEMBER ME FROM...'** Link Baker played Kul in *Living with Monsters*. Peter Stebbings was Marcus Alexander in *Jeremiah*. He also appeared in *On Their Knees*, *Traders* and *Picture Claire*. Kimani Ray Smith was in *Canadian Zombies*.

**LOGIC, LET ME INTRODUCE YOU TO THIS WINDOW** The dead Artok's eyelids briefly flicker open.

**QUOTE/UNQUOTE** Jacob: 'If you can see it, you can shoot it.'
    Bra'tac, holding aloft the Ashrak's knife: 'From the hand of our common enemy, it has made us brothers.'

**NOTES** 'It's history.' What a fantastic episode. An almost Shakespearean story of revenge, mutual mistrust and, ultimately, noble friendship in adversity, 'Allegiance' is one of the best ever examples of *SG-1*'s more cerebral pretensions. Aided by an excellent ensemble cast and Peter DeLuise's fluid direction, this is *SG-1* at its finest.

Jonas has been with SG-2 on P36231 gathering artefacts. SG-12 were wiped out, by a surprise attack by Anubis's forces, whilst helping the Tok'ra to evacuate their base in the Risa system. Teal'c notes that many Jaffa in the service of Apophis were once killed by an Ashrak in the Naqahdah mines of Cowan. A Zatarc detector is used in an attempt to establish the identity of the saboteur. Sam notes that the machine is not infallible and that false positive results have happened before. And she should know (see 'Divide and Conquer'). Nirrti is mentioned, in relation to Goa'uld who possess stealth technology, though Jacob notes that an alliance between her and Anubis is unlikely as she is still an outcast from the System Lords. There are also continuity references to the Ashrak who killed Jolinar (see 'In the Line of Duty').

# 120 CURE

US Transmission Date: 16 Aug 2002
UK Transmission Date:
Writer: Damian Kindler

Director: Andy Mikita

Cast: Teryl Rothery (Dr Janet Fraiser), Peter Stebbings (Malik), Allison Hossack (Zenna Valk), Gwyneth Walsh (Kelmaa/Egeria), Daryl Shuttleworth (Commander Tegar), Malcolm Stewart ( Dollen), Trevor Havixbeck (Pangera Sentry), Andrew Moxham (Pangera Sentry)

On, Pangera, SG-1 are offered a deal for a miracle medicine. They soon discover, however, that the source of this is the offspring of a captured Gou'ald Queen.

**THE WIT AND WISDOM OF JACK O'NEILL** Concerning the Goa'uld reproductive process: 'How's she able to make kids without ... a man friend?'

**ORIGINS OF THE SPECIES** SG-1 make first contact with the Pangerans, who are not far behind Earth in technology. (They have airships and cable cars in their city, for example.) The Pangerans are extremely friendly and keen to explore the universe and find out about their heritage. The SGC is willing to offer Gate co-ordinates for something of value, which the Pangerans quickly produce: Tretonin, a drug that, they claim, offers immunity to virtually all illnesses. Jonas and Teal'c are introduced to Zenna, the Pangerans' Stargate expert, who tries to warn them about the Tretonin. It is soon discovered that a critical element to making Tretonin is Gou'uld symbionts, which the Pangerans have been harvesting specifically for this purpose for the last 30 years. The drug, however, has a high price. It creates bigger problems than it solves as it suppresses the normal immune system of the body, so that one has to keep taking it otherwise one will die. The Pangerans desperately need a new Goa'uld queen to replace their dying one, whom Zenna's father discovered, buried in a canopic jar, 60 years ago (see 'The Curse').

Some Goa'uld queens are able to fertilise their own eggs. It is, Malik tells Jack, essentially an asexual process. Prior to incubating symbionts in the Jaffa, the successful blending of a Goa'uld symbiont and a host body was at a ratio of one in two. The Jaffa race was specifically created to improve the ability of the symbiont to take a host by maturing within a Jaffa. Teal'c notes that a failed blending of symbiont and host normally results in instantaneous death for both.

**THE CONSPIRACY STARTS AT CLOSING TIME** In 'Crossroads', Anise told SG-1 that Egeria spawned the Tok'ra movement 2,000 years ago. She broke from the Goa'uld and went to Earth to stop them from taking humans through the Stargate as slaves. She was an advisor to the Roman leader Numa Pompilius before she was found and killed by Ra. Some Tok'ra scholars speculate that she did not, actually, die. Indeed, Pangera was Ra's base in this sector of space, and she was imprisoned for eternity in the jar and buried in a vault. Some time later, Ra lost the world to another System Lord, Shak'ran. Subsequently, approximately 300 years ago, Shak'ran was killed by Apophis.

Egeria's final gift before death is the salvation of the Pangerans, giving Sam and Malik details of the rogue gene she created to stop the Tretonin working as well as it should have. With this, the Tok'ra will be able to create an antidote to gradually wean the Pangerans off Tretonin. The Pangerans, for their part, look forward to a new alliance with Earth and the Tok'ra.

**POSSIBLE INFLUENCES** *Star Trek: The Next Generation*'s 'First Contact', Hammer's *The Mummy's Shroud, The Spy Who Came in From the Cold, The X-Files* episode 'The Erlenmeyer Flask' and *I Know What You Did.*

**'YOU MIGHT REMEMBER ME FROM...'** Allison Hossack played Sarah in *Two*, and featured in *Anthrax* and *Profit*. Malcolm Stewart was in *Best in Show, Screwed, Jumanji, Dark Angel, Sliders* and *The Littlest Hobo*. Gwynyth Walsh was B'Etor in *Star Trek: The Next Generation* and appeared in *Crossing Fields, The Girl from Mars* and *In the Heat of the Night*. Andrew Moxham was in *The Wicked Season* and *We Can Get That For You Wholesale*.

**LOGIC, LET ME INTRODUCE YOU TO THIS WINDOW** Teal'c describes Ra as 'brother to Apophis'. He wasn't any such thing in Egyptian mythology, and this is the first reference to this link within the series (although the hologram projection seen in 'Seth' *does* suggest that they belong to the same branch of the System Lords' family tree).

**QUOTE/UNQUOTE** Jack, with regard to the Goa'uld: 'We've stayed ahead of the game only because we didn't bite off more than we could chew ... normally.'
    Zenna: 'I am not afraid to die. But I am afraid that my people will not have learned from this.'

**NOTES** 'Here lies Egeria, betrayer of the Goa'uld. May she suffer for all eternity.' Another marvellous little episode that initially promises to be about a sinister alien race and actually turns into a story about making mistakes with the best of motives, and of putting those mistakes right. Good script, well acted and lovely to look at. This series in microcosm.
    Jack speaks a little French.

**DID YOU KNOW?** During this episode's original US broadcast an advert ran for a competition called 'Get in the Gate', the winner of which would have a character in a future *SG-1* episode named after him or her.

## 121 PROMETHEUS

US Transmission Date: 23 Aug 2002
UK Transmission Date:
Writers: Joseph Mallozzi, Paul Mullie
Director: Peter F Woeste
Cast: George Wyner (Al Martell), Ian Tracey (Smith), Kendall Cross (Julia Donovan), Colin Cummingham (Major Paul Davis), Enid-Raye Adams (Jones), John de Lancie (Col Frank Simmons), Bill Marchant (Adrian Conrad), Jason Gaffrey (Sanderson), Catherine Lough Haggquist (Technical Sergeant), Kyle Cassie (Reynolds), Todd Hann (SF Sergeant Gibson), Colby Johansson (SF Sergeant Finney), Michael Shanks (Voice of Thor)

A television journalist learns about 'Project Prometheus', the official government name for the SGC. Hammond's team must quickly create an elaborate ruse to mislead her. But the plan is complicated by the return of not one, but two, old enemies.

**THE CONSPIRACY STARTS AT CLOSING TIME** Journalist Julia Donovan, a reporter for *Inside Access,* contacts Sam concerning a programme she has made and intends to air in four days on Project Prometheus. Donovan clearly has *some* inside information on the SGC's activities, as she knows about the alloy Trinium. Her speculation, that the project involves a fusion reactor in the Nevada desert, is clearly inaccurate however. Hammond gets the President to call the head of the network to have the show indefinitely shelved. Donovan threatens to take her story to a foreign broadcaster, though this would expose her to a charge of treason. However, the SGC, in a show of good faith, agree to give her and a film crew access to a Prometheus facility. This is a mixture of genuine SGC technology - their new warship, the X303 - and complete bullshit. Carter spins an elaborate story about how the X303's key systems were reverse engineered from an alien ship (containing little grey, rather than little green, men) that is pure *The X-Files*. The alien ship, she alleges, crashed one hundred miles north of Fairbanks, Alaska, in 1978. 'It's better than Roswell,' she tells an underwhelmed Jonas.

**IN THE INTERESTS OF NATIONAL SECURITY** Having tapped Donovan's phone and e-mail accounts, and tracked her movements for several days, the SGC agree to the tour of the X303 facility. Once there, however, Donovan's crew, and her producer Al, stage a hijack. They are being paid (a great deal, Al notes), by the rogue NID organisation, supposedly destroyed after the events of 'Shades of Grey', 'Chain Reaction' and '48 Hours'. Their plan is to get Adrian Conrad and Frank Simmons released (see '48 Hours'). Background checks on the crew showed that they had all worked for the TV network for over a year, and the cameraman was a Marine veteran, decorated for bravery in Somalia. However, at least one of the team, (Jones), is clearly an NID veteran; she refers to when Harry Maybourne was 'running our operation.'

During Maybourne's era a tablet written by the Ancients was found off-world. This described a large cache of weapons and technology held at a secret location. Simmons became obsessed with finding this, and his bargain with Adrian Conrad in 'Desperate Measures' was, seemingly, for the co-ordinates of this site in exchange for Conrad's freedom.

**ORIGINS OF THE SPECIES** Simmons shoots Conrad dead, but Conrad's Goa'uld manages to implant itself in Simmons. Sam speculates that the X-303, having jumped to hyperspeed, is at least 1,200 light years from Earth. However, just at this point, Thor turns up, seemingly fully recovered from having his consciousness returned to him (see 'Redemption'). He says that the Asgard monitor all activity in the vicinity of Earth. However, he has not come to help SG-1, but rather to seek *their* help. The Asgard homeworld has been overrun with Replicators.

**POSSIBLE INFLUENCES** *The X-Files* ('Our official policy is deny everything'), specifically the hostage scenario in the episode 'Duane Barry'. *Star Trek* ('inertial dampeners', 'sub light engines', 'Engine Room to Bridge'). Also, *Dog Day Afternoon; Moonraker* (for Simmons's death, sucked out of the airlock into space).

**'YOU MIGHT REMEMBER ME FROM...'** George Wyner played Mr Grinsh in *Not*

SEASON 6

*Another Teen Movie.* He was also in *All the President's Men, The Devil's Advocate, Soap, The Rockford Files, Qunicy* and *Hill Street Blues.* Ian Tracey appeared in *Insomnia, Touched* and *The Commish.* Kendall Cross appeared in *Turbulence 3: Heavy Metal, Fatal Error* and *Andromeda.* Enid-Raye Adams's CV includes *Undercover Brother, The Lone Gunmen* and *Dead Zone.* Catherine Lough Haggquist appeared in *Dark Angel, Doctor Who* and *Rockpoint P.D.*

**LOGIC, LET ME INTRODUCE YOU TO THIS WINDOW** How do Sam, Teal'c and Jack (at various points) manage to survive severe depressurisation? In Sam's case, it seems to consist of her doing a mime of 'running against the wind'. Jack and Teal'c not being sucked into the vacuum of space, when Simmons is, may be the most ridiculous sequence that the series has ever attempted. How convenient that at least one of the death gliders recovered from Anubis's ship is, seemingly, housed at the same secret facility as the X-303, so that Jack and Teal'c can use it.

**QUOTE/UNQUOTE** Teal'c: 'Adrian Conrad has arrived... He was uncharacteristically silent for a Goa'uld.'
    Simmons: 'Spare me the supervillain riff, we're on a clock here.'

**NOTES** 'There are only two ways off this ship. Handcuffs or a bodybag.'
    Jack and Teal'c use one of Anubis's death gliders recovered in 'Descent' to dock with the X-303. Major Davis's first name is finally revealed as Paul. In Greek mythology, Prometheus was the son of a Titan who stole fire from the gods and gave it to men. In punishment, Zeus condemned Prometheus to be chained for eternity in the Caucasus.

**DID YOU KNOW?** The original title of 'Prometheus' was 'X-303, Part 1.'

# 122 UNNATURAL SELECTION

US Transmission Date:
UK Transmission Date:
Writers: Brad Wright, Robert C. Cooper
Director: Andy Mikita

This episode, the second of a two-parter, also concerns the final battle between the Asgard and the Replicators. There are now incredibly advanced forms of Replicators which can adapt into human form, and read the minds of those they touch. SG-1's main hope of defeating them lies in a Replicator that is, in some ways, flawed. Michael Shanks returns to provide the voice of Thor (who, seemingly, didn't die after the events of 'Revelations'). 'That episode also introduces a new villain [who] may have a lot longer life in the franchise,' noted Robert Cooper, enigmatically.

## 123  METAMORPHOSIS

'Metamorphosis' takes place in an off-world laboratory, and will see the return of Nirrti, and (it is promised) the death of semi-regular character.

## 124  SMOKE AND MIRRORS

Writers: Joseph Mallozzi, Paul Mullie

A *JFK*-style political thriller. Jack is accused of assassinating Senator Kinsey after video footage appears to show O'Neill as a lone gunman. SG-1 try to clear Jack's name and, in doing so, discover that the rogue element within the NID is active once more and is using the alien device seen in 'Foothold', allowing the wearer to disguise himself as another person. An NID operative named Agent Devlin is charged with the task of killing Senator Kinsey, perhaps because his shadowy superiors have learned that Jack is holding NID secrets over Kinsey's head (see 'Chain Reaction'). Devlin has also been ordered to put pressure on Hammond to retire once again, so that he can be replaced with someone more suited to the NID programme. But, how far does the conspiracy extend?

## 125  SIGHT UNSEEN

SG-1 track a new race of frightening, but ultimately completely harmless, aliens on Earth. Their tasks is complicated by Vernon, a military veteran and garage attendant, who has been paranoid about the government since the Gulf War. The SGC, subsequently, try to perpetuate a massive cover-up to avert mass hysteria. The aliens are said to resemble large, flying gastropods.

## 126  FORSAKEN

SG-1 arrive on a planet where they find the Seberus, a ship that crashed some years earlier, and her three-man crew including their captain, Corso. They want to return to their homeworld, Hebridan. Aliens attack and the first officer, Tanis Reynard, is wounded. SG-1 take the crew back to the SGC so that Reynard can get medical attention. However, are the crew the real owners of the ship?

## 127  DISCLOSURE

This season's clip-show: Hammond and Major Davis are in Washington, along with Colonel Chekov and Senator Kinsey (who's not dead after all, see 'Smoke and Mirrors') to meet with the French, British and Chinese Ambassadors and brief them on the Stargate programme. It has been decided by the U.S. and Russian governments to ready a joint military venture to combat Anubis if it becomes necessary. Hammond, Davis and Chekov also try to convince the ambassadors that going public and letting the general population know about the Stargate would be a bad idea.

# 128 PARADISE LOST

Joe Mallozzi hints that this episode could see the first appearance of the Furlings, the fourth of the ancient aliens mentioned in 'The Fifth Race'. Harry Maybourne is rumoured to be joining SG-1 on an off-world mission.

# 129 CHANGELING

Writer: Christopher Judge

Some of this episode appears to take the form of a series of a dream scenarios, as SG-1 are involved in a car crash. However, the main focus is on Teal'c who, in his mind, confronts Apophis. Michael Shanks will make his second appearance of the season as Daniel.

# 130 MEMENTO

Writer: Damian Kindler

SG-1 accompany the maiden flight of the Prometheus, a ship commanded by Colonel Renson and Major Gant. However, the Prometheus runs into trouble and is forced to land on Tangea, much to the surprise of the locals. The Tangeans are very suspicious of these aliens. SG-1 know that this planet appeared on the Abydos cartouche. With the Prometheus damaged beyond their ability to repair it, they need the Tangeans to show them where their Stargate is. Unfortunately, the Tangeans have never seen a Stargate and are sure that it's a myth.

# 131 PROPHECY

Writers: Joseph Mallozzi, Paul Mullie

SG-1 visits a backward world where the Goa'uld emissary, Lord Mot, is collecting Naqahdah. Jonas is gifted with a precognitive ability to see glimpses of the future, and his revelations suggest a bad time ahead for Samantha.

# 132 FULL CIRCLE

Writer: Robert C Cooper.

Michael Shanks is scheduled to appear in this episode - the season, and possibly the series, finale. Skaara and Kasuf will also appear. SG-1 returns to where it all began, Abydos, to defend the planet against an attack from Anubis, who is searching for The Eye of Ra. The symbol, which SG-1 have been forewarned that Anubis is seeking, is mentioned in texts on the walls of the Abydonian pyramid, but Daniel and Skaara are unsure what the Eye actually is or does.

# STARGATE AND THE INTERNET

'One of the producers told me there's an [internet element] who like to see Daniel get the shit kicked out of him. I said "Don't they like the character?" He said "No, they *love* the character". What the hell is all *that* about?'
  - Michael Shanks, *SFX*

The internet, via episodes like 'Point of No Return' and 'Desperate Measures', has become a part of *SG-1*'s iconography. Like most good TV series of the Internet age (and lots of bad ones as well), *Stargate* has developed a flourishing and very loyal fan community on the net, with hundreds of websites devoted to it. These are some of the most interesting.

Disclaimer: Websites are transitory things at best and this information, though accurate when written, may be woefully out of date by publication.

Newsgroups: alt.tv.stargate-sg1 is a usenet newsgroup for the discussion of all things *SG-1*. The posters seem very friendly towards newbies (certainly compared with some other usenet groups of this author's acquaintance) but, if you intend to post, it's probably best to spend a few days just lurking and, when you do post, to observe standard *netiquette*. Remember to include spoiler-spaces where appropriate (especially as, because of the way *SG-1* is broadcast around the world, it's probable you've seen episodes that some on the group have not). And try not to *flame* (insult) anybody unnecessarily. Unless they *really* ask for it.

Mailing Lists: These give fans the opportunity to talk in a much more relaxed forum than newsgroups. At http://groups.yahoo.com/ you'll find numerous *Stargate* groups listed. Some are 'members only' like *SG1HC* (for those who like to discuss characters in jeopardy and/or pain and the resulting comfort that can be offered to them), *sg1_spoilme* (devoted to spoilers and news), *danielites* (this list is 'offbeat and adult', apparently), *danandjan* (fan-fiction based on a possible relationship between Daniel and Janet) and *UK-SG1* (primarily for UK and Irish viewers). Amongst the popular public lists are *sg1fans* (with over 2000 members), *tokratimes, majordavisfanclub* (for Colin Cunningham fans) and *danieljacksonfanclub*.

General Websites:
Å *The Official MGM Stargate SG-1 Website* (www.stargate-sg1.com/home.html), like many official sites, this can be somewhat bland, although it has recently undergone a revamp with pages for merchandise and biographies and an interactive section. Features some of the best behind-the-scenes photos you're likely to see.
Å *Gateworld* (www.gateworld.net/) is, quite simply, the best general *SG-1* site. Packed with a complete episode guide, in-depth plot and character synopses, interviews and the most up-to-date news, this is one of the best unofficial sites you'll see for any series. If you're not already a regular, bookmark it today.
Å For British fans *Sphinx Stargâte* (www.sg-1.co.uk/) is an excellent UK-based resource featuring news, character profiles, listings, quizzes, screensavers and pictures. A real gem visually, the layout is very user-friendly.
Å *Starfan* (www.stargatefan.com/) features a bit of everything. A basic episode guide,

fiction, an extensive research section (mainly geared towards fan-fiction authors in search of useful info). This one's also highly recommend.

Å Other impressive general *SG-1* sites include *Gateroom.net* (www.gateroom.net/), a useful database of files on the technology, planets and cultures seen in the series, and *The SGC.org* (www.thesgc.org) which features downloads, fiction, games and an episode guide. *Welcome to the Chappa'ai* (www.internations.net/us/cyber/chappaai/index.html) includes a full episode guide, sections on the characters, mythology, quotes, the movie and news. *The Truth About Stargate* (http://isis_athena1690.tripod.com/index1.html) has an impressive reference archive, whilst *Mission SG-1* (www.ifrance.com/sg1sreports/) features a brilliantly designed front page and a useful collection of guides and specific sections on contact addresses and convention information.

Å *Amanda Tapping Website* (www.amandatapping.qnet.pl/) is *sexy!* A delightful unofficial domain with articles, interviews, a biography, superb galleries and several convention reports. All fans of Major Carter need to check this one out.

Å *Richard Dean Anderson* (http://rdanderson.com/homepage.htm) is a very impressive unauthorised fanpage with a huge content, including a thoroughly-detailed section on *SG-1*. If you're a fan of the main man you can get lost in this site, literally, for days.

Å Numerous Daniel/Michael Shanks sites exist: www.angelfire.com/scifi2/danny_jackson (*Danny Jackson Fan Site!*) is one of the best. *Daniel in the Lion Pit* (www.thespacemonkey.net/) is also lots of fun, with amusing *South Park*-influenced cartoons and a brilliant animated "Dancing Danny".

Å *Joy's Stargate Page* (http://home.kendra.com/urania/stargate_sg1/stargate.htm) features many quotes, graphics and puzzles.

Å By contrast, *The Sam/Jack Horsewomen* (www.sjhw.net/) declare themselves sincere, passionate and (equally) vocal fans dedicated to allowing the production team to be left alone to get on with making the show. Their site features fine episode reviews, fiction and some really good interviews.

Å *Stargate SG-1 Archives* (www.sg1archive.com/) is one of the most popular *SG-1* sites, featuring downloads and images of episodes and bonus videos.

Å *Pink Khaki - The Stargate SG-1 Online Magazine* (www.pink-khaki.net/ index.html) is another superb collection of interviews, the parody adventures of 'PK-14' and lots of amusing subsections for fans with a sense of humour.

Å http://www.site-street.com/members/helenab9/sfxlinks.html has links to the various effects and props houses who work on *SG-1*, most of whom have galleries profiling their work.

Å *ÅSN - The Australian Stargate SG-1 Network* (http://members.tripod.com/~Johnvb/asn.html) is one of Australia's best *SG-1* sites. With a pleasant layout and fast loading, there's an impressive amount of content here, including a forum and a section for fan art. *Orion's Gate* (http://ozstargate.tripod.com) is another excellent Australian domain. Both of these form part of *The Australian Stargate SG-1 Webring*.

Å It's somewhat ironic that, although the series is made in Canada, there don't seem to be many decent Canadian *SG-1* websites. *Canadian Gate* (www.geocities.com/stargate-site/home.htm) is easily the best.

The series, as previously noted, is very popular in many other countries. The following are some of the (literally) hundreds of non-English language domains dedicated to *SG-1*.

French Sites:

Å *Le Stargate Command le pbem* (http://stargaterpg.free.fr/)
Å *Stargate SG-1* (http://perso.wanadoo.fr/yvaine/sommaire.htm)
Å *SG-1 par Jerem* (www.chez.com/stargsg1/)

German Sites:

One of *Stargate*'s biggest fanbases is in Germany and this is reflected by numerous high-quality sites, like:

Å *Amanda Tapping Page* (www.amanda-tapping.de/)
Å *Die Reise durch das Steruentor* (www.stargate-commando.de/)
Å *Mission Stargate* (www.missionstargate.de.vu/)
Å *Stargåte Plånet* (www.stargate-planet.de/)
Å *Nicole's Stargatehomepage* (www.stargate-sg.de/)

Other Foreign Sites:

Å The Austrian domain *Stargatezone* (www.stargatezone.com/) and the Czech page *Welcome to Stargate* (http://stargate.webz.cz/) are also recommended.

Å Norwegian fans will love *SG-1.avd.Norse* (http://home.no.net/stargsg1/). For Spanish and Latino viewers, there's *StarGate Hispano* (http://sghispano.cjb.net/) and *Hispågåte* (www.hispagate.net).

Fan Fiction Sites:

Fan fiction really needs a book of its own to explain all of the nuances, the secret language and the (occasionally bizarre) psychology involved in the topic, but it's a fascinating subject and no review of any series' fandom is truly complete without covering it. So, for those readers yet to discover the delights of *shipper-fic* (relationship-based erotica, some of which is smutty and awful, but much of which is actually superbly well-written) and the like, among the best general-fiction sites are:

Å *Heliopolis* (www.sg1-heliopolis.de/) which carries both German and English fiction.
Å *Chevron 7 Fan Fiction Archives* (www.geocities.com/Hollywood/lot/5076/ sgfan.html)
Å *The Sam & Jack Archive* (www.geocities.com/TelevisionCity/station/ 4335/)
Å *SG-1 Rec-Å-Thon* (http://versaphile.com/sgrecs/index.asp)
Å *Place of Our Legacy* (www.squidge.org/~ancientservant/stargate/stories/)
Å *The Comfort Zone* (www.sg1hc.com/)

Happy surfing!

# BIBLIOGRAPHY

The following books, articles, interviews and reviews were consulted in the preparation of this text:

Abbott, Jon, 'Techno-Arachnophobia' ('Nemesis' review), *TV Zone*, issue 132, November 2000.

Amendola, Tony, 'The Return of Jaffa', interview by Nick Joy, *Xposé*, issue 65, March 2002.

Anderson, Richard Dean, 'Family Man', interview by Steven Eramo, *TV Zone*, Special 38, August 2000.

Anderson, Richard Dean, 'Father Figure', interview by Thomasina Gibson, *Xposé*, issue 53, February 2001.

Anderson, Richard Dean, 'Best of Both Worlds', interview by Jim Swallow, *DreamWatch*, issue 79, April 2001.

Anderson, Richard Dean, 'Lucky Star', interview by Steven Eramo, *TV Zone*, Special 42, May 2001.

Anderson, Richard Dean, 'Actor Follows His Star', interview by Alex Strachan, *Vancouver Sun*, 20 June 2001.

Atherton, Tony, 'Fantasy TV: The New Reality', *The Ottawa Citizen*, 27 January 2000.

'Behind the Scenes: Portal Fun', *SFX*, issue 47, January 1999.

Binns, John, 'Proving Ground' to 'The Summit', *Xposé* 65, March 2002.

Bloom, Jeremy, and Greenspoon, Jaq, 'Gate Crashers', *Sci-Fi Entertainment*, Vol 4 #3, October 1997.

Brown, Rachel, 'Beyond the Stargate', *Sun Herald* (*TV Now*), 7 June 1998.

Campbell, Joseph, *The Masks of Gods*, Penguin, 1982.

Chaikin, Andrew, *A Man on the Moon; The Voyages of the Apollo Astronauts*, Penguin Books, 1995.

'Coming up on *SG-1*', *TV Zone*, Special #46, July 2002.

Cooper, Robert C, 'Born Again', interview by Paul Spragg, *Cult Times*, issue 82, July 2002.

Cope, Julian, *The Modern Antiquarian*, Thorsons/Harper Collins, 1998.

Cornell, Paul, Day, Martin, and Topping, Keith, *The Guinness Book of Classic British TV*, 2nd edition, Guinness Publishing, 1996.

Cornell, Paul, Day, Martin, and Topping, Keith, *X-Treme Possibilities: A Comprehensively Expanded Rummage Through the X-Files*, Virgin Publishing, 1998.

Cruz, Alexis, 'Cruz Control', interview by Steve Eramo, *TV Zone*, issue 136, March 2001.

Davidson, H.R.Ellis, *Gods and Myths of Northern Europe*, Penguin, 1964.

Davis, Don S, Rothery, Teryl and Tapping, Amanda, 'Gate Pride', interview by Jayne Dearsley, *SFX*, issue 74, February 2001.

Davis, Don S, 'An Officer and a Gentleman', interview by Steven Eramo, *TV Zone*, Special 38, August 2000.

Davis, Don S, 'You Have a Go!', interview by Steven Eramo, *TV Zone*, Special 42, May 2001.

Davis, Don S, 'A Good Year, Generally Speaking', interview by Sharon Gosling, *Xposé Yearbook*, December 2001.

Eramo, Steven, 'Mission Briefing: The Adventures of SG-1', *TV Zone*, Special 38, August 2000.

Eramo, Steven, 'Gate Watch', *TV Zone*, Special 42, May 2001.

Farrant, Darrin, 'Green Guide Weekly Recommendation Reviews', *The Age*, 4 December 1997.

Ferguson, Everett, *Backgrounds of Early Christianity* [second edition], William B. Eerdmans Publishing 1993.

French, Marilyn, *Beyond Power: On Men, Women & Morals*, Jonathan Cape, 1985.

Giglione, Joan, 'Some Shows Aren't Big on TV', *Los Angeles Times*, 25 November 2000.

Gibson, Thomasina, 'SG-1 on Location!', *Cult Times*, issue 47, August 1999.

Gibson, Thomasina, 'Write On!', *Cult Times*, issue 59, August 2000.

Gibson, Thomasina, 'Starfate', *sci fi*, April 2002.

Hardy, Phil, *The Encyclopedia of Science Fiction Movies*, Octopus Books, 1986.

Hart, George, *Ancient Egyptian Gods & Goddesses*, British Museum Press, 2001.

Holmes, Richard, *Shelley: The Pursuit*, Elisabeth Sifton Books, 1975.

Hooke, S., *Middle Eastern Mythology*, Penguin, 1963.

Hudolin, Richard, 'By Design', interview by Steve Eramo, *TV Zone*, Special 38, August 2000.

Johnson, RW, 'The Myth of the 20th Century', *New Society*, 9 December 1982.

Jones, Gary, 'The Chevron Man', interview by Steven Eramo, *TV Zone*, Special 38, August 2000.

Juddery, Mark, 'The Show Must Go On', *The Australian*, 7 March 2002.

Judge, Christopher, 'Walking Tall', interview by Steven Eramo, *TV Zone*, Special 38, August 2000.

Judge, Christopher, 'Judge Mental!', interview by Thomasina Gibson, *Xposé*, issue 58, August 2001.

Judge, Christopher, 'Stone Warrior', interview by Steven Eramo, *TV Zone*, Special 42, May 2001.

King, Stephen, *Danse Macabre*, Futura Books, 1981.

Krafchin, Rhonda, 'Through the Stargate SG-1', *Starlog*, issue 12, April 2001.

Lane, Andy, *The Babylon File*, Virgin Publishing, 1997.

Lane, Andy, 'Stargate', *DreamWatch*, issue 76, January 2001.

Lévi-Strauss, Claude, *Myth and Meaning*, Harper and Row, 1978

Levy, David, *Skywtahcing: The Ultimate Guide to the Universe*, HarperCollins, 1995.

Lowry, Brian, 'Actresses Turning Down Roles of Teens' Mothers', *Los Angeles Times*, 29 April 1999.

MacDonald, Ian, *Revolution in the Head*, Fourth Estate Ltd, 1997.

MacKenzie, Donald A, *Teutonic Myths & Legends*, Gresham Publishing, 1984.

McIntee, David, *Delta Quadrant: The Unofficial Guide to Voyager*, Virgin Publishing, 2000.

Mitika, Andy, 'Behind the Cameras', interview by Steve Eramo, *TV Zone*, issue 140, July 2001.

Mosby, John, 'UK-TV', *DreamWatch*, issue 71, August 2000.

Mosby, John, 'From Strength to Strength', *DreamWatch*, issue 74, November 2000.

Mosby, John, 'Desperate Measures' and 'Wormhole X-Treme!', *Impact*, issue 127, July 2002.

Nemec, Corin, 'Very Big Shoes To Fill', interview by Thomasina Gibson, *Xposé*, issue 67, May 2002.

Nemec, Corin, 'Gate Crasher', interview by James G Boutilier, *sci fi*, August 2002.

Nemec, Corin, 'Gate Arrival', interview by Ian Spelling, *DreamWatch*, issue 96, September 2002.

O'Flaherty, Wendy Doniger, *The Origins of Evil in Hindu Mythology*, University of California Press, 1976.

O'Hare, Kate, 'Richard Dean Anderson Looks Beyond Stargate', *St Paul Pioneer Press*, 22 July 2001.

Parks, Steve, 'Stargate's Wormholes Might Hook You', *Newsday*, 27 July 1997.

Peary, Danny, *Guide For the Film Fanatic*, Simon & Schuster, 1986.

Perenson, Melissa J, 'Gate Expectations', *The Hollywood Reporter*, 4 September 2001.

Perowne, S., *Roman Mythology*, Newnes, 1983.

'Redeeming Quinn', *Cult Times*, issue 82, July 2002.

Richardson, David, 'Snyder Remarks', *Xposé*, issue 37, August 1999.

Rose, Rebeeca, 'The Other Side of the Gate', *The West*, 14 April 2001.

Ross, Anne, *Pagen Celtic Britain*, Routledge and Kegan Paul, 1967.

Rothery, Teryl, 'House Calls', interview by Steven Eramo, *TV Zone*, Special 38, August 2000.

Rothery, Teryl, 'Doctor's Orders', interview by Steven Eramo, *TV Zone*, Special 42, May 2001.

Roush, Matt, 'Shows of the Year '99', *TV Guide*, 25 December 1999.

Rundle Clark, R.T., *Myth and Symbol in Ancient Egypt*, Thames and Hudson, 1980.

Ryan, Maureen, 'Sci-Fi shows on the same wavelength', *The Charlotte Observer*, 6 July 2002.

Sangster, Jim and Bailey, David, *Friends Like Us: The Unofficial Guide to Friends* [revised edition], Virgin Publishing, 2000.

Shea, Dan, 'The Fall Guy', interview by Steven Eramo, *TV Zone*, issue 143, October 2001.

'Shanks Back', *SFX*, issue 90, April 2002.

Shanks, Michael, interview by Lisa Coleman, *Prevue*, March-April 1998.

Shanks, Michael, 'Laughing Through the *Stargate*', interview by Jeff Inusi, *Sci-Fi Teen*, issue 9, February 2000.

Shanks, Michael, 'Loss of Innocence', interview by Steven Eramo, *TV Zone*, Special 38, August 2000.

Shanks, Michael, 'Problem Solved', interview by Steven Eramo, *TV Zone*, Special 42, May 2001.

Shanks, Michael, 'Not Lost, But Gone Before...' interview by Thomasina Gibson, *Starlog*, issue 24, March 2002.

Shanks, Michael, 'Daniel in the Lion's Den', interview by Sharon Gosling, *Xposé*, issue 66, April 2002.

Shanks, Michael, 'The Gate Escape', interview by Jayne Dearsley, *SFX*, issue 90, April 2002.

Simpson, Paul , 'The Gatekeepers', *DreamWatch*, issue 63, November 1999.

Smith, Lynn, 'On the Road Again', *TV Zone*, Special 42, May 2001.

Spragg, Paul, '10 Things You Never Knew About Richard Dean Anderson', *Xposé*, issue 37, August 1999.

Spragg, Paul, 'I Gate Around', *Xposé*, issue 39, October 1999.

Spragg, Paul, 'Goa'uld Vibrations', *Xposé*, issue 40, November 1999.

Spragg, Paul, 'Learning Curve' to 'Demons', *Xposé*, issue 39, October 1999.

Spragg, Paul, 'Window of Opportunity' review, *TV Zone*, Special 42, May 2001.

Spragg, Paul, 'Wormhole X-Treme!' review, *Xposé*, issue 61, August 2001.

Stanley, John, *Revenge of the Creature Feature Movie Guide*, Creatures Press, 1988.

Swallow, Jim, 'Double Jeopardy', *DreamWatch*, issue 76, January 2001.

Swallow, Jim, 'Gatekeepers', *SFX* issue 47, January 1999.

Tapping, Amanda, 'Get Carter!', interview by Isabelle Meunier, *SFX*, issue 64, May 2000.

Tapping, Amanda, 'Aye, Aye Captain', interview by Richard Holliss, *Starlog*, issue 1, May 2000.

Tapping, Amanda, 'Major Developments', interview by Steven Eramo, *TV Zone*, Special 38, August 2000.

Tapping, Amanda, 'A Woman Before Whom Gods Themselves Kneel', interview, *TV Mag*, March 2001.

Tapping, Amanda, 'Soul Searching', interview by Steven Eramo, *TV Zone*, Special 42, May 2001.

Tapping, Amanda, 'This is Ground Control to Major Sam', interview by Nick Joy, *Starburst*, issue 284, March 2002.

Tapping, Amanda, 'Tapping a Nerve', interview by Brigid Cherry and Brian J Robb, *DreamWatch*, issue 93, May 2002.

Tichenor, James, 'James & the Giant Mainframe!', interview by Isabelle Meunier, *SFX*, issue 73, January 2001.

Tichenor, James, 'The Cause of Effects', interview by Steven Eramo, *TV Zone*, Special 42, May 2001.

Topping, Keith, 'Stargate SG-1', *DreamWatch*, issue 62, October 1999.

Topping, Keith, Season Three Review, *DreamWatch*, issue 68, April 2000.

Topping, Keith, *High Times: An Unofficial and Unauthorised Guide to Roswell*, Virgin Books, 2001.

Topping, Keith, *Hollywood Vampire: A Revised and Updated Unofficial and Unauthorised Guide to Angel*, Virgin Books, 2001.

Topping, Keith, *Slayer: An Expanded and Updated Unofficial and Unauthorised Guide to Buffy the Vampire Slayer*, Virgin Books, 2002.

Topping, Keith, *Inside Bartlet's White House: An Unofficial and Unauthorised Guide to The West Wing*, Virgin Books, 2002.

Topping, Keith, 'Absolute Power: SG-1, the Development of an SF-Masterpiece', *Intergalactic Enquirer*, June 2001.

Topping, Keith, 'Six... and Out', *TV Zone*, issue 153, July 2002.

'Vancouver subs for aliens in TV spin-off', *Jam Television*, 16 March 1997.

Vincent-Rudzki, Jan, 'Divide and Conquer', 'Window of Opportunity' and 'Watergate', *TV Zone*, issue 136, March 2001.

Vincent-Rudzki, Jan, 'The Fifth Man' to 'Between Two Fires', *TV Zone*, issue 144, November 2001.

Westwood, Jennifer, *Albion*, Paladin Books, 1987.

Wilkerson, Ron, 'Writer Gate', interview by Steven Eramo, *TV Zone*, issue 143, October 2001.

Williams, Peter, 'Playing God', interview by Steven Eramo, *TV Zone*, Special 38, August 2000.

Willis, Roy [Ed], *World Mythology: The Illustrated Guide*, Duncan Baird Publishers, 1993.

Wood, Martin, 'Mr Director', interview by Steven Eramo, *TV Zone*, Special 42, May 2001.

Wood, Martin, 'Lights, camera, action!', interview by Steven Eramo, *TV Zone*, issue 152, June 2002.

Watson, Jeff, 'Secrets' to 'The Fifth Race', *DreamWatch*, issue 72, September 2000.

Wright, Jonathan, 'Beyond Abydos', *Xposé*, issue 35, June 1999

Wright, Matthew, 'Endings and New Beginnings', *Science Fiction World*, issue 2, July 2000.

Zekas, Rita, 'Stargate's Gun-Shy Guy', *Toronto Star*, 13 October 1999.

# FUTURE IMPERFECT

MGM announced as early as October 2000 that a movie version of *SG-1* was under serious consideration. Brad Wright confirmed in September 2001 that a TV spin-off, to be called *Stargate: Atlantis*, was also scheduled after the completion of the first of what would hopefully be a series of *Stargate SG-1* feature films. The movie, it is planned, will be shot immediately following the completion of season six. The spin-off will, as a consequence of events in the movie, take place 'in a slightly altered ... Stargate universe,' Wright noted, adding that it would 'not be based on a military team.' Robert Cooper has also indicated in interviews that the movie will 'evolve the Stargate.' One prevailing fan theory is that the film may introduce the Ancients, the originals builders of the Stargate network (mentioned in 'The Fifth Race'), and identify them as the original inhabitants of Atlantis. 'One of the clues in season five was the elimination of the Tollan,' Robert Cooper told *Cult Times*. 'What we want to happen for the movie is to have many of the options for us eliminated. We want it to be us against the bad guy without having to wonder why we're not calling the Asgard or the Tok'ra or any of the other advanced races we've managed to make friends with. We're going to try and bring some resolution to all of their stories and also help explain why, in the end, we have to face the bad guy alone.'

MGM representatives are rumoured to have approached Fox Studios Australia in the spring of 2001, hoping to shoot *Stargate SG-1: The Motion Picture* there. Interviewed by *TV-Highlights*, Peter DeLuise noted that the writers are currently developing storylines. 'Of course, the story of a movie has to be interesting and understandable for those people who haven't seen the show,' he added. 'But you also have to add certain elements for the fans.' He assured those fans that a theatrical *SG-1* adventure would remain faithful to the series. 'We'd cut into our own flesh [rather than] anger the fans. The *Stargate* movie will be like the show, only much bigger, more elaborate and faster.'

'Brad and Robert will be writing the script,' Joseph Mallozzi told an online chat, whilst Michael Shanks confirmed at the *Best of Both Worlds 12* convention that the movie's plot concerns the lost continent of Atlantis. Shanks also told fans that he would appear in the film.

With regard to the often-mentioned spin-off, casting has not yet even begun (although a persistent fan rumour alleges that Amanda Tapping has already been contracted for the series) and, with *SG-1*'s finale concluding filming around September 2002, if the crew then head straight into production on the movie, *Atlantis* remains unlikely to be seen much before the fall of 2003, and possibly not until 2004. One character whom Brad Wright does intend to use in *Atlantis* is Lantash - the Tok'ra symbiont of Martouf - which Wright confirmed at the 2001 Gatecon convention.

'Season six will build towards a climax that's the *Stargate SG-1* feature film. That will create the milieu and the necessary elements for a spin-off,' noted Wright, in *Cinescape*. MGM are said to have registered internet domain names including *StargateAtlantis.com* and *StargateAtlantis.net* and they are actively shopping the spin-off for both cable and syndication runs, according to *TVinsite.com*. There's no word yet on which network may air the show, though should *SG-1* do well on the Sci-Fi Channel in 2002 and 2003, that would seem to be a likely home for the new series.

'We'd love to see the series develop into a different kind of show, one that evolves the Stargate,' Robert Cooper told *SciFi* magazine. 'It's too early to speculate on how we're going to do it. But we do have some ideas in mind.'

However, *SG-1* will get its first spin-off in September 2002 in the form of *Stargate: Infinity*, a 30-minute animated series on Fox's Saturday morning cartoon line-up.[123] The May 2002 issue of *Impact* confirmed that MGM have ordered 26 episodes, and that *Infinity* would be created by DIC Entertainment, a company famous for such animated series as *Inspector Gadget*, *Captain Planet* and *Sailor Moon*. They have, the report continued, a reputation for producing 'FCC-friendly' educational programming, and for shows based on established properties - from *Sonic the Hedgehog* to an upcoming series based on the movie *Evolution*. *Infinity* will be set 'around 20 years after the events of the *SG-1* movie,' but will try not to violate established continuity, according to the magazine. Though MGM are co-producing the series, the writers and producers of *SG-1* are not thought to be not involved with the project. *Infinity* begins when a beguiling creature named Draga arrives on Earth through the Stargate. The SGC must get her back home when they discover that she is being pursued by a sinister alien race and also by bounty hunters from Earth itself. Led by a veteran soldier named Gus Bonner, a team of four teenage trainees from Stargate Academy head through the Gate each week to explore new worlds and discover new cultures. 'Central to each episode of *Stargate: Infinity* will be the use of [the] Stargate's portals that allow those who master them to travel almost instantaneously to planets all over the universe,' note the producers.

So, it's a packed and diverse future for *Stargate*, seemingly. Not a bad state of affairs for a 'dodgy spin-off from a Bruce Willis-style action movie-in-space,' as this author once less than generously described *SG-1*. We all make snap judgements occasionally and we're often wrong in them. As, first and foremost, a fan of the inventive show that Brad Wright, Robert Cooper, Michael Greenburg, Richard Dean Anderson and co. make, I for one, couldn't be happier.

123 The first episode of *Stargate: Infinity* aired on 20th September 2002.

## HE'S AN URBAN GUERRILLA, HE MAKES BOMBS IN HIS CELLAR

*'If you want, I'll sell you a life story...'*

'A moron' and 'a failed writer' according to some of the more rabid contributors to one usenet forum (don't ask, please, it's a long story), Keith Topping is a freelance journalist and author whose previous work includes co-editing two editions of *The Guinness Book of Classic British TV*, writing numerous guides to television series as diverse as *The X-Files, Star Trek, Doctor Who* and *Roswell* for Virgin Books, four novels and a novella (including the award-winning *The Hollow Men* and Telos's own *Ghost Ship*) and the best-selling volumes *Slayer, Hollywood Vampire* and *Inside Bartlet's White House*. He is a regular contributor to numerous magazines, including *TV Zone* and *Shivers*, and is a former Contributing Editor of *DreamWatch* specialising in coverage of US television. He is currently working on *A Day in the Life: An Unauthorised Guide to 24*, due for publication in 2003.

Notoriously articulate, erudite and a right *wow* with the ladies (allegedly), Keith was born on Tyneside on the same day in 1963 that his beloved Newcastle United lost 3-2 at home to Northampton Town. Everything he's learned in life, he got from Hanif Kureishi's *The Black Album*. Keith also contributed to the BBC television series *I ♥ the 70s* and is currently co-scripting, with Martin Day, a proposed TV series for an independent production company. His hobbies include socialising with friends, foreign travel, loud guitar-based pop music, trashy British horror movies of the 60s and 70s, football, archaeology, military history and lots of other stuff. *Beyond the Gate* is his 25th book. Not at all bad for a failed writer.

# Also Available from Telos Publishing

# DOCTOR WHO
# NOVELLAS

A range of hardback Novellas featuring all new adventures for the
time travelling Doctor. Standard edition: £10
Deluxe signed and numbered edition: £25. P&P £1.50 UK only

## DOCTOR WHO: TIME AND RELATIVE By Kim Newman

The harsh British winter of 1962/3 brings a big freeze and with it comes a new, far
greater menace: terrifying icy creatures are stalking the streets, bringing death and
destruction. The first Doctor and Susan, currently on Earth, are caught up in the crisis. The Doctor seems to know what is going on, but is uncharacteristically detached
and furtive, almost as if he is losing his memory ... Susan, isolated from her grandfather and finding it hard to fit in with the human teenagers at Coal Hill School, tries to
cope by recording her thoughts in a diary. But she too feels her memory slipping away
and her past unravelling. Is she even sure who she is any more?
*An adventure featuring the first Doctor and Susan.*
Standard ISBN: 1-903889-02-2; Deluxe ISBN: 1-903889-03-0

## DOCTOR WHO: CITADEL OF DREAMS By Dave Stone

In the city-state of Hokesh, time plays tricks; the present is unreliable, the future
impossible to intimate. And in an unknowable future the Doctor is busily inciting a
state of bloody unrest. There is worse to come. As both world and time crumble,
Magnus Solaris and Joey Quine will unearth secrets the like of which nobody in
Hokesh could have ever possibly suspected.
*An adventure featuring the seventh Doctor and Ace.*
Standard ISBN: 1-903889-04-9; Deluxe ISBN: 1-903889-05-7

## DOCTOR WHO: NIGHTDREAMERS By Tom Arden

Perihelion Night on the wooded moon Verd. A time of strange sightings, ghosts, and celebration before the morn, when Lord Esnic marries the beautiful Lady Ria. However Ria
has other ideas, and flees through the gravity wells which dot the moon to meet with her
true love Tonio. When the Doctor and Jo arrive on Verd, drawn down by the fluctuating
gravity, they find themselves involved in the unpredictable events of Perihelion. But what
of the mysterious and terrifying Nightdreamers? And of the Nightdreamer King?
*An adventure featuring the third Doctor and Jo.*
Standard ISBN: 1-903889-06-5; Deluxe ISBN: 1-903889-07-3

## DOCTOR WHO: GHOST SHIP By Keith Topping

The TARDIS brings the Doctor to the most haunted place on Earth, the luxury ocean
liner the Queen Mary on its way from Southampton to New York in the year 1963.
But why do ghosts from the past, the present and, perhaps even the future, seek out
the Doctor? What appalling secret is hidden in Cabin 672? And will the Doctor be
able to preserve his sanity as he struggles to save the lives of the passengers against
mighty forces which even he does not fully understand?
*An adventure featuring the fourth Doctor.*
Standard ISBN: 1-903889-08-1; Deluxe ISBN: 1-903889-09-X

**DOCTOR WHO: FOREIGN DEVILS By Andrew Cartmel**
China, 1800, and the Doctor, Jamie and Zoe arrive at the British Trade Concession in Canton. A supposedly harmless relic known as the Spirit Gate becomes active and whisks Jamie and Zoe into the future. The Doctor follows and arrives in England, 1900, where the descendents of an English merchant are gathering. Among their number is a man called Carnacki, an expert in all things mystical, and before long he is helping the Doctor investigate a series of bizarre murders. The spirits of the past have returned, and their attacker may not be all they seem.
*An adventure featuring the second Doctor, Jamie and Zoe.*
Standard ISBN: 1-903889-10-3;  Deluxe ISBN: 1-903889-11-1

# Other Titles

**URBAN GOTHIC: LACUNA AND OTHER TRIPS**
**Edited by David J. Howe**
**Stories by Graham Masterton, Christopher Fowler, Simon Clark, Debbie Bennett, Paul Finch, Steve Lockley & Paul Lewis.**
Based on the Channel 5 horror series.
£9.99 (+ £2.50 p&p) signed and numbered paperback        ISBN: 1-903889-00-6

**THE MANITOU By Graham Masterton**
The 25th Anniversary author's preferred edition of this classic horror novel. An ancient Red Indian medicine man is reincarnated in modern day New York intent on reclaiming his land from the white men.
£9.99 (+ £1.50 p&p)  paperback     £30.00 (+ £1.50 p&p) signed and numbered
ISBN 1-903889-70-7                  limited edition hardback
                                    ISBN: 1-903889-71-5

**CAPE WRATH By Paul Finch**
A party of archaeologists discover the tomb of Ivar Ragnarsson, a vicious Viking war-lord, and bring death and madness to their number. A modern horror/thriller from a major new talent.
£8.00 (+ £1.50 p&p)                            ISBN: 1-903889-60-X

*The prices shown are correct at time of going to press, however, the publishers reserve the right to increase prices from those previously advertised without prior notice.*

**TELOS PUBLISHING**
c/o 5a Church Road, Shortlands, Bromley,
Kent, BR2 0HP, UK
Email: orders@telos.co.uk Web: www.telos.co.uk

To order copies of any Telos books, please visit our website where there are full details of all titles and facilities for worldwide credit card online ordering or send a cheque or postal order (UK only) for the appropriate amount (including postage and packing), together with details of the book(s) you require, plus your name and address to the above address. Overseas readers please send two international reply coupons for details of prices and postage rates.